Seaforth

WORLD NAVAL REVIEW

2026

Seaforth

WORLD NAVAL REVIEW

2026

Seaforth
PUBLISHING

Frontispiece: The Royal Navy aircraft carrier *Prince of Wales* pictured training with the Royal Norwegian Navy *Skjold* class fast attack craft *Gnist* during NATO Exercise 'Nordic Response 24'. The British 2025 Strategic Defence Review has replaced the Royal Navy's previous emphasis on expeditionary operations with a focus on the European and North Atlantic region as part of a return to prioritising its NATO role. *(Catharina Molland Dale/Norwegian Armed Forces)*

First published in Great Britain in 2025 by
Seaforth Publishing,
a division of Pen & Sword Books Ltd,
George House, Beevor Street, Barnsley, S71 1HN

www.seaforthpublishing.com
Email info@seaforthpublishing.com

British Library Cataloguing in Publication Data
A CIP data record for this book is available from the British Library

Hardback 978-1-0361-5076-1

ePub 978-1-0361-5077-8

Pen & Sword Books Limited incorporates the imprints of After the Battle, Archaeology, Atlas, Aviation, Discovery, Family History, Fiction, History, Maritime, Military, Military Classics, Politics, Select, Transport, True Crime, Air World, Frontline Publishing, Leo Cooper, Remember When, Seaforth Publishing, The Praetorian Press, Wharncliffe Local History, Wharncliffe Transport, Wharncliffe True Crime and White Owl.

The Publisher's authorised representative in the EU for product safety is Authorised Rep Compliance Ltd, Ground Floor, 71 Lower Baggot Street, Dublin D02 P593, Ireland.
www.arccompliance.com

Typeset and designed by Stephen Dent

CONTENTS

Section 1: Overview

Section 2: World Fleet Reviews

Section 3: Significant Ships

Section 4: Technological Reviews

Note on Tables: Tables are provided to give a broad indication of fleet sizes and other key information but should be regarded only as a general guide. For example, many published sources differ significantly on the principal particulars of ships, whilst even governmental information can be subject to contradiction. In general terms, the data contained in these tables is based on official information updated as of June 2025, supplemented by reference to a wide range of secondary and corporate sources, such as shipbuilder websites.

1.1 OVERVIEW

INTRODUCTION

Author:
Conrad Waters

'You should have never started it. You could have made a deal.' These were the words of recently elected US President Donald Trump whilst addressing reporters on 18 February 2025 about Ukraine's ongoing defence of its sovereignty against Russia's three year-long invasion.[1] In two short sentences, the American president seemingly lifted the veil on his vision of a new world order and overturned many long-standing security assumptions.

When considered alongside the new administration's many other pronouncements, there is a widespread belief that the United States' long-standing leadership of a rules-based system is increasingly a thing of the past. Supported by an international network of alliances, this framework has been broadly successful in maintaining global stability since the end of the Second World War. Despite this achievement, President Trump is now seen as articulating an alternative philosophy that emphasises a short-term, transactional approach. Under this, the United States' traditional defence partners are frequently viewed as its economic adversaries. Equally, the nation's support for a policy of free trade that has driven prosperity at home and abroad is to be replaced by new tariff regimes. These developments will likely have a fundamental impact both on maritime trade and, also, on the navies that protect the world's sea routes.

It is not the role of this review to examine the rights and wrongs of US domestic politics. At the same time, it seems indisputable that the Trump presidency holds out the potential for profound consequences across the defence and naval sectors.[2] In particular:

- Global defence spending and, with it, naval budgets are set to rise significantly as America's partners respond to new realities. For example, NATO has recently agreed to target spending five percent of GDP on defence by 2035; more than double its previous objective. Whilst this ostensibly reflects acquiescence to the Trump administration's demand that its 'allies' share more of the military burden, the appreciation that the United States can no longer be trusted as a reliable friend in the face of Russian aggression has been an important underlying factor.
- There is likely to be a shift towards growing indigenous industrial capabilities to reduce previous reliance on American technology. The United States' willingness to suspend supplies of defence equipment to Ukraine in their time of need, as well as concerns over a 'kill switch' that might render US-supplied F-35 strike fighters inoperable, are examples of developments that have led to a new-found appreciation of the benefits of military self-sufficiency. The Trump administration's continued willingness to supply *Virginia* (SSN-774) class submarines to Australia as part of the strategically important AUKUS security partnership has even been questioned.[3] Accordingly, American defence manufacturers will doubtless face a more challenging environment when promoting their wares overseas.

Table 1.0.1: COUNTRIES WITH HIGH NATIONAL DEFENCE EXPENDITURES: 2024

RANK 2024	(2023)	COUNTRY	TOTAL US$BN 2024[1]	SHARE OF GDP 2024	WORLD SHARE 2024	TOTAL US$BN 2023[1]	REAL CHANGE 2023–2024[2]	REAL CHANGE 2015–2024[2]
1	(1)	United States	997.0	3.4%	37.0%	916.0	5.7%	19%
2	(2)	China	[314.0]	[1.7%]	[12.0%]	[296.8]	[7.0%]	[59%]
3	(3)	Russia	[149.0]	[7.1%]	[5.5%]	[109.2]	[34%]	[100%]
4	(7)	Germany	88.5	1.9%	3.3%	67.3	28%	89%
5	(4)	India	86.1	2.3%	3.2%	82.3	1.6%	42%
6	(6)	United Kingdom	81.8	2.3%	3.0%	75.3	2.8%	23%
7	(5)	Saudi Arabia	[80.3]	[7.3%]	[3.0%]	77.8	[1.5%]	[-20%]
8	(8)	Ukraine	64.7	34.0%	2.4%	64.9	2.9%	1251%
9	(9)	France	64.7	2.1%	2.4%	59.5	6.1%	21%
10	(10)	Japan	55.3	1.4%	2.0%	48.2	21%	49%
-	(-)	**World Total**	**2718**	**2.5%**	**100%**	**2247**	**9.4%**	**37%**

Information from the Stockholm International Peace Research Institute (SIPRI) – https://www.sipri.org/databases/milex
The SIPRI Military Expenditure Database contains data on countries over the period 1949-2024.

Notes:
1. US$ totals for 2024 and 2023 are based on then current (i.e. non-inflation adjusted) prices and exchange rates for the years in question. Exchange rate movements, in particular, can therefore result in significant movements in the US$ figures and explain apparent discrepancies in the table. SIPRI also adjust previous year calculations when more accurate data becomes available, potentially impacting prior year rankings.
2. The 'real' change figure is based on constant (2023 based) US$ figures. Figures over 10% have been rounded to the nearest percentage.
3. Figures in brackets are SIPRI estimates.

The US Coast Guard medium endurance cutter *Northland* (WMEC-904) pictured operating with the Royal Canadian Navy Arctic patrol ship *Margaret Brooke* (AOPV-431) and the Royal Danish Navy offshore patrol vessel *Lauge Koch* during Operation 'Nanook 2024', a series of exercises aimed at strengthening Arctic security and international partnerships. Recent expansionist statements by the new US Trump administration with respect to Canada and Danish-administered Greenland have exacerbated fears that the United States may no longer be a reliable ally. *(US Coast Guard)*

The dangers of significant military conflict around the world have markedly increased as questions grow over the willingness of the US world 'policeman' to remain on his beat. Indeed, President Trump's threats against the Panama Canal and to Denmark with respect to Greenland suggest that the former agent of law enforcement might even be willing to become a criminal perpetrator in support of an expansionist mindset.

Despite this apparent shifting of the tectonic plates, much remains unchanged in the short term. For now, at least, the United States remains an active military player in defence of allied interests across the globe and, particularly, in the Middle East. Here, on/off hostilities against Houthi rebel forces in defence of Red Sea shipping have seen the US Navy involved in some of its most intensive combat since the end of the Second World War. The navy has also continued to help defend Israel against repeated missile attacks and played an important secondary role in the June 2025 strikes against Iranian nuclear installations. In the course of doing all this it has reportedly expended colossal amounts of precision munitions that might take years to replenish fully.

Most significantly, China looks set to retain its role as the United States' 'pacing challenge' in an updated National Security Strategy expected before the end of the year despite doubts expressed over the new administration's continued commitment to Taiwan's security. Indeed, the additional friction caused by the Trump administration's tariff policies might mean that China has less to lose in pursuing its own expansionist ambitions. Given that well-publicised capacity problems in American shipbuilding – referenced further below – are hindering efforts to rebuild its margin of naval superiority in the vital Pacific region, this might not necessarily play out to the United States' advantage.

The Type 055 'Renhai' class destroyer *Yan'an* leads a flotilla of Chinese PLAN surface combatants in an undated photograph. Whilst much is changing with respect to American foreign policy, China looks set to remain the United States' 'pacing challenge'. *(People's Liberation Army Navy)*

DEFENCE BUDGETS

It is apparent, however, that the Trump administration sees rebuilding the nation's military strength as a top priority. This is most clearly evidenced by its proposal for the first-ever US$1 trillion national security budget for the forthcoming FY2026 budget year. This figure represents a substantial uplift from recent levels of defence spending and maintains the United States' already globally dominant position, as illustrated by the Stockholm International Peace Research Institute's (SIPRI's) annual report on military budgets for 2024 set out in Table 1.0.1.[4]

The SIPRI information is inevitably dominated by the continuing Russo-Ukraine war, with eighth placed Ukraine's expenditure of a third of national income (GDP) on the military only sustainable on the basis of continued international assistance. The spill over from the conflict is also reflected in the very large, 28 percent uplift in the German defence budget that has pushed it to fourth in the list of the world's highest spending nations as it implements the fundamental security transformation heralded by former Chancellor Olaf Scholz's 2022 '*Zeitenwende*' (turning point) speech. Europe is only likely to see this trend accelerate and expand given agreement to the considerably more ambitious NATO spending targets referenced above. However, the trend towards higher military spending extends far beyond the continent, with Japan's 21 percent year-on-year uplift a reflection of the continued tensions driven by Chinese assertiveness. All-in-all, SIPRI noted that the 9.4 percent global increase in expenditure was the highest since 1988 and that military spending per head had reached levels last seen at the end of the Cold War.

FLEET STRENGTHS AND REVIEWS

As has been remarked in previous editions of *Seaforth World Naval Review*, the correlation between military spending and naval power is far from direct. In addition to the fact that some countries – Germany is a good example – are primarily focused on land-based threats, it can take time for higher budgets to feed through to larger or more effective navies. Table 1.0.2, which highlights the composition of the world's leading navies, is a case in point. Although investment in the 'West's' major fleets has been on an upward trajectory for a number of years, the last 12 months have seen an almost across the board decline in the number of warships in their service as older ships are retired before their replacements arrive. The US Navy is facing a particular challenge in this regard as it learns the hard way just how difficult it can be to rebuild industrial infrastructure that has been allowed to erode. The Trump administration seems to be determined to get a grip on the situation, examining ways of how to import overseas best practice into inefficient domestic shipyards and providing incentives to retain crucial workers. Inevitably, it will take time before the results of its endeavours become apparent.

Two other navies that are sustaining challenges to rebuild their capabilities are subject to detailed fleet reviews. James Bosbotinis examines published doctrinal and policy documents to explain the role of the Russian Navy in the country's wider military strategy, assessing how this has shaped the fleet's composition. Although its Black Seas Fleet has taken some hard knocks during the war against Ukraine, the navy provides an important component of Russia's long-range nuclear and conventional strike capabilities. At the same time, a lack of industrial capacity stemming partly through the dislocation caused by the fragmentation of the former Soviet Union means that it is still struggling to replace elements of the Soviet-era fleet despite the promise of very substantial investment.

Meanwhile, Richard Beedall returns to provide his biennial analysis of the British Royal Navy. The fleet has been shrinking at an alarming rate as attempts to extend the lives of elderly warships in the face of delayed implementation of new construction programmes have started to unravel. These problems have been exacerbated by the difficulties of retaining sufficient experienced crews in a reflection of a demographic problem that is having a broad global impact. However, it is not all doom and

TABLE 1.0.2: MAJOR FLEET STRENGTHS 2024–2025[1]

REGION	THE AMERICAS				EUROPE & RUSSIA										ASIA								IND. OCEAN	
COUNTRY	USA		BRAZIL		UK		FRANCE		ITALY		SPAIN		RUSSIA		CHINA		JAPAN		KOREA(S)		AUSTRALIA		INDIA	
	2024	2025	2024	2025	2024	2025	2024	2025	2024	2025	2024	2025	2024	2025	2024	2025	2024	2025	2024	2025	2024	2025	2024	2025
Carriers & Amphibious																								
CV/CVN	11	11	–	–	2	2	1	1	1	1	–	–	1	1	2	2	2	2	–	–	–	–	2	2
CVS/CVH	–	–	–	–	–	–	–	–	1	–	–	–	–	–	–	–	2	2	–	–	–	–	–	–
LHA/LHD/LPH	9	9	1	1	–	–	3	3	–	–	1	1	–	–	3	4	–	–	–	–	2	2	–	–
LPD/LSD	23	23	1	1	5	3	–	–	3	4	2	2	–	–	8	8	3	3	2	2	1	1	1	1
Submarines																								
SSBN	14	14	–	–	4	4	4	4	–	–	–	–	12	12	3	6	–	–	–	–	–	–	1	2
SSN/SSGN	54	51	–	–	6	5	5	5	–	–	–	–	20	20	6	6	–	–	–	–	–	–	–	–
SSK	–	–	4	4	–	–	–	–	8	8	2	2	20	20	50	50	22	22	21	21	6	6	16	17
Surface Combatants																								
BB/BC	–	–	–	–	–	–	–	–	–	–	–	–	2	2	–	–	–	–	–	–	–	–	–	–
CG/DDG/FFG	87	85	6	6	15	14	15	15	17	16	11	11	35	35	100	105	42	43	28	30	10	10	24	27
DD/FGS/FS	24	26	2	2	–	–	11	9	–	–	–	–	45	45	55	50	6	6	3	3	–	–	10	10
FAC[2]	–	–	–	–	–	–	–	–	–	–	–	–	25	20	75	75	6	6	18	18	–	–	7	7
Other (Selected)																								
MCMV	8	8	3	3	7	7	11	11	10	10	6	6	40	40	35	35	18	17	12	12	3	2	–	–

Notes

1 Numbers are based on official sources, where available, supplemented by news reports, published intelligence data and other 'open sources' as appropriate. Given significant variations in available data, numbers should be regarded as indicative, particularly with respect to Russia, China and minor warship categories (which can exclude non-operational vessels and are sometimes rounded). There is also a degree of subjectivity with respect to warship classifications given varying national classifications and this can also lead to inconsistency.

2 FAC numbers relate to ships fitted with or for surface-to-surface missiles.

gloom. Notably, the navy is regarded as one of the main beneficiaries of the United Kingdom's 2025 Strategic Defence Review, being offered the prospect of large numbers of advanced SSN-AUKUS submarines as part of a return to prioritising its NATO role in the so-called 'Atlantic Bastion'. A key part of the new strategy involves the acquisition of numerous autonomous uncrewed surface and underwater vehicles to act as force multipliers for traditional crewed vessels under a programme known as Project Cabot.

SIGNIFICANT SHIPS

The ongoing importance of technological advances are highlighted by returning contributor Tomohiko Tada in his review of the Japan Maritime Self Defence Force's (JMSDF's) *Mogami* (FFM-1) class frigates. Japan faces a particularly severe variant of the demographic challenge referenced above and, accordingly, has used the legendary proficiency of its indigenous electronics sector to create a multi-mission warship that can be crewed by as few as 60 personnel if the circumstances require. As many as 24 of the type and an enlarged 'Upgraded *Mogami*' class are envisaged as part of a major contributor to expanding JMSDF surface warship strength in the face of a fast-growing Chinese People's Liberation Army Navy (PLAN). Japan is also making strenuous efforts to sell the design to Australia in what would be its first major warship export since the end of the Second World War.

Another country that has ambitious plans to expand its indigenous naval industry is Türkiye.[5] Devrim Yaylali returns a decade after his first analysis of the 'Milgem' family of warships to explore how this series of locally-designed and manufactured warships has been successfully developed in the intervening years, describing the various iterations built for both the Turkish Navy and for overseas fleets. Türkiye's aspirations extend far beyond the 'Milgem' programme. On 4 January 2025 it held first steel-cutting ceremonies for a new locally designed air defence destroyer, a lead 'MıLDEN' national submarine, and – most impres-

This photograph shows a busy scene at Huntington Ingalls Industries' Ingalls Shipbuilding on 22 August 2024 as the new amphibious transport dock *Richard M. McCool Jr.* (LPD-29) departs the shipyard on her way to a formal commissioning ceremony at Pensacola, Florida. Despite the obvious extent of the shipbuilding effort underway, the US Navy is struggling to retain its current size as delays in new construction are resulting in warships retiring at a faster rate than they can be replaced. *(Huntington Ingalls Industries)*

The new Royal Navy Type 26 frigate *Cardiff* departs the BAE Systems' Yarrow shipyard on the Malin Augustea barge *CD01* on 30 August 2024 in preparation for her launch. Although the British Royal Navy is facing similar, if not worse problems, to the US Navy in maintaining fleet numbers, a recent 2025 Strategic Defence Review holds out the prospect of better times ahead. *(BAE Systems)*

sively of all – a new indigenous 'MUGEM' aircraft carrier. Whilst there must be questions as to what extent these ceremonies were more than a symbol of future intent, the progress being achieved by Türkiye's naval sector is certainly impressive.

The extent of the challenges involved in designing and constructing a national aircraft carrier are revealed by Mrityunjoy Mazumdar's description of the more than three decades-long journey that eventfully resulted in the commissioning of India's Project 71 Indigenous Aircraft Carrier *Vikrant* on 2 September 2022. Whilst there have been many trials and tribulations along the way, the Indian Navy has eventually received a capable warship that has done much to develop local industrial skills whilst already helping to assert its growing regional maritime dominance.

India's Project 71 Indigenous Aircraft Carrier *Vikrant* was commissioned on 2 September 2022 in a major boost both to the Indian Navy and the country's maritime industrial base. *(Indian Navy)*

TECHNOLOGICAL DEVELOPMENTS

Our final section begins, as always, with David Hobbs' review of developments in world naval aviation. His assessment concludes with a detailed analysis of the current state-of-play with respect to the introduction of the F-35 strike fighter; an aircraft which increasingly forms a crucial part of many countries' naval aviation arms but continues to be beset by developmental problems. By contrast, Richard Scott's overview of the origins and subsequent evolution of the RIM-116 Rolling Airframe Missile (RAM) programme paints a picture of successful international collaboration that continues to maintain a long track record of iterative improvements.

Norman Friedman choses the subject of ship-based anti-submarine warfare (ASW) weapons for his annual technological review. Whilst somewhat overshadowed by the rise of the ubiquitous ASW helicopter, such weapons still have an important rapid response function, particularly against incoming homing torpedoes. It remains unclear, however, as to the extent it has been possible to develop an effective countermeasure against the wake-following torpedoes that were widely adopted by the former Soviet Union and its client states.

This year's annual concludes with a review of changing practices with respect to ship launch, using

the example of the recent roll-out and float-off of the lead Type 31 frigate *Venturer* by Babcock International as an example. The editor had the opportunity to witness the ship's roll-out at first hand. Whilst the process lacks something of the drama of a traditional dynamic launch, it is undoubtedly a less risky and more efficient process. As such, it forms an important part of the jigsaw of improvements to shipbuilding practices that are needed to support the renewal of many navies that is currently underway.

This photograph shows US F-35B strike fighters undertaking trials from the Japan Maritime Self Defence Force (JMSDF) helicopter-carrying destroyer *Kaga* (DDH-184) in November 2024 as part of preparations for Japan to operate her own aircraft of the type at sea. Despite already being in operational service with three navies – the JMSDF will be the fourth – the F-35 still continues to experience developmental difficulties. *(US Navy)*

ACKNOWLEDGEMENTS

Since its inception, production of *Seaforth World Naval Review* (*WNR*) has been supported by a small team comprising publisher Rob Gardiner, designer Stephen Dent and proof reader Stephen Chumbley. The last year has seen Rob's retirement and his replacement by Julian Mannering as the book's new publisher. The editor thanks Rob for his critical role first in driving forward *WNR*'s inception and then promoting it in the years that have followed. He looks forward to working with Julian in the years ahead.

In another change, impacting *WNR*'s author group, this year sees David Hobbs' last year as the contributor of the World Naval Aviation chapter after producing 17 editions. The editor is grateful for David's ever-insightful analysis during this time. More broadly, *WNR* remains dependent on the ongoing work of a wide group of authors, many of whom are regular contributors, illustrator John Jordan, and an increasing range of both official and private photographers. Amongst the last-mentioned, images provided by Lorenz Amiet, Andy Amor, Derek Fox, Vincent Groizeleau, Bruno Huriet, Michael Leek, Marc Piché, Bernard Prézelin, Arjun Sarup, Angad Singh and Peter Whittington have made a significant difference to this and previous editions. The editor also acknowledges with thanks the assistance of the many representatives of navy and industry who have supplied information. As always, he concludes by thanking his wife Susan for her all her help in supporting his work. His debt of gratitude is particularly large this year due to her willingness to drive him to the *Venturer* roll-out at Rosyth after a short bout of illness left him unable to undertake the journey on his own.

The editor continues to welcome engagement with WNR's readership. Please send any comments marked for my attention at info@seaforthpublishing.com.

Conrad Waters, Editor
30 June 2025

Notes

1. Donald J Trump (born 1946) is an American businessman and media celebratory who was the 45th and is currently the 47th president of the United States of America. Depending on one's viewpoint, he can be regarded as the hero of the Make America Great Again (MAGA) movement who is set to restore US economic prosperity or a convicted criminal with dangerous authoritarian tendencies.

2. A good initial overview of the Trump administration's approach to security policy is provided by Will Jessett in 'US Defence Policy And Planning: What To Expect Next?' posted to the Royal United Service Institute's site – rusi.org – on 16 May 2025. Inevitably, however, some of its conclusions have been overtaken by subsequent developments.

3. See, for example, 'Pentagon launches review of US-UK-Australia Aukus security alliance' posted to *The Guardian* newspaper's site – the guardian.com – on 11 June 2025. Most commentators see the review as routine but there are some in the Trump administration who see transfer of *Virginia* class submarines to Australia as part of the phased development of an Australian nuclear-powered submarine flotilla as unwise given America's current inability to produce sufficient boats for its own needs.

4. See Xiao Liang, Nan Tian, Diego Lopes da Silva, Lorenzo Scarazzato, Zubaida A Karim and Jade Guiberteau Ricard, *Trends in World Military Expenditure, 2024* (Stockholm: SIPRI, 2025) and available through sipri.org. Whilst the SIPRI data indicates that United States' defence spending was approaching US$1 trillion as early as 2024, its data includes money not contained within US estimates.

5. *Seaforth World Naval Review* has belatedly changed the spelling of the former Turkey to the new Türkiye following the rebranding campaign launched by President Erdoğan in late 2021 and subsequently adopted by the United Nations in 2022.

2.1 REGIONAL REVIEW

Author:
Conrad Waters

NORTH AND SOUTH AMERICA

On 6 April 2025, President Trump's new administration announced that the United States' national security budget would exceed US$1 trillion for the first time in the country's history. Whilst this headline figure is impressive, the detail is far more complex. When released the following month, the figures in the administration's headline proposal indicated that core Department of Defense spending would actually remain flat year-on-year at US$848.3 billion in non-inflation adjusted, cash terms. A further US$113.3 billion would come from a share of the so-called 'One Big Beautiful Bill', a Trump-sponsored piece of legislation aimed at securing many of his political objectives in a single budget 'reconciliation' bill. Combining these two separate figures together, and then adding in military spending by government agencies beyond the Pentagon, allows the 'magical' US$1 trillion to be reached.[1]

The Trump administration's approach is open to question on a number of grounds. Perhaps most fundamentally, the reconciliation funds are essentially one-off in nature, leaving open the question of the future trajectory of US defence spending beyond the next fiscal year. Without this certainty, military planners will find it difficult to implement the major modernisation and restructuring that, for example, the rise of China as a competing naval power requires.[2]

Whilst the framework for FY2026 defence spending became apparent in May, it was not until 25 June 2025 that details of the proposed Department of the Navy budget were released.[3] The total request is US$292.2 billion. US$248.9 billion is contained in the base budget and US$43.3 billion provided in the reconciliation bill. In total, this is up just over 11 percent from the US$263 billion enacted for FY2025. A major beneficiary of the additional money is procurement, with a material increase in the money spent on shipbuilding reflecting the need to reverse the downward trend in US Navy warship numbers and strengthen the maritime industrial base. Within the overall expansion, there are winners and losers. Notably, there is an acceleration of spending on amphibious warships but a pause in orders for *Constellation* (FFG-62) class frigates. The latter have undergone a problematic design process and the programme's future is seemingly in some doubt.

The new budget aims to stabilise fleet numbers at 287 ships; the same number envisaged at the time of last year's, FY2025 budget request. As is not unusual in the first year of a new presidential administration, there are no five-year Future Years Defense Program figures and this makes it difficult to analyse what the future trajectory of fleet numbers might be. Nevertheless, the decision to take time to work out the optimum way forward seems sensible in light of the administration's acknowledgment that radical action needs to be taken to address deficiencies in American shipbuilding capacity and efficiency. This is reflected in President Trump's March 2025 announcement of his intention to establish an Office of Shipbuilding within the White House; an initiative that could have a profound impact if pursued with enthusiasm and consistency. A seeming willingness to learn from overseas 'best practice' – that could include encouraging foreign investment to revitalise US shipyards – is indicative of the type of flexibility required to achieve the necessary transformation.

One element of the incoming administration's approach has been its disdain for diversity, equity and inclusion (DEI) policies. In a possible – if unlikely – coincidence, its early actions included firing, first, Admiral Linda Fagan, Commandant of the US Coast Guard and, then, Admiral Lisa Franchetti, Chief of Naval Operations; both the first women to hold their posts. Chairman of the Joint Chiefs of Staff, General Charles Q. Brown Jr – only the second African American to hold that role – has been another casualty. New Defense Secretary Pete Hegseth has shown particular determination to rid the US military of 'that DEI woke shit' in favour of embracing a so-called 'warrior culture'. In June 2025 he directed the re-naming of the fleet oiler *Harvey Milk* (T-AO-206) – originally christened in honour of an assassinated gay rights leader – in a move that, seemingly without irony, he described as 'taking the politics out of ship naming'. Whilst the editor looks forward with anticipation to hearing how Secretary Hegseth's philosophy might apply, say, to the naming of US Navy aircraft carriers, he does wonder whether this arguably divisive policy will encourage maintenance of a cohesive and well-motivated force.[4]

Gerald R. Ford (CVN-78) conducts a replenishment at sea with the *John Lewis* class replenishment oiler *Harvey Milk* (T-AO-206) in the Atlantic Ocean on 13 December 2024. Pete Hegseth, the current US Secretary of Defense, has decided to rename *Harvey Milk* – christened in honour of an assassinated gay rights leader – to 'take the politics out of ship naming'. There is, however, no indication that the policy of naming US Navy carriers after American presidents is to be revisited any time soon. *(US Navy)*

Table 2.1.1: FLEET STRENGTHS IN THE AMERICAS – LARGER NAVIES (MID 2025)

COUNTRY	ARGENTINA	BRAZIL	CANADA	CHILE	COLOMBIA	ECUADOR	PERU	USA
Aircraft Carrier (CVN/CV)	–	–	–	–	–	–	–	11
Strategic Missile Submarine (SSBN)	–	–	–	–	–	–	–	14
Attack Submarine (SSN/SSGN)	–	–	–	–	–	–	–	51
Patrol Submarine (SSK)	–[1]	4	4	4	4	2	6	–
Fleet Escort (CG/DDG/FFG)	3	6	12	8	4	2	6	83
Patrol Escort/Corvette (FFG/FSG/FS)	6	2	–	–	2	6	2	26
Missile Armed Attack Craft (PGG/PTG)	2	–	–	3	–	3	4	–
Mine Countermeasures Vessel (MCMV)	–	3	12	–	–	–	–	8
Major Amphibious Units (LHD/LPD/LPH/LSD)	–	2	–	1	–	–	1	32

Note:

1. Argentina's two remaining submarines are non-operational and unlikely to be returned to service. A number of other vessels are of uncertain operational status.

MAJOR NORTH AMERICAN NAVIES – CANADA

The Royal Canadian Navy has seen an acceleration in major procurement developments over the past year as long-awaited projects start to gather momentum. It seems likely that this positive trend will continue into the foreseeable future given the incoming Carney government's pledge to spend two percent of Canadian GDP on defence by 2026 in a substantial expansion of the spending plans announced as recently as April 2024 in the *Our North, Strong and Free* policy review.[5]

The most significant event over the past year was the ceremonial christening of the lead *Protecteur* class joint support ship at Seasapan Shipyards' Vancouver yard on 13 December 2024. She is one of two replenishment oilers based on the German Navy's Type 702 *Berlin* class combat support ship that have been contracted under Canada's costly National Shipbuilding Strategy (NSS). Subsequently technically launched by means of semi-submersible barge on 22 December, the 174m long, 21,600-tonne displacement vessel is reportedly the longest naval vessel ever constructed in Canada. However, some of the gloss was taken off the occasion when it was subsequently announced that *Protecteur*'s planned delivery would be pushed back by six months from the end of 2025 to mid-2026, continuing a record of delays and cost overruns that have impacted the programme. This latest setback does not, however, impact the other member of the class, *Preserver.* This ship seemingly remains on track for delivery in 2027 in a sign that the hard work being put into modernising Canadian shipbuilding might be starting to reap dividends.

Protecteur's launch followed that of *Robert Hampton Gray*, the final member of six *Harry DeWolf* class offshore patrol vessels that have been ordered for Royal Canadian Navy service under the Arctic and Offshore Patrol Vessel (AOPS) programme. She was launched from Irving Shipbuilding's east-coast Halifax shipyard on 9 December 2024. The facility had previously delivered *Frédérick Rolette*, the fifth ship in the class, on 29 August 2024 prior to her official commissioning on 13 June 2025.

The new Royal Canadian Navy joint support ship *Protecteur* seen fitting out at Seaspan's Vancouver shipyard in June 2025. She was launched in December 2024 in a tangible sign of progress with the implementation of Canada's National Shipbuilding Strategy. *(Mike Savage/Seaspan)*

Whilst Irving is currently building two modified variants of the AOPS design for the Canadian Coast Guard, its attention is increasingly turning to the much more significant and costly programme for new Canadian Surface Combatants (CSCs). These are being constructed to a much-modified iteration of the British Type 26 frigate/Global Combat Ship design; a variant that Canada now refers to as the 'River' class destroyer. Fabrication of a production test module commenced in June 2024 and was followed by the award of an 'implementation contract' on 8 March 2025 for the first three of what is eventually planned to be a total of 15 ships. The award has an initial value of C$8 billion (c. US$6 billion) and is intended to support delivery of these three ships during their first six years of construction, as well as the development and delivery of associated training, spares and maintenance. However, this is only part of the total cost – including equipment, systems and ammunition – of C$22.2 billion (c. US$16 billion) – that Canada estimates will eventually need to be spent to bring the three ships into service from the 'early 2030s' onwards. This cost is much higher than for comparable warship designs, including the destroyers' British-built half-sisters, in another indication of the heavy burden that the re-establishment of an indigenous shipbuilding industry is placing on Canada's defence budget.

With renewal of the surface fleet now underway, Canada's next big naval programme will be for replacement submarines under the Canadian Patrol Submarine Project. First established in 2021, this involves the acquisition of up to as many as twelve conventionally-powered boats to replace the existing quartet of *Victoria* (former British Royal Navy *Upholder*) class submarines from 2035 onwards. A request for information (RFI) issued in September 2024 solicited feedback on submarines 'currently in service or in production' that would be able to provide an under-ice capability. It is anticipated that a firm order will be placed by 2028 in order to meet the planned delivery schedule. Unlike the navy's surface vessels, it seems that construction is not expected to take place in Canada, although the RFI seeks suggestions as to how partnerships with Canadian industry could be leveraged to create economic benefits throughout the fleet's life cycle.[6] Predictably, the programme is attracting considerable interest from overseas submarine manufacturers in both Europe and Asia. A strong contender for the

Table 2.1.2: CANADIAN NAVY: PRINCIPAL UNITS AS AT MID 2025

TYPE	CLASS	NUMBER	TONNAGE	DIMENSIONS	PROPULSION	CREW	DATE
Principal Surface Escorts							
Frigate – FFG	**HALIFAX**	12	4,800 tonnes	134m x 16m x 5m	CODOG, 29 knots	225	1992
Submarines							
Submarine – SSK	**VICTORIA** (UPHOLDER)	4	2,500 tonnes	70m x 8m x 6m	Diesel-electric, 20+ knots	50	1990

eventual contract might be South Korea's KSS-3, particularly given the existence of technical cooperation agreements between Korean builders and the UK's Babcock International, holder of the current *Victoria* class in-service support contract.

Pending the eventual realisation of these various programmes, there is unlikely to be any material change to the summary of existing major Royal Canadian Navy warship classes provided in Table 2.1.2.

MAJOR NORTH AMERICAN NAVIES – UNITED STATES

The US Navy's 'ship battle forces' – vessels armed for naval combat or that contribute directly to navy warfighting or support missions – totalled 293 as of mid-2025; a decline of five ships year-on-year. This number is likely to fall further to 287/288 ships in the near future as inadequate funding and the contraction of the US naval industrial base has meant that recent production has proved incapable of keeping pace with the withdrawal of late Cold War-era ships. The navy has been pursuing service life extensions of existing warships 'to keep more ready players in the field' until permanent solutions can be found to address the problem.[7] In late October and early November it made two significant announcements extending the service lives of a further twelve of the *Arleigh Burke* (DDG-51) Flight 1 class destroyers by an average of four years each and three of the *Ticonderoga* (CG-47) class cruisers by an average of a little over three years each to give a total additional 58 years of ship service life through to FY2035. Similar initiatives have previously been taken with respect to aircraft carriers and submarines. Numbers of the latter are under particular pressure due to the block obsolescence of many of the remaining *Los Angeles* (SSN-668) class boats, resulting in a net decline in three submarines in the last year. Whilst long-anticipated, this is a particular problem given that the underwater domain is one of the main areas where the US Navy retains a decisive advantage over its Chinese rival.

The US Navy has big ambitions to include the size and 'lethality' of the fleet in the medium term. The latest Battle Force Ship Assessment and Requirement (BFSAR) – dating from 2023 – envisages a fleet of 381 traditional, crewed vessels. These will be supplemented by large numbers of uncrewed platforms to maintain a decisive warfighting advantage. To date, however, there has been no clear road map as to how this vision will be achieved. Previous analysis from the Congressional Budget Office (CBO) and many others has indicated that the US Navy will require more money and greater shipbuilding capacity to achieve its ambitions. Positively, the new Trump administration seems to have grasped the extent of the challenge. Indeed, the new Secretary of the Navy John Phelan has listed strengthening shipbuilding and the maritime industrial base as the first of his three priorities for shaping the fleet's future direction. This focus on the capacity and efficiency of US naval shipbuilding represents an important, long overdue first step to break the logjam that has seen the number of US warships stagnate for more than two decades.[8]

Inevitably, it will take time to understand the details of how Secretary Phelan intends to achieve his objective and to assess to what extent he is likely to succeed in expanding the US Navy's size. This sense of the new regime's plans being very much

The *Ticonderoga* class cruiser *Gettysburg* (CG-64) – pictured here in January 2025 – is one of three members of the class to have their service lives extended beyond the previous expectation as the US Navy attempts to mitigate delays to the delivery of new warships. In December 2024, she mistakenly shot down a F/A-18F Super Hornet whilst operating with the *Harry S. Truman* (CN-75) carrier strike group during the Red Sea crisis. *(US Navy)*

Table 2.1.3: USN FY2026 SHIPBUILDING BUDGET REQUEST

SHIP TYPE	FY2024 FUNDED[1]	FY2025 REQUEST[2]	FY2026 2025 PLAN[3]	FY2026 CURRENT PLAN[4]	CHANGE FY2026 (NEW V OLD)
Aircraft Carrier (CVN-78)	0	0	0	0	0
Strategic Submarine (SSBN-826)	1	0	1	1	0
Attack Submarine (SSN-774)	2	1	2	2	0
Destroyer (DDG-51)	2	3 (2)	2	2	0
Frigate (FFG-62)	2	0 (1)	2	0	-2
Amphibious Assault Ship (LHA-6)	0	0	0	1	+1
Amphibious Ship (LPD-17 F II)	0	1	0	1	+1
Medium Landing Ship (LSM(X))	0	0 (1)	1	9	+8
Replenishment Oiler (T-AO-205)	1	0	2	2	0
Light Replenishment Oiler (T-AOL(X))	0	0	0	0	0
Submarine Tender (AS(X))	0	0	0	0	0
Surveillance Ship (T-AGOS-25)	0	0	1	1	0
Total [5]	**8 (US$32.5bn)**	**5 (US$34.3bn)**	**11 (N/A)**	**19 (US$41.7bn)**	**+8(N/A)**

Notes

1. Authorised FY2024 construction programme.
2. Authorised FY2025 construction programme (figures in brackets those originally requested by the Biden administration).
3. FY2026 programme in the Biden administration's FY2025 five-year, Future Years Defence Program (FYDP)
4. FY2026 programme requested by second Trump adminisration.
5. US$ figures represent the 'New Construction Total' quoted in the Trump administration's FY2026 budget.

'work in progress' is also reflected in proposed US Navy warship procurement for FY2026; the only year for which the administration's future intentions are currently available. As illustrated by Table 2.1.3, there is a large headline increase in the number of ships requested compared both with FY2025 and the previous administration's plans for the year in question. However, the detail is more nuanced. Additions to the procurement programme all relate to amphibious ships, with the planned expedition of orders for the relatively inexpensive medium landing ship – already being considered by the Biden administration – effectively accounting for the entirety of the net addition. The other changes are a one-year acceleration in the planned procurement of a LHA-6 type amphibious assault ship and a LPD-17 Flight II amphibious transport dock, counterbalanced by the omission of two FFG-62 *Constellation* class frigates that were previously included in the FYDP for FY2026.

Alongside the future of the *Constellation* class, there is also considerable uncertainty over the next generation F/A-XX fighter programme. This has essentially been shelved for the time being to focus funding and technical resources on the US Air Force's F-47; a decision that will potentially significantly erode the capacity of the navy's air groups in a decade or so from now. In truth, the Trump administration's plans for the navy remain open to considerable uncertainty despite the seeming willingness to address long-standing problems. Many questions will only be answered as longer term procurement priorities are revealed. In the meantime, Table 2.1.4 summarises the major components of current US Navy fleet strength as of mid-2025, with more detailed analysis of recent developments provided under the following category headings.

Aircraft Carriers: In addition to the negative news with respect to the F/A-XX programme referenced above, the US Navy is continuing to experience delays in the expected delivery dates of its *Ford* class aircraft carriers. In April 2025, it emerged that the arrival of *John F. Kennedy* (CVN-79) would be pushed back until at least 2026 due to problems with her advanced weapons elevators and arresting gear, issues that also impacted *Gerald R. Ford* (CVN-78). Construction of the next ship in the class, *Enterprise* (CVN-80), has also experienced further slippage and she will not now be delivered until 2030. More positively, the FY2026 budget accelerates advanced procurement funding for the future CVN-82 in a sign of the continued importance attached to the nuclear-powered carrier fleet. In January 2025, President Joe Biden announced that CVN-82 would be named *William J. Clinton* and the future CVN-83 *George W. Bush* in a reversion to the practice of naming aircraft carriers after former US presidents.

Surface Combatants: The US Navy's force of large combatants has continued its recent decline over the past year despite the efforts to extend the lives of some ships. Four further *Ticonderoga* class cruisers – *Antietam* (CG-54), *Leyte Gulf* (CG-55), *Cowpens* (CG-63) and *Vicksburg* (CG-69) – have been decommissioned since 28 June 2024 whilst the only new arrival has been that of the *Arleigh Burke* Flight IIA class destroyer *John Basilone* (DDG-122). The ongoing DDG-51 programme is one of a number that are struggling to meet staff hiring, training, and retention targets, with the US Government Accountability Office's (GAO's) latest, June 2025, report noting that construction of the latest, Flight III iteration, had experienced additional delivery delays since its last assessment. Each of the first 13 follow-on Flight IIIs – the prototype, *Jack H. Lucas* (DDG-125), has already been delivered – being built at General Dynamics Bath Iron Works (BIW) and Huntington Ingalls Industries' (HHI's) Ingalls Shipbuilding had suffered further slippage. Deliveries are now ranging from eight to as much as 41 months behind their contracted dates. The start of operational testing and evaluation for DDG-125

The *Arleigh Burke* class destroyer *John Basilone* (DDG-122) is seen passing the Statue of Liberty whilst arriving at New York prior to her commissioning ceremony on 9 November 2024. She is the only large US Navy surface combatant to be delivered in the last year. *(US Navy)*

is also running behind schedule. Despite these problems, deliveries are expected to pick up in the year ahead. The FY2026 budget request sustains funding for the class at its typical two p.a. 'drumbeat' in line with a previous multi-year procurement agreement.[9]

The modernisation of the lead *Zumwalt* (DDG-1000) class destroyer to integrate the hypersonic Conventional Prompt Strike (CPS) weapon system continues to make good progress at Ingalls Shipbuilding. However, live testing has been pushed back to 2027. Meanwhile, *Michael Monsoor* (DDG-1001) has officially joined the 'battle force' and will commence CPS modernisation in mid-2026 after an initial operational deployment. The third ship, *Lyndon B. Johnson* (DDG-1002), will be delivered around the end of 2026 with CPS-capability installed, finally bringing the three ships actually built under a costly and troubled programme into front-line service.

Initial design development work continues on the DDG(X) guided missile destroyer, which will eventually follow the Flight III *Burke* class into production at BIW and Ingalls Shipbuilding. In contrast to previous recent practice, the US Navy plans to complete the ship's functional design prior to transferring the design effort to the shipbuilders. It is also evaluating the costs and benefits of using a so-called 'digital twin' to assist design changes and technology upgrades throughout the project's life.[10]

The force of smaller surface combatants has been bolstered by the deliveries of the *Freedom* (LCS-1) class Littoral Combat Ships *Nantucket* (LCS-27) and *Beloit* (LCS-29). This means that this class has reached its ten-ship target, with *Fort Worth* (LCS-3) still likely to be decommissioned after the final ship in the class, *Cleveland* (LCS-31), is delivered. There were no further deliveries of *Independence* (LCS-2) class variants over the last year but this iteration's final vessel, *Pierre* (LCS-38), was launched on 5 August 2024 prior to completing acceptance trials in June 2025. Her imminent arrival will take this class to 17 units, two above the previously declared target. It had been intended to decommission *Jackson* (LCS-6) and *Montgomery* (LCS-8), the oldest two members of the class still in service, but it seems that the current administration has decided to

Deliveries of both variants of the US Navy's Littoral Combat Ship type are drawing towards a conclusion, with only one vessel of each of the *Freedom* (LCS-1) and *Independence* (LCS-2) classes still to be delivered as of mid-2025. This photograph shows The *Freedom* variant *Nantucket* (LCS-27) alongside the historic frigate *Constitution* in Boston on 8 November 2024, a few days before her 16 November commissioning ceremony. *(US Navy)*

Table 2.1.4: UNITED STATES NAVY: PRINCIPAL UNITS AS AT MID 2025

TYPE	CLASS	NUMBER	TONNAGE	DIMENSIONS	PROPULSION	CREW	DATE
Aircraft Carriers							
Aircraft Carrier – CVN	**FORD** (CVN-78)	1	100,000 tonnes+	333m x 41/78m x 12m	Nuclear, 30+ knots	4,600	2017
Aircraft Carrier – CVN	**NIMITZ** (CVN-68)	10	100,000 tonnes+	333m x 41/78m x 12m	Nuclear, 30+ knots	5,200	1975
Principal Surface Escorts							
Cruiser – CG	**TICONDEROGA** (CG-47)	9	9,900 tonnes	173m x 17m x 7m	COGAG, 30+ knots	365	1983
Destroyer – DDG	**ZUMWALT** (DDG-1000)	2	15,800 tonnes	186m x 25m x 8m	IEP, 30+ knots	175	2016
Destroyer – DDG	**ARLEIGH BURKE** (DDG-51) – Flight III	1	9,700 tonnes	155m x 20m x 7m	COGAG, 30 knots	360	2023
Destroyer – DDG	**ARLEIGH BURKE** (DDG-51) – Flight II-A	44	9,400 tonnes	155m x 20m x 7m	COGAG, 30 knots	330	2000
Destroyer – DDG	**ARLEIGH BURKE** (DDG-51) – Flights I/II	29	8,900 tonnes	154m x 20m x 7m	COGAG, 30+ knots	305	1991
Littoral Combat Ship – FS	**FREEDOM** (LCS-1)	10	3,500 tonnes	115m x 17m x 4m	CODAG, 45+ knots	<50[1]	2008
Littoral Combat Ship – FS	**INDEPENDENCE** (LCS-2)	16	3,000 tonnes	127m x 32m x 5m	CODAG, 45+ knots	<50[1]	2010
Submarines							
Submarine – SSBN	**OHIO** (SSBN-726)	14	18,800 tonnes	171m x 13m x 12m	Nuclear, 20+ knots	155	1981
Submarine – SSGN	**OHIO** (SSGN-726)	4	18,800 tonnes	171m x 13m x 12m	Nuclear, 20+ knots	160	1981
Submarine – SSN	**VIRGINIA** (SSN-774)	24	8,000 tonnes	115m x 10m x 9m	Nuclear, 25+ knots	135	2004
Submarine – SSN	**SEAWOLF** (SSN-21)	3[2]	9,000 tonnes	108m x 12m x 11m	Nuclear, 25+ knots	140	1997
Submarine – SSN	**LOS ANGELES** (SSN-688)	20	7,000 tonnes	110m x 10m x 9m	Nuclear, 25+ knots	145	1976
Major Amphibious Units							
Amph. Assault Ship – LHD	**AMERICA** (LHA-6)	2	45,000 tonnes	257m x 32/42m x 9m	COGAG, 22+ knots	1,050	2014
Amph Assault Ship – LHD	**WASP** (LHD-1)	7[3]	41,000 tonnes	253m x 32/42m x 9m	Steam, 20+ knots	1,100	1989
Landing Platform Dock – LPD	**SAN ANTONIO** (LPD-17)	13	25,000 tonnes	209m x 32m x 7m	Diesel, 22+ knots	360	2005
Landing Ship Dock – LSD	**WHIDBEY ISLAND** (LSD-41)	10[4]	16,000 tonnes	186m x 26m x 6m	Diesel, 20 knots	420	1985

Notes:

1 Plus mission-related crew.

2 Third of class, SSN-23, is longer and heavier.

3 LHD-8 has many differences.

4 Includes four LSD-49 HARPERS FERRY variants.

abandon this plan. Despite the Littoral Combat Ships' modular, adaptable design it remains the intention to dedicate the LCS-1 class to anti-surface operations and their LCS-2 counterparts to the mine countermeasures role.

The follow-on *Constellation* class frigate programme continues to be beset by problems. Their primary cause seems to have been the US Navy's insistence on overlaying its own requirements on the 'parent' Italian FREMM design to the extent that it is essentially a different vessel. Although construction of the lead ship started in August 2022, its functional design was only 70 percent complete at the end of 2024. Moreover there has been unplanned weight growth of nearly 760 tonnes or 13 percent from initial estimates, limiting the scope for enhancements throughout the type's service life. Currently planned delivery of the lead ship is April 2029; three years later than first agreed. Whilst six members of the class have been contracted to date, no additional ships have been funded since FY2024. Indeed, the failure to include the type in the latest budget request suggests a full-scale review of the project's future is now underway.

Amphibious & Support Shipping: There have been no year-on-year changes to the numbers of major warships that form the core of the US Navy's amphibious fleet. There is a Congressional requirement to maintain a minimum force of 31 large amphibious ships, of which ten must be 'big deck' LHA/LHD type amphibious assault ships. This numerical total is currently exceeded by the 32 ships in service, albeit that the force of ten LHAs/LHDs will not be achieved until *Bougainville* (LHA-6) – the first, modified Flight I iteration of the *America* (LHA-6) class – is delivered. After some prevarication, the navy now appears committed to investing in the current large ship amphibious force and has resumed orders for the LPD-17 Flight II variant amphibious transport docks after a temporary pause in procurement of the type. In September 2024, HII Ingalls was awarded a block-buy contract for three LPD-17s – the fourth, fifth and sixth Flight II vessels – in addition to a modification of a separate contract for LHA-10, the third Flight I variant of the *America* class. Actual funding for *Travis Manion* (LPD-33), the fourth LPD-17 Flight II ship, was approved in the FY2025 budget whilst the FY2026 accelerates funding for *Helmand Province* (LHA-10) and the as yet-unnamed LPD-34.[11]

The US Navy's larger amphibious ships are due to be supplemented by a new class of medium landing ship (LSM-1). These are supposed to be relatively cheap but numerous vessels – at least 18 are envisaged – to support the US Marine Corps' Expeditionary Advanced Base Operations concept; a complement to the wider Distributed Maritime Operations (DMO) philosophy. It was originally intended to acquire a new design to meet the requirement. However, a request for proposals from five builders who had previously completed concept studies for the type was abandoned in December 2024 after costs were much higher than anticipated. Instead, an alternative approach is now being pursued that will seek to use an existing design. It seems that Bollinger Shipyards' *Nahshon* class landing ship design – itself a derivative of the US Army's *General Frank S. Besson* class logistics support vessels – built for the Israeli Navy and Damen's LST-100 are both being considered. This opens up the possibility that the two types might be constructed in parallel to the meet the requirement for nine vessels contained in the FY2026 budget.[12]

Meanwhile deliveries continue of the cheaper, commercially-based designs that have been procured to flesh out frontline amphibious ship numbers. These included *Robert E. Simanek* (ESB-7), the fifth of six expeditionary mobile bases that provide operating platforms for Special Forces and other maritime security missions, and *Point Loma* (T-EPF-15), the second of three Flight 1 variants of the numerous *Spearhead* (T-EPF-1) class of expeditionary fast transports operated by the US Military Sealift Command. The fact that three of the older members of the class have already been laid up in inactive status is, perhaps, indicative of the consequences of Congressional action forcing the navy to acquire more ships of a type than it really needs in order to support local industrial interests.

The FY2026 budget request also reflects ongoing procurement of *John Lewis* (T-AO-205) class replenishment oilers and *Don Walsh* (T-AGOS-25) class ocean surveillance ships. The former programme has suffered from delays and cost overruns in the past but now seems to be on a more stable course.[13] The two ships in the FY2026 budget will be the eleventh and twelfth members of a planned 20-ship class and will form part of an eight-vessel block buy agreed with General Dynamics NASSCO in September 2024. The fourth member of the class, *John F. Kennedy* (T-AO-208), was delivered in December 2024, whilst *Lucy Stone* (T-AO-209) and *Sojourner Truth* (T-AO-210) were launched, respectively, in September 2024 and April 2025. The T-AGOS-25 programme is far less advanced, with construction of the lead ship by Austal USA yet to start against a backdrop of design delays and an over 80 percent

Harrisburg (LPD-30) is the first Flight II iteration of the longstanding *San Antonio* amphibious transport dock class. After some prevarication, the US Navy has resumed construction of these vessels and a block buy contract for three of the Flight II variant was agreed with Huntington Ingalls Industries in September 2024. This photograph was taken at the time of *Harrisburg's* float off on 5 October 2024. *(Huntington Ingalls Industries)*

increase in projected cost to an eye-watering US$790 million. Given this, the decision to seek funding for the second ship – *Victor Vescovo* (T-AGOS 26) – in FY2026 is possibly premature.

Submarines: It is arguably the US Navy's submarine flotilla that is suffering most from the current problems being experienced by America's naval industrial base. The need to replace the navy's strategic submarines – its ongoing top priority – has coincided with an increased demand for new nuclear-powered attack submarines to replenish the quickly-diminishing number of Cold War boats. This has created something of a perfect storm that has seen a growing backlog of ordered but uncompleted submarines, highlighting the difficulties of expanding capacity in a particularly complex industry. Whilst large amounts are being allocated to strengthening industrial capacity – for example the FY2026 budget includes a further US$2.5 billion for 'productivity and wage enhancements' – the situation is likely to deteriorate before it gets better. It is particularly damming that the potential problem was identified as long as 30 years ago but not addressed until the damage had already been done.[14]

Despite having the highest priority for resource allocation, the expected delivery date for the first of the new *Columbia* (SSBN-826) class strategic submarines has continued to slip backwards in the past year. As of April 2024, completion of *District of Columbia* was running 12–16 months behind schedule. However, this delay had increased to around 17 months – to March 2029 – by mid-2025. Costs were also reported as running considerably above the US$15.2 billion currently allocated for the first boat's completion; a figure which does, however, encompasses many one-off, developmental expenses. The FY2026 budget includes funding for *Groton* (SSBN-828), the third member of the class, in line with a previously planned shift to annual procurement of the twelve-strong class.

The extent of delays impacting the lower, but still high priority, *Virginia* (SSN-774) class is significantly worse, averaging between 24 months (for the Block V variant) and 36 months (for the earlier Block IV variant) in April 2024. The current objective is to increase production rates from the existing 1.2 submarines each year to two boats each year by

The American naval industrial base continues to struggle to deliver sufficient submarines in a timely manner and large amounts of money are being invested in an attempt to rectify the problem. This photograph shows *Arkansas* (SSN-800) – the latest member of the *Virginia* class to be launched – at the time of being floated out from Huntington Ingalls Industries' Newport News shipyard in mid-2025. *(Huntington Ingalls Industries)*

The US Navy is acquiring large numbers of attritable uncrewed surface vessels (USVs) to explore the offensive and defensive potential of using swarms of such vessels as part of its broader evaluation of the future role of USVs in the fleet. This photograph shows a Global Autonomous Reconnaissance Craft (GARC) operating with the British Royal Navy patrol boat *Pursuer* during the BALTOPS 2025 exercises. The US Navy anticipates taking delivery of as many as 32 GRARCs a month before the end of 2025. *(US Navy)*

2028 and, thereafter, to 2.33 each year. However, there has been little evidence of tangible progress towards meeting this objective, with recent news reports highlighting production delays at General Dynamics Electric Boat (GDEB) due to supply train issues. GDEB shares construction of the navy's nuclear-powered submarines with HII's Newport News shipyard, which has also attracted negative press from the emergence of defective welding techniques in some of its construction. The FY2025 construction programme reduced procurement of the *Virginia* class to just one unit to try to give industry some breathing space to get back on track but the usual two annual SSN-774s are included in the FY2026 request. Hopefully this is a sign of confidence that construction performance will improve in the foreseeable future.

In the interim, the lack of foresight in addressing capacity problems has been demonstrated by a net fall of three in submarine numbers over the past year. The *Los Angeles* class boats *Helena* (SSN-725), *San Juan* (SSN-751), *Pasadena* (SSN-752) and *Topeka* (SSN-754) all retired from active service whilst the GDEB-built *Virginia* class submarine *Iowa* (SSN-797) was the only new boat to be delivered. Industry did, however, manage to launch two new members of the class; GDEB's *Idaho* (SSN-799) in August 2024 and Newport News' *Arkansas* (SSN-800) in June 2025.

Uncrewed Vessels: The US Navy continues to experiment with a wide range of uncrewed vessels as it evolves its thinking on how such ships will operate as part of a distributed fleet. Its previous plans for larger uncrewed surface types envisaged both a Large Unmanned Surface Vehicle (LUSV) for distributed missile capacity and a Medium Unmanned Surface Vehicle (MUSV) for surveillance and targeting sensors. However, in April 2025, it emerged that the two types will likely be combined into a single programme for autonomous surface craft that can carry either type of payload. An industry briefing suggests that the revised 'future unmanned surface vessel' programme will be comprised of high endurance, 'non-exquisite' autonomous vessels with a maximum speed in excess of 25 knots and a capacity to ship two 40ft equivalent containerised payloads. It appears that procurement of the new ships will commence in FY2027 but it is not yet clear when initial operational capability will be achieved. [15] Another area of US Navy USV development relates to the potential application of large volumes of cheap, attritable vessels that could adopt swarm tactics in both offence and defence. In January 2025, the navy announced that it would stand-up a third specialised USV squadron – Unmanned Surface Vessel Squadron 7 (USVRON 7) – to join the previously established USVRON 3 in experimenting with and evaluating the value of such small surface drones in the fleet.

The underwater equivalent of the future unmanned surface vessel is the 'Orca' Extra-Large Unmanned Undersea Vehicle (XLUUV), which is intended to supplement crewed submarines in missions such as minelaying. A total of six prototype XLUUVs – including one so-called 'test asset' – have been ordered from Boeing and all should be delivered before the end of 2025 despite developmental problems that have included battery endurance and the operation of its autonomous systems. At this stage, it seems unclear whether or not the navy will actually adopt the platform for operational use given the costs that this might involve. The US Navy is also considering the acquisition of alternative underwater systems, notably an ultra-large uncrewed undersea vehicle known as the Combat Autonomous Maritime Platform (CAMP). It is unclear whether this is seen as an alternative or supplement to the 'Orca' line of development. The navy also continues to expand its use of smaller UUVs across a large number of mission requirements.

OPERATIONAL HIGHLIGHTS

The last year has seen the US Navy continue to be engaged in extensive 'real life' warfighting against asymmetrical threats in the Red Sea whilst preparing for a possible future confrontation against a 'near peer' rival in the form of China's People's Liberation Army Navy (PLAN) in the Pacific. The Red Sea operations against the Houthis have been described as seeing the highest tempo of US Navy warfighting since the end of the Second World War. These have involved the first-time use of new weapons such as the Standard SM-3 ballistic missile interceptor in combat scenarios.

The new – as well as older – technology has generally worked well in defeating the threats posed by well-supplied rebel Houthi forces despite the adverse publicity generated by accidental losses of a number of aircraft from the *Harry S. Truman* (CVN-75) and the costly drain on expensive munitions, often expended against attritable drones. Whilst little is known of the detailed operational lessons that have been learned from the fighting, the experience gained will undoubtedly be of value in refining future US Navy tactics. One development the conflict has seemingly accelerated is exploration of the possibility of replenishing vertical launch systems (VLS) at sea. In October 2024, the technique was successfully practiced by the dry cargo ship *Washington Chambers* (T-AKE-11) and the cruiser *Chosin* (CG-65) whilst the two ships were operating in the Pacific using prototype equipment that had first been produced in the 1990s but never subsequently developed. If adopted, it would be part of the solution to countering the risk of magazine depletion that the Red Sea actions have highlighted.

In addition to revealing the challenges posed by protracted naval operations in a hostile littoral environment, the Red Sea engagements have had the

The *Nimitz* class aircraft carrier *Harry S. Truman* (CVN-75) and *Arleigh Burke* class destroyer *Jason Dunham* (DDG-109)sail together in the Mediterranean in May 2025 towards the end of an eventful deployment for the *Truman* strike group that saw intensive 'real world' warfighting against asymmetrical *Houthi* threats in the Red Sea. *(US Navy)*

The *Ticonderoga* class cruiser *Chosin* (CG-65) carries out an at-sea demonstration of the Transferrable Reload At-sea Method (TRAM) with the *Lewis and Clark* class dry cargo ship *Washington Chambers* (T-AKE-11) during an underway replenishment in the Pacific Ocean on 11 October 2024. The method opens up the possibility of replenishing the missile capacity of VLS-equipped ships at sea. *(US Navy)*

negative effect of draining US Navy resources away from the higher priority Pacific theatre. This will undoubtedly have delayed the actualisation of the new operating concepts that form part of the DMO philosophy. Despite this, the US Navy have expanded operations with a range of Allied navies, including joint carrier operations with visiting French and Italian carrier strike groups. US Navy submarines have also been periodically visiting the HMAS *Stirling* base in Western Australia as part of preparations for the Submarine Rotational Force-West that will be stood up from 2027 under the AUKUS strategic partnership.

Although the commitments in Middle East and Pacific have dominated US Navy activity, it maintains an extensive presence across the rest of the globe. For example, June 2025 saw the navy's newest carriers – *George H. W. Bush* (CVN-77) and *Gerald R. Ford* (CVN-78) – carry out rare dual carrier operations in the North Atlantic in a mirror image of a similar contemporaneous set of exercises by China's two carriers off Japan. At the other end of the scale, the mine countermeasures-equipped *Independence* (LCS-2) variant littoral combat ships have started forward deployment with the arrival of *Canberra* (LCS-30) at Bahrain in May 2025. *Tulsa* (LCS-16) and *Santa Barbara* (LCS-32) are also expected to be based at Bahrain and other vessels of the type in Japan, allowing the remaining wooden-hulled members of the *Avenger* (MCM-1) class to pass into retirement.

US COAST GUARD

The US Coast Guard's (USCG's) longstanding fleet replacement programme suffered several setbacks over the last year in a vivid illustration of the performance issues impacting the US shipbuilding industry. Originally devised in 2004, the initial programme envisaged procurement of (i) eight large 'WHEC' designated national security cutters, (ii) 25 slightly smaller 'WMSM' offshore patrol cutters, and (iii) 58 'WPC' fast response cutters in a comprehensive renewal of the USCG fleet.

Construction of the 'Legend' or *Bertholf* (WMSL-750) class national security cutters has been carried out by HII's Ingalls Shipbuilding under a largely successful programme that saw orders expand to eleven vessels. However, it is clear that things went seriously awry with the eleventh and final cutter, *Friedman* (WMSL-760), on which work began in May 2021 for planned delivery in 2024. In June 2025, it was announced that it had been agreed to terminate the ship's construction against a backdrop of a dispute relating to project delays and cost overruns. To the editor, it is astonishing that a problem of this magnitude could have emerged so late in the overall programme's history.

The US Coast Guard has been struggling with multiple problems impacting its cutter procurement programmes. The much delayed *Argus* ((WMSM-915) – the lead ship of a new class of offshore patrol cutters – was launched by Eastern Shipbuilding Group from its Panama City, Florida shipyard on 27 October 2023 but has yet to be delivered. *(US Coast Guard)*

Unfortunately, problems with executing the programme for the Heritage' or *Argus* (WMSM-915) offshore patrol cutters have been much more significant. The selected contractor, Eastern Shipbuilding Group (ESG), has struggled to execute the contract after suffering significant damage from a hurricane. It had originally been awarded a deal that included options for up to nine ships but production from the fifth cutter onwards was subsequently re-allocated to Austal USA under a July 2022 agreement that could extend to eleven vessels. As of mid-2025, delivery of the lead ship was scheduled for December 2025 – more than four years late – but this date could be further deferred. In June 2025 ESG was also ordered to suspend work on the third and fourth vessels against a backdrop of continued problems that could see completion of these ships also being re-assigned to another yard. Meanwhile, Austal commenced fabrication of the first of its offshore patrol cutters, *Pickering* (WSMM-919), on 24 August 2024.

By contrast, construction of the 'Sentinel' or *Bernard C. Webber* (WPC-1101) fast response cutters to a Damen Stan Patrol 4708 design by Bollinger Shipyards has been much more straightforward. *Frederick Mann* (WPC-1160) became the 60th member of the class to be delivered on 27 June 2025 as the number of the type required has crept steadily upwards to meet expanding USCG requirements both at home and overseas.

In addition to these three main programmes, the USCG also has a pressing need for new heavy and medium icebreakers as polar operations steadily grow in importance. A start was made in 2019 when the then VT Halter Marine – now acquired by Bollinger – was awarded a design and build contract for lead ship – subsequently named *Polar Sentinel* (WMSP-21) – of a heavy, polar security cutter class. This has turned out to be another botched project. As of March 2025, the ship's projected cost had increased from US$940 million to US$2.4 billion and planned delivery postponed from 2024 to 2030. Whilst Bollinger has a contract for a second vessel of the class, future procurement is currently up in the air amidst reports that the Trump administration intends to turn to Finland's experienced shipyards to expedite expansion of the coast guard's cutter fleet.

In the interim, the force has taken delivery of the second-hand icebreaking supply vessel *Aivq* – now renamed *Storis* (WAGB-21) – as an immediate reinforcement for its meagre icebreaking flotilla.

Despite these various woes, the Trump administration's One Big Beautiful Bill holds out the prospect of a significant reinforcement to coast guard capabilities, allocating as much as US$14.6 billion for expedited cutter construction. This figure includes at least two polar security cutters, three medium-sized arctic security cutters, eight offshore patrol cutters and as many as 15 fast response cutters. These would be accompanied by additional investment in aircraft and infrastructure to allow the USCG to escape a seeming spiral of decline.[16]

OTHER NORTH AND CENTRAL AMERICAN NAVIES

Mexico's navy hit the headlines for all the wrong reasons on 17 May 2025 when its sail training ship *Cuauhtémoc* collided with New York's Brooklyn Bridge in an accident that claimed the lives of two crew members. More broadly, the fleet has been starved of procurement funding by recent governments, ending an increasingly ambitious programme of indigenous naval construction that extended the Damen Sigma 10514 frigate-like oceanic patrol vessel *Benito Juárez.* The navy hopes to resume construction of offshore patrol ships alongside that of smaller coastal vessels and interceptors in the 2025-2030 timeframe. However, it is unclear if the current Sheinbaum administration will provide the funding to secure this ambition.

There have been few other significant regional developments. Ongoing deliveries of the 13 planned Metal Shark '85 Defiant' near coastal patrol vessels (NCPVs) – based on Damen Stan Patrol 2606 design – to Caribbean navies under a US military assistance programme continue at a slow rate. The **Dominican Republic** received its second vessel – and the seventh vessel in the overall programme – in June 2025. The country also reportedly hopes to receive larger second-hand patrol ships from Portugal in the near future.

MAJOR SOUTH AMERICAN NAVIES - BRAZIL

As indicated by Table 2.1.5, there have been no significant changes to the Brazilian Navy's composition over the last year. *Tonelero*, the third *Riachuelo* class submarine being built to the Naval Group 'Scorpène' design under the PROSUB project commenced sea trials in October 2024 and should be delivered before the end of 2025. By that time, the fourth and final boat in the programme - the renamed *Almirante Karam* (formerly *Angostura*) – should also have been launched. However, budgetary cuts are reportedly impacting the overall project, threatening progress with the country's first nuclear-powered attack submarine, *Álvaro Alberto.* Although much preliminary work has been undertaken on this high profile project, it will be the mid-2030s at the earliest before she becomes operational.[17]

Construction of surface combatants is also progressing against a backdrop of further disruption due to funding constraints. Notably, the lead *Tamandaré* class frigate was christened at the TKMS Estaleiro Brasil Sul yard in Itajaí on 9 August 2024 prior to being floated out on the 17th of that month.[18] Although widely described as a MEKO A-100BR design, she is somewhat larger than TKMS standard A-100 corvette/light frigate designs, with her reported length of 107 metres and displacement of 3,500 tonnes falling between these ships and the company's larger A-200 series. The second member of the class, *Jerônimo de Albuquerque,* was subsequently rolled out of her construction hall in May 2025 prior to her planned launch and the keel of the third vessel, *Cunha Moreira*, was laid the same month. The Brazilian Navy would like to add an additional quartet of the class to the four that have been ordered so far to complete replacement of the remaining *Niterói* and *Greenhalgh* (former British Type 22 *Broadsword*) class frigates but it is unclear whether the budget will be available. *Greenhalgh* herself was disposed of in a SINKEX on 13 September 2024, bringing the Falkland War veteran's career to a watery end. The navy's continued use of former British warships does, however, look set to continue into the foreseeable future with the proposed acquisition of the amphibious transport docks *Albion* and *Bulwark*, which have been prematurely retired from Royal Navy service. Together with the existing *Atlântico* (ex HMS *Ocean*), these former British ships provide a considerable reinforcement to the navy's amphibious capacity.

Other projects underway include the rejuvenated programme for the 500 tonne *Macaé* class patrol vessels. After a considerable delay caused by the collapse of the original builder, the third member of the class – *Maracanã* – was completed at the Rio de Janeiro Naval Arsenal in 2022. The facility is

Table 2.1.5: BRAZILIAN NAVY: PRINCIPAL UNITS AS AT MID 2025

TYPE	CLASS	NUMBER	TONNAGE	DIMENSIONS	PROPULSION	CREW	DATE
Principal Surface Escorts							
Frigate – FFG	**GREENHALGH** (Batch I Type 22)	1	4,700 tonnes	131m x 15m x 4m	COGOG, 30 knots	270	1979
Frigate – FFG	**NITERÓI**	5	3,700 tonnes	129m x 14m x 4m	CODOG, 30 knots	220	1976
Corvette – FSG	**BARROSO**	1	2,400 tonnes	103m x 11m x 4m	CODOG, 30 knots	145	2008
Corvette – FSG	**INHAÚMA**	1	2,100 tonnes	96m x 11m x 4m	CODOG, 27 knots	120	1989
Submarines							
Submarine – SSK	**RIACHUELO** (Scorpène)	2	1,900 tonnes	71m x 6m x 6m	Diesel-electric, 20+ knots	35	2022
Submarine – SSK	**TIKUNA** (Type 209/1400 – modified)	1	1,600 tonnes	62m x 6m x 6m	Diesel-electric, 22 knots	40	2005
Submarine – SSK	**TUPI** (Type 209/1400)	1	1,500 tonnes	61m x 6m x 6m	Diesel-electric, 22+ knots	30	1989
Major Amphibious Units							
Helicopter Carrier – LPH	**ATLÂNTICO** (OCEAN)	1	22,500 tonnes	203m x 35m x 7m	Diesel, 18 knots	490	1998
Landing Ship Dock – LSD	**BAHIA** (FOUDRE)	1	12,000 tonnes	168m x 24m x 5m	Diesel, 20 knots	160	1998

In a case of 'out with the old and in with the new', the Brazilian Navy launched the first of its four *Tamandaré* class frigates from TKMS Estaleiro Brasil Sul shipyard on 17 August 2024 before disposing of the decommissioned Type 22 frigate *Greenhalgh* in a SINKEX the following month. *Greenhalgh* was formerly the British Royal Navy frigate *Broadsword*; a veteran of the Falklands War. *(Brazilian Navy)*

currently completing *Mangaratiba*, the fourth ship in the class, and commenced work on a fifth vessel, *Miramar*, on 8 August 2024. Construction also continues on a new Antarctic support ship, *Almirante Saldanha,* at the Jurong Aracruz shipyard in Aracruz-Espirito Santo. It was originally anticipated that she would be delivered before the end of 2025 but this schedule may be subject to some delay.

OTHER SOUTH AMERICAN NAVIES

Amongst the two other traditional leading South American 'ABC' navies, **Argentina's** fleet retains aspirations to reinstate a submarine capacity and acquire new amphibious ships. There have been a number of reports of ongoing discussions with Naval Group and TKMS to progress the former requirement. In practice, however, the Milei administration's ambitions to increase defence spending are likely to be constrained by economic conditions, whilst there have been higher priorities – such as the purchase of combat aircraft – for the limited pool of available funds. As such, it is a matter of speculation as to whether Argentina will realise its naval objectives in the foreseeable future. Indeed, the navy's strength has continued to decline over the past year with the retirement of the three *Drummond* (French A69) class corvettes. *Granville* was the last of the trio to leave Argentine service when decommissioned on 31 August 2024.

The third 'ABC' navy, **Chile**, is in a far better position, with its fleet of eight major surface combatants and four submarines a rival to the Brazilian Navy for the claim to be South America's leading naval power. Naval modernisation is being bolstered by a 'Continuous Plan of Naval Construction' that intends to steadily enhance the capacity of local shipbuilder ASMAR. The shipbuilder delivered the icebreaker *Almirante Viel* in July 2024 and is now working on the 'Escotillón IV' project for up to four amphibious transport docks that, like the icebreaker, are based on a VARD design. These will, in turn, pave the way for a national frigate programme in due course. Construction of the first amphibious ship was reportedly approaching the half way mark in mid-2025, when the second vessel was laid down.

Peru's naval modernisation is also gaining pace. In June 2025, local shipyard SIMA returned the Type 209/1200 submarine *Chipana* back to Peruvian naval service after completion of a comprehensive and protracted life extension programme. The navy's other three Type 209/1200 boats are also scheduled to undergo similar modernisation, with work on *Antofagasta* reportedly now well advanced. The country's two older Type 209/1100 submarines will likely be retired as the modernised vessels return to service.

In the longer term, SIMA looks set to work in conjunction with HD Hyundai Heavy Industries (HD HHI) to develop a replacement 1,500 tonne submarine design. The memorandum of understanding for this programme follows the 2024 contract with the South Korean shipbuilder that encompasses the construction of a frigate, an offshore patrol vessel and two logistics support ships in SIMA's yards as the first instalment of a major programme of fleet renewal. In the interim, *Paita* – the second South Korean designed *Makassar* class amphibious transport dock – built at SIMA's Callao yard was reportedly close to completion in mid-2025. Additionally, two *Río Pativilca* patrol ships – *Río Huarmey* and *Río Nepeña* – were launched from the company's facility at Chimbote in January 2025. Respectively the seventh and eighth members of the class, they are another licensed South Korean design manufactured under a transfer of technology agreement with K Shipbuilding Co (formerly STX).

In another sign of South Korea's efforts to gain a stranglehold over South America's naval sector**,** **Ecuador's** navy took delivery of a second-hand Korea Coast Guard *Tae Pyung Yang* offshore patrol vessel in April 2025. Renamed *Jambeli,* the donated c. 4,000 tonne vessel has been transferred to help develop industrial ties and will be the largest vessel in naval service. It has also been reported that talks have been held with Italy to explore the transfer of decommissioned *Maestrale* class frigates to replace the pair of life-expired *Leander* class vessels previously obtained from Chile. Meanwhile, there has been little news of further progress with the Fassmer MPV70 Mk III multi-role vessel ordered in 2020 and being built by local yard ASTINAVE.

Columbia concluded lengthy negotiations with Damen for the build phase of its lead Sigma 10514 light frigate in August 2024. She is intended to be the first of five ships built under the navy's *Plataforma Estratégica de Superficie* (PES) programme to replace the existing quartet of *Almirante Padilla*, class frigates. The ship will be constructed locally by the COCTEMAR shipyard, with Damen seemingly being well placed to support delivery of the project by a yard that has no previous experience of frigate construction given its success in similar situations in both Mexico and Indonesia. COTECMAR will also shortly launch POC-93, the first of four planned oceanic patrol vessels, and is building a series of coastal hospital ships to provide medical services to remote littoral regions.

Venezuela's cash-strapped navy continues to focus on refitting existing vessels against a backdrop of territorial tensions with neighbouring **Guyana.** The latter country took delivery of a 35 metre patrol ship from the United States' Metal Shark in 2024 and is reportedly awaiting delivery of a larger 58 metre offshore patrol vessel from France's OCEA under a reported €39.5 million (c. US$47 million) deal.

Uruguay's drawn out acquisition of new patrol vessels has started to see tangible fruit with a first-steel cutting ceremony for the lead ship at the Spanish Cardama group's Vigo shipyard in March 2025. The event was followed by the ship's keel laying on 15 May, with commencement of work on her sister said to be imminent. The arrival of the two new ships cannot come quickly enough given that the bulk of the existing fleet has been reported as being no longer seaworthy.[19]

Notes:

1. The politically-charged US budget process is always challenging to decipher and this year's 'reconciliation' process – essentially a mechanism to expedite a budget's approval by allowing it to be approved by a simple majority – makes this doubly so. It is important to note that the US Department of Defense does not account for all US military spending; for example, the National Nuclear Security Administration also has a substantial, defence-related budget.

2. A good critique of the US budget proposal was provided by Shaun McDougall, 'A Trillion-Dollar Defense Budget That Isn't' posted to Forecast International's *Defense and Security Monitor* – dsm.forecastinternational.com – on 7 May 2025.

3. The details of the defence and, hence, navy budgets were revealed much later in the year than is normally the case, causing some Congressional disquiet. This also gave the editor very limited time to analyse the detailed proposals before the publisher's deadlines; he apologies for any errors that might have resulted from the rush.

4. Secretary Hegseth's remark criticising DEI policy was referenced in an article carried by *The Guardian* newspaper, 'Trump fires Black joint chiefs chair Hegseth accused of promoting diversity' that was posted to the guardian.com on 22 February 2025. His subsequent justification for the fleet replenishment oiler re-naming was reported on the *ABC News* site - abcnews.go.com – in an article by Anne Flaherty and Chris Boccia, 'Hegseth announces USNS Harvey Milk is being renamed USNS Oscar V. Peterson' posted on 27 June 2025. It is worth noting that the current US administration is not the first to turn to revising warship names to further a political agenda. For example, the former *Chancellorsville* (CG-62) was renamed *Robert Smalls* in March 2023 following the establishment of a commission to examine the use of Confederate symbols across the US military. Whilst acknowledging this – and having some sympathy with the drive to focus America's armed forces on their core, warfighting mission – the editor would argue that the highly-politicised way in which the Trump administration is pursuing its objectives for the military is open to significant objection.

5. See, *Our North, Strong and Free: A Renewed Vision for Canada's Defence* (Ottawa: Department of National Defence, 2024) which is readily available by searching the web.

6. Details of the RFI were provided in a press release, 'Government of Canada announces progress on the Canadian Patrol Submarine procurement' posted by Public Services and Procurement Canada on 17 September 2024.

7. See the US Navy press release, 'SECNAV Announces Service Life Extensions for 12 Destroyers to "Keep More Ready Players on the Field"' dated 31 October 2024.

8. The emphasis on shipbuilding and the naval industrial base is made clear in the US Navy's *FY 2026 Budget Highlights* (Washington DC: Office of Budget, 2025). The other two priority objectives are fostering an adaptive, accountable and innovative war-fighter culture, and the health, welfare and training of sailors and their Families. A good overview of the current US government's approach to the navy is provided by Sidney E Dean in, 'Race against time: The naval policy of the second Trump administration', *Maritime Defence Monitor* 012025 (Bonn, Mittler Report, 2025) and currently available at euro-sd.com.

9. For progress with the DDG-51 programme and other major US Navy projects, see the GAO's *Weapon Systems Annual Assessment* (Washington DC: United States Government Accountability Office, 2025). Exceptionally, the approved FY2025 budget added a third destroyer to planned procurement.

10. An explanation of the digital twin concept, albeit in a British context, was provided by the *Navy Lookout* site – navylookout.com – in an article, 'Synthetic battlespace – digital twins and the Royal Navy's new training era' posted on 17 June 2025.

11. A thorough summary of amphibious assault ship procurement is provided by Ronald O' Rourke, *Navy LPD-17 Flight II and LHA Amphibious Ship Programs: Background and Issues for Congress R43543* (Washington DC: Congressional Research Service, 2025). This is one of numerous periodically updated reports by Mr O'Rourke, the Congressional Research Service's (CRS's) longstanding Specialist in Naval Affairs. They can be accessed by searching the Congressional Research Service's website at crsreports.congress.gov.

12. Another Ronald O'Rourke CRS report, *Navy Medium Landing Ship (LSM) Program: Background and Issues for Congress R46374,* provides a comprehensive analysis of the project's progress.

13. The programme was detailed by Sidney E. Dean in 'John Lewis (TA-205) class oilers', *Seaforth World Naval Review* 2025 (Barnsley: Seaforth Publishing, 2024), pp. 100-111.

14. See, for example, Ronald O'Rourke's CRS report, *Navy Virginia-Class Submarine Program and AUKUS Submarine (Pillar 1) Project: Background and Issues for Congress RL32418,* page 4.

15. For further information on the new vessel, see Justin Katz, 'Navy to host industry for talks about "Future Unmanned Surface Vessel" program' posted to the *Breaking Defense* site – breakingdefense.com – on 16 May 2025.

16. See Sam LaGrone, 'Reconciliation Bill Calls for $14.6B in Coast Guard Cutters, New Arctic Icebreakers' posted to the *USNI News* site – usninews.org – on 29 April 2025.

17. The *Poder Naval* site – naval.com.br – remains an invaluable source of information for Brazilian naval developments.

18. thyssenkrupp Marine Systems was rebranded as TKMS in June 2025 as part of preparations for its demerger from the broader thyssenkrupp AG group.

19. The Spanish-language defensa.com and its rival infodefensa.com remain invaluable sources of additional information on naval developments in Latin America.

2.2 REGIONAL REVIEW

ASIA AND THE PACIFIC

Author:
Conrad Waters

Although the world's attention has been diverted by conflicts in Europe and the Middle East, it is the ongoing development of China's People's Liberation Army Navy (PLAN) that continues to have the most profound effect on the balance of world naval power. It is true that events of the past 12 months have lacked some of the drama that surrounded the commencement of sea trials by *Fujian*, China's first catapult-assisted take-off but arrested recovery (CATOBAR) configured aircraft carrier, in May 2024. Despite the lack of eye-catching headlines driven by such an event, the PLAN has made further progress from both a technical and operational perspective over the last year.

Much of this progress is being driven by the almost overwhelming strength of China's industrial base. A March 2025 report from the Center for Strategic and International Studies (CSIS), a leading American think tank, noted that China's shipbuilding sector now accounts for more than half of the world's total commercial shipbuilding production in terms of gross tonnage.[1] Its analysis highlighted the 'dual use' nature of this enterprise, with the integration of commercial and naval shipbuilding activities helping to facilitate the PLAN's rapid expansion. The last year has seen more evidence of this trend, with significant developments including commissioning of the lead ships of a new Type 54B frigate class, the launch of the first of a larger, Type 076 amphibious assault ship design and, perhaps most notably, material progress in the field of nuclear-powered submarine construction. Meanwhile, production of established designs continued at a rapid pace. All-in-all, the PLAN continues to expand its quantitative lead over the US Navy and is also narrowing the qualitative gap.

The most important question – posed repeatedly in previous editions of *Seaforth World Naval Review* – is what China intends to do with its costly investment in building a world-class navy. Sinophobes highlight China's desire to use its new-found power to further its territorial and political objectives, starting with the long-held ambition to achieve Chinese reunification through the return of Taiwan to the mainland's control. Proponents of this line of thinking were strengthened in their beliefs in January 2025, when news emerged of construction of a series of amphibious assault barges that could facilitate a cross-strait landing.[2] Described by some commentators as 'Shuiqiao ships' (water bridges), they are conceptually similar to the Mulberry harbour system that supported the 1944 Allied invasion of Normandy during the Second World War.

The PLAN's operational reach is increasingly stretching far beyond the Taiwan Strait. In October 2024, the PLAN's two existing aircraft carriers *Liaoning* and *Shandong* carried out China's inaugural dual carrier strike group exercise in the sensitive waters of the South China Sea. This was followed in June 2025 by the first simultaneous deployment of the two ships beyond the First Island Chain, with both carrier groups conducting intensive training in the Philippine Sea for an extended period. During this deployment, Japanese maritime patrol aircraft monitoring the manoeuvres were harassed by PLAN jets on multiple occasions. Another sign of the PLAN's long-arm came in April 2025 with the opening of a new, Chinese-funded joint logistics and training centre at Ream Naval Base adjoining the Gulf of Thailand in Cambodia.[3] The facility is only China's second overseas base, the first being opened in Djibouti in 2017.

The ongoing growth in the PLAN's regional maritime influence is accelerating a reaction from China's somewhat conflicted Asian-Pacific neighbours. These countries often regard China as a valued economic partner but view its expanding military prowess – often combined with assertive diplomacy – with a degree of concern. The need to prepare for this potential threat, increasingly a focal point of regional defence reviews, is being reflected in an accelerated pace of naval investment that is leading to the acquisition of expensive new capabilities across the region. Amongst prominent examples of this trend are Australia's pursuit of the trilateral SSN-AUKUS submarine project and the work Japan is undertaking to equip its existing *Izumo* (DDH-183) class 'destroyers' as short take-off and vertical landing (STOVL) 'Lightning carriers'. Many other countries have significant, if less ambitious, projects underway. Whilst foreign shipbuilders are gaining significant benefits from this investment splurge, another consequence is the expansion of the regional naval sector beyond established players such as South Korea due to technological transfer and other co-production agreements.

A US F-35B Lightning II strike fighter lands on the flight deck of the Japanese 'helicopter-carrying destroyer' *Kaga* (DDH-184) on 2 November 2024 during preparatory trials for the eventual embarkation of Japan Air Self Defence Force Lightning IIs on the two ships of the class. The rapid expansion of the capability and reach of China's PLAN is a major factor behind other regional navies acquiring expensive new capabilities. *(US Navy)*

Table 2.2.1: FLEET STRENGTHS IN ASIA AND THE PACIFIC – LARGER NAVIES (MID 2025)

COUNTRY	AUSTRALIA	CHINA[1]	INDONESIA	JAPAN	S KOREA	SINGAPORE	TAIWAN	THAILAND
Aircraft Carrier (CV)	–	2	–	2	–	–	–	–
Support/Helicopter Carrier (CVS/CVH)	–	–	–	2	–	–	–	1
Strategic Missile Submarine (SSBN)	–	6	–	–	–	–	–	–
Attack Submarine (SSN)	–	6	–	–	–	–	–	–
Patrol Submarine (SSK/SS)	6	50	4	22	21	4	4[4]	–
Fleet Escort (DDG/FFG)	10	105	7	43	30	6	25	7
Patrol Escort/Corvette (FFG/FSG/FS)	–	50	24	6	3	14	7	10
Missile Armed Attack Craft (PGG/PTG)	–	75	24[2]	6	18	–	c. 30	–
Mine Countermeasures Vessel (MCMV)	2	35	8	17	12	4	c. 6	5
Major Amphibious Units (LHD/LPD/LSD)	3	12	8[3]	3	2	4	2	2

Notes:
1: Chinese numbers approximate and exclude some obsolescent vessels.
2: Some additional Indonesian patrol gunboats are able to ship missiles.
3: Includes three vessels configured as hospital ships.
4: Taiwan's submarines are reported to have limited operational availability.

The Royal Australian Navy *Anzac* class frigate *Arunta* pictured in the Captain Cook Graving Dock at Fleet Base East, Sydney, during the course of a scheduled refit in June 2023. The decision to retire some members of the *Anzac* class earlier than previously scheduled and to cancel the TransCAP life-extension programme means that numbers of Australian major surface combatants are likely to fall in the short term despite plans for longer-term growth. *(Australian Department of Defence)*

MAJOR REGIONAL POWERS – AUSTRALIA

The Royal Australian Navy's (RAN's) likely future trajectory has been set by a series of major policy decisions that commenced with signature of the trilateral AUKUS strategic partnership in September 2021. The acquisition of, first, *Virginia* (SSN-774) and, ultimately, SSN-AUKUS submarines under the so-called Pillar 1 of the agreement was subsequently detailed in the publication of the *AUKUS Nuclear-Powered Submarine Pathway* in March 2023. This should start to see the RAN transition to a nuclear-powered submarine flotilla from the early 2030s onwards at an estimated cost over the next decade (2024-34) alone of up to AU$63 billion (c. US$41 billion). Modernisation of the existing *Collins* class patrol submarines and investment in other underwater capabilities such as uncrewed vehicles will add a further AUS$13 billion (c. US$8.5 billion) to the total. Meanwhile, the fleet of surface combatants will transition to the structure focused on the three existing *Hobart* class destroyers, six new *Hunter* class frigates and eleven, cheaper general purpose frigates – all supplemented by six optionally crewed large surface vessels – under the plans set out in the *Enhanced Lethality Surface Combatant Fleet* review published in February 2024. When combined with spending on investments in other ships, equipment and support facilities, this could cost up to an additional AUS$69 billion (c. US$45 billion) in the ten years to 2034. Overall investment in the maritime domain over this timescale is estimated to around 38 percent of the Australian Department of Defence's investment programme; well over double that individually allocated to its land and air counterparts.[4]

Whilst these investments are unquestionably substantial, major questions remain. In the immediate term, a decision needs to be taken on the design of the new general purpose frigates, for which the German TKMS MEKO A-200 and the Japanese Mitsubishi Heavy Industries 'Upgraded *Mogami*' were shortlisted in November 2024. A decision is expected before the end of 2025 in the hope of bringing the first of the new ships into service around the end of the decade. More significantly, the decision to abandon the planned TransCAP life-extension programme for the existing *Anzac* class means that the number of major surface combatants will fall to no more than ten ships before new vessels start to be delivered. *Anzac* herself was decommissioned in May 2024. Her sister, *Arunta*, will likely follow during 2026, subject to an assessment of her condition. Similarly, it is also questionable whether

Table 2.2.2: ROYAL AUSTRALIAN NAVY: PRINCIPAL UNITS AS AT MID 2025

TYPE	CLASS	NUMBER	TONNAGE	DIMENSIONS	PROPULSION	CREW	DATE
Principal Surface Escorts							
Frigate – FFG	**HOBART** (F-100)	3	6,300 tonnes	147m x 19m x 5m	CODOG, 28 knots	200	2017
Frigate – FFG	**ANZAC**	7	3,600 tonnes	118m x 15m x 4m	CODOG, 28 knots	175	1996
Submarines							
Submarine – SSK	**COLLINS**	6	3,400 tonnes	78m x 8m x 7m	Diesel-electric, 20 knots	45	1996
Major Amphibious Units							
Amph Assault Ship – LHD	**CANBERRA** (JUAN CARLOS I)	2	27,100 tonnes	231m x 32m x 7m	IEP, 21 knots	290	2014
Landing Ship Dock – LSD	**CHOULES** (LARGS BAY)	1	16,200 tonnes	176m x 26m x 6m	Diesel-electric, 18 knots	160	2006

the elderly *Collins* class submarines can be kept fully operational until their planned nuclear-powered replacements arrive. An AU$2.2 billion (c. US$1.5 billion) contract to fund the initial phase of a planned AU$4–5 billion life extension programme was signed in July 2024. However, the project has been listed as a 'product of concern' against a backdrop of reports of significant corrosion emerging in the class.

In the meantime, the core fleet structure outlined in Table 2.2.2 has remained unchanged over the past year. There does, however, continue to be more adjustment with respect to smaller warships, with the minehunter *Gascoyne* and the patrol vessel *Broome* both being decommissioned during the second half of 2024. The latter's departure leaves just three of the once 14-strong *Armidale* class in commission. Their steady withdrawal is being counterbalanced by ongoing deliveries of the new 'Evolved Cape' class patrol vessels; an enhanced variant of the original 'Cape' class boats that were initially ordered for Australian Boarder Force (ABF). Eight of the type – plus two 'Capes' operated on lease – are now in RAN service following the deliveries of *Cape Solander* and *Cape Schanck* from Austal in, respectively, August and November 2024.[5] Two further members of the class are being built for the RAN to meet a total requirement for ten 'Evolved Capes', two of which will be used for training. In a change to previous policy, many of the RAN vessels are losing their previous 'ADV' (Australian Defence Vessel) prefix and being commissioned as Australian warships with an 'HMAS' (His Majesty's Australian Ship) designation. This reflects the fact that – following the decisions taken in the *Enhanced Lethality Surface Combatant Fleet* review – the class is now seen as forming a long-term part of the fleet rather than a temporary expedient pending delivery of the *Arafura* class.

Ordered under Project SEA1180 Phase 1 in 2018, the original requirement for the NVL-designed *Arafura* class has been overtaken by changes in Australian defence policy. Now seen as too complex for constabulary patrol operations but insufficiently lethal for front-line service, their planned numbers were cut from twelve to six in the revamped 2024 surface fleet plan. Completion of the lead vessel, launched back in December 2021, has also proved problematic, although she was finally accepted in January 2025 prior to being formally commissioned on 28 June that year. The five remaining vessels of the class remain under construction at what is now

The 'Evolved Cape' class patrol vessels *Cape Solander* (left) and *Cape Schanck* (right) seen during their commissioning ceremony held at HMAS *Coonawarra*, Darwin, on 8 May 2025. In a change to previous policy, the Royal Australian Navy is commissioning many of these vessels, giving them the prefix 'HMAS'. *(Australian Department of Defence)*

After long delays, the Royal Australian Navy commissioned the lead *Arafura* class offshore patrol vessel – pictured here during sea trials in August 2024 – on 28 June 2025. Changes in proposed future fleet structure mean that orders for the class have been reduced to just six vessels and their future utility is somewhat questionable. *(Australian Department of Defence)*

BAE Systems Maritime Australia at Osbourne, Adelaide and Cimvec's shipyard at Henderson, Perth. NVL has now sold its stake in what was Lürssen Australia to Cimvec and withdrawn from the country after becoming another casualty of a seemingly ever-changing Australian naval procurement strategy.

MAJOR REGIONAL POWERS – CHINA

As already noted in the introduction to this chapter, China's PLAN continues to expand both its force capabilities and operational experience at a rapid rate. Notably, serial production of various warship classes of all types across China's numerous shipyards has now allowed the withdrawal of the vast proportion of the fleet's 'legacy' types. As such, the once wide qualitative gap that existed with comparative 'Western' warships has been steadily eroded. Table 2.2.3 provides an overview of the current status of the PLAN's major vessels as of mid-2025, with commentary on specific categories following:

Aircraft Carriers & Amphibious Vessels: The PLAN's carrier force continues to be centred on the two short take-off but arrested recovery (STOBAR) configured carriers *Liaoning* and *Shandong*. Both have been extremely active in the past year as the navy steadily expands its knowledge of carrier operating techniques. The two vessels are essentially providing an interim capability pending the arrival of the CATOBAR configured Type 003 carrier, *Fujian*. The new ship had completed eight separate sea trial phases from Shanghai's Jiangnang shipyard by June 2025 and is expected to be commissioned into PLAN service within the next 12 months. Estimated to displace over 80,000 tonnes in full load condition, she will be second only to the US Navy's aircraft carriers in size once delivered. It is believed that an even larger Type 004 aircraft carrier, possibly

Table 2.2.3: PEOPLE'S LIBERATION ARMY NAVY: PRINCIPAL UNITS AS AT MID 2025

TYPE	CLASS	NUMBER	TONNAGE	DIMENSIONS	PROPULSION	CREW	DATE
Aircraft Carriers							
Aircraft Carrier – CV	Type 002 **SHANDONG** (Mod Kuznetsov)	1	65,000 tonnes	315m x 35/75m x 10m	Steam, 32 knots	Unknown	2019
Aircraft Carrier – CV	Type 001 **LIAONING** (Kuznetsov)	1	60,000 tonnes	306m x 35/73m x 10m	Steam, 32 knots	Unknown	2012
Principal Surface Escorts							
Destroyer – DDG	Type 055 **NANCHANG** ('Renhai')	8	c. 12,000 tonnes	180m x 20m x 7m	COGAG, 30 knots	c. 300	2019
Destroyer – DDG	Type 052D **KUNMING** ('Luyang III')	30	7,500 tonnes	156m x 17m x 6m	CODOG, 28 knots	280	2014
Destroyer – DDG	Type 051C **SHENYANG** ('Luzhou')	2	7,100 tonnes	155m x 17m x 6m	Steam, 29 knots	250	2006
Destroyer – DDG	Type 052C **LANZHOU** ('Luyang II')	6	7,000 tonnes	154m x 17m x 6m	CODOG, 28 knots	280	2005
Destroyer – DDG	Type 052B **GUANGZHOU** ('Luyang I')	2	6,500 tonnes	154m x 17m x 6m	CODOG, 29 knots	280	2004
Destroyer – DDG	Project 956E/EM **HANGZHOU** (Sovremenny)	4	8,000 tonnes	156m x 17m x 6m	Steam, 32 knots	300	1999
Destroyer – DDG	Type 051B **SHENZHEN** ('Luhai')	1	6,000 tonnes	154m x 16m x 6m	Steam, 31 knots	250	1998
Destroyer – DDG	Type 052 **HARBIN** ('Luhu')	2	4,800 tonnes	143m x 15m x 5m	CODOG, 31 knots	260	1994
Frigate – FFG	Type 054B **LUHOE** (('Jiangkai III')	2	5,500 tonnes	150m x 17m x 5m	CODAD, 28 knots+	Unknown	2025
Frigate – FFG	Type 054A **XUZHOU** ('Jiangkai II')	40	4,100 tonnes	132m x 15m x 5m	CODAD, 28 knots	190	2008
Frigate – FFG	Type 054 **MA'ANSHAN** ('Jiangkai I')	2	4,000 tonnes	132m x 15m x 5m	CODAD, 28 knots	190	2005
Frigate – FFG	Type 053 H3 **LIANYUNGANG** ('Jiangwei II')	6	2,500 tonnes	112m x 12m x 5m	CODAD, 27 knots	170	1992
Frigate – FSG	Type 056/056A **BENGBU** ('Jiangdao')	50[1]	1,500 tonnes	89m x 12m x 4m	CODAD, 28 knots	60	2013
Submarines							
Submarine – SSBN	Type 094/094A ('Jin')	c. 6	9,000 tonnes	133m x 11m x 8m	Nuclear, 20+ knots	Unknown	2008
Submarine – SSBN	Type 092 ('Xia')	1[2]	6,500 tonnes	120m x 10m x 8m	Nuclear, 22 knots	140	1987
Submarine – SSN	Type 093/093A ('Shang')	c. 6	6,000 tonnes	107m x 11m x 8m	Nuclear, 30 knots	100	2006
Submarine – SSN	Type 091 ('Han')	3[2]	5,500 tonnes	106m x 10m x 7m	Nuclear, 25 knots	75	1974
Submarine – SSK	Type 039A/039B/039C (Type 041 'Yuan')	c. 25+	2,500 tonnes	75m x 8m x 5m	AIP, 20+ knots	Unknown	2006
Submarine – SSK	Type 039/039G ('Song')	13	2,300 tonnes	75m x 8m x 5m	Diesel-electric, 22 knots	60	1999
Submarine – SSK	Project 636 ('Kilo')	10	3,000 tonnes	73m x 10m x 7m	Diesel-electric, 20 knots	55	1997
Plus c. 5–10 obsolescent patrol submarines of the Type 035 ('Ming' Class), many in reserve. A Type 032 'Qing' trials submarine has also been commissioned for strategic missile trials.							
Major Amphibious Units							
Amph. Assault Ship – LHD	Type 075 HAINAN ('Yushen')	4	40,000 tonnes	237m x 36m x 8m	CODAD, 20+ knots	Unknown	2021
Landing Platform Dock – LPD	Type 071 KULUN SHAN ('Yuzhao')	8	25,000 tonnes	210m x 27m x 7m	CODAD, 20 knots	Unknown	2007

Notes:

1. The 22-strong Type 056 variant has been transferred to the Coast Guard after refit.

2. The operational status of these vessels is highly questionable if they are not already retired.

equipped with nuclear propulsion, is at an advanced stage of development.

The PLAN's amphibious flotilla will shortly be bolstered by the delivery of *Hubei*, the fourth and likely final member of the Type 075 'Yushen' class amphibious assault ships. Production is already transitioning to a larger Type 076 'Yulan' class. The first of these, named *Sichuan*, was launched from Hudong–Zhonghua Shipbuilding in Shanghai on 27 December 2024. Broadly similar in configuration to the British *Queen Elizabeth* class but equipped with an electromagnetic catapult rather than a ski jump, she is reportedly intended to operate both helicopters and uncrewed aerial vehicles (UAVs). If previous PLAN practice is followed, she is likely to be the first of an extended class.[6]

Surface Combatants: China continues to pursue a massive programme of surface warship construction. Following completion of the large programme of diminutive Type 056A anti-submarine warfare (ASW) corvettes in early 2021, production has increasingly trended towards larger and more complex combatants. As of mid-2025, projects for four classes of major surface warship – encompassing both destroyers and frigates – were ongoing.

The largest ships are the Type 055 'Renhai' destroyers, which displace around 12,000 tonnes. Eight of these were delivered from the Jiangnan Shipyard and Dalian Shipbuilding Industry Corporation (DSIC) between 2020 and 2023. At least six of a further batch are at various stages of construction in the two yards. At this stage it is not certain if the new batch will be identical to the earlier ships or include iterative improvements.

The smaller Type 052D 'Luyang III' class – displacing around 7,500 tonnes and derived from a hull which dates back around 20 years to the pair of Type 052B 'Luyang I' class destroyers commissioned in 2004 – also remain in production at the two shipyards. Completion of deliveries of a third batch of slightly lengthened variants took total production to 25 ships by the end of 2022 but at least 13 of a fourth batch are now being delivered. Much of DSIC's destroyer construction has recently migrated to a newly-built yard at neighbouring Dagushan in a movement reminiscent of the shift in Shanghai warship construction to the new shipyards established on Changxingdao Island

The latest PLAN surface combatant is the new Type 054B 'Jiangkai III' class frigate. The lead ship

The Chinese People's Liberation Army Navy Type 002 aircraft carrier *Shandong* launches a Shenyang J-15 multi-role fighter during an operational deployment. The PLAN's two existing STOBAR-equipped carriers are paving the way for the arrival of more capable vessels. *(People's Liberation Army Navy)*

The PLAN destroyer *Lhasa* was commissioned in March 2021 as the second member of the powerful Type 055 'Renhai' class. This overhead image gives a good impression of the ship's extensive array of 112 VLS cells, located forward and amidships. They can be used to launch a wide range of anti-air, anti-ship, anti-submarine and land attack misisles. *(People's Liberation Army Navy)*

of the class, named *Luhoe*, was delivered from the Hudong–Zhonghua shipyard in January 2025. She was followed some months later by a sister, *Qinzhou*, that had been completed by China's other frigate builder, Huangpu Wenchong Shipbuilding of Guangzhou. Although categorised as forming part of the Type 054 series, these new ships are longer and heavier than their predecessors and have significant differences to their equipment outfit that extend to a new, rotating active phased-array type radar. At present, it seems that no more of the new ships are under construction; perhaps reflecting a desire to thoroughly evaluate the new design in a similar fashion to which the pair of original Type 054 frigates were subsequently followed by the series-produced Type 054As.

In a somewhat surprising development given the pending transition to production of the Type 054B, a further batch of at least six Type 054A frigates have also been launched by the two shipyards over the past year. This takes total production of the class to 46 vessels, this number excluding the two Type 054 prototypes and additional iterations built for the coast guard. The latest batch, sometimes referred to as the Type 054AG, includes adjustments to the flight deck and hangar to allow operation of the new Z-20 series helicopter, as well as minor changes to weapons and sensors.

The influx of new equipment has allowed withdrawal of older ships, with the veteran Type 053H1G 'Jiangu V' class frigates all now decommissioned or allocated secondary roles. Many of the once ten-strong Type 053 H3 'Jiangwei II' class are also starting to be withdrawn from front-line service, with some of the motley collection of 1990s-era destroyer expecting to follow them in the near term. This will essentially complete the transition to a much more homogenous front-line fleet.

Submarines: US Navy intelligence analysis as of December 2024 estimated that the PLAN had six strategic submarines, six nuclear-powered attack submarines and 48 diesel-electric submarines in its frontline fleet.[7] This total of 60 is expected to expand to 65 by the end of 2025 and to as many as 80 by 2035 as new submarines are commissioned at a faster rate than the withdrawal of older units.

The last year has seen further news emerge of the production of the new Type 093B 'Shang III' nuclear-powered attack submarine type. This is regarded as a much modified variant of the existing two Type 093 'Shang I' and four Type 093A 'Shang II' boats delivered between 2006 and 2018 but arguably incorporates sufficient differences to be regarded as a new class. Satellite imagery and rare internet images of the design on trials suggest that this new variant is significantly more streamlined than earlier members of the Type 093 series and, in addition to being equipped with a pump jet propulsor, will be armed with a vertical launch system (VLS) silo for submarine-launched cruise missiles. The US Navy estimates that four Type 093Bs were launched during 2022-3 and that up to three of them could be in service before the end of 2025. Some analysts believe that the class might prove to be an extended one, although speculation about an entirely new Type 095 design continues. There is also an expectation that a new Type 096 strategic submarine is under development, although there has been no tangible news over the last year.[8]

The diesel-electric submarine fleet is increasingly dominated by the Type 039A/B/C 'Yuan' series. In similar fashion to its Type 093 nuclear-powered counterpart, this has now gone through several iterations. The latest Type 039C variant is currently in series production, taking total class numbers of all iterations to around 25. When combined with the 13 earlier Type 039 'Song' and ten Project 636 Russian-built 'Kilo' class boats in service, this has likely allowed withdrawal of the few remaining elderly 'Ming' class from frontline duties.

There has been much speculation over the past year with respect to a new Type 041 'Zhou' class submarine, which some sources suggest might be a

Luhoe is the lead ship of an initial class of two new Type 054B 'Jiangkai III' class frigates. Significantly larger than the previous Type 054A frigate design, she is equipped with a rotating, two-faced active phased-array radar atop her forward mast. *(China Military Online)*

hybrid diesel-electric boat equipped with an auxiliary nuclear plant. News of the new boat's launch from the Wuchang Shipyard in Wuhan emerged in mid-2024 was followed by reports that it may have sunk pierside following an industrial accident. Given the previous concentration of PLAN nuclear-powered submarine construction at the expanded Bohai shipyard in Huludao, the nature of the new boat's propulsion must be regarded as speculative until more definitive information emerges.

Other Ships: Whilst the pace of Chinese major combatant delivery often serves to obscure other developments, the PLAN's construction activities extend to a wide range of smaller vessels and non-combatants. Significantly, it is reported that construction has resumed of additional Type 901 'Fuyu' class combat support ships and the somewhat smaller and slower Type 903 'Fuchi' class replenishment tankers. These ships are vital for expanding the PLAN's operational reach and more will be required as the planned new aircraft carriers and amphibious ships enter service.

China's shipbuilding industry is also noteworthy for developing a range of experimental ships, including at least two types of bespoke UAV 'drone carriers'. The Chinese Armed Forces have already developed extensive, largely land-based drone capabilities, many of which would have particular relevance in providing the intelligence and communications capacity required to make maximum use of their long-range anti-ship missiles. Also reportedly undergoing trials are a new design of stealth corvette – a possible successor to the Type 056 corvettes – and a trimaran-type uncrewed surface vessel referred to as the 'Jari USV-A'.

MAJOR REGIONAL POWERS – JAPAN

Although lacking the spectacular growth experienced by the rival Chinese PLAN, the Japan Maritime Self Defence Force (JMSDF) continues a process of steady expansion in line with national security and defence strategies published at the end of 2022. Japanese defence spending is now rising strongly but demographic constraints mean that an underlying imperative is to increase overall force 'lethality' within the existing headcount of roughly 45,000 personnel.

The main components of the current JMSDF fleet are listed in Table 2.2.4. The main change over the last year was an increase in the number of major surface warships by one unit. Two new vessels were delivered, whilst the *Asagiri* (DD-151) class destroyer *Yamagiri* (DD-152) was shifted to a training role to replace the veteran *Hatakaze* (TV-3520, formerly DDG-171), which was retired in March 2025.

A key element of the naval expansion programme is increasing the fleet of surface warships through the series construction of the compact and minimally

Table 2.2.4: JAPAN MARITIME SELF-DEFENCE FORCE: PRINCIPAL UNITS AS AT MID 2025

TYPE	CLASS	NUMBER[1]	TONNAGE	DIMENSIONS	PROPULSION	CREW	DATE
Support and Helicopter Carriers							
Aircraft Carrier – CV[2]	**IZUMO** (DDH-183)	2	27,000 tonnes	248m x 38m x 7m	COGAG, 30 knots	470	2015
Helicopter Carrier – CVH	**HYUGA** (DDH-181)	2	19,000 tonnes	197m x 33m x 7m	COGAG, 30 knots	340	2009
Principal Surface Escorts							
Destroyer – DDG	**MAYA** (DDG-179)	2	10,500 tonnes	170m x 21m x 6m	COGLAG, 30 knots	300	2020
Destroyer – DDG	**ATAGO** (DDG-177)	2	10,000 tonnes	165m x 21m x 6m	COGAG, 30 knots	300	2007
Destroyer – DDG	**KONGOU** (DDG-173)	4	9,500 tonnes	161m x 21m x 6m	COGAG, 30 knots	300	1993
Destroyer – DDG	**HATAKAZE** (DDG-171)	0 (1)	6,300 tonnes	150m x 16m x 5m	COGAG, 30 knots	260	1986
Destroyer – DDG	**ASAHI** (DD-119)	2	6,800 tonnes	151m x 18m x 5m	COGLAG, 30 knots	230	2017
Destroyer – DD	**AKIZUKI** (DD-115)	4	6,800 tonnes	151m x 18m x 5m	COGAG, 30 Knots	200	2012
Destroyer – DDG	**TAKANAMI** (DD-110)	5	6,300 tonnes	151m x 17m x 5m	COGAG, 30 knots	175	2003
Destroyer – DDG	**MURASAME** (DD-101)	9	6,200 tonnes	151m x 17m x 5m	COGAG, 30 knots	165	1996
Destroyer – DDG	**ASAGIRI** (DD-151)	7 (1)	4,900 tonnes	137m x 15m x 5m	COGAG, 30 knots	220	1988
Frigate – FFG	**MOGAMI** (FFM-1)	8	5,300 tonnes	133m x 16m x 5m	CODAG, 30+ knots	90	2022
Frigate – FFG	**ABUKUMA** (DE-229)	6	2,500 tonnes	109m x 13m x 4m	CODOG, 27 knots	120	1989
Submarines							
Submarine – SSK[3]	**TAGEI** (SS-513)	3 (1)	4,300 tonnes	84m x 9m x 8m	Diesel-electric, 20+ knots	70	2022
Submarine – SSK	**SORYU** (SS-501)	12	4,200 tonnes	84m x 9m x 8m	AIP, 20+ knots[4]	65	2009
Submarine – SSK	**OYASHIO** (SS-590)	7 (2)	4,000 tonnes	82m x 9m x 8m	Diesel-electric, 20+ knots	70	1998
Major Amphibious Units							
Landing Platform Dock – LPD	**OSUMI** (LST-4001)	3	14,000 tonnes	178m x 26m x 6m	Diesel, 22 knots	135	1998

Notes:

1. Figures in brackets refer to trials or training ships.

2. In the course of conversion to operate F-35B STOVL strike fighters.

3. The lead unit is now operated as a dedicated trials submarine.

4. The last two units of the class have their AIP plant replaced by lithium-ion batteries; an arrangement also adopted in the follow-on *Tagei* class

Japan's JMSDF continues to take annual deliveries of a range of new ships as it steadily grows in terms of size and capability. These photographs were taken at the time of delivery of the new submarine *Raigei* and the mine countermeasures vessel *Nomi*, the fourth members of – respectively – the *Taigei* and *Awaji* classes. *(JMSDF)*

crewed *Mogami* (FFM-1) class frigates. These are multi-role vessels that will use uncrewed systems to take on some of the work previously performed by traditional mine countermeasures vessels in addition to their frigate-like functions.[9] The frigates have been entering service at the rate of approximately two each year since 2022, with the seventh and eighth members of the class being commissioned in May and June 2025. The Japanese FY2024 defence budget saw orders transition to a larger, 'Upgraded *Mogami*' variant after twelve of the original class had been ordered, with twelve of the new class also envisaged. It is hoped to complete orders for this variant by FY2028 and the FY2025 budget approved three of these as part of this planned acceleration.[10] Rapid construction of the FFMs will allow the JMSDF's force of surface combatants to increase to a targeted total of 50 – in addition to four carrier-like 'helicopter-carrying destroyers' and two new Aegis System Equipped Vessels (ASEVs) – whilst allowing retirement of obsolescent and crew-heavy older types.

The underwater flotilla has already reached its planned total of 22 front-line boats (plus two training and one trials submarine). Accordingly, the current plan is based on a rolling programme that sees one submarine ordered, one delivered and one retired (after a period as a training asset) each year. In line with this approach, the FY2025 budget saw approval for the ninth *Tagei* (SS-513) class submarine at a cost of 114 billion Japanese yen (c. US$780 million). The fourth member of the class, *Raigei* (SS-516), was delivered by Kawasaki Heavy Industries on 6 March 2025 whilst the second *Oyashio* (SS-590) class boat, *Michishio* (TS-3609, formerly SS-591), was withdrawn later that month after ending her final years as a training submarine.

The only other new ships authorised in the FY2025 budget were three landing and transport ships for joint Self Defence Force Maritime Transport Group, which was established on 24 March 2025. Significant amounts were, however, allocated to missile production, with the introduction of both Tomahawk cruise missiles and the new Type 12 surface-to-surface missile both accelerated a year on previous plans. Additional money was approved to support the introduction of the two ASEVs that are likely to enter service in 2027-8, whilst research funding was committed to prepare for eventual replacements for the four *Kongou* (DDG-173) Aegis-equipped destroyers.

The flotilla of minor warships was reinforced by the arrival of *Nomi* (MSO-307), the fourth *Awaji* (MSO-304) class mine countermeasures vessel. Two further units have been ordered and a total of nine vessels is ultimately planned, supplementing the FFM type frigates with a bespoke mine countermeasures capability. However, the overall number of minehunters fell by one to 17, with *Naoshima* (MSC-684) being decommissioned in March 2025 and her sister *Ukishima* (MSC-686) capsizing and sinking after an engine room fire on 10 November 2024 in a rare total loss of an operational JMSDF warship.

MAJOR REGIONAL POWERS – SOUTH KOREA

The Republic of Korea Navy's ongoing modernisation programme continues to make progress against a backdrop of political crisis and fears over the future of the protective US military presence in the country given the uncertainties of the Trump regime. Whilst these developments have the potential to see a large shift in defence priorities, there has been little alteration to the navy's direction of travel over the last year. This has seen continued investment in capabilities linked to South Korea's 'Three Axis' deterrent system against its hostile neighbour to the north whilst steadily enhancing the fleet's 'blue water' capabilities.[11]

A summary of current major combatants is provided in Table 2.2.5. The last year has seen the arrival of the lead ships of two new warship classes; the initial KDX-3 Batch 2 destroyer, *Jeongjo the Great,* and the first FFX-3 class frigate, *Chungnam.* The former is an enlarged variant of the existing three KDX-3 Batch I *Sejong the Great* class Aegis-equipped destroyers. Delivered by the re-named HD Hyundai Heavy Industries (HD HHI) in November

Table 2.2.5: REPUBLIC OF KOREA NAVY: PRINCIPAL UNITS AS AT MID 2025

TYPE	CLASS	NUMBER	TONNAGE	DIMENSIONS	PROPULSION	CREW	DATE
Principal Surface Escorts							
Destroyer – DDG	KDX-3 Batch 2 **JEONGJO THE GREAT**	1	11,000 tonnes	170m x 21m x 6m	COGAG, 30 knots	300	2024
Destroyer – DDG	KDX-3 Batch 1 **SEJONG THE GREAT**	3	10,000 tonnes	166m x 21m x 6m	COGAG, 30 knots	300	2008
Destroyer – DDG	KDX-2 **CHUNGMUGONG YI SUN-SHIN**	6	5,500 tonnes	150m x 17m x 5m	CODOG, 30 knots	200	2003
Destroyer – DDG	KDX-1 **GWANGGAETO THE GREAT**	3	3,900 tonnes	135m x 14m x 4m	CODOG, 30 knots	170	1998
Frigate – FFG	FFX-3 **CHUNGNAM**	1	4,300 tonnes	129m x 15m x 4m	CODLOG, 30 knots	Not Known	2024
Frigate – FFG	FFX-2 **DAEGU**	8	3,600 tonnes	122m x 14m x 4m	CODLOG, 30 knots	140	2017
Frigate – FFG	FFX-1 **INCHEON**	6	3,000 tonnes	114m x 14m x 4m	CODOG, 30 knots	140	2013
Frigate – FFG	**ULSAN**	2	2,300 tonnes	102m x 12m x 4m	CODOG, 35 knots	150	1981
Corvette – FSG	**POHANG**	3	1,200 tonnes	88m x 10m x 3m	CODOG, 32 knots	95	1984
Submarines							
Submarine – SSK	KSS-3 **DOSAN AHN CHANG-HO**	3	3,800 tonnes	84m x 8m x 8m	AIP, 20+ knots	50	2021
Submarine – SSK	KSS-2 **SON WON-IL** (Type 214)	9	1,800 tonnes	65m x 6m x 6m	AIP, 20+ knots	30	2007
Submarine – SSK	KSS-1 **CHANG BOGO** (Type 209/1200)	9	1,300 tonnes	56m x 6m x 6m	Diesel-electric, 22 knots	35	1993
Major Amphibious Units							
Amph Assault Ship – LHD	LPX **DOKDO**	2[1]	18,900 tonnes	200m x 32m x 7m	Diesel, 22 knots	425	2007

Notes:
1. *Marado*, the second ship of the class, is built to a slightly different design.

2024, she will be followed by two sister-ships by 2027. In contrast to her predecessors, she is fully equipped for integrated air and missile defence (IAMD) and is also fitted with the deeper, KVLS-II variant of South Korea's indigenous vertical launch system. This combination of advanced missile defence and land attack capabilities makes the design particularly relevant to the maritime component of the 'Three Axis' deterrent referenced above. *Jeongjo the Great* has also been assigned the role of flagship of the Republic of Korea Navy's new Task Fleet Command, the navy's blue water, rapid-response force. Inaugurated at the new Jeju Island naval base in February 2025, this comprises three squadrons of the navy's largest combatants – its KDX-3 and KDX-2 destroyers – supported by logistic support ship assets.[12]

In contrast to the larger destroyers, *Chungnam* is the latest iteration of a series of FFX designated frigates intended to serve with South Korea's three regionally-based fleets operating in the East, South and West Seas. Delivered by HD HHI on 18 December 2024, she shares similarities with the previous FFX-2 *Daegu* class iteration of the series but is larger and heavier. A notable addition is the use of a four-faced active phased-array radar developed by Hanwha Systems that is similar to the Elta EL/M-2248 MF-STAR installed in the amphibious

A computer-generated graphic of the Republic of Korea Navy's FFX-4 frigate design; the latest iteration of a series of littoral warfare frigates that includes the previous *Incheon, Daegu* and *Chungnam* classes. The FFX-4 has the same dimensions and appearance as the previous FFX-3 *Chungnam* class frigates but is said to incorporate improved integration of equipment and a reduced crewing requirement. *(Hanwha Ocean)*

assault ship *Marado.* The second member of the class, *Gyeongbukham*, was launched by SK Ocean Plant on 20 June 2025 and four further members of the class have been ordered.[13]

Production of the FFX-3 class will be followed by a new FFX-4 variant that continues the process of iterative improvement. On 19 December 2024, Hanwha Ocean announced that it had been contracted to build the first two units of what will be another six-ship class. The FFX-4 will be of the same size and general appearance of the preceding FFX-3 design but is described as a 'smart ship' with better integration and a reduced crewing requirement. The latter is reflective of the fact that, like many developed nations, South Korea is also facing a demographic challenge that will start to impact the number of naval personnel. This consideration will also influence the design of a proposed new KDDX destroyer class being developed by HD HHI and is also spurring interest in a wide range of uncrewed systems.

There were no changes in the composition of the navy's submarine flotilla year-on-year following completion of the first batch of KSS-3 *Dosan Ahn Chang-Ho* class submarines in April 2024. The three KSS-3 Batch 2 variants are now all under construction by Hanwha Ocean following commencement of work on the third member of the class in October 2024.

The Indonesian Navy is due to take delivery of two *Paolo Thaon di Revel* class multi-role frigates before the end of 2025. This photograph shows the new KRI *Brawijaya*. She was previously launched as the Italian Navy's *Marcantonio Colonna* before transfer to Indonesia to expedite fulfilment of the Indonesian Navy's requirement. *(Fincantieri)*

OTHER REGIONAL FLEETS

Indonesia: After the announcement of significant contracts for French submarines and Italian frigates in the first half of 2024, the last year has been much quieter with respect to Indonesian naval procurement. The arrival of former defence minister Prabowo Subianto as the nation's eighth president in October 2024 is expected to see military spending embark on an upward trajectory in line with an aspiration almost to increase the defence budget from 0.8 percent to 1.5 percent of GDP over time. However, with major purchases of jets and other expensive equipment already approved under the previous presidency, it remains unclear as to how much of the navy's extensive wish list will be affordable.

In broad terms, the navy continues to pursue a longstanding two tier fleet strategy. The high end of this force increasingly comprises newly built warships that are largely of overseas design, albeit with a steady trend towards emphasising local assembly. The €1.2 billion (c. US$1.4 billion) contract for two Italian *Paolo Thaon di Revel* class multi-role frigates announced in March 2024 was something of an exception to this direction of travel and may have been driven by a desire to accelerate the fielding of modern capabilities in the light of ongoing tensions in the South China Sea. The two ships – renamed KRI *Brawijaya* and KRI *Prabu Siliwangi* – are expected to arrive in Indonesia in, respectively, September and December 2025 after completion of crew training. It is possible that more of the type might be assembled in Indonesia to meet a requirement for new large surface combatants. However, France and Japan are pressing the competing merits of their *Amiral Ronarc'h* (FDI) and *Mogami* (FFM-1) designs.

For the time being, the most important indigenous surface warship programme remains the construction at Surabaya-based PT PAL of two Babcock-designed 'Arrowhead 140' frigates under the *Merah Putih* (red and white) frigate programme. Although based on an Anglo-Danish platform, the ships will incorporate a considerable amount of Turkish equipment that includes Havelsan's ADVENT combat management system and a 64-cell MİDLAS VLS supplied by Roketsan. This is reflective of growing links between Indonesia and the Turkish defence sector that also extend to the construction of two large KCR-70M fast attack craft at the Sefine shipyard in Türkiye and the selection of ADVENT for two 90m *Raja Haji Fisabilillah* offshore patrol vessels being built at the Noahtu Shipyard (formerly PT Daya Radar Utama) at Bandar Lampungm in Sumatra. The latter two vessels were launched within two days of each other in September 2024.

The arrival of the new Italian and indigenous frigates will give rise to a marked increase in the combat power of the navy's surface flotilla. This currently comprises five elderly *Van Speijk* (*Leander*) and two modern 'Sigma 10514' frigates supplemented by 24 corvettes of various ages and effectiveness. However, the navy's ambitions extend beyond the recapitalisation of this rather motley assortment to encompass the operation of 'big deck' amphibious assault ships of similar type to the Spanish *Juan Carlos I* design. It has been reported that there have been talks with Italy to explore the possible acquisition of the recently retired STOVL carrier *Giuseppe Garibaldi* to provide an interim capability. If the deal goes through, she would likely be equipped with helicopters and drones.

Meanwhile, preparations continue to implement the April 2024 agreement to acquire two 'Scorpène Evolved Full LiB' submarines from France's Naval Group. The contract involves at least some assembly by PT PAL and it seems that the complexities of the deal mean that it will be quite some time before the new boats are completed. Accordingly, the Indonesian Navy is seeking the acquisition of additional 'interim submarines' to fill the gap and bolster its small current four boat flotilla. Designs from China, Italy, South Korea and Türkiye are amongst those reportedly under consideration.

The fleet's second tier is largely formed of various patrol and logistic support ships of increasingly indigenous design and construction. These vessels are largely focused on constabulary and humanitarian missions across the vast Indonesian archipelago, although some 'KCR' iterations have been equipped with surface-to-surface missiles for territorial defence. Built by numerous shipyards, they range in size from the extended *Makassar* series of amphibious transport docks and hospital ships through to relatively small 'KAL' designated patrol craft. Amongst more significant recent deliveries are the 60m PC-60M *Dorang* class patrol boats *Hampala and Lumba-Lumba* – completed by PT Caputra Mitra Sejati in December 2024 – and the smaller PC-40M type *Butana* and *Selar* accepted from PT Citra Shipyard in September that year. Taken together, there are now around 25 of the two classes in service. A somewhat larger and more complex type is represented by the two 73 metre helicopter-capable *Bung Karno* class patrol ships – officially categorised as corvettes – built by PT Karimun Anugrah Sejati of Batam. *Bung Hatta*, the second of these c. 650-tonne vessels, was commissioned in April 2025.[14]

Malaysia: It has been a somewhat mixed year for the Royal Malaysian Navy as it struggles to transform its disparate fleet of elderly warships into a more homogenous and modern fleet under the overarching rationalisation strategy adopted under its '15 to 5 Transformation Plan'.[15]

Positively, the previously troubled and long-delayed littoral mission ship programme focused on the construction of five *Maharaja Lela* class 'Gowind' type frigates at the renamed Lumut Naval Shipyard (LUMAS) is seemingly gaining traction.

The Royal Malaysian Navy fast attack craft *Pendekar* pictured sinking off the coast of Johore in August 2024 after a navigating error saw her make contact with a reef. Although subsequently salvaged, she was decommissioned as a constructive total loss. *(Royal Malaysian Navy)*

The lead ship has now commenced the setting to work phase and is expected to commence sea trials in December 2025 prior to delivery the following year. The second ship, *Raja Muda Nala*, was subject to technical launch in May 2025, when the overall project was said to be over 70 percent complete. Current plans envisage all five ships being in service by the end of the decade.

Good progress is also being made on the second batch of smaller littoral mission ships (LMS), which are being built in Türkiye to a modified 'Ada' class design.[16] Work on the lead ship commenced in December 2024 and was followed by a formal keel-laying ceremony at the private Istanbul Shipyard on 8 April 2025. Deliveries of all three ships are expected by the end of 2027, a seemingly challenging target. Orders for a third batch of LMS are anticipated within the lifespan of the 2026-30 13th Malaysia Plan, with a number of rival firms offering proposals for the order. The navy also hoped to proceed with orders for two LPD-like multi-role support ships within the same timeframe.

On the negative side of the ledger, June 2025 saw the decommissioning of three major warships without immediate replacement. The ships comprised the two 'Laksamana' class corvettes *Hang Nadim* and *Tun Pusmah* along with the *Handalan* fast attack craft, *Pendekar*. The last-mentioned ship had sunk off the coast of Johore on 25 August 2024 after an engine-room leak – caused by a collision with the Stork Reef after a navigational error – resulted in an uncontrollable flood that resulted in the ship's loss. Fortunately, all her crew were safely rescued. Although subsequently salvaged in October that year, the 45-year-old vessel was considered unsuitable for economic repair.[17]

New Zealand: The New Zealand government published its long-awaited Defence Capability Plan in April 2025.[18] Set against a backdrop of a more volatile regional security situation that had previously been highlighted by Chinese naval exercises in the Tasman Sea between Australia and New Zealand earlier that year, it holds out the prospect of a material boost to defence resources. Promising NZ$12 billion (c. US$7.2 billion) of funding over the next four years – three-quarters of which will be new money – it also held out the prospect of a near doubling of the defence budget to two percent of GDP by the early 2030s.

Naval capabilities selected for immediate investment include replacement of the SH-2G(I) Super Seasprite helicopters at a cost of over NZ$2 billion (c. US$1.2 billion), investment in uncrewed surveillance drones, and a life extension programme for the two elderly *Anzac* class frigates. A programme to replace these ships and the two 'Protector' class offshore patrol vessels – potentially with a common hull – will follow in the medium term. A replacement for the multi-role vessel *Canterbury* is also envisaged. An intention to acquire upgraded strike capabilities for the overall New Zealand Defence Force could potentially see the purchase of Naval Strike Missiles for the frigates or Lockheed Martin's AGM-158C Long-Range Anti-Ship Missile (LRASM) for the air force's P-8A maritime patrol aircraft.

The new investment is urgently needed for a Royal New Zealand Navy that continues to struggle from a long period of relative neglect. Its misfortunes have been exacerbated by the loss of the relatively-recently acquired survey vessel *Manawanui*, which was lost after running aground on a reef off Samoa on 5 October 2024 in an incident attributed to human error. News reports suggest that the patrol vessel *Otago*, one of three vessels currently laid up for lack of crew, will return to service in order to pick up some of the duties previously undertaken by the lost vessel.

North Korea: The Korean People's Navy (KPN) has been another Asian fleet to suffer a high-profile mishap during the course of the last year. On 21 May 2025, *Kang Kon* – second of the new *Choe Hyon* class destroyers – partly capsized during a launch ceremony at Chongjin's Hambuk Shipyard attended by North Korean Premier Kim Jong Un. The destroyer was being launched by the sideways method when the launch bogies seemingly failed to move in parallel. As a result, her bow failed to leave the slipway and the ship flipped onto its side. Impressively, it proved possible to right the destroyer over the course of the next two weeks, allowing a second official, face-saving 'launch' event to be held on 12 June. Despite this progress, it seems unlikely that the underlying damage to the vessel will have been anything other than substantial.

Nevertheless, the accident served to highlight the KPN's recent progress in developing new surface warship classes to modernise its overwhelmingly elderly fleet. *Kang Kon*'s launch followed the delivery of the lead ship of the *Choe Hyon* class, which had commenced sea trials at the end of April 2025 after a launch ceremony held at the Nampo Shipyard on the 25th of that month. Open source information suggests that the c. 5,000-tonne vessels have a length of around 145ms and a beam of about 16m, making them equivalent in size to a European frigate. They are seemingly equipped with phased array radar and over 70 VLS cells for a range of surface-to-surface and surface-to-air missiles. Their arrival follows the previous delivery of the modern *Amnok* type corvette/light frigate, whilst more of the larger destroyer class are reportedly under construction.

Meanwhile, in March 2025, news emerged of the construction of a nuclear-powered strategic submarine (SSBN) at the Sinpo South Shipyard. Little tangible information is available on this new boat – described as 'A mystery wrapped around a riddle and an enigma' – which is likely several years away from completion.[19] In the interim, work reportedly continues to prepare the 'Sinpo-C' class tactical ballistic missile submarine (SSB) *Hero Kim Kun Ok,* launched on 6 September 2023, for operational service.

Diego Silang is the second of two *Miguel Malvar* class frigates built by HD HHI for the Philippine Navy. This photograph was taken at the time of her official 'launch' ceremony on 27 March 2025. The Philippine Navy's surface fleet is increasingly formed of a core of modern, South Korean-built ships. *(HD HHI)*

The Philippines: The Philippine Navy marked a further step forward in its programme of fleet renewal at a ceremony to mark the arrival of the new frigate *Miguel Malvar* (FFG-06) at the Naval Operating Base Subic, Zambales on 8 April 2025. Subsequently commissioned on 25 May, she is the lead vessel of a two-strong class of what were first referred to as 'corvettes'. They were ordered from HD HHI in December 2021 under the 'Horizon 2' phase of the Philippine Armed Forces' three phase modernisation programme. The ships are based on the HD HHI HDC-3100 design and – at c. 3,100 tonnes with a length of 118 metres – they are actually larger and better equipped than the two preceding *Jose Rizal* (FF-150) class frigates that were also built by HD HHI and delivered in 2020-21. This reality is now reflected in their FFG designation.

Miguel Malvar will shortly be joined by her sister, *Diego Silang* (FFG-07), which was officially launched on 27 March 2025 and is also due for delivery before the year's end. Also under construction at HD HHI are a class of six *Rajah Sulayman* offshore patrol vessels, the first of which was launched in 11 June 2025. Based on the company's HDP-2200 design, these c. 2,400-tonne vessels are somewhat smaller than the frigates and will only be gun-armed. Nevertheless, the total flotilla of ten newly-build HD HHI vessels will bring a welcome degree of homogeneity to the Philippine fleet.

Other modernisation efforts underway include

ongoing deliveries of *Acero* (PG-901) fast attack craft based on the Israeli 'Shaldag V' design. Notably, *Tomas Campo* (PG-908) and *Albert Maljini* (PG-909), respectively the seventh and eighth vessels of the nine-strong class, were both commissioned over the last year. The latter was assembled locally at the Naval Shipbuilding Center in Cavite, where the ninth and – to date – final member of the class remains under construction.

Although the AFP has now moved into the 'Horizon 3' phase of its modernisation programme, it seems that further major procurement may need to wait integration of the significant amount of new equipment that is already in the course of delivery. The navy has hopes of acquiring submarines in this phase of the programme but these would represent a costly and ambitious purchase.

Singapore: The Republic of Singapore Navy's (RSN's) short-term focus is on bringing its new German TKMS-built Type 218SG submarines into service. Dating back to 2013, the first phase of the programme reached its conclusion on 24 September 2024 when the two boats – *Invincible* and *Impeccable* – ordered under the initial contract were commissioned into RSN service. A second pair of submarines – *Illustrious* and *Impeccable* – contracted in 2017 have both been launched but remain in Germany for final outfitting and trials. In March 2025, Singapore's defence minister announced plans to procure a third batch of *Invincible* class boats and the relevant contract was subsequently signed on 7 May. This latest order is probably intended to replace the existing Swedish-built *Archer* class submarines to ensure a six-strong underwater flotilla. Meanwhile, the two remaining *Challenger* (former Swedish *Sjöormen*) class boats were both decommissioned at a ceremony on 25 November 2024

German industry is also involved in the construction of a new class of four offshore patrol vessels (OPVs). The vessels are based on the German Federal Police's Fassmer-built *Potsdam* class and will replace the re-rolled *Fearless* class patrol vessels that now serve in Singapore's Maritime Security and Response flotilla. A first steel-cutting ceremony was held for the lead vessel on 11 October 2024 at Lithuania's Western Baltic Shipyard, which is constructing the ships' hulls prior to final outfitting in Germany. The keels of the initial two vessels were subsequently laid in April 2025, with deliveries expected to commence in 2028.

Albert Majini is the eighth of nine *Acero* class fast attack craft ordered by the Philippine Navy to the Israeli 'Shaldag V' design. She is one of two members of the class to be assembled in the Philippines at Naval Shipbuilding Center in Cavite. *(Philippine Navy)*

The commissioning of Singapore's first Type 218SG *Invincible* class submarines in September 2024 was followed by the formal retirement of the remaining pair of *Challenger* class boats two months later. This picture shows the decommissioning pennant of RSS *Chieftain* – the former Swedish *Sjöhunden* – being lowered at a ceremony at Changi Naval Base on 25 November 2024. *(Singapore Ministry of Defence)*

Pending the arrival of new submarines, Taiwan is dependent on its *Tuo Chang* catamarans (left) and 'Kuang Hua VI' fast attack craft (right) to deter any invasion from mainland China across the Taiwan Strait. *(Republic of China Navy)*

The allocation of the OPV project to Fassmer may reflect the use of much of local company ST Engineering's capacity in the contemporaneous Multi-Role Combat Ship programme. Encompassing six frigate-sized vessels under a contract signed in March 2023, the programme saw the laying-down of the lead ship on 22 October 2024 and steel being cut for the second unit on 24 April 2025. Reportedly displacing around 8,500 tonnes and having a length of some 150 metres, the new ships will be large, leanly-crewed vessels optimised to act as 'mother-ships' for an assortment of uncrewed vehicles.[20] The lead vessel is expected to be launched within the next 12 months and enter service in 2028.

Taiwan: The Republic of China Navy's priority programme remains the prototype indigenous submarine *Hai Kung* (SS-711). She commenced initial sea trials from CSBC's Kaohsiung shipyard on 17 June 2025 prior to her scheduled delivery by the year's end. Successful completion of what is likely to be an exhaustive series of tests would likely lead to orders for the seven, series-built boats that are intended to follow.

Pending revitalisation of its small submarine flotilla, Taiwan largely relies on its force of *Tuo Chiang* stealth corvettes and 'Kuang Hua VI' class missile attack craft to deter the PLAN from any cross-strait incursion. Its relatively numerous but elderly flotilla of larger warships are no longer a match for China's modern equivalents and replacements are urgently needed. A planned force of twelve light frigates – six in ASW and six in anti-air warfare configurations – will go some way to filling the shortfall. Local press reports suggest that two prototypes – one of each variant – that are now under construction could be delivered as soon as 2026; a target that seems optimistic. In the meantime, the flotilla of destroyers and frigates has fallen by one ship to 25 vessels in the last year as a result of the withdrawal of the *Knox* (FF-1052) class frigate *Lan Yang* (FFG-935), the former US Navy *Joseph Hewes* (FF-1078), on 23 January 2025.

Thailand: The Royal Thai Navy's longstanding ambitions to acquire a submarine capacity continue to be thwarted by political indecision with respect to the single S26T boat – an export variant of the PLAN's 'Yuan' class – ordered in 2017. China's failure to supply the contracted German MTU396 diesel engine intended to power the boat combined with Thailand's reluctance to accept a Chinese-made CHD620 alternative have resulted in an ongoing impasse despite several false dawns. As of June 2025, a decision was said to be imminent with respect to a programme that has already incurred substantial 'sunk' costs with respect to advance payments, training and supporting infrastructure.

In the meantime, the navy is firming up plans for what it describes as four new 'high performance frigates'. Local news reports suggest that it is hoped to obtain funding for two pairs of vessels in the FY2026 and FY2027 Thai budgets and that half the class would be assembled locally under transfer of technology arrangements. The Royal Thai Navy undoubtedly requires modern surface combatants, with the Hanwha Ocean (formerly DSME) built *Bhumibol Adulyadej* the only frigate-sized ship delivered in recent years. It, along with Türkiye's STM, are amongst leading contenders for the new project. However, it remains highly questionable as to whether the money required will be made available given competing requirements that extend to expensive new fighter jets.

Vietnam: The Vietnam People's Navy (VPN) marked the 70th anniversary of its foundation on 7 May 2025. Despite the significance of the event, there has been little news of further force development, with some commentators speculating that the ongoing Russo-Ukrainian War has disrupted plans to acquire additional Russian equipment. Indeed, the Vietnamese armed forces – officially the People's Army of Vietnam – are increasingly expanding their base of potential suppliers. India, in particular, is making significant efforts to engage with the VPN against a backdrop of reports that Vietnam may soon acquire the BrahMos supersonic cruise missile; perhaps ironically, a jointly-developed Indo-Russian project.

Notes:

1. See Matthew P. Funaiole, Brian Hart, and Aidan Powers-Riggs, *Ship Wars: Confronting China's Dual-Use Shipbuilding Empire* (Washington D.C., Center for Strategic and International Studies, 2025). The report is currently readily available by searching the web. The authors note that China accounted for 53.3 percent of global commercial shipbuilding tonnage in 2024 compared with 29.1 percent for South Korea and 13.1 percent for Japan. This left just 4.5 percent to be completed in the rest of the world, of which 0.1 percent was in the United States.

2. See H I Sutton, 'China Suddenly Building Fleet Of Special Barges Suitable For Taiwan Landings' posted to the *Naval News* website – navalnews.com – on 10 January 2025.

3. The base's opening was officially reported in a Chinese Ministry of Defence press release, 'China-Cambodia joint logistics, training center officially launched', dated 5 April 2025.

4. See, *The AUKUS Nuclear-Powered Submarine Pathway: A Partnership for the Future* jointly published by the three partner nations and *Enhanced Lethality Surface Combatant Fleet: Independent Analysis of Navy's Surface Combatant Fleet* (Canberra: Australian Government, 2024). Additional detail of planned procurement, including estimated costs is contained in the *Integrated Investment Program 2024* (Canberra: Australian Government, 2024). All these documents can currently be found by searching the web.

5. These numbers related to the RAN. Two additional 'Evolved Capes' have been ordered for the ABF, supplementing eight original 'Capes' already operated by the service. More vessels of the type are planned.

6. Further information on Chinese naval aviation, including aircraft under development, is contained in Chapter 4.1.

7. This information is drawn from the annual report *Military and Security Developments Involving the People's Republic of China* (Washington DC: US Department of Defense, 2024), p.52. The report is an invaluable source of intelligence on PLAN developments.

8. News related to the Type 093B submarine programme has appeared in several sources. For example, see Alex Luck, 'Chinese Type 09IIIB nuclear powered attack submarine surfaces in clearest image yet' posted to the *Naval News* site on 13 October 2024. The 'X' posts of Tom Shugart, a former US Navy submariner and Adjunct Senior Fellow at the Center for a New American Security (CNAS) have also provided much new analysis.

9. A full review of the *Mogami* class is contained in Chapter 3.2.

10. See, *Progress and Budget in Fundamental Reinforcement of Defense Capabilities: Overview of FY2025 Budget* (Tokyo: Ministry of Defence, 2024)

11. The 'Three Axis' deterrent system comprises (i) a 'Kill Chain' to launch pre-emptive strikes on enemy missile sites, (ii) a 'Korea Air and Missile Defence' to intercept incoming missiles, and (iii) a 'Korea Massive Punishment and Retaliation' to strike at North Korea's leadership and command and control structure. For an interesting analysis and critique, see Doyeong Jung, 'South Korea's Revitalized "Three-Axis" System' posted to the US-based Council on Foreign Relations think tank site – cfr.org – on 4 January 2023.

12. Further analysis – including reference to ongoing local opposition to the Jeju Island base – is provided in an article by Hwang Joo-young, 'S. Korea Navy launches task fleet command', posted to *The Korea Herald* site – koreaherald.com – on 3 February 2025. The article incorrectly suggests that South Korea has ten Aegis-equipped ships.

13. Ongoing posts by the researcher Eunhyuk Cha to the *Naval News* site are a good source of information on this and other South Korean programmes.

14. A good source of information on Indonesian (and other local naval) developments, particularly with respect to smaller vessels, is the *Defense Studies* news site, defense-studies.blogspot.com

15. The original '15 to 5 Transformation Plan' envisaged the navy being re-structured to comprise 55 major combatants in five classes. Whilst the broad fundamentals of the plan still hold good, its details have been subject to subsequent revision.

16. The 'Ada' class design, including the Royal Malaysian Navy variant, is described in chapter 3.1.

17. The age of the ship's hull was regarded as a contributory factor in her ultimate loss. See, 'Report: Malaysian Patrol Boat Lost Due to Navigation Error and Hull Fatigue' published to the *Maritime Executive* site - maritime-executive.com – on 29 October 2024.

18. See, *2025 Defence Capability Plan* (Wellington: New Zealand Government, 2025).

19. See Van H Can Diepen, "North Korea's Nuclear-Powered Missile Submarine: A Mystery Wrapped Around a Riddle and an Enigma" posted to the Henry L. Stimson Center's 38 North site – 38north.org – on 21 March 2025. The site contains much information about North Korean military programmes, including also the Choe Hyon class destroyers.

20. See Gordon Arthur, 'Details of Singapore's MRCV emerge from the shadows' posted to the *Naval News* site on 14 May 2025.

2.3 REGIONAL REVIEW

Author:
Conrad Waters

THE INDIAN OCEAN AND AFRICA

In a world where widespread instability and even open hostilities are fast becoming the norm, the Middle East and its surrounds can stake an unenviable claim for leading the world in armed conflict. The last year's events were inevitably dominated by Israel's expanding campaign against Iran's Islamic Republic and its network of regional proxies. Prominent amongst these Iranian allies are Houthi rebel forces in Yemen. Their ongoing attacks on merchant shipping in the Red Sea have caused few casualties but extensive disruption, whilst highlighting limitations of the magazine capacity of escorting warships conducting protracted defensive operations. In March 2025, the new US Trump administration decided to intensify its counter-offensive against rebel forces, undertaking an extensive series of strikes against Houthi targets in which the *Harry S. Truman* (CVN-75) carrier strike group played a leading part. The resulting Operation 'Rough Rider' campaign – ending in a ceasefire at the start of May – did not entirely go the United States' way. In addition to American losses of several MQ-9 Reaper drones, the US Navy reportedly burned through over US$1 billion worth of weaponry in less than two months, causing a worrying dent in its stockpile of precision munitions.[1]

Whilst the May ceasefire brought a temporary halt to the US Navy's involvement in regional hostilities, the conflict between the Houthis and Israel continued. On 10 June 2025, this saw the Israeli Navy engage targets in Yemen for the first time. Reportedly using at least one of the new SA'AR 6 corvettes, the navy conducted long-range strikes against the Houthi-held port of Hodeidah, supplementing a continuing Israeli Air Force campaign against military and logistic assets.[2] These attacks were soon followed by the launch of Israel's full-scale attack on Iran's atomic weapons programme and military leadership on 13 June 2025, significantly escalating a series of direct confrontations that had commenced in April 2024. On 22 June 2025, the United States re-entered the conflict to carry out precision strikes – led by US Air Force B2 bombers but also involving US Navy submarine-launched Tomahawk cruise missiles – on Iranian nuclear infrastructure under Operation 'Midnight Hammer'. Suffering mounting pressure, the Iranian regime agreed to a ceasefire on 24 June after conducting a token attack against US military facilities in Qatar. As of the end of June 2025, the ceasefire still held.

At this moment in time, it is still too early to assess the likely future direction of a war that has severely weakened Iran's leadership without, seemingly, dealing a decisive blow to its ambitions or regional hegemony. From a naval perspective, however, the recent operations have some important lessons – both negative and positive – for the exercise of naval power when taking account of the current state of military technology. Significantly, the Red Sea engagements have reinforced the previous experience of Russia's Black Sea Fleet in highlighting many of the practical challenges inherent in sustaining protracted operations in littoral waters against a well-equipped, land-based opponent. These difficulties have been exacerbated by the increasing availability of attritable drones to improve intelligence surveillance and reconnaissance (ISR) capabilities and hold out the threat of swarm attack. At the same time, both the US Navy and Israeli strikes suggest the utility of warships as platforms for low-risk, long-range missile strikes, reinforcing another lesson of the Russo-Ukrainian War.[3]

Another regional hotspot that re-ignited in 2025 also demonstrated the potential of naval power. On 7 May, India launched Operation 'Sindoor', a series of missile and air strikes on what it claimed were terrorist-related targets in neighbouring Pakistan. Mutual attacks on air bases and other military installations soon followed. An Indian Navy strike group led by its new indigenous aircraft carrier *Vikrant* was deployed into the Arabian Sea. Here it was held ready to blockade Pakistan's coast and undertake strikes on the port city of Karachi. Fortunately, a ceasefire between the two nuclear-armed nations was arranged on 10 May 2025 before a spiral of escalation developed. Nevertheless, the Indian Navy deployment – which reportedly encompassed 36 warships and submarines (including those supporting the carrier group) armed with integrated air defences and equipped with long-range strike missiles – vividly demonstrated its growing capacity. The Indian Navy is increasingly the dominant naval power in a vast and volatile region; and a strategic instrument of national policy to match.[4]

The Indian Navy's *Deepak* class replenishment tanker *Shakti* pictured refuelling the Project 11356 class frigate *Tabar* and the Royal Australian Navy *Anzac* class frigate *Stuart* during exercise 'Malabar' 2024 in the Indian Ocean. An increasingly capable Indian Navy – notably demonstrated by the size and extent of its deployments during the short conflict with Pakistan in May 2025 – is steadily expanding its regional influence. *(Australian Department of Defence)*

Table 2.3.1: FLEET STRENGTHS IN THE INDIAN OCEAN, AFRICA AND THE MIDDLE EAST – LARGER NAVIES (MID 2025)

COUNTRY	ALGERIA[1]	EGYPT[1]	INDIA	IRAN[2]	ISRAEL	PAKISTAN	SAUDI ARABIA	SOUTH AFRICA
Aircraft Carrier (CV)	–	–	2	–	–	–	–	–
Strategic Missile Submarine (SSBN)	–	–	2	–	–	–	–	–
Attack Submarine (SSN/SSGN)	–	–	–	–	–	–	–	–
Patrol Submarine (SSK/SS)	6	8	17	4	5	5	–	3
Fleet Escort (DDG/FFG)	2	16	27	–	–	10	12	4
Patrol Escort/Corvette (FFG/FSG/FS)	11	3	10	9	7	4	4	–
Missile Armed Attack Craft (PGG/PTG)	c. 10	c. 25	7	c. 30	8	10	9	1[3]
Mine Countermeasures Vessel (MCMV)	3	c. 10	–	1	–	5	3	2[3]
Major Amphibious (LPD)	1	2	1	–	–	–	–	–

Notes:

1 Algerian fast attack craft and Egyptian fast attack craft and mine-countermeasures numbers approximate.

2 Iranian fleet numbers exclude large numbers of indigenously-built midget and coastal submarines, as well as numerous additional missile-armed patrol boats operated both by the Iranian Navy and Revolutionary Guard.

3 The South African attack craft and mine countermeasures vessels serve in patrol vessel roles.

INDIA

India remains in the top five countries with the largest military budgets, albeit the share of its national wealth allocated to defence has declined slightly over time and is a little below the global average. An examination of the 2025/26 budget – INR 8.81 trillion (c. US$78 billion) – shows a continuation of the previous balance towards revenue spending, with the capital budget only around a quarter of the total allocation. Unusually, however, the Indian Navy actually managed to cut through bureaucratic delays and spend its allotted capital budget for the naval fleet in 2024/25, possibly reflecting the realisation of a number of long-delayed projects.[5] This progress is reflected in Table 2.3.2 highlighting the major components of fleet strength, which saw increased force levels under several headings. An analysis of the fleet's major components follows.

Submarines: The most significant, if relatively little publicised, event impacting the Indian Navy over the last year was the commissioning of India's second *Arihant* class strategic submarine, *Arighaat,* at a ceremony at Visakhapatnam on 29 August 2024. Reportedly incorporating a number of improvements over her sister, she later conducted a test launch of the K4 submarine-launched ballistic missile towards the end of September. At least two further improved variants of the design are under construction at the secretive Ship Building Centre (SBC) in Visakhapatnam, from where the fourth boat in the series was reportedly launched in October 2024.

The SBC also looks set to play a leading role in the delivery of India's first nuclear-powered attack submarine (SSN) programme. Now known as Project 77 (previously Project 75A), a plan for as many as six of these submarines received preliminary government approval as long ago as 2015 but has subsequently been subject to protracted design development. More recently, in October 2024, government authorisation was received to build the first two boats at a reported cost of c. US$4.7 billion. The Indian Navy believes that these submarines can be completed by 2036-7 but this seems wildly optimistic. Another Russian-built nuclear-powered submarine – a successor to the Project 971 'Akula' class *Chakra* returned in 2021 – is to be leased to build operating experience until the new units are delivered.

Meanwhile, on 15 January 2025, *Vaghsheer*, the sixth Project 75 *Kalvari* class submarine, was officially commissioned into the Indian Navy during a ceremony attended by Indian Prime Minister Narendra Modi and other dignitaries. Built at Mumbai-based Mazagon Dock Shipbuilders Ltd (MDSL) under a technology of transfer agreement with what is now Naval Group in 2025, the entire class is scheduled to receive indigenously-developed air-independent propulsion (AIP) hull plugs under a contract signed in December 2024. As of mid-2025, negotiations for an additional batch of three submarines of the class were reportedly close to conclusion. In the longer term, MDSL hope to transition to producing next generation Project 75I series boats under a partnership with Germany's TKMS, which currently appears to have the upper hand over a competing Navantia-Larsen & Toubro (L&T) alliance.

Major Surface Warships: The last year has seen the

Table 2.3.2: INDIAN NAVY: PRINCIPAL UNITS AS AT MID 2025

TYPE	CLASS	NUMBER	TONNAGE	DIMENSIONS	PROPULSION	CREW	DATE
Aircraft Carriers							
Aircraft Carrier (CV)	**VIKRANT**	1	45,000 tonnes	263m x 62m x 9m	COGAG, 28 knots	1,650	2022
Aircraft Carrier (CV)	Project 1143.4 **VIKRAMADITYA** (KIEV)	1	45,000 tonnes	283m x 60m x 10m	Steam, 30 knots	1,600	1987
Principal Surface Escorts							
Destroyer – DDG	Project 15B **VISAKHAPATNAM**	4	7,400 tonnes	163m x 17m x 7m	COGAG, 30+ knots	300	2021
Destroyer – DDG	Project 15A **KOLKATA**	3	7,400 tonnes	163m x 17m x 7m	COGAG, 30+knots	330	2014
Destroyer – DDG	Project 15 **DELHI**	3	6,700 tonnes	163m x 17m x 7m	COGAG, 32 knots	350	1997
Destroyer – DDG	Project 61 ME **RAJPUT** ('Kashin')	3	5,000 tonnes	147m x 16m x 5m	COGAG, 35 knots	320	1980
Frigate – FFG	Project 17A **NILGIRI**	1	6,700 tonnes	149m x 18m x 5m	CODAG, 32 knots	225	2025
Frigate – FFG	Project 17 **SHIVALIK**	3	6,200 tonnes	143m x 17m x 5m	CODOG, 30 knots	265	2010
Frigate – FFG	Project 11356 **TALWAR**	7	4,000 tonnes	125m x 15m x 5m	COGAG, 30 knots	180	2003
Frigate – FFG	Project 16A **BRAHMAPUTRA**	3	4,000 tonnes	127m x 15m x 5m	Steam, 30 knots	350	2000
Corvette – FSG	Project 28 **KAMORTA**	4	3,400 tonnes	109m x 13m x 4m	Diesel, 25 knots	195	2014
Corvette – FSG	Project 25A **KORA**	4	1,400 tonnes	91m x 11m x 5m	Diesel, 25 knots	125	1998
Corvette – FSG	Project 25 **KHUKRI**	2	1,400 tonnes	91m x 11m x 5m	Diesel, 25 knots	110	1989
Submarines							
Submarine – SSBN	**ARIHANT**	2	7,500+ tonnes	112m x 11m x 10m	Nuclear, 25+ knots	100	2016
Submarine – SSK	Project 75 **KALVARI** ('Scorpène)	6	1,800 tonnes	68m x 6m x 6m	Diesel-electric, 20 knots	45	2017
Submarine – SSK	Project 877 EKM **SINDHUGHOSH** ('Kilo')	7	3,000 tonnes	73m x 10m x 7m	Diesel-electric, 17 knots	55	1986
Submarine – SSK	**SHISHUMAR** (Type 209/1500)	4	1,900 tonnes	64m x 7m x 6m	Diesel-electric, 22 knots	40	1986
Major Amphibious Units							
Landing Platform Dock – LPD	**JALASHWA** (AUSTIN)	1	17,000 tonnes	173m x 26/30m x 7m	Steam, 21 knots	405	1971

Indian Navy's construction of major surface combatants take tangible steps forward on several fronts. Notably, three new destroyers and frigates have been delivered. On 15 January 2025, at the same ceremony that marked the arrival of the submarine *Vagsheer*, the navy commissioned both the destroyer *Surat* and frigate *Nilgiri*. *Surat* is the last of four Project 15B *Visakhapatnam* class destroyers ordered from MDSL in 2011 and completed from 2021 onwards. The quartet is closely related to three earlier Project 15A *Kolkata* class destroyers commissioned between 2014 and 2016, which were themselves derived from the previous three members of the Project 15 *Delhi* class.[6] *Surat*'s delivery is likely the end of this design line, as future production is scheduled to switch to a much larger Project 18 type 'Next Generation Destroyer' later this decade.

Nilgiri is the first of seven Project 17A frigates ordered in February 2015 as a follow-on design to the previous Project 17 *Shivalik* class. Four of the frigates are being built by MDSL and three by Garden Reach Shipbuilders & Engineers (GRSE) in Kolkata. Displacing approximately 7,000 tonnes in full load condition, the vessels are equipped with the Israeli EL/M-2248 MF-STAR multifunction radar and Barak 8 surface-to-air missiles also used in the Project 15A/15B series destroyers, as well as the carrier *Vikrant*. Interestingly, the MDSL-built *Nilgiri* was commissioned a little over seven years after keel laying; a marked improvement over similar previous Indian Navy ships. Moreover, both the second MDSL Project 17A, *Udaygiri*, and her first GRSE-built sister, *Himgiri*, have successfully completed contractor sea trials and are also expected to be delivered imminently. It is hoped that the remaining four ships will be commissioned by 2027, after which production will transition to a further enhanced Project 17B design.

The other new arrival was the Project 11536 *Talwar* class frigate *Tushil*. She is one of two former Russian-ordered ships purchased by India when Russia's occupation of Crimea interrupted the supply of their Ukrainian-manufactured gas turbines. Built by the Yantar shipyard in Kaliningrad, *Tushil* was commissioned on 9 December 2024. Her sister, *Tamala*, is due to follow on 1 July 2025. A further pair of the type is being built under licence at Goa Shipyard Ltd (GSL), which launched *Triput* in July 2024 and *Tavasya* in March 2025. GSL has little previous experience of outfitting such complex combatants and it will be interesting to see whether planned deliveries in late 2026 and early 2027 will be achieved. When the two ships are completed, there will be ten of the Project 11536 series in Indian Navy service.

On 15 January 2025, the Indian Navy held a joint commissioning ceremony to welcome three major new vessels to the fleet. The event marked the arrival of the lead Project 17A class frigate *Nilgiri* (foreground), the sixth and final *Kalvari* class submarine *Vagsheer* (right), and the fourth and last Project 15B destroyer *Surat* (rear). *(Indian Navy)*

There have been few tangible developments with respect to other major warship programmes beyond the confirmation of the order for French Rafale M jets to operate from India's aircraft carriers, which is covered in more detail elsewhere in this volume. Proposals for new 'big deck' amphibious assault ships remain under consideration. In November 2024, the Indian and British Ministries of Defence signed a statement of intent with respect to cooperation on the design and development of electric propulsion systems, which are intended to be used in the new vessels.

In the latest of a long line of accidents to impact the Indian Navy, the lead Project 16A class frigate *Brahmaputra* caught fire whilst under refit at Naval Dockyard, Mumbai on 21 July 2024. Although the blaze was successfully extinguished, the frigate suffered a partial capsize the following day due to a loss of stability following the fire-fighting efforts. One sailor lost his life in the incident. The frigate was subsequently righted in a major salvage operation and is expected to return to service by the end of 2026.

Other Ships: Another major highlight of 2024-5 was the commissioning of *Arnala* – the first of eight Anti-Submarine Warfare Shallow Water Craft (ASW-SWC) ordered from GRSE in 2019 – on 18 June 2025. Displacing around 900 tonnes, she is armed with a RBU-6000 ASW rocket launcher and tubes for lightweight torpedoes in addition to a 30mm Naval Service Gun. Sea trials of the second ship, *Androth*, have also been completed and work on many of their sisters is now well advanced. Cochin Shipyard Ltd (CSL) has been contracted to build a further eight of the type to its own design, with delivery of its lead ship expected within the next year. All 16 vessels are equipped with diesel-powered waterjets and indigenously developed sonar.

CSL has also started work on a programme for six larger Next Generation Missile Vessels, which are to be optimised for anti-surface warfare. A first steel-cutting ceremony for the as yet unnamed lead ship was held in Kochi on 16 December 2024. Her delivery is scheduled for March 2027.

Arnala is the first of eight Anti-Submarine Warfare Shallow Water Craft (ASW-SWC) ordered from GRSE of Kolkata for the Indian Navy. Eight further vessels with a similar mission but of different design are being built by CSL of Kochi. *(Indian Navy)*

November 2024 saw a keel-laying ceremony for the first of the navy's long-delayed fleet support ships at Hindustan Shipyard Ltd (HSL) in Visakhapatnam. The event was followed in December by a first steel-cutting event for the second vessel at the L&T shipyard in Kattupalli, which has been sub-contracted to build the hulls of two of the five-strong class. The arrangement with L&T mirrors a similar, successful arrangement with respect to four of the ASW-SWC vessels ordered from GRSE and likely reflects an aggressive delivery schedule for the programme's completion. By June 2025, work had also commenced on the third and fourth members of the class.

OTHER INDIAN OCEAN NAVIES

Bangladesh: There are few tangible developments to report with respect to the Bangladesh Navy over the last year, with the collapse of the country's Hasina government in August 2024 resulting in the departure of an administration that had done much to promote naval development. Reports suggest that the replacement interim government led by Muhammad Yunus is likely to take a much more overtly pro-China stance than its predecessor, potentially threatening a previously expanding relationship between the Bangladesh and Indian navies.

The most significant recent reinforcement to Bangladesh's fleet has been the 350-tonne *Padama* class patrol vessel *Bishkhali*. Commissioned on 30 November 2024, she is the fifth and final unit of a second batch of the type ordered from the Khulna Shipyard in May 2019 and the tenth member of the class overall. The Bangladesh Navy is also reportedly in the final stages of acquiring the former British survey vessel *Enterprise*, thereby adding to its extensive inventory of second-hand former Royal Navy warships.

Myanmar: In December 2024 the Myanmar Navy launched *King Thalun*, the latest iteration of a series of indigenously designed frigates. Reported having a length of 135m and a displacement of 3,500 tonnes, the frigate is larger than the two previous *Kyan Sittha* commissioned between 2014 and 2015. Two smaller, 63m ASW-configured patrol ships were commissioned during the same occasion.

In spite of this technical progress, the Myanmar's military junta continues to struggle countering multiple insurgencies in the country's ongoing civil war. In September 2024, it was reported that the Maung Shwe Lay navy training base in Rakhine (formerly known as Arakan) had fallen to the separatist Arakan Army, the first major naval facility to be lost to insurrectionist forces.

Pakistan: Whilst Pakistan's defence budget is reportedly increasing by 20 percent to c. US$9 billion in 2025-6, this is dwarfed by that of its Indian neighbour. This disparity has forced the Pakistan Navy to follow an asymmetrical anti-access/ area denial (A2/AD) in which an enhanced submarine force will play an increasingly important part. This revitalisation is based on a 2015 agreement with China to acquire eight *Hangor* class submarines; reportedly a S26 export variant of the People's Liberation Army Navy Type 039A/B/C 'Yuan' series. The programme – which encompasses four Chinese-built boats and four assembled in Pakistan by Karachi Shipyard & Engineering Works (KSEW) – has proved slow to implement. However, the second Chinese-built unit, named *Shushuk*, was launched at Wuchang Shipbuilding on 15 March 2025. Delivery of the lead submarine is also said to be imminent.[7]

Faster progress has been made with surface fleet modernisation. This has been based on a three tier approach encompassing procurement of Chinese-built Type 054A/P frigates, Turkish-designed *Babur* (stretched 'Ada') class corvettes, and offshore patrol vessels (OPVs) constructed in Damen's Romanian shipyard. Deliveries of the four Type 054A/P *Tughril* class frigates were completed in 2023. They were followed in 2024 by a second batch of two, enlarged *Yarmook* class OPVs; *Hunain* commissioned on 26 July and *Yamama* on 17 December. Meanwhile, three of the four *Babur* class corvettes remain under construction in Türkiye and at KSEW following the official induction of the lead, Turkish-built vessel in September 2024. Further details of the class are provided in Chapter 3.1.

AFRICAN NAVIES

In back-to-back events held on 24 and 25 April 2024, **South Africa** saw, respectively, the formal commissioning of its second Damen Stan Patrol 6211 inshore patrol vessel, *King Shaka Zulu*, and the naming of the final member of the class as *Adam Kok III*. The ceremonies marked a rare moment of good news for a navy that is struggling to retain operational effectiveness against a backdrop of underfunding and alleged corruption. The small frontline fleet of four MEKO A200-SAN frigates and three Type 209 submarines has seen poor availability due to a lack of scheduled refits, with *Amatola*, the lead MEKO, being forced to cancel a planned deployment to attend the 2024 Russian Navy Day due to technical defects. The completion of *Nelson Mandela*, the hydrographic survey ship being built under Project Hotel by Sandock Austral

Adam Kok III is the third of three locally-built Damen Stan Patrol 6211 inshore patrol vessels delivered to the Republic of South Africa Navy. *(Damen)*

The as-yet unnamed offshore patrol vessel pennant number 502 is launched from Navantia's San Fernando shipyard in the Bay of Cadiz on 27 May 2025. Laid down in September 2024, she is being built for the Royal Moroccan Navy to the company's 'Avante 1800' design. *(Navantia)*

Shipyards continues to make only slow progress, whilst it seems unlikely an option for a fourth inshore patrol vessel will be taken up in the current financial climate.[8]

Amongst the other more significant navies in Sub-Saharan Africa, **Angola** has been taking delivery of further vessels under its longstanding partnership with France's Constructions Mécaniques de Normandie (CMN). These have included the second of a pair of tank landing ships and additional 'Ocean Eagle' catamaran-type inshore patrol vessels, which were delivered by heavy-lift ship early in 2025. Work on a more significant contract – reportedly valued at nearly €1 billion (c, US$1.2 billion) – for three BR71 Mk II corvettes derived from the CMN *Baynunah* class design agreed with Abu Dhabi Ship Building (ADSB) is ongoing, with construction of the two lead vessels being split between the French and Emirati shipyards. Deliveries are expected to commence before the end of 2026 under what is likely the region's most expensive current naval programme.

Nigeria also continues to bolster its fleet, holding a formal induction ceremony for three new patrol vessels and three Leonardo AW109 helicopters during a ceremony on 31 May 2025 that coincided with its 69th anniversary. The ships in question were a second-hand, former South Korean 'Chamsuri' class fast patrol craft and two new, Singapore-built 'Sea Eagle' patrol boats. Deliveries of larger Turkish-built patrol vessels and further French Ocea-built patrol boats are also said to be imminent, whilst construction of indigenous 'seaward defence vessels' is also ongoing.

In North Africa, there has seemingly been a pause in the wave of warship procurement activity that has previously seen the wholesale rejuvenation of both **Algeria's** and **Egypt's** fleets. However, in March 2025, it emerged that the Algerian Navy had signed a contract for three AW159 Wildcat helicopters, becoming only the fourth country after the United Kingdom, South Korea and the Philippines to operate the successor to the highly popular Lynx.[9] Elsewhere in the region, **Tunisia** has taken delivery of two former US Coast Guard 'Island' class cutters, which were commissioned as *Tazarka* and *Menzel Bourguiba* at a ceremony at La Goulette on 17 April 2025. However, it is **Morocco** that looks set to see the greatest imminent boost to its strength following the launch of its as yet-unnamed offshore patrol vessel pennant number 502 on 27 May 2025. Being constructed by Navantia's San Fernando shipyard in the Bay of Cadiz, the ship is an 'Avante 1800' variant of the series of patrol ships and corvettes previously delivered to both Saudi Arabia and Venezuela.

MIDDLE EASTERN NAVIES

As noted in the introduction, **Israel** has continued to be engaged on multiple fronts across the Middle East. The Israeli Navy has been active in support of a number of these operations, including the June 2025 attack against Hodeidah in Yemen. Previously, in December 2024, it carried out a pre-emptive strike on **Syria's** naval base in the port of Laktakia in the aftermath of the collapse of that country's Assad regime. The aim of the mission was to destroy a number of obsolete missile-armed 'Osa' class fast attack craft to prevent them falling into the insurrectionists' hands.

Israel's own naval forces continue to be bolstered

Drakon is the third and final member of three Israeli 'Dolphin II' submarines built by TKMS at Kiel with financial assistance from the German government. She incorporates a number of differences from the other boats of the class; notably an enlarged fin (sail) that has been rumoured to incorporate VLS tubes for long range missiles. Formally christened in November 2024, she is expected to be delivered before the end of 2025. *(TKMS)*

A large number of HIS-32 patrol boats have been built by Constructions Mécaniques de Normandie (CMN) in France and Zamil Offshore Services in Saudi Arabia for the Royal Saudi Navy under a joint construction programme. In a significant expansion of its indigenous naval sector, Saudi Arabia now intends that local industry will manufacture block assemblies for one of three additional 'Avante 2200' light frigates ordered from Spain's Navantia. *(Peter Whittington)*

by new procurement programmes. The most recent development has seen the signature of a long-awaited contract with Israel Shipyards for five 'Reshef' fast attack craft – a variant of its SA'AR-72 design – at a cost approaching the equivalent of US$800 million. Work on the first vessel commenced with a first steel-cutting ceremony held on 18 February 2025 in what was claimed to be the first indigenous construction programme for a major Israeli warship for two decades. Earlier, on 12 November 2024, the final Israeli 'Dolphin II' class AIP-equipped submarine, *Drakon*, was the focal point of a ceremonial launching event at TKMS Kiel. It has long been speculated that Israel's submarines are equipped with nuclear-armed missiles to provide a 'second strike' capability, with *Drakon*'s enlarged fin (sail) rumoured to be equipped with a vertical launch system (VLS) for this purpose. An IDF press release at the time of the launch lent credibility to this speculation, stating that the submarine is 'equipped with unique systems, including ground-breaking technologies that expand the range of the IDF's capabilities across various arenas'.[10] The ceremony was combined with the start of production of the lead boat of a new series of Israeli submarines that are to be known as the *Dakar* class. These will eventually replace the three original 'Dolphin I' class boats that were commissioned between 1999 and 2000 on a numerical like-for-like basis, thereby maintaining a six-strong submarine flotilla.

In December 2024, **Saudi Arabia** marked a further extension of its relationship with Spain's Navantia through a contract for an additional three 'Avante 2200' *Al Jubail* class corvettes; essentially frigates in all but name. They will supplement the first batch of five delivered between 2022 and 2024. The new contract involves an extension of Saudi Arabian industrial involvement in the project, including supply of the complete combat management system by the SAMI-Navantia joint venture and the manufacture of blocks for the third of the corvettes in Saudi Arabia. A first steel-cutting ceremony for the first of the new vessels was held within a week of contract signature, with work on the second ship starting in March 2025. Saudi Arabia's increased involvement in the new corvettes' construction represents a significant expansion of its naval shipbuilding ambitions. These have previously been limited to the assembly of HSI-32 patrol boats by Zamil Offshore Services in a joint programme with CMN of France.

Elsewhere in the Middle East, the **United Arab Emirates** demonstrated the growing prowess of its indigenous naval sector through the launch of the first of its 'Falaj 3' OPVs from ADSB's yard on 14 January 2025. Subsequently commissioned as *Altaf* at the NAVDEX 2025 naval exhibition the following month, she is one of four 60m (62.7m overall) missile-armed patrol vessels built with design support from Singapore's ST Engineering under an AED 3.5 billion (c. US$950 million) contract signed in 2021. In May 2025, ABSD's parent Company EDGE announced that **Kuwait** had agreed to purchase eight 'Falaj 3' type vessels through an AED 9 billion (c. US$ 2.5 billion) deal that includes integrated logistical and in-service support.

November 2024 brought a successful conclusion to Fincantieri's agreement to rebuild **Qatar's** navy with the delivery of the hybrid amphibious transport dock *Al Fulk*, the final vessel in a seven ship contract initially agreed in 2016. Broadly similar to the Algerian Navy's *Kalaat Beni Abbes*, the c. 9,000 tonne vessel is noteworthy in being equipped with a powerful Aster missile-based SAAM-ESD air defence system to supplement her amphibious capabilities. Whilst Fincantieri hopes to expand its relationship with Qatar for further warships, the country has also developed ties with the growing Turkish naval sector for missile-armed fast attack craft and armed uncrewed surface vessels.

Italy's Fincantieri delivered the amphibious transport dock *Al Fulk* to the Qatar Emirati Navy in November 2024, completing a large seven-ship order that also encompassed frigate-sized 'corvettes' and fast attack craft-like patrol vessels. *(Fincantieri)*

It has been far from a good year for **Iran's** regime, whose military leadership has suffered partial 'decapitation' from targeted Israeli strikes. Whilst it appears that the Iranian Navy has escaped significant destruction during hostilities, it has been weakened by significant damage sustained to the frigate *Sahand*. The 'Moudge' class vessel – a derivative of Iran's British Vosper Thornycroft designed *Alvand* class – capsized in the port of Bandar Abbas on 7 July 2024 in an accident ascribed to a technical fault. Although subsequently salvaged, it is unclear to what extent the resultant damage can be successfully repaired. The class has already suffered a series of mishaps, including the total loss of *Damavand* after striking a breakwater during a storm in 2018 and an industrial accident suffered by *Talaiyeh* whilst under construction. The latter vessel was reportedly delivered in January 2025 under a changed name as the intelligence gathering vessel *Zagros*.

Notes:

1. See, for example, 'Fight With Houthis Left a Dent in U.S. Navy's Weapons Inventory' posted to the *Maritime Executive* site – martime-executive.com – on 15 May 2025.

2. Amongst numerous reports on the attack was Yonah Jeremy Bob & Amichai Stein, 'Israel Navy attacks Houthis for first time in Hodeidah Port strike' posted to the *Jerusalem Post* site – jpost.com – on 10 June 2025.

3. Further analysis of the challenges encountered by navies in the essentially littoral campaigns in the Black and Red Seas is provided in the editor's 'Naval operations: Lessons from recent conflicts' posted to the *European Security & Defence* site – euro-sd.com – on 31 March 2025.

4. A broader analysis of the significance of the Indian Navy's deployment is provided by Captain Sarabjeet S Parmar (retd.), 'The Indian Navy's role and impact in Operation Sindoor: Historical precedents and future imperatives' posted to the New Delhi based Council for Strategic and Defense Research (CSDR) think tank – csdr online.com – on 30 May 2025.

5. For further analysis, Deependra Singh Hooda's 'Policy Brief: India's Defence Budget 2025-26' posted to the Delhi Policy Group's site – delhipolicygroup.org – on 12 February 2025 provides a concise overview.

6. The Project 15A and Project 15B designs were described in detail by Mrityunjoy Mazumdar in the 2024 edition of *Seaforth World Naval Review*.

7. See, Liu Xuanzun and Guo Yuandan, 'Exclusive: Submarines from China-Pakistan cooperation project to join Pakistan Navy fleet soon, says Pakistani naval chief' posted to the Chinese Communist party-affiliated *Global Times* website – globaltimes.cn – on 15 January 2025.

8. More details of the current status of South Africa's naval modernisation can be found on the *defenceWeb* site – defenceweb.co.za – which remains an excellent source of news on naval developments across the African continent.

9. This news was reported by Dominic Perry in, 'Leonardo mulls Wildcat's future amid dwindling backlog' posted to the *FlightGlobal* –flightglobal.com – on 13 March 2025.

10. These remarks are contained in an Israel Ministry of Defense social media post, dated 12 November 2024.

2.4 REGIONAL REVIEW

EUROPE AND RUSSIA

Author:
Conrad Waters

On 25 June 2025, Europe's NATO members made a historic pledge to raise defence spending to five percent of gross domestic product; an increase from the previous target of two percent in a decision described in an official NATO communique as an 'ironclad commitment to collective defence'.[1] Primarily driven by fears that US President Donald Trump would walk away from the alliance if the agreement was not reached, the goodwill generated by the announcement appears to have assuaged concerns of NATO's imminent demise; at least for the time being. Moreover, the promise of increased money holds out the prospect of a reversal of a decades-long atrophy of European military power, including the revitalisation of its much-weakened naval forces.

As is often the case in these circumstances, the truth is a good deal more nuanced. In reality, continued American military support for its NATO partners is far from assured given the Trump administration's mercurial nature, its often ill-concealed disdain for many traditional allies, and its broader ambivalence towards mutual defence commitments. Moreover, the pledge by NATO members is not quite as robust as the headlines suggest. Just 3.5 percent of the commitment relates to 'core defence spending' – the remainder comprising rather loosely defined 'defence and security-related investments' – and even this has only to be achieved in 2035; a decade from now. As such, there is plenty of scope for backsliding. Notably, Spain has already achieved a carve-out from the new target in a concession that hardly strengthens the NATO alliance's overall cohesion.

It is also questionable to what extent the new largesse will benefit naval forces as compared with other branches of the military. Understandably, many of the countries that are seemingly most committed to the new objective have the greatest proximity to Russia and the conflict in Ukraine. For example, Germany reportedly intends to achieve the new NATO 3.5 percent 'core' target in just four years, increasing its defence budget by more than two thirds from €95 billion (c. US$110 billion) to €162 billion (c. US$190 billion) in the process. Many of these Central and Eastern European countries are primarily land-based powers, suggesting that new investment might be disproportionately weighted towards this domain. In contrast, leading naval powers such as France and the United Kingdom – both of which face significant financial constraints – are expected to grow their spending at a much slower rate.[2]

Nevertheless, it appears certain that the expansion in European naval spending that has already become established since Russia's initial annexation of Crimea in 2014 is likely to see further acceleration. This has already driven the emergence of new naval programmes from the Baltic to the Black Sea, as well as a significant upsurge in investment in infrastructure. The latter was most recently marked by the official opening on 25 June 2025 of the new Janet Harvey Hall at BAE Systems' Govan shipyard in Glasgow –currently used for the construction of the British Royal Navy's Type 26 frigates – but has been replicated in similar upgrades to shipyards across Europe.[3] The high quality jobs and economic prosperity brought by these new facilities is increasingly being used to justify the politically 'difficult choices' being made with respect to other elements of government spending and taxation.

From a naval perspective, other difficult choices are likely to arise with respect to the future configuration of naval fleets. Having only recently completed the transformation from a focus on Cold War European warfighting towards equipment optimised for worldwide expeditionary stabilisation missions, many navies are now faced with the potentially expensive need to reverse tack. This gives rise to an associated dilemma with respect to the new missions that have been taken on and which, for example, have seen lengthy deployments to the Indo-Pacific by carrier groups led by *Cavour* (Italy), *Charles de Gaulle* (France) and *Prince of Wales* (United Kingdom) during 2024-5. A hint of the future direction of travel is provided by Britain's 2025 Strategic Defence Review. This has prioritised, inter alia, a very substantial investment in expanding the Royal Navy's nuclear-powered attack submarine (SSN) fleet as part of a return to a 'NATO first' strategy. One consequence is that the only recently expanded Royal Navy presence in Far Eastern waters may soon be largely a thing of the past.

The British Royal Navy aircraft carrier *Prince of Wales* arrives at Singapore on 23 June 2025 during the CSG-25 deployment. Her arrival marked the first time a warship of the name had been seen in the city since the Royal Navy's Force Z sailed to its doom at the start of the Pacific phase of the Second World War on 8 December 1941. Whilst three European carrier groups have deployed to the Far East over the past 12 months, the deteriorating security environment in Europe may make such deployments more of a rarity. *(Crown Copyright 2025)*

TABLE 2.4.1: FLEET STRENGTHS IN WESTERN EUROPE – LARGER NAVIES (MID 2025)

COUNTRY	FRANCE	GERMANY	GREECE	ITALY	NETHERLANDS	SPAIN	TURKEY	UK
Aircraft Carrier (CVN/CV)	1	–	–	1	–	–	–	2
Support/Helicopter Carrier (CVS/CVH)	–	–	–	–	–	–	–	–
Strategic Missile Submarine (SSBN)	4	–	–	–	–	–	–	4
Attack Submarine (SSN)	5	–	–	–	–	–	–	5
Patrol Submarine (SSK)	–	6	9[2]	8	3	2	13	–
Fleet Escort (DDG/FFG)	15	11	13[2]	16	6	11	17	14
Patrol Escort/Corvette (FFG/FSG/FS)	9	5	–	–	–	–	9	–
Missile Armed Attack Craft (PGG/PTG)	–	–	15				17	
Mine Countermeasures Vessel (MCMV)	11	8[1]	3	10	3	6	11	7
Major Amphibious (LHD/LPD/LPH/LSD)	3	–	–	4	2[3]	3	1	3

Notes:

1 Two further units used as support vessels and two as recruitment platforms.

2 Headline figures may overstate the actual position, as some old units are of doubtful operational status.

3 Also one joint support ship with amphibious capabilities.

MAJOR REGIONAL POWERS – FRANCE

There has been relatively little change to the French Navy's planned development since the approval of the *Loi de Programmation Militaire* 2024-2030 (LPM 2024-30) in July 2023, which set out the future structure and funding of the French Armed Forces until the end of the decade. Whilst the subsequent deterioration in the global security environment has driven demands for a further increase in defence investment, France's stretched finances and fractured political climate suggest further movement may be difficult to achieve in the short term. As noted in last year's edition of *Seaforth World Naval Review*, this leaves the French Navy in a position where it is able to modernise its existing equipment but is unlikely to afford much in the way of material expansion.

The lack of substantial change is reflected in Table 2.4.2, which summarises the navy's major warship classes. With the exception of the long-planned decline in light frigate/corvette numbers, there has been no change in overall fleet structure. A summary of major developments follows.

Aircraft Carriers: A formal contract for construction of the new generation aircraft carrier (PANG) is now expected to be signed before the end of 2025. This will be followed by the start of construction at the Chantiers de l'Atlantique in Saint Nazaire during 2026. Latest design details of the as yet unnamed ship suggest she will have a full load displacement of 78,000 tonnes and a length of 310m, making her broadly similar to China's Type 003 *Fujian* in overall size. Her 17,200m² flight deck will be equipped with three electromagnetic launch system (EMALS) type catapults and – unlike the existing *Charles de Gaulle* – she will be capable of launching and landing aircraft simultaneously. Her notional air group is sized at 30 fast jets and uncrewed air vehicles (UAVs) in addition to early airborne warning aircraft and helicopters. The construction programme envisages the commencement of sea trials in 2036 so as to allow *Charles de Gaulle* to be retired from operational service in 2038.[3]

Submarines: The underwater flotilla has seen the continued transition to the new *Suffren* class SSN-type submarines at the expense of the remaining *Rubis* class boats. In line with this process, the third member of the *Suffren* class, *Tourville*, was delivered in November 2024 – although she has yet to be declared fully operational – whilst the fourth *Rubis* class submarine, *Émeraude*, was decommissioned on 12 December. The transition will continue throughout the rest of the decade until the nuclear-powered attack submarine is comprised solely of the six *Suffren* class units.

Attention is already turning to the renewal of the strategic submarine force following the commencement of work on the lead third-generation strategic submarine (SNLE 3G) at Cherbourg in March 2024. This programme will dominate shipyard activities through to the planned delivery of the last of four planned boats – replacements for the four existing members of the *Le Triomphant* class – until around 2050. Given this, it seems unlikely that there will be the capacity to consider any expansion of submarine numbers in the foreseeable future.

Surface Combatants: The lead defence and intervention frigate (FDI) *Amiral Ronarc'h* commenced the first phase of her sea trials from Lorient on 7 October 2024. Subsequent phases have continued into 2025, with delivery expected before the end of the year. The arrival of further French members of the class will be delayed by priority being given to the export for the Hellenic Navy's *Kimon* class variant, albeit that a further three of the French vessels are now in various stages of construction. Completion of deliveries around the end of the decade will give the navy a modern surface fleet of two 'Horizon', eight FREMM, and five FDI frigates, thereby meeting the current objective of a 15-strong 'first rank' force of major combatants. An increase in this number back to a previous objective of 18 vessels has been floated by the French defence minister. However, the likely difficulty of further

TABLE 2.4.2: FRENCH NAVY: PRINCIPAL UNITS AS AT MID 2025

TYPE	CLASS	NUMBER	TONNAGE	DIMENSIONS	PROPULSION	CREW	DATE
Aircraft Carriers							
Aircraft Carrier – CVN	**CHARLES DE GAULLE**	1	42,000 tonnes	262m x 33/64m x 9m	Nuclear, 27 knots	1,950	2001
Principal Surface Escorts							
Frigate – FFG	**AQUITAINE** (FREMM)	8[1]	6,000 tonnes	142m x 20m x 5m	CODLOG, 27 knots	110	2012
Frigate – FFG	**FORBIN** ('Horizon')	2	7,100 tonnes	153m x 20m x 5m	CODOG, 29+ knots	195	2008
Frigate – FFG	**LA FAYETTE**	5	3,600 tonnes	125m x 15m x 5m	CODAD, 25 knots	150	1996
Frigate – FSG	**FLORÉAL**	6	3,000 tonnes	94m x 14m x 4m	CODAD, 20 knots	90	1992
Frigate – FS[2]	**D'ESTIENNE D'ORVES** (A-69)	3	1,300 tonnes	80m x 10m x 3m	Diesel, 24 knots	90	1976
Submarines							
Submarine – SSBN	**LE TRIOMPHANT**	4	14,400 tonnes	138m x 13m x 11m	Nuclear, 25 knots	110	1997
Submarine – SSN	**SUFFREN**	3	5,300 tonnes	100m x 9m x 7m	Nuclear, 25+knots	65	2020
Submarine – SSN	**RUBIS**	2	2,700 tonnes	74m x 8m x 6m	Nuclear, 25+ knots	70	1983
Major Amphibious Units							
Amph Assault Ship – LHD	**MISTRAL**	3	21,500 tonnes	199m x 32m x 6m	Diesel-electric, 19 knots	160	2006

Note:

1 Includes two slightly-modified *Alsace* variants.

2 Now officially reclassified as offshore patrol vessels.

Amiral Ronarc'h, the first of at least five planned French FDI type frigates, pictured departing Lorient on 7 October 2024 at the start of her sea trials. *(Naval Group)*

extending the service lives of the existing *La Fayette* class 'stealth' frigates – that the FDIs are being built to replace – makes this aim look challenging in the immediate term.

The remaining flotilla of *D'Estienne d'Orves* class corvettes – now officially regarded as offshore patrol vessels (OPVs) – continues to decline in line with previous plans. *Commandant Birot* and *Commandant Ducuing* have both completed their final operational deployments prior to retirement, leaving just three of the elderly vessels in *Marine Nationale* service. The six larger *Floréal* class vessels – all built to commercial standards and delivered in the early 1990s – are also starting to show their age and will likely be replaced through the European Union's European Patrol Corvette (EPC) project in due course.

Minor Warships & Auxiliaries: In the meantime, the programme for the OPVs – referred to by the French Navy as *patrouilleurs hauturiers* (PHs) – that are intended to form the *D'Estienne d'Orves* class's replacement is now underway after considerable delay. The vessels are being built in a number of smaller French shipyards under the overall direction of Naval Group, with the first three of an initial batch of seven now under construction. Orders for three more are anticipated in the next LPM to meet a total requirement for ten ships, all of which will be based in Metropolitan France. It is hoped that delivery of the first vessel may be achieved before the end of 2026 but this seems optimistic. Work also continues on the *patrouilleurs outre-mer* (POMs) that undertake similar duties in France's overseas territories. *Auguste Techer*, the third member of the six-strong class, was reported as being close to delivery from builders Socarenam in June 2025. The remaining vessels should all follow her into service in the next 12 to 18 months.

The new French logistic support ship *Jacques Chevallier* pictured refuelling the Royal Australian Navy destroyer *Hobart* in the course of the *Charles de Gaulle* carrier strike group's deployment to the Indian Ocean and Pacific in 2024-5. She had been declared as fully operational on 20 November 2024, shortly before the start of the mission. *(Australian Department of Defence)*

December 2024 saw the French Navy take delivery of its first uncrewed mine warfare module under a joint project with the United Kingdom known as SLAM-F in France.[4] A further seven of the modules should be delivered by 2030 as part of a wider programme that also includes eight BGDM mine countermeasures motherships and five BBPD-NG next generation diving support vessels. An agreement signed in February 2025 has confirmed France's use of the rMCM mothership design already jointly purchased by Belgium and the Netherlands as the basis for the BGDM element of the programme.

The lead BRF type replenishment tanker *Jacques Chevallier* was declared fully operational in November 2024 prior to accompanying the *Charles de Gaulle* carrier strike group's 2024-5 Indo-Pacific deployment. The second member of the four-ship class, *Jacques Stosskopf*, was launched from Chantiers de l'Atlantique in August 2024 prior to commencing sea trials in April 2025. Her arrival, together with that of the remainder of the class, is increasingly pressing given the current lack of replenishment vessels to support the French Navy's longer distance deployments.

MAJOR REGIONAL POWERS – ITALY

Italy's *Marina Militare* has continued to demonstrate its expanding global reach during the past year, most notably evidenced by the five-month deployment of a carrier strike group focused on *Cavour* and the FREMM-type frigate *Alpino* to the Indian Ocean and Pacific between June and October 2024. The mission, just one of a number of international deployments highlighted in the Italian Navy's annual report, is indicative of the shift in the navy's outlook beyond its traditional Mediterranean focus to encompass a *Mediterraneo allargato*, an 'enlarged Mediterranean' extending, particularly, into the Indian Ocean.[5]

As illustrated by Table 2.4.3 summarising the fleet's main components, the Italian Navy increasingly possesses the means to pursue this strategy. The last year marked something of a shift from old to new in terms of equipment, with a number of significant warship decommissionings being balanced by some important new arrivals. The most noteworthy withdrawal was that of the veteran aircraft carrier *Giuseppe Garibaldi*, the first Italian carrier actually to enter service. She was placed in reserve at the Taranto naval base on 1 October 2024 after completing a 29-year career but may be sold to Indonesia for further service. Another important milestone was marked on 1 April 2025 when *Grecale,* the last of the eight *Maestrale* class frigates in operational service, returned to La Spezia at the end of her final mission. The lead *Durand de la Penne* class destroyer also left the active fleet in October 2024; many years before her replacement in the form of the planned DDX destroyer programme is likely to be delivered.

Despite the undoubted significance of these departures, they were more than counterbalanced by the ships that were delivered. Heading the roster was the amphibious assault ship, *Trieste*, which was accepted from Fincantieri on 7 December 2024 after completing an extensive series of trials. At nearly 37,500 tonnes displacement, she is the largest Italian warship built since the Second World War and, in addition to her primary amphibious mission, has a secondary role as a substitute aircraft carrier for *Cavour*.

The Italian multi-purpose combat ship *Giovanni delle Bande Nere* is the first fully-configured member of the *Paolo Thaon di Revel* class to be commissioned into the Italian Navy. This photograph was taken after she completed a short visit to Portsmouth naval base in the United Kingdom in June 2025. *(Conrad Waters)*

Also joining the fleet was the FREMM type frigate *Spartaco Schergat*, a replacement for a previous member of the class transferred to Egypt before delivery. Delivered on 15 April 2025 as the ninth member of ten planned Italian members of the class, she combines capabilities found in the previous *Bergamini* general purpose and *Fasan* anti-submarine warfare (ASW) variants. Her arrival was preceded by that of *Giovanni delle Bande Nere*, the fourth member of the *Paolo Thaon di Revel* PPA multi-purpose combat ship class and the first to be completed in the enhanced 'full' equipment configuration. Delivered on 2 October 2024, she subsequently deployed to British waters to participate in the NATO 'At Sea Demonstration/Formidable Shield 25' (ASD/FS25) exercises, where she undertook a test firing of her Aster surface-to-air missile system.[6]

The last year has also seen broader progress across a wide range of construction programmes that are noteworthy both for their cost and ambition. Key developments included:

- **FREMM EVO Frigate:** A follow-on from the FREMM frigate programme incorporating new technologies, this initially encompasses two ships. A c. €1.5 billion (c. US$1.75 billion) contract for the vessels was signed in July 2024, with construction of the lead vessel commencing at Fincantieri's Riva Trigoso shipyard on 3 April 2025.
- **PPA Multi-Role Combat Ship:** *Domenico Millelire*, the fifth Italian member of the class, was launched at Riva Trigoso on 13 July 2024. Subsequently, on 26 June 2025, Fincantieri and its partner Leonardo received a €700 million (c. US$820 million) contract to replace the two members of the class sold to Indonesia in 2024.
- **PPX Offshore Patrol Vessel:** A steel-cutting ceremony for the first of these next-generation OPVs was held at Riva Trigoso on 24 September 2024. A contract for three of these ships with an additional three options was signed in July 2023, with one of the options subsequently being exercised in

Table 2.4.3: ITALIAN NAVY: PRINCIPAL UNITS AS AT MID 2025

TYPE	CLASS	NUMBER	TONNAGE	DIMENSIONS	PROPULSION	CREW	DATE
Aircraft Carriers							
Aircraft Carrier – CV	**CAVOUR**	1	28,100 tonnes	244m x 30/39m x 9m	COGAG, 29 knots	800	2008
Principal Surface Escorts							
Frigate – FFG	**CARLO BERGAMINI** (FREMM)[1]	9	6,700 tonnes	144m x 20m x 5m	CODLOG, 27 knots	145	2013
Frigate – FFG	**ANDREA DORIA** ('Horizon')	2	7,100 tonnes	153m x 20m x 5m	CODOG, 29+ knots	190	2007
Destroyer – DDG	**DE LA PENNE**	1	5,400 tonnes	148m x 16m x 5m	CODOG, 31 knots	375	1993
Frigate – FFG/FF[2]	**PAOLO THAON DI REVEL**	4	6,250 tonnes[2]	143m x 17m x 5m	CODAGOL, 32+ knots	[2]	2022
Submarines							
Submarine – SSK	**TODARO** (Type 212A)	4	1,800 tonnes	56m x 7m x 6m	AIP, 20+ knots	30	2006
Submarine – SSK	**PELOSI** (Improved SAURO)	4	1,700 tonnes	64m x 7m x 6m	Diesel-electric, 20 knots	50	1988
Major Amphibious Units							
Amph. Assault Ship – LHD	**TRIESTE**	1	37,500 tonnes	245m x 36m/55m x 9m	CODOGOL, 25 knots	450	2024
Landing Platform Dock – LPD	**SAN GIORGIO**	3	8,000 tonnes	133m x 21m x 5m	Diesel, 20 knots	165	1987

Note:

1. Class includes *Bergamini* (GP), *Fasan* (ASW) and *Schergat* (combined) variants.

2. Varies dependent on armament configuration.

August 2024. The value of the four ships on order to date is estimated at €1.2 billion (c. US$1.4 billion), giving some idea of the complexity of the vessels involved.

- **NGN-C Next Generation Minehunter-Coastal:** A firm order for five vessels, together with three options, was placed with Intermarine and Leonardo in July 2024. Displacing around 1,300 tonnes, the new ships will replace many of the current *Lerici* class and combine many of the features of traditional mine countermeasures vessels with those of the new generation of 'motherships'. If all three options are exercised, total programme cost will be €2.6 billion (c. US$3 billion). A separate class of new-generation oceanic minehunters is also envisaged.
- **LSS Logistic Support Ship:** *Atlante*, the second member of up to four *Vulcano* class logistic support ships, commenced sea trials in March 2025. She is expected to be delivered before the end of 2025.
- **Type 212 NFS:** Following signature of the contract for the fourth and final Type 212 Near Future Submarine (NFS) in June 2024, a study has been funded to retrofit NFS technologies to the existing quartet of *Todaro* class Type 212A boats as part of a mid-life upgrade. The Italian Navy continues to plan the procurement of two Type 212 NFS EVO variants to expand the future submarine flotilla from eight to ten boats.

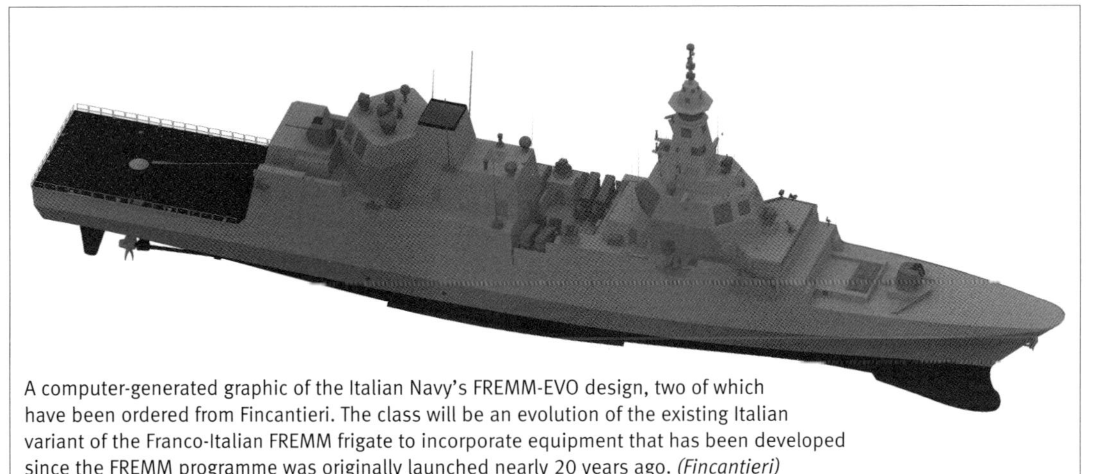

A computer-generated graphic of the Italian Navy's FREMM-EVO design, two of which have been ordered from Fincantieri. The class will be an evolution of the existing Italian variant of the Franco-Italian FREMM frigate to incorporate equipment that has been developed since the FREMM programme was originally launched nearly 20 years ago. *(Fincantieri)*

All-in-all, the *Marina Militare* continues to modernise and expand its overall force structure, increasingly rivalling the conventional capabilities of the France's *Marine Nationale* and the British Royal Navy.

MAJOR REGIONAL POWERS – RUSSIA

A detailed review of the Russian Navy's place in the country's overall military strategy, as well as the force structure that this has produced, is provided in Chapter 2.4A. The war against Ukraine has, however, arguably served to impede implementation of this structure due to the toll that it has taken at both an operational and economic level. Positively for Russia, the heavy attrition experienced by the Black Sea Fleet in previous stages of the war has been far less marked over the last year, probably because of a far more cautious use of its remaining assets. Russia has also been able to demonstrate the largely undiminished capacity of its three remaining fleets through an extensive series of deployments and exercises, most notably the global 'Ocean 2024' serials that took place in September 2024. Claimed to involve more than 400 ships, 125 aircraft and over 90,000 personnel – a likely spurious assertion – the exercises were reportedly held simultaneously across 13 maritime zones in the Pacific and Arctic Oceans, as well as in the Mediterranean, Caspian and Baltic seas.[7] Whilst certainly putting on an impressive show, this demonstration failed to hide Russia's patchy progress in transition from a legacy Soviet-era fleet to an up-to-date force. The diversion of productive resources to meet the demands of the Ukraine War is likely acting as a further impediment to this transformation. Meanwhile, the collapse of the Assad regime in Syria is another blow to Russia's naval ambitions, with the likely abandonment of the naval base at Tartus threatening its Mediterranean presence.

Table 2.4.4 highlighting the major components of the current Russian Fleet is suggestive of increasing industrial constraints, with few changes to the number of major vessels year-on-year. The only significant additions have been to the submarine flotilla which – by dint of its importance to Russia's strategic (nuclear) and conventional strike capacity – has long been afforded priority for investment. More specifically, the nuclear-powered guided missile/attack submarine *Arkhangelsk* – fifth members of the Project 855/855M *Severodvinsk* class – was delivered on 27 December 2024 and the diesel electric *Yakutsk* – the twelfth and, to date, final Project 636.3 boat – on 11 June 2025. In addition, *Knyaz Pozharsky* – the eighth of the Project 955/955A series of strategic submarines – is undergoing sea trials.

Whilst, therefore, the underwater flotilla's modernisation is making some headway, there is less positive news with respect to the surface fleet. All vessels above frigate size date from the Soviet era and – as suggested by the protracted nature of the Project 1143.5 aircraft carrier *Admiral Kuznetsov*'s refit – they are proving increasingly difficult to retain in operational service. Although September 2024 saw the launch of the fourth modern Project 22350 *Admiral Gorshkov* class frigate, *Admiral Isakov*, her completion is likely to be at least two years away. It also seems that there have been no new launches of Project 20380 *Steregushchiy* class light frigates in the past 12 months.

Given this state of affairs, the surface fleet is increasingly reliant on continued deliveries of the smaller corvette-like missile boats that Russia has increasingly turned towards to compensate for its limited ability to complete larger surface combatants. Deliveries of more of the relatively numerous Project 22800 'Karakurt' class should be able to perform some of the heavy lifting, as their UKSV vertical launch system (VLS) gives them a strike capacity that is disproportionate to their size. However, the class has already proved hideously vulnerable to damage during the Ukraine War,

TABLE 2.4.4: RUSSIAN NAVY: SELECTED PRINCIPAL UNITS AS AT MID 2025

TYPE	CLASS	NUMBER[1]	TONNAGE	DIMENSIONS	PROPULSION	CREW	DATE
Aircraft carriers							
Aircraft Carrier – CV	Project 1143.5 **KUZNETSOV**	1	60,000 tonnes	306m x 35/73m x 10m	Steam, 32 knots	2,600	1991
Principal Surface Escorts							
Battlecruiser – BCGN	Project 1144.2 **KIROV**	2	25,000 tonnes	252m x 29m x 9m	CONAS, 32 knots	740	1980
Cruiser – CG	Project 1164 **MOSKVA** ('Slava')	2	12,500 tonnes	186m x 21m x 8m	COGAG, 32 knots	530	1982
Destroyer – DDG	Project 956/956A **SOVREMENNY**	c. 2	8,000 tonnes	156m x 17m x 6m	Steam, 32 knots	300	1980
Destroyer – DDG	Project 1155.1 **CHABANENKO** ('Udaloy II')	1	9,000 tonnes	163m x 19m x 6m	COGAG, 29 knots	250	1999
Destroyer – DDG	Project 1155 **UDALOY**	c. 7	8.500 tonnes	163m x 19m x 6m	COGAG, 30 knots	300	1980
Frigate – FFG	Project 22350 **GORSHKOV**	3	5,500 tonnes	135m x 16m x 5m	CODAG, 30 knots	210	2018
Frigate – FFG	Project 11366R **GRIGOROVICH**	3	4,000 tonnes	125m x 15m x 4m	COGAG, 30 knots	200	2016
Frigate – FFG	Project 1154 **NEUSTRASHIMY**	2	4,400 tonnes	139m x 16m x 6m	COGAG, 30 knots	210	1993
Frigate – FFG	Project 1135 **BDITELNNY** ('Krivak I/II')	c. 2	3,700 tonnes	123m x 14m x 5m	COGAG, 32 knots	180	1970
Frigate – FFG	Project 20385 **GREMYASHCHIY**	1	2,500 tonnes	106m x 11m x 5m	CODAD, 27 knots	100	2020
Frigate – FFG	Project 20380 **STERGUSHCHIY**	9	2,200 tonnes	105m x 11m x 4m	CODAD, 27 knots	100	2008
Frigate – FFG	Project 11611 **TATARSTAN** ('Gepard')	2	2,000 tonnes	102m x 13m x 4m	CODOG, 27 knots	100	2002
Submarines							
Submarine – SSBN	Project 95/955A **YURY DOLGORUKY** ('Borey')	7	20,000+ tonnes	170m x 13m x 10m	Nuclear, 25+ knots	110	2010
Submarine – SSBN	Project 677BDRM **VERKHOTURYE** ('Delta IV')	5[2]	18,000 tonnes	167m x 12m x 9m	Nuclear, 24 knots	130	1985
Submarine – SSGN	Project 855/855M **SEVERODVINSK** ('Yasen')	5	13,500+ tonnes	120m x 14m x 9m	Nuclear, 30+ knots	90	2013
Submarine – SSGN	Project 949A ('Oscar II')	c. 7	17,500 tonnes	154m x 8m x 9m	Nuclear, 30+ knots	100	1986
Submarine – SSN	Project 971 ('Akula I/II')	c. 8	9,500 tonnes	110m x 14m x 10m	Nuclear, 30+ knots	60	1986
Submarine – SSK	Project 677 **KRONSTADT** ('Lada')	1	2,700 tonnes	72m x 7m x 7m	Diesel-electric, 21 knots	40	2024
Submarine – SSK	Project 636.3 (Improved 'Kilo')	11	3,200 tonnes	73m x 10m x 7m	Diesel-electric, 20 knots	55	2014
Submarine – SSK	Project 877 ('Kilo')	c. 8	3,000 tonnes	73m x 10m x 7m	Diesel-electric, 20 knots	55	1981

Notes:

1. Table only includes main types and focuses on operational units and/or ships believed to be under active modernisation or refit.

2. One additional unit is being used in an experimental role.

during which two are believed to have been destroyed to date. Moreover, they hardly provide the 'blue water' capacity that the Russian Navy requires to maintain Russia's pretence of 'great maritime power' status.

MAJOR REGIONAL POWERS – SPAIN

Spain remains a laggard amongst its NATO peers in terms of defence spending and the navy's size has shrunk as a result. However, a major programme of investment announced in April 2025 as part of plans to accelerate the country's achievement of the alliance's (then) two percent of GDP spending target holds out the prospect of accelerated implementation of a number of naval programmes. Prominent amongst these is the acquisition of a second *Cantabria* class combat supply ship to replace the elderly *Patiño.* A contract for the new vessel, which will benefit from improvements to the original design incorporated in the subsequent Australian *Supply* class variants, was signed with Navantia on 10 June 2025. Construction has been allocated to the company's shipyard at Ferrol in Galicia and delivery is expected by 2030. Reported cost is in the region of €650 million (c. US$750 million). Other proposed new construction includes a new intelligence-gathering ship to replace the existing, *Alerta*, and an additional hydrographic survey vessel. Although details have not been released, it is possible that new variants of the ever-expanding series of 'BAM' type maritime action vessels may fulfil the requirement. In the meantime, a firm order for two ASW variants of the type – approved in 2023 – is still awaited.

For the time being, there has been no change to the list of major Spanish Navy warships listed in Table 2.4.5. Current construction remains dominated by the programmes for S-80 *Isaac Peral* class submarines and F-110 *Bonifaz* class frigates. The second member of the four-strong submarine class, *Narcisco Monturiol*, is scheduled for formal naming and launch at Navantia Cartagena in July 2025. Her delivery is expected in 2026, marking further progress towards completing the much-delayed programme. In contrast, construction of the new F-110 frigates at Ferrol appears to be progressing much more smoothly. A keel-laying event for the second member of the class, *Roger de Lauria*, on 25 April 2025 coincided with the start of work on *Menéndez de Avilés*, the third member of the five-ship class. The lead ship is expected to be launched

Spain is making good progress constructing the first F110 *Bonifaz* class frigate at its shipyard in Ferrol in Galicia, where this photograph was taken in mid-2025. She is expected to be launched before the end of 2025. *(Navantia)*

Table 2.4.5: SPANISH NAVY: PRINCIPAL UNITS AS AT MID 2025

TYPE	CLASS	NUMBER	TONNAGE	DIMENSIONS	PROPULSION	CREW	DATE
Principal Surface Escorts							
Frigate – FFG	**ÁLVARO DE BAZÁN** (F-100)	5	6,300 tonnes	147m x 19m x 5m	CODOG, 28 knots	200	2002
Frigate – FFG	**SANTA MARÍA** (FFG-7)	6	4,100 tonnes	138m x 14m x 5m	COGAG, 30 knots	225	1986
Submarines							
Submarine – SSK	**ISAAC PERAL** (S-80)	1	3,000 tonnes	81m x 12m x 6m	DE and AIP, 19+ knots	35	2023
Submarine – SSK	**GALERNA** (S-70/AGOSTA)	1	1,800 tonnes	68m x 7m x 6m	Diesel-electric, 21 knots	45	1983
Major Amphibious Units							
Amph Assault Ship – LHD	**JUAN CARLOS I**	1	27,100 tonnes	231m x 32m x 7m	IEP, 21 knots	245	2010
Landing Platform Dock – LPD	**GALICIA**	2	13,000 tonnes	160m x 25m x 6m	Diesel, 20 knots	185	1998

in the second half of 2025 and delivered in 2028.

In spite of past financial austerity, the Spanish Navy continues to be active in support of national and collaborative deployments across the glove. An interesting development in 2025 was the integration of the F-110 class frigate *Méndez Núñez* in the British Royal Navy's 'Operation Highmast' carrier strike group deployment to the Indo-Pacific. The Spanish Ministry of Defence highlighted the four month-long deployment as an opportunity to, 'showcase Spain's technological capability and independence, as well as its ability to project force across diverse geographical areas, reaffirming Spain's commitment to global stability'.[8]

MAJOR REGIONAL POWERS – UNITED KINGDOM

A summary of the Royal Navy's major warships is provided in Table 2.4.6. The last year saw further retirements of major vessels before the arrival of planned replacements. Heading the list was the last *Trafalgar* class submarine, *Triumph*, which made the final voyage from her base at Faslane to Devonport in December 2024 to prepare for final decommissioning after completing over 33 years of operational service. Also leaving the fleet was the 30-year-old Type 23 frigate *Northumberland,* which was retired after it was ascertained that structural damage discovered during her refit made it uneconomical to complete intended life-extension work. This leaves just eight of the class in Royal Navy service, reducing the flotilla of major surface combatants to a new low of 14. Whilst it is difficult to dispute the rationale for these withdrawals, decisions to dispose of the amphibious transport docks *Albion* and *Bulwark* as well as the replenishment tankers *Wave Knight* and *Wave Ruler* – which were all being held in maintained reserve – is somewhat more questionable. It has subsequently emerged that the two amphibious ships are likely to be sold to Brazil for further service, suggesting that there is still plenty of life in them.

Triumph, the last of the Royal Navy's *Trafalgar* class nuclear-powered attack submarines, departed the Faslane naval base in Scotland for the final time on 10 December 2024 to make the short voyage to Devonport prior to formal decommissioning. *(Crown Copyright 2024)*

Part of the reason for the decline in the fleet's size has been delays to new construction. Here there is the prospect of better news. Construction of the eight new Type 26 *Glasgow* class frigates on the Clyde is gaining traction, with the second of the class, *Cardiff,* launched in September 2024 and first steel for the fifth vessel, *Sheffield,* cut the following November. *Glasgow* herself was ceremonially named in May 2025 and is due to commence sea trials during 2026. Meanwhile, over on Scotland's east coast, the lead Type 31 frigate, *Venturer,* was floated off from her launch barge in June 2025 and should also begin trials before the end of 2026.[9] Fabrication of *Formidable,* the third ship of the five ship class began the previous October. The same month saw the launch of the sixth *Astute* class submarine, *Agamemnon,* whose delivery was believed to be imminent as of mid-2025. There is more uncer-

Table 2.4.6: BRITISH ROYAL NAVY: PRINCIPAL UNITS AS AT MID 2025

TYPE	CLASS	NUMBER	TONNAGE	DIMENSIONS	PROPULSION	CREW	DATE
Aircraft Carriers							
Aircraft Carrier – CV	QUEEN ELIZABETH	2	65,000 tonnes	284m x 73m x 11m	IEP, 26 knots+	1,600	2017
Principal Surface Escorts							
Destroyer – DDG	DARING (Type 45)	6	7,500 tonnes	152m x 21m x 5m	IEP, 30 knots	190	2008
Frigate – FFG	NORFOLK (Type 23)	8	4,900 tonnes	133m x 16m x 5m	CODLAG, 30 knots	185	1990
Submarines							
Submarine – SSBN	VANGUARD	4	16,000 tonnes	150m x 13m x 12m	Nuclear, 25+ knots	135	1993
Submarine – SSN	ASTUTE	5	7,800 tonnes	93m x 11m x 10m	Nuclear, 30+ knots	100	2010
Major Amphibious Units							
Landing Ship Dock – LSD (A)	LARGS BAY	3	16,200 tonnes	176m x 26m x 6m	Diesel-electric, 18 knots	60	2006

tainty over progress with the seventh boat, *Achilles* (formerly *Agincourt*), following potential delays as a result of a major fire on 29 October 2024 in the Devonshire Dock Hall at Barrow-in-Furness where she is being built.

Looking further to the future, the Royal Navy seems to be a major winner from the latest British Strategic Defence Review (SDR), published in June 2025. Amongst headline announcements were plans to increase numbers of nuclear-powered attack submarines to as many as twelve as part of a reorientation of British defence capabilities towards the 'Euro-Atlantic'. However, many questions remain over other elements of the navy's future structure; some of which may be answered in the publication of a Defence Investment Plan scheduled for the autumn of 2025. In the interim, a more detailed assessment of the Royal Navy's current status and likely future trajectory is contained in Chapter 2.4B.

MID-SIZED REGIONAL FLEETS

Germany: The marked increase in defence spending being implemented by the current German government is being accompanied by upward growth in the *Deutsche Marine*'s force structure ambitions. This was evidenced in the May 2025 publication of its *Kurs Marine 2025* (*Navy Course 2025*) vision document; essentially an update on the March 2023 'Vision 2035+' fleet plan.[10] The document largely maintains the earlier plan's consistent use of a multiple of three for major force elements, reflecting a calculation that each deployable vessel needs the support of two additional units undergoing training or maintenance. However, targeted numbers of some equipment – mostly uncrewed elements but also, for example, submarines – are higher than previously forecast. There are also new items on the shopping list, most notably large uncrewed missile vessels to supplement the capacity of the planned F127 air defence frigates. Further details of the steady growth in the navy's aspirations are provided in Table 2.4.7.

Current surface warship construction is dominated by the F126 *Niedersachsen* class frigate programme. These ships are being built in German shipyards to a Dutch Damen design. Predictably, there are reports that the programme for the six ship class is running behind schedule, with the ambitious target for the lead ship's delivery seemingly postponed from 2028 until at least 2030. The delay

Table 2.4.7: GERMAN NAVY: PLANNED CHANGES IN FLEET STRCTURE

VESSEL TYPE TIMESCALE	MISSION	CURRENT (2025)	PLAN PRE-2023 (UNSPECIFIED)	VISION 2035 (2023) (BY 2035)	NAVY COURSE 2025 (BY 2035)
F127 Frigate	Air defence/strike	0	5	6	6
F126 Frigate	ASW/strike	0	6	6	6
F125 Frigate	Stabilisation/strike	4	4	3	3–4
F124 Frigate	Air defence	3	0	0	0
F123 Frigate	Anti-submarine warfare	4	0	0	0
K130 Corvette	Surface/strike	5	10	6-9	6–9
Large Remote Missile Vessel	Air defence/strike (uncrewed)	0	0	0	3
Future Surface Combat System	Surface/strike (uncrewed)	0	0	Up to 18	18+
MCMV	Mine warfare	10	11	Up to 12	12+
MCMV Toolbox Systems	Mine warfare (uncrewed)	0	0	To be decided	24+
T212A/CD Submarine	Surface/sub-surface warfare	6	8	6–9	9–12
Large uncrewed Submarine	Intelligence gathering	0	0	Up to 6	12+
T423/424 Auxiliary	Intelligence gathering	0	3	3	3
T702 Auxiliary	Fleet replenishment vessel	3	3	3	3
T704/T707 Auxiliary	Fleet tanker	2	2	3	3
T404 Auxiliary/T404 Successor	Supply/support vessel	6	6	6	6
Multi-role Combat Boats	Amphibious	0	0	0	40+

Germany is close to completing its assessment of designs for its new F127 air defence 'frigates'. TKMS has been promoting its MEKO A-400 AMD concept – displacing around 10,000 tonnes at full load – as the basis for the new design. *(TKMS)*

follows the protracted construction of the second batch of K130 class corvettes, which were ordered in September 2017 to maintain continuity of activity in the naval sector prior to the start of work on the new frigates. The fourth member of the class, *Augsburg*, was christened at NVL's Blohm & Voss Hamburg shipyard in May 2025 and the first two vessels have already carried out sea trials. However, problems with integrating their combat management systems have seen actual delivery postponed.

The next major surface warship construction programme will encompass the planned F127 class frigates, which are intended to replace the three existing F124 *Sachsen* class ships. The current official requirement is for five F127 frigates but *Navy Course 2025* envisages procurement of a sixth ship. In addition to renewing the maritime and theatre air defence capacity offered by the F124s, the new ships are expected to provide a sea-based capability to defend against hypersonic and ballistic missile threats in the lower interception layer. This will allow them to play a significant role in homeland defence and to form part of a NATO ballistic missile shield. An additional mission is to provide a long-range precision strike capability against hardened targets. 'In principle decisions' to use the US Navy Aegis combat system and AN/SPY-6 radar have already been taken, whilst a TKMS-NVL consortium looks likely to be awarded the contract to build the ships. TKMS has been promoting its MEKO A-400 AMD concept – a c. 160m ship with a full load displacement of c. 10,000 tonnes – as the basis for the design. A selection from the German defence procurement organisation, BAAINBw, was believed to be imminent as of mid-2025 prior the formal award of contracts during 2026.[11]

Meanwhile, Germany's greater appetite for defence spending saw Bundestag (parliamentary) approval in December 2024 to triple the *Deutsche Marine*'s order for Type 212CD submarines from two to six boats at an estimated cost €4.7 billion (c. US$5.4 billion). Their construction forms part of a joint project between Germany and Norway that now comprises ten boats but could increase to twelve if Norwegian plans for an additional two submarines of their own are finalised. In another

A computer-generated image of the German Navy's new Type 424 intelligence-gathering ship. Three of the class have been ordered from Germany's NVL, which laid the keel for the first at its Wolgast Peene Shipyard on 25 February 2025. *(NVL)*

The first of Greece's three FDI-type *Kimon* class frigates commenced sea trials from Naval Group's Lorient shipyard on 21 May 2025. Negotiations to exercise an option for a fourth member of the class are likely to be completed soon. *(Bruno Huriet)*

development, the Bundestag also approved acquisition of the IDAS (Interactive Defence and Attack System for Submarines) missile system that, inter alia, provides a submerged defensive capability against low flying aircraft.

In addition to its projects for major surface and underwater combatants, Germany is also undertaking a number of programmes for second line vessels. Notably, NVL has made a start fulfilling a contract for three Type 424 intelligence-gathering ships, laying the keel for the lead vessel at a ceremony at its Wolgast Peene Shipyard on 25 February 2025. The company has also been entrusted with the delivery of two Type 707 replenishment tankers; replacements for the life-expired Type 704 *Rhön* class. Much of the actual construction effort has been allocated to Meyer Werft's shipyards in Rostock and Papenburg, who seem to be struggling to meet the project's deadlines in another indication of the difficulties shipyards are facing in ramping up production to meet higher demand. The force structure set out in *Navy Course 2025* suggests an additional vessel will be ordered to allow the 'rule of three' to be met.

Greece: In April 2025, Greek Prime Minister Kyriakos Mitsotakis announced a €25 billion (c. US$29 billion) 'Long Term Defence Armaments Plan' for the period 2025-37. Marking the latest stage of a rebound in Greek defence investment after a period of previous austerity, the headline announcement was the development of an integrated air and missile defence system to be known as 'Achilles Shield'. However, the programme also heralds further significant investment in the Hellenic Navy following on from the procurement of Naval Group FDI type *Kimon* class frigates that is already underway.[12]

The most significant naval investment will likely be in the recapitalisation of the Hellenic Navy's submarine flotilla. This has been steadily shrinking as its elderly Type 209 submarines are slowly withdrawn, with the Type 209/1100 class *Triton* the latest to be retired when she was decommissioned on 15 May 2025. The plan envisages the eventual procurement of four new submarines – initially two plus two options – to serve alongside the existing Type 214 air-independent propulsion (AIP) equipped boats of the *Papanikolis* class, which will all receive midlife modernisations. This will give the Hellenic Navy a modern, eight-strong underwater flotilla.

Turning to the surface fleet, the immediate objective is to bring the three members of the *Kimon* class that are currently on order into service. The lead ship commenced sea trials from Lorient on 21 May 2025 and is expected to be delivered before the year's end. Both of her sisters are now also in the water, with *Nearchos* entering the River Scorff on 18 September 2024 and *Formion* being floated out on 28 May 2025.[13] As of June 2025, negotiations were at an advanced stage to exercise the option for a fourth member of the class. The composition of the remainder of the fleet's major surface combatants remains open to a degree of conjecture. However, local reports suggest that Italy is willing to provide at least two second-hand FREMM frigates as an interim step towards Greece's eventual participation in the US Navy's *Constellation* (FFG-62) class programme, which is based on the same design. The planned midlife upgrades of the four MEKO 200HN *Hydra* class frigates will also go ahead, whilst the requirement for new corvettes may be wrapped into the European Union's EPC project. All-in-all, it seems that a future surface fleet of around 16 frigates and corvettes is envisaged. However, the increasing obsolescence of the numerous *Elli* (Dutch *Kortenaer*) class frigates may mean that numbers will drop in the short term.

The fast attack craft flotilla is also experiencing a decline as increasing numbers of 'La Combattante IIB' and 'La Combattante IIIB' are withdrawn from service. The armaments plan envisages midlife modernisation of the seven, most recent fast attack craft of the *Roussen* class. However, hoped-for new construction to replace the older vessels is open to more doubt. The news with respect to the navy's patrol ship fleet has been more positive, with four upgraded former US Coast Guard 'Island' class coastal patrol vessels delivered from Salamis Shipyards in January 2025 after extensive refurbishment. The Hellenic Navy hope to acquire additional second-hand US Coast Guard patrol ships as they become available for transfer.

The Netherlands & Belgium: The fast-moving pace of the international security environment was reflected in the publication of a new Dutch *Defence White Paper 2024* in September 2024, little more than two years after its previous iteration was released.[14] Intended to accelerate the Netherlands' achievement of the (now outdated) NATO two percent of GDP target, the white paper offers the prospect of

The newly-arrived combat support ship *Den Helder* seen at Damen's Vlissingen yard in December 2024 after her delivery voyage from Galati in Romania. Her subsequent christening ceremony held on 22 February 2025 was the first for a Dutch warship in over a decade. *(Damen)*

The lead Belgian *Castor* class coastal patrol vessel seen entering Portsmouth Harbour, United Kingdom on 26 June 2025. An order for a third member of the class was placed with France's Socarenam in November 2024 as part of moves to 'beef up' the Belgian Naval Component's maritime surveillance capabilities. *(Derek Fox)*

achieving a noteworthy increase in the size of the Dutch fleet after years of progressive decline. A list of enhancements is headed by the proposed acquisition of an additional pair of 'ASWF' anti-submarine warfare frigates under the joint programme being undertaken with Belgium, increasing the proposed Dutch order to four ships. The Royal Netherlands Navy will also receive two minimally-crewed modular, multi-functional support vessels, which will initially assist surveillance activities in the North Sea but can also be configured to provide additional magazine capacity for the four *De Zeven Provinciën* air defence and command frigates. The ships will be based on a commercial standard Damen hull and be outfitted with containerised missile and electronic warfare equipment supplied by Israel Aerospace Industries.[15] An interim North Sea surveillance capacity based on a chartered vessel and operating crew provided by a partnership between Dutch-based companies Damen and Fugro will be acquired before the two new vessels become fully operational in 2026-7.

Meanwhile, on 30 September 2024, the delivery agreement for the Replacement Netherlands Submarine Capability (RNSC) programme was signed at a ceremony in Den Helder. The contract followed a March 2024 announcement that Naval Group's diesel-electric 'Blacksword' variant of its 'Barracuda' family had been provisionally selected to replace the four *Walrus* class boats on a numerical like-for-like basis. The new submarines are to be known as the *Orka* class and deliveries should start within ten years of contract signature. The project's framework includes an industrial cooperation agreement committing Naval Group to collaborate with various Dutch companies and institutions in the supply of systems and components. The contract's signature marks a welcome conclusion to a protracted procurement process that has forced the Royal Netherlands Navy to start withdrawing the existing submarines to provide spare parts to sustain the remainder in service. Other programmes currently in the developmental stage include four new replacement air defence ships and six amphibious vessels, the latter to take over the missions of not only the *Rotterdam* class amphibious transport docks but also the *Holland* class OPVs.

Another positive event took place on 22 February 2025 when the new combat support ship *Den Helder* was christened by Catharina-Amalia, Princess of Orange at a ceremony held at the Damen Naval shipyard in Vlissingen. The vessel had previously arrived in the Netherlands in December 2024 after undertaking her maiden voyage and initial sea trials from Damen's facility in Galati, Romania. The ship was subsequently handed over to the Dutch Ministry of Defence's Materiel and IT Command in March 2025 and is due to complete final outfitting before entering operational service during 2026. *Den Helder* was the first Dutch warship to be christened since the multi-role support ship *Karel Doorman* in 2014.

The closely associated Belgium Naval Component is also likely to join its Dutch counterpart in expanding its overall size. A statement issued by the incoming Belgian coalition in September 2024 indicated that it would also increase its ASWF procurement through acquisition of a third ship. The Belgian Ministry of Defence also concluded negotiations with France's Socarenam for a third *Castor* class coastal patrol vessel in November 2024 in a further sign of the need to enhance maritime surveillance in the face of hostile state actors.

The existing joint Belgo-Dutch programme for rMCM 'City' class mine countermeasures 'motherships', encompassing six for each navy, has continued to make progress following previous delays. *Oostende*, the lead Belgian ship and first member of the class overall, is due for delivery in the summer of 2025 whilst *Vlissingen*, the initial Dutch unit, commenced sea trials on 27 March 2025. Another three members of the class – the Belgian *Tournai* and *Brugge*, as well as the Dutch *Scheveningen* – have been launched to date. Construction is being carried out both in France and Romania, where the Giurgiu shipyard has been contracted to fabricate the hulls of many of the later ships. The future ASWF frigates that form part of the joint procurement framework will also be built in Romania – at Damen's Galati yard – prior to final outfitting in Vlissingen. As of mid-2025, the start of their construction was believed to be imminent.

Türkiye: Türkiye increasingly sees its future fortunes being linked to the maritime domain, with the existence of various overlapping economic interests and claims across the Eastern Mediterranean placing a high premium on maintaining a strong navy. The extent of the country's naval ambitions was made clear on 2 January 2025 with the announcement of the start of work on three important naval construction projects on the same day. In line with the emphasis on developing a strong indigenous naval industry evidenced in the previous Milgem 'national ship' programme, the three new projects all have a distinctly national emphasis.[16]

The most remarkable of these three new naval programmes is that for a National Aircraft Carrier ('MUGEM'). This national endeavour has gained momentum over the past 18 months and follows on from the commissioning of the 'big deck' amphibious assault ship *Anadolu* in April 2023. The planned c. 60,000-tonne vessel is designed to embark and operate a range of indigenously produced crewed and uncrewed aerial vehicles in short take-off but arrested recovery (STOTAR) configuration. Further details are provided in Chapter 4.1.

A second project – that for a new National Submarine (MİLDEN) – is equally ambitious. Design development for the programme commenced in 2019 and will have benefitted from construction of the six Type 214 air-independent propulsion (AIP) equipped 'Reis' class boats under a license agreement with Germany's TKMS. *Pirireis*, the lead member of this class, was finally commissioned in August 2024 after a protracted build period at Gölcük Naval Shipyard that was extended, inter alia, by Turkish-specific changes to the design. As of mid-2025, the second member of the class – *Hizirreis* – was undergoing sea trials, whilst the third boat, *Muratreis*, was floated out on 29 May 2025. Current plans envisage all six submarines being in service by the end of the decade. The planned construction timeline pertaining to the lead MİLDEN, about which few details have been publicly released, have not been published. However, the experience of other countries transitioning to a wholly indigenous submarine design suggests Gölcük Naval Shipyard, which has been assigned construction of the new class, faces a challenging road ahead.

The final vessel on which work commenced on 4 January was the long-planned TF-2000 air defence destroyer. Like the new aircraft carrier, she is being built at Istanbul Naval Shipyard. Work on the project began in earnest in 2017 after previous false starts, and the destroyer's configuration has evolved through several iterations. The current design envisages a ship of 149m in length with a full-load

Pirireis is the first of six 'Reis' class submarines based on the TKMS Type 214 AIP equipped design that are being built locally at the Gölcük Naval Shipyard. *Pirireis* was commissioned in August 2024 after a lengthy period under construction. *(Devrim Yaylali)*

The recently modernised MEKO 200-TN *Barbaros* class frigate *Oruçreis* (right) makes an interesting comparison with her younger but as yet unmodernised sister *Salihreis* in this January 2025 photograph. Led by Türkiye's Aselsan and Havelsan, the midlife upgrade saw the installation of much new equipment – including the CENK surveillance array atop the forward mast, the Akrep fire control radar on the bridge roof, and Gökdeniz CIWS in 'B' position that are all prominent in the photograph – that is common with the new 'İstif' class frigates. *(Devrim Yaylali)*

displacement of around 8,300 tonnes armed with a total of 96 MIDLAS VLS cells and fitted with Aselsan's Çafrad multi-function active phased array radar. The design will also have doubtless benefited from the mid-life upgrade recently completed on the MEKO 200-TN *Barbaros* class frigate *Oruçreis* that, in turn, has some commonality with the electronics outfit installed in the lead the 'İstif' class frigate, *İstanbul.* These frigates are now in series production, as further detailed in chapter 3.1.

OTHER REGIONAL FLEETS

Black Sea and Mediterranean: The ongoing naval war in the Black Sea has tended to attract less attention over the past year as Russia's ships have largely been pulled back from the front line following previous heavy attrition. **Ukraine** does, however, continue to show considerable innovation in the production and use of uncrewed surface drones.[17] Steps are also progressing to develop the new navy that will be needed when the war is over and the Turkish straits are re-opened. Notably, the recent transfers of the former 'Tripartite' type minehunters *Narcis* and *Vlaardingen* from, respectively, Belgium and the Netherlands will reinforce the former British *Sandown* class vessels previously transferred. Ukraine has also taken delivery of *Hetman Ivan Mazepa*, the lead ship of two 'Ada' type corvettes ordered from Türkiye.

Elsewhere in the Black Sea, **Bulgaria's** Varna-based MTG Dolphin shipyard is seemingly making good progress with the construction of two corvette-like multipurpose modular patrol vessels based on NVL's OPV-90 design. The second of these vessels, *Smeli,* was reportedly launched ahead of schedule on 12 December 2024. Her sister, *Habri*, had previously been launched in August 2023 and is expected to be delivered before the end of 2025.

Naval modernisation in neighbouring **Romania** has been significantly set back by the collapse in August 2023 of a deal to acquire four French Naval Group 'Gowind' type corvettes as part of an agreement that would also have seen modernisation of its existing pair of Type 22 frigates. It seems that a phased naval procurement programme is now envisaged under which the acquisition of two new OPVs would be followed by construction of more sophisticated ships under the European Union's EPC project in due course. Whilst Dame's Galati shipyard would seem the ideal location for both projects given its considerable expertise of naval construction, reports of the purchase of Turkish-built 'Hisar' type OPVs have also been circulating in local media. In the meantime, the Romanian Navy awaits the imminent arrival of *Căpitan Constantin Dumitrescu* (the ex-HMS *Pembroke*) – the second of two *Sandown* class minehunters transferred from the Royal Navy – which was close to completing refit at Babcock's Rosyth shipyard as of mid-2025.

Turning to the Mediterranean, **Croatia** received *Umag,* the first series-produced variant of its five planned *Omiš* class patrol boats from the Brodosplit yard on 17 January 2025. Local media suggest the procurement of large, corvette-sized vessels is also on the horizon. **Montenegro** is also buying new patrol ships, ordering two 60m OPVs from the Naval Group-Piriou Kership joint venture during the 'Euronaval 2024' exhibition. Construction of the lead ship commenced at Lorient on 24 April 2025.

The Atlantic & Northern Europe: Although the significant crewing crisis that has impacted **Ireland's** navy has shown signs of stabilising in the past year, the Irish Naval Service is still struggling to put ships to sea. The number of patrol days carried out by the service's ships fell to just 428 in 2024; a 57 percent decline on the 1,007 achieved as recently as 2020.[18] LÉ *Gobnait* (formerly HMNZS *Pukaki*) – one of two former New Zealand 'Lake' class coastal patrol vessels purchased in 2022 and subsequently commissioned in September 2024 was reported as having failed to undertake a single operational sea day as of June 2025 due to lack of sailors to crew her. The ongoing problems are set against a backdrop of increased Russian surveillance of critical undersea assets in Irish waters. In June 2025 it was announced that the navy would acquire its first towed array sonar to improve its underwater monitoring capabilities.

Portugal's naval modernisation has made progress on several fronts over the last year. In December 2024, it became the latest country to turn to Türkiye's growing naval export sector to place an order for two logistics support ships, officially referred to as 'auxiliary oiler replenisher and logistics ships'. Some 137m in length and displacing

Bulgaria's MTG Dolphin shipyard launched *Smeli*, the second member of the *Habri* multi-role corvette class, on 12 December 2024. Her sister-ship, now in the later stages of outfitting, can be seen in the background. The ships are based on NVL's OPV-90 hull, an enlarged version of the OPV-80 design in service in Australia and Brunei as, respectively, the *Arafura* and *Darussalam* classes. *(MTG Dolphin)*

c. 11,000 tonnes, the new vessels have command and control, as well as limited amphibious transportation capabilities, in addition to their primary replenishment role. Later, on 31 March 2025, construction commenced at the West Sea Viana shipyard on the first of the six new batch of *Viana do Castello* class OPVs ordered in December 2023. Deliveries of this third batch are expected to commence in 2027. By that time, Portugal should also have received *D. João II*, its innovative, multi-functional drone carrier. A keel-laying ceremony was held on 3 October 2024 at Damen's Galati shipyard, which has been contracted to build the ship.

Seemingly threatened both by Russia and the US Trump regime, **Denmark** is accelerating the pace of its previously planned naval modernisation. This process has been facilitated by the allocation of an additional 120 billion Danish kroner (c. US$19 billion) to the ten-year 2024-33 Danish Defence

Portugal ordered two new logistic support ships from Türkiye's STM in December 2024. The contract is claimed to be the first time that Türkiye has exported a warship to either a NATO or European Union member state. *(STM)*

Saab Kockums re-launched *Halland*, the third and final member of the *Gotland* submarine class to be subject to a midlife upgrade, at the Karlskrona shipyard on 13 February 2025. Delays to the construction of the follow-on *Blekingke* class suggest that a further life extension of the 30-year-old *Gotland* class boats will be required. *(Saab)*

Agreement and has gained greater clarity through a series of announcements in the first half of 2025. More specifically:

- The design of the patrol vessels intended to replace the existing *Thetis* class light frigates will be re-orientated to focus on Arctic mission requirements.
- The first phase of a fleet plan has been agreed that will see the construction of 26 minor vessels at a cost of 3.6 billion Danish kroner (c. US$570 million). The programme will encompass a surveillance vessel and associated drones; four dual use environmental control ships with a secondary wartime minelaying capability, and 21 patrol boats for the Danish Marine Home Guard. Realisation of the plan is intended to have a strong element of indigenous construction.
- A second phase of this 'naval agreement' will agree a way forward for the construction of replacement frigates. Some reports have subsequently suggested that the existing *Iver Huitfeldt* class frigates will be retired without receiving mid-life upgrades to accelerate the introduction of the new ships.
- Funds have been allocated to purchase coastal missile batteries to protect Danish internal waters.

The announcement of Denmark's naval plans follows on from the greater clarity provided with respect to **Norway's** future fleet structure under the 2024 Long-term Defence Plan described in last year's edition. An important element of the plan is the acquisition of at least five new frigates equipped with anti-submarine helicopters to replace the Royal Norwegian Navy's four remaining *Fridtjof Nansen* class frigates. In November 2024, France, Germany, the United Kingdom and the United States were all invited to offer proposals to meet the requirement. A decision will be taken before the end of 2025. Germany is already a likely winner from the defence plan, with TKMS set to receive an order for two additional Type 212CD submarines to supplement the Norwegian quartet already contracted under the joint programme.

Finland's lead *Pohjanmaa* class corvette pictured in the course of being loaded onto a semi-submersible barge for float-off at the Rauma Marine Constructions shipyard in May 2025.For members of the class have been ordered under the 'Squadron 2020' project. *(Tuukka Salo/ Rauma Marine Constructions)*

Sweden became the latest Scandinavian country to agree an updated defence strategy when the Swedish parliament adopted the country's *Totalförsvaret 2025–2030* (*Total Defence 2025-2030*) resolution in December 2024. The update largely prioritised enhancements to land-based and civil defence, with little offered in the way of new naval programmes. However, the modernisation of the *Visby* class corvettes with a surface-to-air missile capability (CAMM) is confirmed, as is the procurement of the new *Luleå* class. In June 2025, Babcock International, which is helping Saab develop the new ships' design, confirmed its involvement in the project was proceeding to schedule. Whilst preparatory work on a replacement for the existing *Gotland* class submarines will begin before 2030, nothing was said about the navy's hopes to increase the size of the underwater flotilla. This may have been influenced by further delays to the construction of the pair of new *Blekingke* class, whose delivery has now reportedly been pushed back into the 2030s. It seems that this might result in a requirement for a further life-extension of the existing *Gotland* class. In February 2025, Saab Kockums' Karlskrona shipyard relaunched *Halland*, the third and final member of the class to complete the previous upgrade cycle.

Elsewhere in the Nordic region, **Finland** marked an important milestone in the production of the new *Pohjanmaa* class corvettes with a formal launching ceremony at the Rauma Marine Constructions Oy (RMC) shipyard on 21 May 2025. The ship had previously been rolled out of the yard's construction hall and floated off by barge prior to installation of its Saab-supplied integrated mast. The construction of the second multi-purpose corvette began several weeks ahead of schedule during October 2024 and its keel was laid on 8 May 2025.

Across the Baltic, **Poland** is also making progress with its 'Miecznik' frigate programme, which is based on the Babcock International 'Arrowhead 140' design. *Wicher*, the lead ship, is expected to be launched in the summer of 2026, whilst a first-steel cutting ceremony was held for *Burza,* the second member of the three-ship class, at the PGZ Naval Shipyard in Gdynia on 5 May 2025. Work also continues on the second batch of three 'Kormoran II' minehunters being built by the Remontowa shipyard in neighbouring Gdansk. The second ship, *Rybitwa*, was launched on 19 March 2025 whilst production got underway on *Czajka*, the third and final ship, the preceding October. Attention is now increasingly turning to the long-delayed 'Orka' submarine programme, which reportedly encompasses the acquisition of three new boats at a cost of c. €2.5 billion (c. US$1.9 billion) to revitalise Poland's underwater flotilla. South Korea's Hanwha Ocean and HD HII are joining European shipyards in positioning themselves to compete for the potentially lucrative contract.

Notes:

1. See the NATO press release, 'The Hague Summit Declaration' issued on 25 June 2025.

2. The marked upward trajectory of German military spending, not necessarily always viewed as a positive thing in the past, has been noted by several sources. For example, see Anne-Sylvaine Chassany 'Germany to boost defence spending at faster rate than France or UK' posted to the *Financial Times* website – ft.com – on 23 June 2025.

3. For further detail see Richard Scott, 'PA-Ng aircraft carrier programme approaches key decision point' posted to the *Naval News* site – navalnews.com – on 9 June 2025.

4. See the Organisation for Joint Armament Cooperation (OCCAR) press release 'OCCAR Delivers First MMCM System to France' posted on 19 December 2024.

5. The Italian language annual review, *Rapporto Marina 2024*, is available on the Italian Navy's website, marina.difesa.it. An interesting review of the Italian Navy's expanding horizons was provided by David Scott in, 'On wider seas: Italian naval deployments and maritime outreach to the Indo-Pacific' posted to the Center for International Maritime Security *CIMSEC* site – cimsec.org – on 5 March 2025.

6. A full review of the Italian navy's *Paolo Thaon di Revel* class was provided by the editor in *Seaforth World Naval Review 2025* (Barnsley: Seaforth Publishing, 2024) pp. 112-31.

7. The 'Ocean 2024' designation is reminiscent of the large scale naval exercises of the Soviet era. An interesting assessment was provided by Captain Chris Bott, USN (retired) in 'Okean Returns: A Battered Russian Navy Brings Back a Soviet-Era Exercise' published in the October 2024 USNI *Proceedings* journal (Annapolis MD: US Naval Institute, 2024) and currently available by searching the web.

8. Spanish Ministry of Defence press release dated 9 April 2025.

9. A description of *Venturer's* launch process is contained in Chapter 4.4.

10. See the German language, *Kurs Marine* (Rostock: Inspekteur der Marine, 2025) which is currently available by searching the web.

11. The editor's 'German F127 frigate programme: Important decisions ahead' in *Maritime Defence Monitor* 012025 (Bonn: Mittler Report, 2025) provides a more detailed status report on the frigate project as of May 2025. An online version was posted to the *European Security & Defence* site – euro-sd.com – on 20 May 2025.

12. A good overview of the programme is provided by Peter Felstead, 'Hellenic defence procurement poised to embark on new modernisation plan' posted to the *European Security & Defence* site on 28 April 2025.

13. A formal 'launching' ceremony for *Nearchos* was held on 19 September 2024, the day after she had been floated out.

14. See, *2024 Defence White Paper: Strong, Smart and Together* (The Hague: Netherlands Ministry of Defence, 2024). The English language version is currently readily available by searching the web.

15. A detailed description of the multi-functional support vessel concept was provided, again, by Richard Scott in, 'Netherlands firms up plans for multifunction support vessels' posted to the *Naval News* site on 27 September 2024.

16. Türkiye's focus on the maritime domain is underlined by the so-called 'Blue Homeland' doctrine of 2019, which shifted the traditional emphasis from Türkiye as a land power towards the importance of protecting the country's maritime zones and interests. Meanwhile, a more detailed assessment of the programmes summarised in this section can be found in Devrim Yaylali's, 'Turkish naval programmes: Status report', *Maritime Defence Monitor* 012025 (Bonn: Mittler Report, 2025) and available at euro-sd.com.

17. The *Naval News* site regularly carries reports by H I Sutton detailing Ukrainian drone developments.

18. The number of patrol days was reported by Cormack O'Keeffe in an article, 'Number of patrol days carried out by naval service more than halved' posted to the *Irish Examiner's* site – irishexaminer.com – on 16 February 2025.

2.4A FLEET REVIEW

THE RUSSIAN NAVY

Retaining Strategic Importance

Author:
James Bosbotinis

Russia's continuing war against Ukraine dramatically illustrates the scale and brutality of Moscow's neo-imperial ambitions, whilst also setting in motion developments that constitute a substantial challenge to global order. Notably, in order to sustain its war against Ukraine, Russia has been forced to turn to Iran and North Korea for the supply of missiles, artillery and loitering munitions, underpinning the emergence of a Moscow-Tehran-Pyongyang axis. This has included the signing of a Russia-North Korea treaty, which includes a mutual defence clause. Moreover, the re-election of Donald Trump as President of the United States has seen his adoption of an increasingly pro-Russian position. For Moscow, the potential for a US-Russia rapprochement holds out the prospect of a major strategic victory. This would have significant implications for Russian military, including naval, development.

A photograph of the Project 20380 frigate *Boikiy* taken against the backdrop of the historic Russian Admiralty building in Saint Petersburg in August 2016. Russia continues to view its status as a 'great maritime power' as being a national interest. *(Conrad Waters)*

THE NAVY IN RUSSIAN STRATEGY

As explained by the renowned defence analyst, Michael Kofman, 'Russia does not formally have a naval strategy: unlike Western counterparts, the Russian military system is not one where services independently develop their own strategies.'[1] Instead, 'Doctrine and strategy development are integrated within the General Staff...Consequently, there is a military doctrine, national security strategies, and defence plans, but the navy does not have its own and distinct formulation of these ideas'. Thus, according to Kofman, 'Russian naval strategy is therefore more a discussion on operational art in the maritime domain, roles, and missions of naval forces in strategic operations, and the purpose of military actions at sea in achieving political goals in peacetime'.

Naval Doctrine: At the grand strategic level, Russian maritime policy broadly defined is set out within the *Maritime Doctrine of the Russian Federation*, with *The Fundamentals of the State Policy of the Russian Federation in the Field of Naval Operations for the Period Until 2030* providing the core naval policy document. The updated maritime doctrine was promulgated in 2022, replacing the previous 2015 edition. It sets out the overarching strategic framework within which the economic, scientific, industrial and naval aspects of Russian sea power are developed, defining the 'national maritime policy of the Russian Federation...the goals, principles, directions, objectives, and methods of achieving the national interests of the Russian Federation in the World Ocean, as well as the implementation of maritime activities as defined by the state and society'.[2] It 'specifies and expands on the main provi-

The US Navy *Nimitz* class aircraft carrier *Harry S. Truman* (CVN-75) pictured from the deck of the Royal Norwegian Navy frigate *Roald Amundsen* whilst the two ships were operating off the Norwegian coast in November 2024. Russian strategy views the actions of the US Navy and its allies as the main threats to its maritime security. *(Ørjan Andreassen/Norwegian Armed Forces)*

sions of the National Security Strategy...Military Doctrine...and other strategic planning documents relevant to maritime activities.'

The geographic scope and ambition underpinning Russian maritime thinking is stated clearly: 'the national interests of the Russian Federation as a great maritime power extend over the entire World Ocean and Caspian Sea'. The preservation of Russia's 'status as a great maritime power' is defined as a national interest, with the 'development of the Russian Federation as a great maritime power and strengthening of its position among the leading maritime powers of the world', listed as the primary strategic objective of national maritime policy. The doctrine calls for the 'development of maritime potential and strengthening defence capabilities', as well as 'conducting naval operations in the World Ocean to ensure and protect' Russian interests and 'maintain strategic and regional stability'. It also asserts that the,

> Development of the Russian Federation in the modern world occurs against the background of existing and new challenges and threats to its national security...[its] independent foreign and domestic policy is opposed by the United States and its allies, who seek to maintain their dominance in the world...They have implemented a policy of containment...which includes political, economic, military and informational pressure against the state.

In this context, the doctrine identifies the 'main challenges and threats' to Russia's national security and development as the 'US strategic course for dominance in the world's oceans', the US 'desire to achieve overwhelming' naval superiority, wider US and allied activities aimed at limiting Russian access 'to the resources of the world's oceans and maritime transport communications', claims to Russian coastal and island territories, 'economic, political, international legal, informational and military pressure' to 'discredit and reduce the effectiveness of Russian maritime activity', and efforts 'by a number of states' to weaken Russian control over the Northern Sea Route and an increase in the foreign naval presence in the Arctic.

In terms of regional priorities, Arctic and Atlantic 'directions' – the latter including the Baltic, Black and Azov, and Mediterranean Seas – are arguably the most important areas for Russia, with the doctrine

The veteran Soviet-era Project 1155 *Udaloy* class destroyer *Vice-Admiral Kulakov*, first commissioned in 1981, seen operating in the North Atlantic in November 2020. Arctic and Atlantic 'directions' are arguably the most important for Russian naval strategy and the country's Northern Fleet is, accordingly, the most powerful of the navy's four principal formations. *(Crown Copyright 2020)*

referring to, in the case of the Arctic, the growing importance of the Navy in 'ensuring national defence' and the need to strengthen Russia's 'leading position'. This includes enhancing the combat capabilities of the Northern and Pacific Fleets, 'exercising control' over foreign naval activities along the Northern Sea Route, and the 'diversification and activation of maritime activities on the archipelagos of Spitsbergen, Franz Josef Land, Novaya Zemlya and Wrangel Island'. In the Atlantic, national policy is 'determined by the existence of NATO', the 'unacceptability for the Russian Federation of plans to move NATO military infrastructure to its borders and attempts to give the alliance global functions', with the objective of Russian policy being to 'vigorously defend and reliably ensure' Russia's national interests. The doctrine calls for 'ensuring the capability of the shipbuilding complex to build heavy-tonnage vessels, including modern aircraft carriers for the Navy', in particular in the Russian Far East, and the 'development of advanced systems and weapons, military and special equipment, including marine robotic complexes for various purposes based on artificial intelligence, and ensuring advanced development of the Navy and the competitiveness of domestic naval products'.

The doctrine concludes by affirming that 'The modern Russian Federation cannot exist without a strong Navy' and that its attributes 'predetermine its existence and development in the 21st century as a great continental and maritime power'.

Naval Policy: The claim to 'great maritime power' status is also central to *The Fundamentals of the State Policy of the Russian Federation in the Field of Naval Operations for the Period Until 2030,* which was published in 2017.[3] This asserts:

> The Russian Federation still maintains the status of a great maritime power, possessing maritime potential that supports the implementation and defence of its national interests in any area of the World Ocean, is an important factor of international stability and strategic deterrence, and allows the pursuit of an independent national maritime policy as an equal participant in international maritime activities.

Moreover, the State Policy ambitiously declares, with regard to 'Naval Strategic Requirements, Objectives and Priorities for its Modernisation and Development', that 'The Russian Federation will not allow significant superiority of naval forces of other states over its Navy and will strive to secure its position as the second most combat capable Navy in the world'. It sets out the 'Military Risks and Threats' to Russian national interests, focusing particularly on the increasingly contested and competitive nature of the international system, and the 'aspiration of a range of states, primarily the United States of America…and its allies, to dominate on the World Ocean, including the Arctic, and to achieve overwhelming superiority of their naval forces'. In this regard, one of the threats that the State Policy highlights is the 'deployment (build-up) of strategic high-precision sea-based non-nuclear weapons systems, as well as sea-based ballistic missile defence systems by foreign states in the waters adjacent to the territory of the Russian Federation'. As Kofman explains in his previously referenced chapter, 'the policy on naval activity is more specific than the maritime doctrine in defining the threat environment, and prescriptions for how naval power can help address the challenges or security grievances'.

The policy document also lays out naval modernisation priorities and the evolving contribution of the Russian Navy to wider Russian strategy. Of particular note – and, arguably, mirroring the threat assessment highlighted above – is the development of a conventional strategic strike role:

> The Navy is one of the most effective instruments of strategic (nuclear and non-nuclear) deterrence, including preventing 'global strike'. This is due to the Navy possessing strategic nuclear and conventional naval forces and the ability to implement its combat potential in virtually any area of the World Ocean…With the development of high-precision weapons, the Navy faces a qualitatively new objective: destruction of the enemy's military and economic potential by striking its vital facilities from the sea.

The development of a long-range precision strike capability, highlighted by the 3M14 'Kalibr' (NATO: SS-N-30A 'Sagaris') and the 3M22 'Tsirkon' (SS-N-33) subsonic and hypersonic cruise missiles respectively, is defined, after the naval strategic nuclear forces, as the principal priority for naval development: that is, 'to develop conventional naval force task groups with capabilities to fulfil strategic non-nuclear deterrence missions', with 'long-range high-precision cruise missiles' forming the 'primary armament of the undersea, surface and coastal forces…through 2025', and hypersonic missiles 'and various unmanned autonomous systems' to be deployed from 2025. The development of a naval conventional strategic strike capability is intended to provide the means to threaten an adversary's critical military facilities and economic infrastructure, as part of a 'strategy based

Two views of an unidentified 'Kilo' class submarine transiting the English Channel in October 2018. The deployment of 3M14 'Kalibr' (NATO: SS-N-30A 'Sagaris') cruise missiles on new-build and modernised 'Kilo' class submarines has formed part of wider Russian Navy plans that have resulted in the development of a potent, long-range precision strike capability. *(Crown Copyright 2018)*

The sole Russian aircraft carrier, the Project 1143.5 class *Admiral Kuznetsov* pictured transiting the English Channel in January 2017 whilst returning to Russia after a Mediterranean deployment in support of the then Syrian government. She has been under lengthy refit and repair since October that year and, with some of her crew reportedly deployed to the war in Ukraine, there are now significant questions over when, or even if, she will return to service. *(Crown Copyright 2017)*

on cost imposition to deter would be opponents from conducting large-scale strikes against the Russian homeland'. More broadly, 'the Russian Navy's operational concepts reflect a plan to attrit opponent forces at longer ranges, such that they do not have the freedom of action' to strike Russia directly, a key concern given, for example, the US Navy's strength in carrier airpower and ship-launched cruise missiles.

Perhaps most significantly, the development of a conventional strategic strike capability has enabled the Russian Navy to establish a distinct contribution to wider Russian strategy:

> The Russian Navy attained a strong role within current strategic deterrence concepts and associated missions…[it] provides for the strategic conventional component…via long-range strike land-attack cruise missiles. The Navy also fields a substantial percentage of Russia's non-strategic nuclear weapons, able to employ them demonstratively or against military or economic targets…rather than return to a secondary role supporting the Russian ground troops in continental operations, it has instead evolved into a major component of the strategic deterrence forces at sea.

Whilst the development of a long-range precision strike capability is relatively new for the Russian Navy, the intellectual underpinnings of this policy are not. This was made clear by the authors David Fields and Robert Avery in their recent book, *The Royal and Russian Navies: Cooperation, Competition and Confrontation.* Writing with respect to Russian state policy, they state, 'the core aim of the policy remains consistent with that of Admiral Gorshkov: to protect Russia with a set of capabilities that can be

Russia's frigates and corvettes are increasingly of modern origin. This photograph of *Soobrazitelniy*, the second unit of the Project 20380 *Steregushchiy* class, was taken in December 2024. *(Crown Copyright 2024)*

deployed at range to deter and to defeat an adversary'.[4] This thinking is in line with other authors who declare that the legacy of Gorshkov runs deep. This is also reflected in the policy document's own declaration that:

> The Russian Federation, as a great sea and land power, must take into account all aspects of the geopolitical processes that take place on the World Ocean, coastal territories, and surrounding waters. Trends in the development of the current geopolitical situation in the world convincingly confirm that only the presence of a strong Navy will secure the Russian Federation a leading position in a multipolar world in the 21st century, as well as enable the state to effectively implement and protect its national interests.

Currently, Russia's Council for the Strategic Development of the Navy, established in August 2024 as part of the Maritime Board, and under the auspices of Presidential Aide Nikolai Patrushev, is developing a draft 'Strategy for the Development of the Navy', which 'will formulate the Russian Navy's immediate and long-term goals and objectives, as well as priorities in terms of shaping and developing the Navy'. It is taking into account lessons from the Ukraine war, and is intended to 'safeguard Russia's status as a great maritime power'.[5]

CURRENT NAVAL FORCES

Although the war against Ukraine has taken its toll on the Black Sea Fleet and the Russian economy, the major part of the Russian Navy is not committed to operations against Ukraine. Notably, the other Russian fleets – the Northern Fleet, the Pacific Fleet and the Baltic Fleet, as well as the Caspian Flotilla – have only seen peripheral involvement in the conflict. Moreover, shipbuilding and the delivery of new vessels, in particular small surface combatants and submarines, is continuing. A summary of current fleet strength is provided in Table 2.4A.1, with comments on the main types set out below.

Surface Combatants: Over 30 years after the Soviet Union's collapse, the Russian Navy's surface forces remain centred on a core of former Soviet vessels. These include the Project 1144.2 *Kirov* class nuclear-powered battlecruisers *Pyotr Velikiy* and *Admiral Nakhimov*, two Project 1164 'Atlant' ('Slava') class cruisers, and eight Project 1155/Project 1155.1 *Udaloy*/'Udaloy II' class (comprising six *Udaloy*, one 'Udaloy II', and one modernised *Udaloy*) and, perhaps, two active Project 956 *Sovremenny* class destroyers. The aircraft carrier *Admiral Kuznetsov*, currently undergoing a refit, is

The Project 955/955A series of 'Borey' class strategic submarines form a core element of Russia's nuclear deterrent. This is a photograph of the lead boat of the class, *Yury Dolgoruky*, in March 2017. She is currently in service with Russia's Northern Fleet. (*Russian Ministry of Defence*)

intended to return to service at some point. This is despite the ship only providing a limited capability and at least some of its crew being formed into a mechanised battalion for deployment in Ukraine.[6]

The frigate force, in contrast, is comprised principally of new ships. These include three Project 11356R *Admiral Grigorovich*, nine Project 20380 *Steregushchiy* and one Project 20385 *Gremyashchiy* class vessels, with more of the last two types under construction. These are supplemented by a handful of Soviet-era Project 11540 and Project 1135/1135M *Neustrashimy* class and 'Krivak' series ships. Most notably, the first three of the larger Project 22350 *Admiral Gorshkov* class frigates have been commissioned, with a fourth – the first unit intended for the Pacific Fleet – launched. At least six more *Admiral Gorshkov* class frigates are under construction or on order. It is reported that these ships will incorporate a 32-cell UKSK vertical launch system (VLS) rather than the 16-cell system on the first four ships.

The Russian Navy has also received, and continues to receive, smaller corvettes. These include the Project 21631 'Buyan-M' class, of which eleven out of a planned twelve have been delivered to date, and the Project 22800 'Karakurt' class. Six out of a projected class of 16 of the latter type have been delivered to date, one of which – *Tsiklon* – was reportedly destroyed in a Ukrainian missile attack in May 2024. These modern vessels are supplemented by significant numbers of Soviet-era corvettes and fast attack craft, many of dubious operational status.

The importance of the Arctic to Russian strategy highlighted above is reflected in the imminent arrival of two Project 23550 *Ivan Papanin* class Arctic patrol ships. The lead ship is undergoing sea trials and likely to commission in 2025, with the second ship, *Nikolai Zubov*, due in 2026. Two additional, slightly modified variants are being built for the coast guard of Russia's FSB Border Service.

Many of the recently-built ships – and some modernised vessels – are armed with the 'Kalibr' family of missiles. This is a multi-role weapon that can be launched from a wide range of platforms and encompasses anti-ship, land attack and anti-submarine variants. 'Kalibr' widespread installation reflects Russian efforts to deploy a long-range strike capability across as many platforms as possible. Its adoption is being supported by increasing use of the UKSK VLS 'universal shipborne firing system, which can also accommodate the SS-N-26 'Strobile' supersonic and SS-N-33 'Tsirkon' hypersonic missiles.

Submarines: Russia's submarine force is a key component of the country's nuclear deterrent and a major contributor to the navy's development of a conventional strategic strike capability. Whilst still comprising a mix of former Soviet and new boats, it has been the primary beneficiary of recent Russian naval investment, with around 25 new submarines – both nuclear and diesel-electric powered – delivered since 2010.

The Russian Navy currently operates twelve ballistic missile-armed, nuclear-powered strategic submarines (SSBNs) forming the naval strategic nuclear deterrent force. These comprise five Project 667BDRM 'Delta IV' class and seven Project 955 'Borey' – including four, improved Project 955A 'Borey A' – class boats. They are armed, respectively, with 16 SS-N-23 (either 'Sineva' or 'Liner' variants) and 16 SS-N-32 'Bulava' submarine-launched ballistic missiles. A further five 'Borey' class boats are planned to replace the 'Delta IV' submarines and maintain a twelve-strong SSBN force, split equally between the Northern and Pacific Fleets.

The core of the conventionally-armed, submarine force is approximately twelve nuclear-powered guided missile submarines (SSGNs). These comprise around seven, Soviet-era Project 949A 'Antey'

Two tranches of Project 636.3 Improved 'Kilo' class submarines have been ordered for, respectively, the Black Sea and Pacific Fleets. This is the second member of the class, *Krasnodar*, pictured in 2016. *(Conrad Waters)*

('Oscar II') and the first five of twelve planned, modern Project 885/885M 'Yasen/Yasen-M' class boats. It seems that four of the Project 949As will be modernised to a Project 949AM standard, receiving launchers for 72 'Kalibr', 'Strobile' and Tsirkon missiles in place of the current armament of 24 SS-N-19 'Shipwreck' missiles. It has been reported that *Orel* was the first boat to receive this upgrade with a second, *Irkutsk*, possibly due to re-enter service in 2025. Meanwhile, the Project 885/885M class represent the apex of current Russian nuclear submarine development. They are reportedly extremely quiet, and are armed with 32 'Kalibr' and 'Strobile' missiles, also being due to receive the 'Tsirkon' in due course. The first 'Tsirkon' armed boat, and sixth in class, *Perm*, was launched on 27 March 2025. On the same day, President Putin visited the 'Yasen-M'-class *Arkhangelsk*, where it was noted that there are two 'Tsirkon' variants, and that 'one of them has a slightly bigger range'.[7] The SSGNs are supplemented by around ten Soviet-era nuclear-powered attack submarines from various classes.

There are also around 20 diesel-electric submarines (SSKs). Eleven of these are Project 636.3 'Varshavyanka' (Improved 'Kilo') boats, ordered in batches of six for, firstly, the Black Sea Fleet, and, then, the Pacific Fleet. One of the Black Sea Fleet units – *Rostov-on-Don* – has been sunk by Ukraine whilst the last Pacific Fleet boat, launched in October 2024, has just been delivered. There are plans for a third batch, possibly for the Northern Fleet. The balance is formed by around eight original Project 877 'Paltus' ('Kilo') class boats from the Soviet era and *Kronstadt*, the first production variant of five planned Project 677 'Lada' class SSKs.[8] The newly built submarines – and at least one modernised 'Kilo' – are armed with 'Kalibr' cruise missiles. The Russian Navy, together with the Main Directorate for Deep Sea Research ('GUGI'), also operate a variety of special mission assets, including submarines which are employed for intelligence and other roles, such as targeting undersea cables.

Table 2.4A.1: RUSSIAN NAVY (MID 2025) – ORIGIN OF MAJOR COMBATANTS[1]

TYPE	SOVIET ERA[2]	POST SOVIET ERA[2]
Aircraft Carriers (CVs)		
Project 1143.5 **KUZNETSOV**	1	0
Cruisers and Destroyers (CGs/DDGs)		
Project 1144.2 **KIROV**	2	0
Project 1164 **MOSKVA** ('Slava')	2	0
Project 956/956A **SOVREMENNY**	2	0
Project 1155/1155.1 **UDALOY**/'Udaloy II'	8	0
Frigates and Corvettes (FFGs/FFs)		
Project 22350 **GORSHKOV**	0	3
Project 11366R **GRIGOROVICH**	0	3
Project 1154 **NEUSTRASHIMY**	2	0
Project 20385 **GREMYASHCHIY**	0	1
Project 20380 **STERGUSHCHIY**	0	9
Other Frigates	2	2
Project 21361 'Buyan M'	0	11
Project 22800 'Karakurt'	0	5
Other Corvettes	27[3]	3[4]
Strategic Submarines (SSBNs)		
Project 955/955A **YURY DOLGORUKY** ('Borey')	0	7
Project 667BDRM **VERKHOTURIE** (Delta IV)	5	0
Attack Submarines (SSGNs/SSNs)		
Project 855/855M **SEVERODVINSK** ('Yasen')	0	5
Project 949A ('Oscar II')	7	0
Other nuclear-powered Submarines	10	0
Patrol Submarines (SSKs)		
Project 677 **KRONSTADT** ('Lada')	0	1
Project 636.3 (Improved 'Kilo')	0	11
Project 877 ('Kilo')	8	0

Notes
1. Ship numbers, particularly older ships of the Soviet-era, are often approximations given difficulties establishing operational status.
2. In broad terms, Soviet-era ships refer to those ships laid down before 1991, even if completed afterwards.
3. Encompasses corvettes of the Project 1124/1124M 'Grisha', Project 1239 BORA and Project 1331M 'Parchim II' classes.
4. Project 21360 'Buyan' class corvettes.

Amphibious Ships: The Russian Navy's amphibious shipping remains dependent on ex-Soviet vessels of the Project 775 'Ropucha', and Project 1171 'Tapir' ('Alligator') class landing ship types. These are bolstered by two, modern and larger Project 11711 *Ivan Gren* landing ships, which are being followed by others of a modified type. The amphibious ships deployed to the Black Sea in support of operations against Ukraine have suffered badly in the war, with at least five being badly damaged or destroyed.

OPERATIONS

More broadly, the war against Ukraine has had a significant impact on the overall strength of the Black Sea Fleet, with at least 15 vessels – headed by the cruiser *Moskva* and the submarine *Rostov-on-Don* – either sunk or severely damaged. Shore-based infrastructure, for example in Sevastopol, has also suffered extensive destruction. However, overall assessments of the overall impact vary. For example, Fields and Avery highlight that Russia still 'remains

Russia's largely Soviet-era amphibious forces have suffered badly during the Ukraine war, with at least five major units destroyed or heavily damaged. These losses include four members of the once numerous Project 775 'Ropucha' class, of which *Aleksandr Otrakovsky* – pictured here in February 2025 – is one of the survivors. *(Crown Copyright 2025)*

able to project force within the Black Sea', conduct strikes with 'Kalibr' cruise missiles, and 'has yet to escalate to targeting vessels with torpedoes fired from its submarines', suggesting that claims of 'the "functional defeat of the Black Sea Fleet" should be treated with caution'.[9] Moreover, the Russian Navy undertook a number of notable deployments in the course of 2024. These included June exercises in the Caribbean and Atlantic with the frigate *Admiral Gorshkov* and 'Yasen-M'-class submarine *Kazan*, the large-scale 'Ocean-2024' exercise held in September, and the navy's first joint exercise with the Indonesian Navy in November.

There are nonetheless, significant constraints on Russian naval capability. In particular, these encompass:

- Deficiencies in anti-submarine warfare and mine countermeasures
- Weaknesses in logistics support and replenishment at sea
- Lack of access to overseas basing, a factor that is identified in The Maritime Doctrine, and compounded by recent developments in Syria
- Limitations in key enablers for maritime strike, especially relating to supporting over-the-horizon intelligence, surveillance, reconnaissance and targeting (ISR-T) functions.

The last-mentioned are critical to the successful prosecution of attacks against mobile targets at extended ranges. This is in part offset by an emphasis on the targeting of critical national infrastructure on land. As Kofman explains, 'Russian thinking about the contribution of naval power to military strategy has also shifted the accent from the defensive, destroying combat groupings at sea, to offensive operations targeting objects on land'.[10]

FUTURE PROSPECTS

Whilst Russia, including the Russian Navy, is confronted by a highly challenging strategic environment, there appears to be no diminishing of Russian national, or naval, ambition. On 11 April 2025, President Putin, chairing a meeting on the development strategy for the navy until 2050, announced that 8.4 trillion roubles (c. US$107 billion at current exchange rates) 'have been allocated to build new warships for the Navy over the next decade', as

The Russian Project 20380 *Steregushchiy* class frigate *Hero of the Russian Federation Aldar Tsydenzhapov* – part of Russia's Pacific Fleet – photographed whilst taking part in an exercise with China's People's Liberation Army Navy in October 2020. Although Russia's Black Sea Fleet has been degraded by losses suffered from the war against Ukraine, units of the country's other fleets have remained active. *(China Military Online)*

part of a wider, continued naval development programme. Total Russian military expenditure for 2025 is forecast by the Institute for Strategic Studies to be 15.6 trillion roubles (c. USD198 billion) or 7.5 percent of GDP, some 39 percent of total Russian federal budget spending. Putin identified priorities including precision and hypersonic weapons, uncrewed systems (air, surface and sub-surface), and ISR-T, stating that 'all these systems operating in the air, under water and on the surface must be closely integrated into a single reconnaissance and strike circuit and linked to our satellite constellation'.[11]

Russian merchant vessel *General Skobelev* transiting through the English Channel in February 2025 whilst supporting Russian naval forces being withdrawn from Syria following the collapse of that country's Assad regime. Weaknesses in logistics support and replenishment at sea are amongst a number of factors holding back Russian ambitions. *(Crown Copyright 2025)*

The Russian oceanic research ship *Admiral Vladimirsky*, which has been widely reported as being used for intelligence gathering activities, is seen being shadowed by the Royal Navy minehunter *Cattistock* in March 2025. Russian President Vladimir Putin has stated that improved intelligence, search, reconnaissance and tracking (ISR-T) capabilities are key priorities for the Russian Navy's future development. *(Crown Copyright 2025)*

Although President Putin described Russia's naval plans as 'ambitious' in his March 2025 visit to the submarine *Arkhangelsk*, Presidential Aide Nikolai Patrushev notably stated in a February 2025 interview that: 'Gigantomania [sic] of the fleet or its neglect are unacceptable'.[12] This, perhaps, suggests that the Russian Navy will resist the vision articulated by proponents of large nuclear-powered aircraft carriers and surface combatants, such as the mooted Project 23560 'Lider' class destroyers. Despite this, plans for some form of next generation aircraft carrier persist. In this regard, work continues on two 'big deck' Project 23900 *Ivan Rogov* class amphibious assault ships under construction at the Zaliv shipyard in Crimea. The ships were both laid down in July 2020 but the subsequent war has meant that planned delivery has slipped towards the end of the decade. The next major surface combatant is likely to be the enlarged, Project 22350M derivative of the *Admiral Gorshkov* class, which may be started once upgrade work at the Severnaya Verf shipyard in Saint Petersburg is completed. The status of a proposed Project 545 'Laika' next-generation nuclear-powered attack submarine is uncertain.

Publication of the forthcoming development strategy for the Russian Navy will shed much light on Russian thinking towards the roles of maritime power for the coming decades. However, until the war against Ukraine is concluded, Russian strategy will inevitably remain focused on the conflict, clouding longer term strategy with uncertainty. For the Russian Navy, resolution of the conflict may also yield the challenge of competing against the army

The diminutive Russian Project 21631'Buyan M' class corvette *Zelenyy Dol* pictured being replenished from a Russian tug during a long-distance deployment in 2016. Remarks by influential Russian Presidential Aide Nikolai Patrushev suggest that the Russian Navy will maintain its recent focus on smaller warships which – despite being equipped with powerful strike weapons – suffer from limited capacity to undertake oceanic missions. *(Crown Copyright 2016)*

for budgetary resources, especially given the need to replace the substantial losses incurred in Ukraine. The means by which the war ends will also be critical: a negotiated settlement that leaves Russia in control of Crimea and potentially southern Ukraine will maintain a position of Russian strength in the Black Sea region, whilst necessitating a continued focus by both Kyiv and the wider European region on deterring renewed aggression by Moscow.

Moreover, the continued apparent Russian influence on the White House and, with it, the potential for a radical shift in US-Russia relations may result in a significant improvement in Russian fortunes. An easing of American sanctions would greatly aid the Russian economy, thus helping military and naval modernisation, and most importantly, would enable a substantial shift in military thinking. As the preceding discussion of Russian maritime doctrine highlighted, the United States is currently identified as the principal threat to Russian interests; if this were no longer to be the case, Russia's room for manoeuvre, particularly with respect to Europe, would significantly improve. Although Russia may not be able to fulfil all of its naval ambitions, it will nevertheless pose a substantial threat, especially through its long-range strike capabilities. Those will ensure that the Russian Navy remains central to wider Russian military strategic and national policy objectives as the Kremlin pursues its neo-imperial and great power ambitions.

The Project 11356R frigate *Admiral Makarov* cuts an impressive figure whilst operating in the English Channel in August 2018. Now assigned to the Black Sea Fleet, she has participated in 'Kalibr' cruise missile strikes against Ukrainian targets. Her future, along with that of the rest of the Russian Fleet, will be heavily influenced by the outcome of the Ukraine War and the future trajectory of relations with the United States. *(Crown Copyright 2018)*

Notes

1. See, Michael Kofman, 'Evolution of Russian Naval Strategy', in Andrew Monaghan and Richard Connolly (editors), *The Sea in Russian Strategy* (Manchester: Manchester University Press, 2023), pp.94-123.

2. An unofficial translation by Anna Davis and Ryan Vest of the 2022 *Maritime Doctrine of the Russian Federation* can currently be found on the website of the US Naval War College's Russia Maritime Studies Institute at: usnwc.edu/Research-and-Wargaming/Research-Centers/Russia-Maritime-Studies-Institute.html

3. Again, an unofficial translation by Anna Davis can be found on US Naval War College's Russia Maritime Studies Institute's website.

4. See David Fields and Robert Avery, *The Royal and Russian Navies: Cooperation, Competition and Confrontation* (Manchester: Manchester University Press, 2025), p.154. Admiral of the Fleet Sergey Georgyevich Gorshkov (1910-88) was Commander-in-Chief of the Soviet Navy between 1956 and 1985, overseeing its expansion into a powerful, 'blue water' force.

5. See, President of the Russia, 'Meeting of the Council for Strategic Development of the Navy', 21 March 2025, currently available at: en.kremlin.ru/events/administration/76522

6. See, for example, George Allison, 'Russian Aircraft Carrier Crew Sent to Frontline in Ukraine' posted to the *UK Defence Journal* site – ukdefencejournal.org.uk – on 21 September 2024. There has been recent speculation that *Admiral Kuznetsov*'s current refit will be abandoned and the ship scrapped.

7. See, President of Russia, 'Vladimir Putin visited Arkhangelsk nuclear-powered cruiser submarine', 27 March 2025, currently available at: en.kremlin.ru/catalog/keywords/91/events/76557

8. The prototype Project 677 submarine, *Sankt Petersburg*, was decommissioned in 2024 after over a decade of sub-standard performance.

9. See, David Fields and Robert Avery, *The Royal and Russian Navies: Cooperation, Competition and Confrontation*, p.156.

10. See, Michael Kofman, 'Evolution of Russian Naval Strategy', p.113.

11. See, President of Russia, 'Meeting on development strategy for the Navy', 11 April 2025, currently available at: en.kremlin.ru/events/president/news/76673

12. See, 'Russian Presidential Aide Calls for Balanced Navy Development' posted to the *TASS* site on 18 February 2025 and currently available at: https://tass.com/defense/1914783

2.4B FLEET REVIEW

UNITED KINGDOM: ROYAL NAVY

New Roles for a New Hybrid RN

Author:
Richard Beedall

The last twenty years have been difficult for the Royal Navy (RN). World events have resulted in the RN facing a level of threats and operational demands unprecedented since the 1980s, but a declining budget has resulted in an ever-smaller fleet. Indeed, the last few years have seen a perfect storm of insufficient funding, worn-out or mechanically unreliable ships, delays in the delivery of new vessels, and a crewing crisis.

When Russia invaded Ukraine on 24 February 2022 the British naval services had about 60 major vessels, excluding minor units such as patrol ships and craft.[1] Between then and June 2025, no fewer than 17 of these were decommissioned, namely:

- Three nuclear-powered attack submarines (SSNs)
- Two amphibious assault ships (LPDs)
- Four frigates (FFGs)
- Four mine countermeasure vessels (MCMVs)
- Two hydrographic survey ships
- Two fast fleet tankers

During the same period just one SSN and two auxiliary ships entered service. Another MCMV and a frigate are scheduled to decommission in late 2025, without immediate replacement.[2] It was therefore a relief that when the latest British defence review promised some investment in the RN, it didn't also demand the immediate cuts and savings that have become the norm in such exercises.

The Type 23 frigate *Monmouth* departs Portsmouth Harbour for the final time on 3 April 2025 en route for the shipbreakers in Turkey. The first Type 23 frigate to be scrapped, she will soon be joined by increasing numbers of her Royal Navy sister ships whose withdrawals have been accelerated after life extensions have been found to be prohibitively costly. The Royal Navy has suffered a very extensive reduction in fleet numbers over recent years in the face of insufficient funding and crew numbers, worn-out ships, and delays to their replacements. *(Andy Amor)*

STRATEGIC DEFENCE REVIEW 2025 (SDR 2025)

When a new Labour Government was elected in June 2024, one of its first actions was to announce a strategic defence review, led by a former NATO Secretary-General, Lord Robertson.

A major constraint on the review was that it must be achievable within the available funding. On 25 February 2025, Prime Minister Keir Starmer pledged that British defence spending would increase from the current 2.3 percent of gross domestic product (GDP) to 2.5 percent from April 2027, with an ambition of 3 percent by the end of the next Parliament in 2034. He claimed that the defence budget would therefore increase by £13.4 billion p.a. in 2027-8 compared to 2024-5, with the prospect of further growth thereafter.[3] Lord Robertson and his team later confirmed that SDR 2025 had been developed and its affordability assessed using the 3 percent ambition. This had 'made an enormous difference', as the decision had established the affordability of the review's recommendations across a ten-year period.[4] Even then, SDR 2025 still had little financial headroom for major new initiatives or force-level increases, as much of the extra money would be consumed by pay increases, procurement cost overruns, rebuilding munition stocks, military aid to Ukraine, essential infrastructure upgrades, improving military housing, and – unexpectedly – payments to Mauritius.[5]

The review was published on 2 June 2025.[6] It set the context as being, 'The UK is entering a new era of threat and challenge…The UK and its allies are once again directly threatened by other states with advanced military forces.' It noted Russia is an immediate and pressing threat, with China being a sophisticated and persistent challenge. In response, the review prioritises the security of Britain's own backyard, recommending a NATO-first approach as 'there is an unequivocal need for the UK to redouble its efforts within the alliance and to step up its contribution to Euro-Atlantic security more broadly – particularly as Russian aggression across Europe grows and as the United States of America adapts its regional priorities'.

Along with the rest of the British Armed Forces, the Royal Navy is assigned three core roles. These are:

- Defend, protect, and enhance the resilience of the United Kingdom, its Overseas Territories, and Crown Dependencies.
- Deter and defend in the Euro-Atlantic.
- Shape the global security environment.

This effectively focuses the RN on tasks such as protecting critical underwater infrastructure and improving its anti-submarine warfare (ASW) capabilities in British and northern European waters. It has been largely pulled back from the expeditionary operations and a tilt to the Indo-Pacific and global power projection that was envisaged in the previous 2021 Integrated Review and which, indeed, dates as far back as the SDR of 1998.

Astute, lead boat of her class of nuclear-powered attack submarines, briefly surfaced for photos on 28 April 2025 as it accompanied the UK Carrier Strike Group 25 (CSG25) on Operation Highmast. A significant increase in Royal Navy submarine numbers is envisaged in the British 2025 Strategic Defence Review, although they are likely to be increasingly focused on defending a planned 'Atlantic Bastion'. *(Crown Copyright 2025)*

The review determined that the RN must change the way it fights and move towards a cheaper and simpler fleet. It must evolve into a new type of hybrid navy with a mix of crewed, uncrewed, and increasingly autonomous surface and sub-surface vessels and aircraft. As an example, the evolution of 'hybrid' carrier air wings is recommended, whereby crewed combat aircraft such as the F-35B strike fighter are complemented in the air by autonomous collaborative platforms, expendable single-use drones, and even long-range precision missiles fired from the carriers' decks. Other key points affecting the RN are:

- The importance of maintaining and refreshing the United Kingdom's Continuous at Sea Deterrent, including construction of the *Dreadnought* class strategic submarines (SSBNs).
- A recommendation that work begins by 2029 on a post-*Dreadnought* system, to enter service from the mid-2050s.
- Infrastructure investments to allow the United Kingdom to produce a submarine every 18 months, and through the AUKUS submarine programme grow the SSN fleet to up to twelve.
- A faster shift towards a high-low equipment mix and the greater use of autonomy and artificial intelligence (AI), in particular the 'Atlantic Bastion' concept for securing the North Atlantic.
- An evolution to mine-hunting delivered using autonomous platforms.
- Exploring the development of a minimally crewed or autonomous air dominance system to form part of the United Kingdom's Integrated Air and Missile Defence system.
- Using commercial vessels and burden-sharing with NATO allies to augment Royal Fleet Auxiliary (RFA) ships in non-contested environments.
- Use of the multi-role ocean survey ship (*Proteus*) and fleets of autonomous vehicles to counter threats to critical undersea infrastructure.
- A focus by the Royal Marines Commando Force on supporting NATO requirements, including integration into the Strategic Reserve Corps when appropriate.

Two notable omissions that the review does not mention are the RN's desire to expand its frigate force to at least 18 vessels and the requirement for new amphibious ships. However, these may yet feature in future implementation documents that are scheduled to be published in the autumn of 2025.

If SDR 2025 is fully implemented, by the 2040s the Royal will be a 'Hybrid Navy', centred on *Dreadnought* and SSN-AUKUS submarines, a modest number of cutting-edge warships and support ships, transformed aircraft carriers, plus autonomous vessels to patrol the North Atlantic and beyond.

THE 'ATLANTIC BASTION'

The Royal Navy's 'Atlantic Bastion' plan was given particular emphasis in SDR 2025. This plan came to prominence in February 2025, when the Ministry of Defence (MoD) publicly launched 'Project Cabot', an ambitious initiative to achieve the quick and affordable delivery of a persistent remotely operated and autonomous anti-submarine warfare (ASW) barrier in the North Atlantic and across the Greenland-Iceland-UK (GIUK) gap. The project is to be implemented in two phases.

In May 2025 it was confirmed that tenders would soon be sought for the first phase known as 'Atlantic Net'. This will deliver 'ASW as a service' via contractor owned and operated lean-crewed or uncrewed systems. In essence, these systems will collect acoustic data which will be sent to a RN-operated remote operations centre for classification and analysis. It is hoped that the first elements of the service will be operational as soon as the end of 2025, under a four-and-a-half year contract budgeted at £20 million (c. US$27 million).

Subsequently, around 2029, a second phase known as 'Atlantic Bastion' will see a transition to a RN owned and operated force. This will include the addition of uncrewed surface vessels (USVs) that will be designated as Type 92 ASW sloops and uncrewed underwater vehicles (UUVs) known as Type 93 ASW chariots. This phase may also introduce UK-developed underwater battlespace area denial (UBAD) capabilities; probably sea mines and lightweight torpedoes carried by drones. The trials ship XV *Patrick Blackett* is already testing prototype systems and technologies for the Type 92, whilst the extra-large UUV XV *Excalibur* will do similar for the Type 93. 'Atlantic Bastion' aims to combine a comprehensive layered network of acoustic detection systems leveraging AI with integrated decision-support systems for targeting.[7]

On 15 May 2025, the Royal Navy accepted and named the new Extra-Large Uncrewed Underwater Vessel (XLUUV) XV *Excalibur* at Devonport. She will join the Fleet Experimentation Squadron for the testing of her intelligence, surveillance and reconnaissance capabilities, informing the design of a production standard Type 93 uncrewed submarine that will form a key part of the operational concept envisaged for the planned 'Atlantic Bastion'. *(Crown Copyright 2025)*

A REDUCED GLOBAL PRESENCE

A consequence of the renewed focus on home waters and the Atlantic is likely to be a reduced RN global presence. Previous British governments have prioritised the RN's deployments beyond European waters, particularly in the Arabian Gulf and Indo-Pacific region. While SDR 2025 emphasises that its NATO-first policy is not 'NATO only' because of the connection between Euro-Atlantic security and other regions such as the Middle East, it certainly gives these a lower priority. Accordingly, whilst deployments such as the United Kingdom's Carrier Strike Group's (CSG25's) Operation Highmast deployment 'East of Suez' to, amongst other places, India, Singapore, Australia and Japan, are not ruled out in the future, they will likely be given less focus.

The RN's presence in the Arabian Gulf, operating from the United Kingdom Naval Support Facility (UKNSF) in Bahrain, may also decline. This was the base for six ships and nearly 1,000 personnel in the early 2020s but has been significantly reduced recently. SDR 2025 implies that the facility will be retained, but there is no clarity as to what ships – if any – will remain based there.

Since late 2021 the Batch 2 'River' class patrol vessels *Spey* and *Tamar* have been forward deployed with great success to the Indo-Pacific region. The ships engage in activities with local states, ranging from 'showing the flag', disaster relief, and participation in military exercises. However, by 2028 at the latest, they are due to return to the United Kingdom to replace the old Batch 1 patrol ships *Tyne* and *Mersey* for fishery protection and EEZ duties in British waters. SDR 2025 is silent as to whether or how they might, in turn, be replaced in the Indo-Pacific.[8]

An important exception to this retrenchment is that the plan for an *Astute* class submarine to be forward deployed to Perth in Australia from 2027 will be maintained. This reflects the political and industrial significance of the Australia-UK-US (AUKUS) alliance, including the SSN-AUKUS project.

EQUIPMENT: SUBMARINES

The biggest single component of British defence spending relates to the Defence Nuclear Enterprise (DNE), described as a partnership or organisations from government and industry that operate, maintain, renew and sustain the UK's nuclear deterrent. In addition to the Royal Navy, key government participants include the Defence Nuclear Organisation (DNO), the Submarine Development Agency (SDA) and the Atomic Weapons Establishment (AWE). For national security reasons, the enterprise has limited public accountability.

The largest programme managed by the SDA is the construction of four new *Dreadnought* class ballistic missile submarines. Displacing 17,200 tonnes and some 153.6m in length, they will replace the aging *Vanguard* class. In a May 2025 report, the MoD stated that the *Dreadnought* programme remained within its £31bn (c. US$42 billion) budget and additional £10 billion (c. US$13.5 billion) contingency.[9] The hull of the first-of-class submarine, *Dreadnought*, has now been joined into a single unit. However, the report also acknowledged that '…risks remain on the *Dreadnought* programme and across the enterprise, notably in infrastructure delivery, the workforce, and the programme to replace the UK's nuclear warhead'. In February 2020, the United Kingdom committed to replacing its existing warheads with a new Astraea A21/Mk 7 warhead, which is expected to be used throughout the life of the *Dreadnought* class. The British sovereign nuclear warhead programme will cost a separate £15 billion (c. US$20 billion).

Pending the arrival of the *Dreadnought* submarines, the four aging *Vanguard* class boats are struggling to maintain the UK's Continuous At Sea Deterrent (CASD). In 2023 and 2024 *Vigilant* and *Vengeance* had to undertake unusually long patrols of over six months. *Vanguard* – finally operational

The Royal Navy's Batch 2 'River' class patrol vessels have been largely tasked with maintaining an overseas presence, with two undertaking an extended deployment in the Asia-Pacific region. Here, *Tamar* is seen on exercises with the Japanese *Mogami* class frigate *Noshiro* (FFM-3) in July 2024. It is currently unclear as to whether or not this mission will be maintained in the medium term as the Royal Navy's NATO role becomes paramount. *(Australian Department of Defence)*

Nearly nine years after her construction started, and with her pressure hull already complete, a ceremony attended by Prime Minister Keir Starmer and Defence Secretary John Healey was performed on 20 March 2025 to lay down the keel of the strategic submarine *Dreadnought*. No external photographers were allowed, and the few moderate quality official photographs released showed little more than the spectators in front of a large plastic sheet. *(BAE Systems)*

again after a seven-year refit – then completed a gruelling 204-day patrol ending in March 2025. The fourth boat, *Victorious*, hasn't been operational since 2022; in June 2023 she arrived at Devonport dockyard prior to beginning a Deep Maintenance Period (DMP) expected to cost at least £560 million (c. US$760 million). It's hoped that she will recommission by 2027 and then be good for another ten years of service. As noted below, significant improvements to the maintenance and refit facilities available for the *Vanguard* class and other submarines are being made in order to improve their availability.

The last of the *Trafalgar* class hunter killer, or nuclear-powered attack submarine, *Triumph*, arrived in Devonport for decommissioning on 12 December 2024, just two years after completing a major and expensive four-year long refit. This left the RN with five *Astute* class submarines in service, although due to a lack of maintenance facilities it is suspected that often only one is deployable. The sixth boat, *Agamemnon*, should be operational by 2026 after being launched on 3 October 2024. There is uncertainty as to when the seventh and final boat, *Achilles* – renamed from *Agincourt* in January 2025 – will enter service. She is officially expected to be delivered by the end of 2026 but this seems unlikely. As of mid-2025 she had yet to be launched, possibly due to damage from a substantial fire that occurred on 29 October 2024 in the Devonshire Dock Hall at Barrow-in-Furness where she is being constructed.

One part of SDA's work that has gained media attention is the AUKUS submarine programme. Whilst the United States and United Kingdom have published very little information about this, Australia has been slightly more forthcoming because of the political need to justify the substantial spending involved. Although SSN-AUKUS (or SSN-A) may only be built for the RN and Royal Australian Navy, the design will incorporate many American systems, including the selection of an evolved version of the AN/BYG1 Combat Management System instead of the BAE Systems-developed Submarine Command System Next Generation (SMCS NG), and the fitting of a vertical launch system that is expected to be based on the Virginia Payload Module. It is currently planned

The four aging *Vanguard* class strategic submarines are struggling to maintain the UK's Continuous At Sea Deterrent (CASD). Here *Vengeance* navigates through Gare Loch in February 2025 as she departs HM Naval Base Clyde in Faslane to conduct sea trials. *(Crown Copyright 2025)*

The sixth *Astute* class submarine, *Agamemnon*, pictured outside the Devonshire Dock Hall at Barrow-in-Furness in October 2024, shortly before her launch. She is expected to enter service in 2026. *(BAE Systems)*

A computer-generated rendering of the SSN-AUKUS submarine design. The SSN-AUKUS, also known as the SSN-A, is intended to enter service with the United Kingdom's Royal Navy in the late 2030s and Royal Australian Navy in the early 2040s. *(BAE Systems)*

that the first RN SSN-A will enter service in the late 2030s, with further boats following at 18-month intervals.[10]

In order to supplement its manned nuclear submarines, the RN has long been investigating autonomous UUVs for use in ASW patrols, infrastructure surveillance, intelligence gathering, and even combat. A milestone was reached when, on 15 May 2025, the RN unveiled the MSubs Ltd-manufactured XV *Excalibur*; an experimental 12 metre long extra-large UUV displacing 19 tonnes and costing £15.4million (c. US$21 million). *Excalibur* will now undergo three years of sea trials and tests, which will inform the design of a production standard Type 93 UUV. They will also likely inform the capabilities of SSN-A, which is intended to collaborate with networked UUVs.

EQUIPMENT: AIRCRAFT CARRIERS & THE FLEET AIR ARM

The pride of the Royal Navy remains the two *Queen Elizabeth* Class aircraft carriers. However, their operational usefulness has been hampered by accidents and mechanical failures. For example, *Queen Elizabeth* was about to sail for a NATO exercise in February 2024 when a critical fault was identified with a propeller shaft, forcing her sister *Prince of Wales,* to take her place. Another major problem is the lack of aircraft, escorts and support ships required to form a combat-capable carrier strike group.

On 2 December 2024 *Queen Elizabeth* handed over the role of Fleet Flagship and High Readiness Carrier to *Prince of Wales*. Although *Prince of Wales* commissioned in 2019, CSG25 was her first significant deployment. Moreover, observers noted that many of her accompanying vessels were provided by allies such as Canada, Norway, and Spain.

The Fleet Air Arm (FAA) is currently in a stable state. The highlight of the last few years was the re-establishment of 809 Naval Air Squadron on 8 December 2023, operating F-35B Lightning strike fighters, whilst the extension of the end of service date for the Merlin MH.2 helicopter from 2030 to 2040 removed its biggest procurement challenge. The focus is now on two projects.

An Airborne Surveillance and Control (ASaC) Merlin Mk2 Helicopter from 820 Naval Air Squadron conducts training from the aircraft carrier *Queen Elizabeth* in June 2021. The ASaC Crowsnest system finally achieved full operating capability in March 2025 but is widely regarded as a costly disappointment that will soon be replaced. *(Crown Copyright 2021)*

The Type 45 destroyers are starting to emerge from a protracted power improvement programme and are also receiving other major upgrades to their weapons and combat systems. This May 2025 image shows *Defender* (foreground) in the course of refit at Portsmouth; the forward part of her missile silo is under canvass as part of work to install CAMM missiles. In the background is the decommissioned Type 82 destroyer *Bristol,* a veteran of the 1982 Falkland Islands campaign and seen in the course of preparation for her final voyage to the scrapyard after finishing a lengthy second career as a training hulk. *(Andy Amor)*

A fine photo of the Type 23 frigate *St. Albans* commencing sea trials in March 2024 after a four-and-a-half-year refit and life extension at Devonport. Designed in the 1980s, her cluttered upperworks look incongruous in an age of stealth, but replacements have been delayed. *(Babcock International Group)*

The first is replacing the Crowsnest Airborne Surveillance and Control (ASaC) system, although it only entered operational service in 2025. It is a costly disappointment – with £426 million (c. US$575 million) spent as of December 2023 – and will be taken out of service on 31 December 2029. A replacement is being sought, with an airborne early warning (AEW) version of the MQ-9B uncrewed aerial vehicle (UAV) a contender.

A second priority is bulking out the air groups of the *Queen Elizabeth* class aircraft carriers. SDR 2025 implied that the United Kingdom will never have enough F-35Bs to form two full-strength carrier air groups. Instead, to gain mass and capability, it strongly backed the formation of hybrid air groups including both crewed aircraft, and unmanned drones and autonomous air vehicles.

The RN has already purchased a significant number of UAVs and drones, which are primarily operated by 700X NAS, and its Maritime Aviation Transformation strategy is ambitious. It aims, by 2040, to transform the RN's maritime aviation capabilities by introducing a range of high-performance UAVs and uncrewed combat aerial vehicles (UCAVs) for missions such as air-to-air refuelling, electronic warfare, air combat and strike. Operating these larger and heavier air vehicles may require the aircraft carriers to be fitted with an electromagnetic catapult and arresting gear.

EQUIPMENT: DESTROYERS AND FRIGATES

The RN's shortage of escort vessels has escalated to a crisis as it tries to fulfil competing urgent operational demands from an ever-shrinking pool. There were 19 destroyers and frigates in 2020; just 14 in 2025.

The availability of the six Type 45 destroyers continues to be badly impacted by a decade-long power improvement programme. Three ships – *Dauntless*, *Daring* and *Dragon* – have now completed this (although *Daring* has yet to return to service) and the remaining ships should follow by 2028. The destroyers are also in the process of receiving significant upgrades to their weapons fit, including improved Sea Viper (Aster 30 Block 1) missiles with a limited anti-ballistic missile capability and the addition of a silo of 24 Sea Ceptor missiles. Some ships will also benefit from the replacement of Harpoon with the Naval Strike Missile, and the fitting of Sea Dragon directed-energy weapons. Although now roughly halfway

On 22 May 2025 Her Royal Highness the Princess of Wales, formally named the first of eight Type 26 ASW frigates as *Glasgow* at the BAE Systems shipbuilding facility in Scotstoun. The ship is expected to commence sea trials in 2026. *(BAE Systems)*

through their service life, the destroyers are finally becoming well-armed and formidable opponents.

A new class of destroyer, the Type 83, should start replacing the Type 45s from the late 2030s. Although announced in 2021, details about the Type 83 project are only just starting to emerge. It will form part of the Future Air Dominance System (FADS) – a system of air defence systems – and will, inter alia, be capable of countering hypersonic missiles. The project had entered the concept and assessment phase by March 2025, with current plans suggesting actual procurement around 2028. SDR 2025 also recommended exploring '…a minimally crewed or autonomous air dominance system that could integrate directed energy weapons…', with BAE Systems and Babcock promoting, respectively, variants of the Type 26 (the Global Air Warfare Command Ship) and Type 31 (Arrowhead 160) to meet the requirement. The Type 83 may well be operated in conjunction with an uncrewed surface vessel –the Type 91 arsenal ship – to increase magazine depth. Whilst an entry into service by 2035 is targeted, past experience makes this target look optimistic.[11]

The last few years have seen an unexpectedly rapid run down of the Type 23 frigate force, which consisted of 13 ships as recently as 2020. *Monmouth* (2021), *Montrose* (2023), *Westminster* (2024), *Argyll* (2025) and *Northumberland* (2025) have all been decommissioned as worn out and uneconomic to refit, with *Lancaster* expected to follow shortly. Most of the decommissionings have occurred years before previously-announced planned dates, for example, *Northumberland* had been expected to remain in service to 2029. Replacement of the Type 23s by eight Type 26 'City' class high-end ASW frigates built by BAE Systems and five Type 31 'Inspiration' class lower-end general purpose (GP) frigates built by Babcock International is running at least a year behind the schedules stated in 2022.

The first Type 26, *Glasgow*, is now due to start contractor sea trials in 2026 and to reach initial operating capability in October 2028. Construction

The auxiliary dock landing ship *Lyme Bay* is one of a dwindling pool of British amphibious assets. This photograph was taken during the Joint Viking 2025 exercise on 12 March. *(Thomas Haraldsen/Norwegian Armed Forces)*

RFA crewing difficulties have led to a decision to transfer the auxiliary mine countermeasures mother-ship *Stirling Castle* to the Royal Navy. This overhead image was taken in Portland Harbour in July 2024. *(Andy Amor)*

of her seven sister-ships is expected to be complete by the mid-2030s, subject to any impact from a potential export sale of Type 26s to Norway. To increase productivity and reduce Type 26 build times, BAE Systems have invested £300 million (c. US$410 million) in new facilities at its Clyde shipyards, including the 'Janet Harvey' shipbuilding hall at Govan. This enables the construction of two frigates undercover simultaneously, starting with the third of the Type 26 class, *Belfast*.

The first Type 31, *Venturer*, was rolled out for launch on 27 May 2025 and is now due to commission in 2027, with her four sister-ships all following by the early 2030s. They will enter service with some now desired equipment missing and the MoD will pay Babcock to complete a capability insertion period for the frigates. This covers the fitting of equipment over and above that specified in the original fixed-price contract, likely including Mk 41 vertical launch cells, Ancilia decoy launchers and additional electronic warfare equipment.

In November 2020 plans to build up to five Type 32 general purpose frigates were announced, but this project was never adequately funded, with just £4 million (c. US$5 million) being allocated for the concept phase. There has been speculation that the programme has effectively been abandoned and there was no mention of it in SDR 2025. The focus is now on the uncrewed Type 92 sloop. The limited information so far available suggests that this will be a small, 40 metre (130ft) long unmanned autonomous drone ship that can spend months on patrol towing a sonar array.

EQUIPMENT: AMPHIBIOUS SHIPS

On 20 November 2024, the new government reversed a May 2024 decision by their predecessors and announced that the two *Albion* class assault ships would be retired by March 2025, nearly a decade earlier than previously planned. *Bulwark* was completing a £72 million (c. US$100 million) refit in mid-2023 when it was determined that there were not enough sailors available to recommission her as the flagship of Littoral Response Group (North), leaving both members of the class in maintained reserve. In April 2025, it emerged that the United Kingdom had signed a letter of intent to sell the two ships to Brazil for a reported £20 million (US$27 million). They will join the RN's last amphibious helicopter carrier, *Ocean*, which was sold to Brazil in 2018 after 19 years of service.

This updated graphic of their successful FSS design was released by Team Resolute in September 2023. It shows a few changes to the superstructure compared to earlier images. *(Team Resolute)*

With the demise of the *Albion* class, the only specialist amphibious ships left in UK service are the three far less capable 'Bay' class auxiliary landing ships, which are in demand for other duties. Whilst the aging but versatile *Argus* now officially has an amphibious, 'littoral strike' role, she also still serves as a primary casualty receiving ship and as an aviation support/training ship. The lack of suitable ships suggests previous plans to maintain two amphibious Littoral Response Groups (LRGs) – LRG (North) and LRG (South) – is unlikely to be maintained.

Looking to the future, at least three and up to six Multi-Role Strike Ships (MRSS) – previously known as Multi-Role Support Ships – are due to enter service from 2033/34. In May 2024 the MRSS programme entered the concept phase, and the MoD is finalising the requirements before moving into the assessment phase in 2026, when the detailed design will be developed. The ships are expected to incorporate a well dock for landing craft, davits for a new Commando Insertion Craft (CIC), a hangar for helicopters and uncrewed systems, and a large flight desk capable of accommodating a Chinook helicopter. The ships will be fitted with self-defence and offensive capabilities, as well as combat and command support systems. Unlike the 'Bay' class they will be classified as military vessels and will be manned and operated by the Royal Navy rather than the RFA. SDR 2025 made no further mention of the MRSS project but subsequent official statements have confirmed that it is still progressing.

In January 2025 the MoD began the procurement process for a future strategic sealift service (SSL-F), replacing the aging 'Point' class ships provided by Foreland Shipping Limited. The new ships, probably four, will enter service around 2032.

ROYAL MARINES

The previous 2021 Integrated Review set out a modest but coherent vision for the Royal Marines' transformation into the Future Commando Force, essentially moving from providing an amphibious infantry brigade (3 Commando Brigade) to a smaller formation (UK Commando Force, or UKCF) focused on special operations. However, implementation was dogged by a lack of the money required for new equipment and the procurement or conversion of one or two specialist Littoral Strike Ships for sea-based operations.

Whilst SDR2025 complimented the UKFC on offering political choices for 'action worldwide', it recommended that it should now focus on NATO operations and eventually become part of a land-based strategic reserve led by the British Army. This threatens to mark the beginning of the end of the Royal Marine Corps (which now numbers less than 5,800 personnel) as a distinct naval arm.

THE ROYAL FLEET AUXILIARY SERVICE

The last few years have been challenging for the RFA, with a shortage of personnel resulting in ships being laid up. Particularly embarrassing was its inability to crew the supply ship *Fort Victoria* for the CSG25 deployment, or *Stirling Castle* as a mother-ship for autonomous minehunting systems. Indeed the latter will now be crewed and operated by the Royal Navy.

Difficulties also emerged with the operation of the Multi-Role Ocean Surveillance Ship (MROSS) *Proteus*, which was hurriedly purchased in 2023 to counter threats to the UK's underwater infrastructure. She was built to commercial standards and key

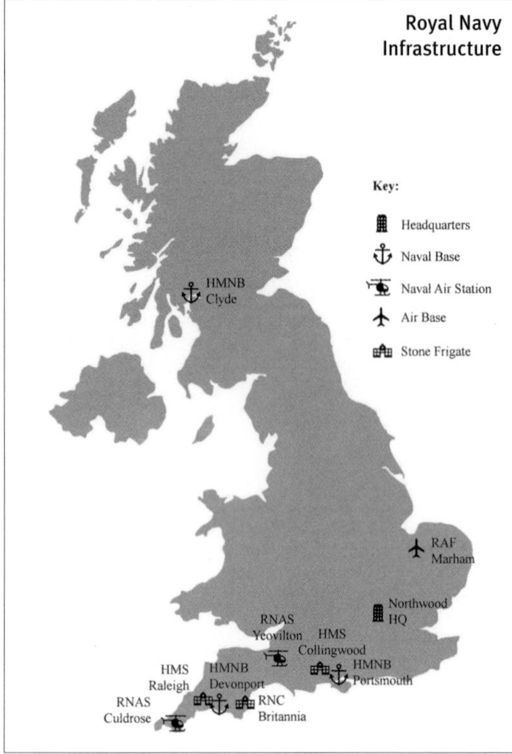

systems failed under the more rigorous demands of quasi-military service; she has spent much of her RFA service under repair and maintenance.

In November 2024 it was announced that the fast fleet tankers *Wave Knight* and *Wave Ruler* would be sold, reversing an announcement the previous year that they would be retained until 2028. They have spent much of their 20-year lives in extended readiness and potentially represent a bargain buy.

In January 2023 a £1.6 billion (c. US$2.2 billion) contract was awarded to Team Resolute (BMT, Harland & Wolff, and Navantia UK) to construct three Fleet Solid Support (FSS) ships. Unfortunately, Harland & Wolf went into administration in September 2024; to salvage the project the MoD facilitated the purchase of the company by the Spanish company Navantia. The first vessel is now expected to enter service in the early 2030s, with overall costs subject to renegotiation.

NAVAL INFRASTRUCTURE

The Royal Navy's shore infrastructure has shrunk significantly since the end of the Cold War in 1989. However, it still possesses some of the most important naval facilities in Europe, and significant investments are currently being made to modernise these.

The three main operating bases are:

HM Naval Base Portsmouth: This is the homeport for the two *Queen Elizabeth* class aircraft carriers and the six Type 45 destroyers, and the future base for five Type 31 frigates. A programme to refurbish its aging facilities and increase its number of operational jetties and berths – known as Project Bentham – was announced in April 2025.

HM Naval Base Devonport: By area, the base and the adjacent Babcock-run Royal Dockyard Devonport form the largest naval facility in Europe. The base is the home of the RN's Type 23 and future Type 26 frigates, with the dockyard taking care of the refit of the Type 23 frigates and all the RN's nuclear-powered submarines. Work on the latter is concentrated on a Submarine Refit Complex centred on the dockyard's No. 5 Basin. At present, No. 9 Dock is used for SSBN refits and No. 15 Dock for SSN refits, with No. 14 Dock being prepared for defuelling decommissioned submarines. In addition, No. 10 Dock is being rebuilt to provide an additional refitting facility, including for the future SSN-As.

An image of No. 5 Basin at Royal Dockyard Devonport taken in April 2020 showing the main elements of the facility's Submarine Refit Complex. Dock Nos. 8,9,10 and 11 can be seen from left to right at the top of the image, with the strategic submarine *Vanguard* in the course of her protracted life extension in No. 9 Dock. The two closest docks are, from left to right, Nos. 14 and 15 Docks. The former is being prepared for the defuelling of redundant submarines whilst the latter is now being used for *Astute* class refits, although it is likely that it is *Triumph* that is in the dock in this image. *(Andy Amor)*

Devonport also houses the Fleet Operational Standards and Training (FOST) organisation. A steady stream of RN and other NATO warships are trained and tested by FOST before they are considered ready for operations by their respective navies.

The complex has already benefitted from around £2.5 billion (c. US$3.4 billion) of investment in recent years, including the £750 million (c. US$1 billion) Submarine Waterfront Infrastructure (SWIF) programme contracted in November 2023. In September 2024 the Ministry of Defence announced an additional £4.4 billion investment over ten years into the two facilities to support a further strengthening of submarine support infrastructure.

HM Naval Base Clyde: Located near Faslane, this is the homeport for all operational RN submarines, currently the *Vanguard* and *Astute* classes. Work has been progressing for some time on the £1.8 billion (c.US$2.4 billion) Clyde Infrastructure Programme (CIP), which will upgrade facilities at both Faslane and the nearby Royal Naval Armaments Depot Coulport to support Dreadnought and SSN-A type submarines from 2032 onwards. At present, the base relies on a single shiplift for out-of-water submarine maintenance, creating significant problems when unavailable. Consequently, the MoD is seeking to acquire two floating docks for Faslane under the Additional Fleet Time Docking Capability (AFTDC) programme.

Other important shore facilities include:

- **Northwood HQ**: the UK's principal military headquarters, home to five operational headquarters including NATO's Allied Maritime Command (MARCOM). It is located in Northwood, Middlesex.
- **HMS *Raleigh***: Located across the River Tamar from Devonport near Torpoint in Cornwall, this is a 'stone frigate' that trains about 2,000 new entry ratings a year.
- **Britannia RNC:** Located in Dartmouth in Devon, the naval college trains around 300 RN and overseas officer cadets a year.
- **HMS *Collingwood***: Multiple RN training establishments have been federated under the aegis of Collingwood, making it the largest in Western Europe. Located in Fareham, near Portsmouth, about 5,000 personnel a year pass through its doors.
- **RNAS Culdrose & RNAS Yeovilton:** Located, respectively, in Cornwall and Dorset, these two naval air stations house both front-line squadrons and training units for the FAA's helicopter force.
- **RAF Marham:** This Norfolk air base is the home of the United Kingdom's jointly operated RAF-RN F-35B strike fighters, including the FAA's 809 NAS.

CONCLUSION

Despite the siren warnings accompanying it, SDR 2025 was constrained by the government announcing only a relatively small real increase in core British defence spending. Even three percent of GDP is an aspiration rather than a firm commitment. The RN thus failed to gain a clear recommendation for an overall increase in its size; indeed, its amphibious warfare capabilities have already been greatly reduced, its forward deployed presence is declining, and the number of frigates may not recover above the 13 seen as recently as 2020. Instead, the highest priority assigned to the RN is rebuilding its ASW and underwater surveillance capabilities in northern European waters via autonomous platforms with, eventually, the prospect of more attack submarines.

Notes

1. His Majesty's Naval Service consists of the Royal Navy (including the Fleet Air Arm), Royal Marines, Royal Fleet Auxiliary, Royal Naval Reserve, Royal Marines Reserve and the Naval Careers Service. This article uses the term 'Royal Navy' as a commonly accepted title for all of these, unless a branch is explicitly named.

2. A useful summary on the current status of the RN/RFA surface fleet is provided by Louisa Brooke-Holland, *UK defence in 2025: Warships and the surface fleet* (London: House of Commons Library, May 2025), which is currently readily accessible by searching the web.

3. The £13.4 billion claim has been subject to significant challenge, as it was based on existing defence spending being frozen in cash terms. It has since been calculated that the real increase in lifting the defence budget from 2.3 percent to 2.5 percent is around £6.4 billion p.a. Obtaining consistent and comparable figures for UK defence spending is difficult given differing definitions of expenditure and the need to adjust for inflation. A good analysis of the current position is provided by another House of Commons Library publication, Niamh Foley, Louisa Brooke-Holland and Claire Mills, *UK defence spending* (London: House of Commons Library, May 2025).

4. The team's comments were reported by the BBC's Chris Mason in a report 'Starmer's 'ambition' to increase defence spending to 3% won't be easy' posted to the broadcaster's website – bbc.co.uk.news – on 2 June 2025, citing a *Daily Telegraph* article.

5. On 22 May 2025 the United Kingdom controversially signed a treaty which transferred sovereignty of the Chagos Islands in the Indian Ocean to Mauritius. It also agreed to pay an average of £101 million (c. US$137 million) a year to retain the use of a military base on the island of Diego Garcia for 99 years; a base primarily used by the United States of America.

6. See, *Strategic Defence Review: Making Britain Safer: secure at home, strong abroad*, (London: Ministry of Defence, 2025), available by searching gov.uk

7. A good overview of Project Cabot was provided by Richard Scott in, 'UK sets out Project CABOT ambition to deploy autonomous ASW screen in the North Atlantic' posted to the *Naval News* site – navalnews.com – on 18 February 2025.

8. Previous reports have suggested that the patrol vessels' overseas tasking – that also includes operations off the Falkland Islands and in the Caribbean – will be replaced by the new Type 31 frigates.

9. See, *Defence Nuclear Enterprise 2025 Annual Update to Parliament,* published on 29 May 2025 and, again, available on gov.uk.

10. The Australian Submarine Agency's site – asa.gov.au – provides regular updates on AUKUS from an official government perspective. Alternative, less positive, views are easy to find. Canada is often suggested as a potential addition to the SSN-AUKUS programme, as the design is well suited to operations under the Arctic ice. However, the Canadian Patrol Submarine Project (CPSP) is currently limited to non-nuclear solutions.

11. Some of the first detailed information on the Type 83 destroyer programme was revealed in briefings at the Navy Leaders CNE 2025 conference in Farnborough on 21 May. Amongst articles covering the briefing were Richard Scott's 'Royal Navy details ambitions for FADS programme, Type 83 destroyer' posted to the *Naval News* site on 5 June 2025 and 'Royal Navy presents bold ambitions for the Future Air Dominance System' posted to the Navy Lookout site – navylookout.com – on 26 May 2025. The latter, well-respected site provides a regular stream of authoritative reports on RN developments.

F 515
F515

3.1 SIGNIFICANT SHIPS

THE MİLGEM FAMILY

Spearheading Türkiye's Naval Renaissance

Author:
Devrim Yaylali

The Milgem family of warships illustrates the rise of Türkiye as a capable designer, builder and exporter of modern naval platforms.[1] What began as a national initiative to reduce dependence on foreign suppliers has grown into a strategic capability that has been spearheaded by the Turkish Navy and supported by key national industrial partners such as state-owned defence manufacturer ASFAT and security conglomerate STM. Through their efforts, the Milgem program has not only produced an indigenous fleet of surface combatants but has also enabled Türkiye to provide tailored warship solutions to countries as far afield as Malaysia, Pakistan and Ukraine. This chapter explores the evolution of the Milgem design, highlighting its application across several fleets.

BACKGROUND

The origins of many of Türkiye's current naval shipbuilding projects can be traced back to the Milgem project. In 1996, the Turkish Navy sought to procure eight corvettes to replace older coastal patrol and anti-submarine warfare (ASW) vessels. This project set the groundwork for future Turkish Navy warship development by emphasising indigenous design and national control over the programme. A senior Turkish naval officer, still in active service and who has commanded one of the ships during his career, shared the following perspective on the significance of what were to become known as the 'Ada' class corvettes, including their impact both on the Turkish Navy and the broader national defence ecosystem:

> For decades, Türkiye relied on foreign suppliers for its warships – larger frigates and destroyers were mostly US-built, while lighter units came from Germany. Today, that landscape has changed. Various derivatives of the indigenous 'Ada' class corvettes increasingly form the backbone of the new Turkish fleet, from offshore patrol vessels (OPVs) to destroyers. The design's modularity is a game-changer, allowing for the seamless integration of additional

Left: The Turkish Navy frigate *İstanbul* pictured transiting the Bosphorus Strait during the course of initial sea trials in July 2023. The lead ship of the 'İstif' class, she is the latest iteration of Türkiye's increasingly successful Milgem family of surface combatants. *(Turkish Navy)*

The 'Ada' class corvette *Burgazada* (foreground) and MEKO 200TN type frigate *Barbaros* seen exercising together in the Mediterranean in August 2020 during joint operations with the US Navy. The delivery of 'Ada' class corvettes under the Milgem national ship project marked an important first step towards reducing the Turkish Navy's previous reliance on foreign designs, such as the German MEKO type. *(US Navy)*

sensors and weapons based on a particular navy's needs. This adaptability was demonstrated during the construction of Pakistan's PNS *Babur*, which received a vertical launch system by means of an extended hull.

It once seemed a distant dream for a Turkish officer to command a nationally built warship, fully equipped to operate across all warfare domains, under the national flag. That dream is now a reality. 'Ada' class corvettes are widely acknowledged as reliable, seaworthy, and technologically advanced, with cutting-edge C4ISR systems centred on the ADVENT combat management system (CMS).

With shrinking naval manpower worldwide, 'Ada' class ships offer an efficient solution; they have nearly half the displacement and crew size of a frigate, but offer equivalent capabilities. Their multitude of integrated sensors and smart monitoring architecture reduce workload while maintaining full combat readiness. Beyond their operational value, these ships mark a milestone for Türkiye's defence industry and have already been adopted by several foreign navies.

'ADA' CLASS CORVETTES

After significant delays caused by the economic crises of the late 1990s and a subsequent abortive tender process, the Milgem programme gained traction in July 2005 when steel for the first 'Ada' class corvette was cut at what is now the ASFAT-managed Istanbul Naval Shipyard (INS).[2] This lead ship,

Kınalıada was the final Turkish member of the original 'Ada' class when commissioned in September 2019. She utilised some equipment, most importantly the Havelsan ADVENT combat management system, that was to be subsequently deployed in the following 'İstif' class frigates. *(STM)*

TCG *Heybeliada* (F511), was commissioned into the Turkish Navy on 27 September 2011. She was joined by *Büyükada* (F512) on 27 September 2013. Their sister *Burgazada* (F513) entered service on 4 November 2018 and the final unit, *Kınalıada* (F514), followed on 29 September 2019. Although initial plans envisaged transfer of production to a private shipyard after the completion of the first two ships, a variety of factors meant that all four vessels were eventually completed at INS. Similarly, the original intention to build eight corvettes was also overtaken by developments.[3]

Each 'Ada' class corvette has a full load displacement of around 2,400 tonnes, measures 99.5m in length, and utilises a stealthy hull and superstructure design to reduce radar cross-section. The ships are powered by a combined diesel and gas (CODAG) propulsion system consisting of one 25MW GE LM2500 gas turbine and two 4.3MW MTU 16V595 TE90 diesels. This arrangement enables speeds of almost 30 knots to be achieved on a two-shaft propulsion arrangement, whilst range is 3,500 nautical miles at an economical 15 knots.[4]

The main armament encompasses a 76mm Leonardo OTO Super Rapid gun, Harpoon or Atmaca anti-ship missiles, RIM-116 RAM short-range air defence missiles, and fixed lightweight torpedo launchers. The corvettes are also equipped with two Aselsan STAMP stabilised weapon stations for close-range defence. Aviation facilities include a hangar and flight deck able to support an S-70B Seahawk helicopter.

The class's advanced sensor suite includes a license-produced Thales SMART-S Mk 2 3D surveillance radar, as well as a range of locally designed equipment that includes the Mekesan TBT-01 YAKAMOS bow sonar and various other surveillance and electronic warfare systems. Weapons and sensors are integrated through an indigenous CMS; initially the G-MSYS variant of the Havelsan GENESIS system. This was superseded from build by the company's more recent ADVENT in *Kınalıada,* which undertook sea acceptance trials for this new CMS. A scalable, open architecture system, ADVENT is likely to be used across all future Turkish Navy combatants and is also being widely exported.

Physical construction work on the lead 'İstif' class frigate, *İstanbul*, commenced in January 2017 after several years of design development. This model provides a good indication of the final design, which is essentially a stretched iteration of the previous 'Ada' class retaining the same general propulsion configuration. The actual ship shows several detailed differences from the model. *(STM)*

'İSTİF' CLASS FRIGATES

It is possible to argue that the Turkish Navy's long-term goal for the Milgem project was ultimately to produce an indigenous frigate. However, launching a domestically-built frigate programme would have been highly ambitious for a country with no prior experience in designing and constructing warships using indigenous resources. Instead, the programme began with the more modest and feasible 'Ada' class corvettes. Their successful completion laid a strong foundation for the development of larger, more capable warships in the form of the 'İstif' class frigates. This ambition reached fruition with the delivery of TCG *İstanbul* (F515), the lead ship of the class, in January 2024.

In another sign of progress, the design and construction framework initially intended for the 'Ada' class – involving the transfer of production to private shipyards after the prototype was completed – was actually applied to the 'İstif' class. Accordingly, the first ship was built at INS while the remaining seven vessels have been ordered from the TAIS Shipyards consortium comprising Anadolu Shipyard (three units), Sefine Shipyard (two units), and Sedef Shipyard (two units). Under an agreement signed in April 2019, STM is undertaking oversight of the overall programme as prime contractor.

Programme Status: Construction of *İstanbul* began in January 2017 with a first steel-cutting ceremony. She was launched in January 2021, starting sea trials in June 2023 prior to her January 2024 delivery.

In December 2022, Türkiye's Defence Industry Executive Committee authorised the construction of three additional 'İstif' class frigates. Work on the contract commenced in 2023, and construction of these series-production ships is progressing steadily. The most advanced of these, *İzmir* and *İzmit*, were both launched in January 2025 from, respectively, the Anadolu and Sedef yards.

In January 2024, the committee approved four more 'İstif' class ships. While specific details have not been released, it is expected that these vessels will be optimised for ASW and will incorporate the DÜFAS low-frequency towed sonar system developed by Aselsan.

Another view of *İstanbul* on sea trials in July 2023. She commenced her maiden voyage from Istanbul Naval Shipyard on 20 June 2023 and was subsequently commissioned on 19 January 2024. Some items of electronic equipment had not yet been installed at this stage. Seven additional members of the class have been ordered. *(Turkish Navy)*

Platform Description: *İstanbul* is 113.2m long, 14.4m in beam, and has a draft of 4.1m. Her full-load displacement is approximately 3,000 tonnes. Core complement is 112 but she can accommodate 144 personnel. Full technical details are provided in Table 3.1.1.

While their overall design resembles the preceding 'Ada' class, the 'İstif' class frigates are larger and incorporate several structural differences. These include an extended forecastle to accommodate the indigenous MIDLAS vertical launch system (VLS) between the bridge and main gun. The main mast houses multiple antennas, including those for the ARES 2-N electronic support measures (ESM) system carried over from the previous ships. Additional short masts fore and aft of the funnel carry supplementary antennas and shield against heat from exhaust. Other distinguishing features include the aft-facing fire-control radar and the prominent Gökdeniz CIWS turret mounted on the hangar roof.

Propulsion and Performance: The 'İstif' class retains broadly the same propulsion arrangement as the 'Ada' class.[5] Two shafts fitted with controllable-pitch propellers are powered by two 4.3MW MTU 20V 4000 M93L diesel engines and one 23MW GE LM2500 gas turbine in a CODAG configuration, generating a combined 32MW. Maximum speed is 29 knots and range 4,000 nautical miles at 18 knots, with up to 5,700 nautical miles being achievable at an economical 14 knots. The ships can remain fully operational up to Sea State 5 and have a minimum endurance of 15 days without replenishment.

Weapons*:* *İstanbul*'s main gun is a 76mm/62 calibre OTO mounting located in the 'A' position.[6] An indigenous 16-cell MİDLAS vertical launching system comprising two eight cell modules is positioned immediately aft, between the gun and the bridge. This was substituted for the US-manufactured Mk 41 VLS that was incorporated in the vessels' initial design when delays in American export approval drove Türkiye to develop its own launcher, thereby impacting the overall project timeline.[7] The VLS is equipped with the locally-produced Hisar D air defence missile, which is the class's primary air defence weapon. The Hisar D RF missile is the naval version of the Hisar O air defence missile developed for the Turkish Land Forces, with the imaging IR seeker of the original missile being

Displacing approximately 3,000 tonnes and some 113m in length, the 'İstif' class frigates are significantly larger ships than their 2,400-tonne 'Ada' class predecessors. In spite of having a comparable power output, their finer lines mean that they have a roughly equivalent top speed. In addition to being more powerfully armed than the earlier class, they have seen considerably increased utilisation of indigenous equipment. These two photographs of *İstanbul* were taken off her namesake city on 2 March 2024. *(Devrim Yaylali)*

replaced with an active RF seeker in the naval derivative. The missile has a dual-pulse engine and has been reported to have an approximate 25km range. It was first test launched from *İstanbul* in March 2024.

Ships of the class are equipped with an Aselsan Gökdeniz close-in weapons system (CIWS) positioned atop the hanger for close range defence. This unmanned mounting is fitted with twin 35mm KDC-02 autocannons, capable of firing 1,100 rounds per minute. It integrates a CENK 200-N surveillance radar, a fire-control radar, and electro-optical sensors. Gökdeniz can engage aerial targets up to 4 kilometres away and intercept incoming missiles at distances of up to 2.5km. The system is supplemented by two Aselsan STOP remotely-controlled weapon stations (RCWS); located to port and starboard abreast the funnel. Each is armed with a 25mm KBA cannon with a firing rate of 450–600 rounds per minute.

The class's primary offensive armament consists of 16 Roketsan Atmaca anti-ship missiles housed between the main mast and funnel. The launchers are enclosed in panels to protect them from environmental conditions and minimise radar signature. Each missile is 5.2m long, weighs 750kg, and carries a 220kg warhead. Guidance is provided by radar and infrared seekers, along with inertial navigation, GPS, and altimeter systems. Their maximum range is 250km.

The frigates are equipped with two fixed twin torpedo tubes to combat underwater threats. The 324mm tubes of can fire US Navy Mk 46 and Mk 54 lightweight torpedoes, as well as the newly developed indigenous Roketsan Orka weapon. There is also Aselsan Hızır torpedo counter measures system onboard each vessel. This system utilises an active array launched from the stern to listen for incoming torpedoes and includes a towed decoy. There are also

Table 3.1.1.

İSTANBUL PRINCIPAL PARTICULARS

Building Information:	
Laid Down:	3 July 2017[1] Launched: 23 January 2021 Commissioned: 19 January 2024
Builders:	Istanbul Naval Shipyard
Dimensions:	
Displacement:	3,000 tonnes full load displacement.
Overall Hull Dimensions:	113.2m x 14.4m x 4.1m
Equipment:	
Armament:	4 x quad launchers for Roketsan Atmaca surface-to-surface missiles. 2 x 8-cell MİDLAS vertical launchers for Hisar D RF surface-to-air missiles. 1 x 76mm OTO gun. 1 x twin 35mm Aselsan Gökdeniz CIWS. 2 x 25mm Aselsan STOP mountings. 2 x twin 324mm Zıpkın anti-submarine torpedo tubes.
Aircraft:	1 x S-70B Seahawk.
Countermeasures:	Include Aselsan ARES-2N ESM system & Aselsan Hızır torpedo defence system.
Principal Sensors:	1 x Aselsan CENK 400-N air/surface-search radar. 1 x Aselsan ALPER LPI intercept navigation radar. 2 x navigation radars. 2 x Aselsan Akrep 300-N fire control directors. 1 x Aselsan Denizgözü Ahtapot electro-optical surveillance tracker. 1 x Aselsan FERSAH 100-N/MF hull mounted sonar.
Combat System:	Havelsan ADVENT integrated combat management system.
Propulsion Systems:	
Machinery:	CODAG. 2 x MTU 20V 4000 M93L diesels each rated at 4.3MW 1 x GE LM-2500 gas turbine rated at 23MW. 2 shafts.
Speed:	Designed speed is 29 knots in full CODAG configuration. Range is 5,700 nautical miles at 14 knots.
Other Details:	
Complement:	Normal crew is 112. There are sufficient berths for up to 144 personnel.
Class:	One ship – *İstanbul* (F515) – completed. Seven further ships ordered, of which *İzmir* (F516) and *İzmit* (F517) had been launched as of mid-2025. *İçel* (F518), *Akdeniz* (F519), *Karadeniz* (F520), *Ege* (F521) and *Marmara* (F522) are the names of the other ships.

Notes

1. First steel was cut on 19 January 2017

two countermeasures launchers located at either side of the funnel to fire expendable decoys.

The 'İstif' class frigates also incorporate a helicopter hangar and flight deck capable of supporting a 10-tonne Sea Hawk S-70B, as well as future uncrewed aerial vehicles (UAVs). Helicopter operations can be carried out by day and night and be sustained in meteorological conditions up to Sea State 4. Additional ammunition and JP-5 fuel stowage are provided to support shipboard aviation.

Sensors: The main surveillance radar is Aselsan's CENK 400-N. Located on top of the forward mast, CENK 400-N is an active electronically-scanned array (AESA) operating in the S band (NATO E/F bands). It incorporates an integrated IFF interrogator and provides 70-degree elevation coverage. The single array rotates at 30 RPM, can track up to 1,000 targets out to a reported instrumented range of 400km, and encompasses electronic counter-countermeasures (ECCM) functions and jammer detection. The system is liquid-cooled, weighing less than 1,750kg above deck.

Fire control functions are provided by Aselsan's Akrep 300-N radar, which the manufacturer claims delivers 'high accuracy and high update rate 3D target track data to meet the track quality requirements of fire control systems'.[8] The system is equipped with a complementary electro-optical (E/O) suite that includes an infrared (IR) camera, a daylight TV camera, and a laser rangefinder. The radar and E/O suite can operate together or independently, depending on mission requirements. Each frigate is equipped with two of these radars; one forward above the bridge and one on a superstructure mast aft of the funnel.

Operating in both the X and Ka bands (NATO I/J and K bands), Akrep 300-N provides accurate range and angular data. It is equipped with ECCM

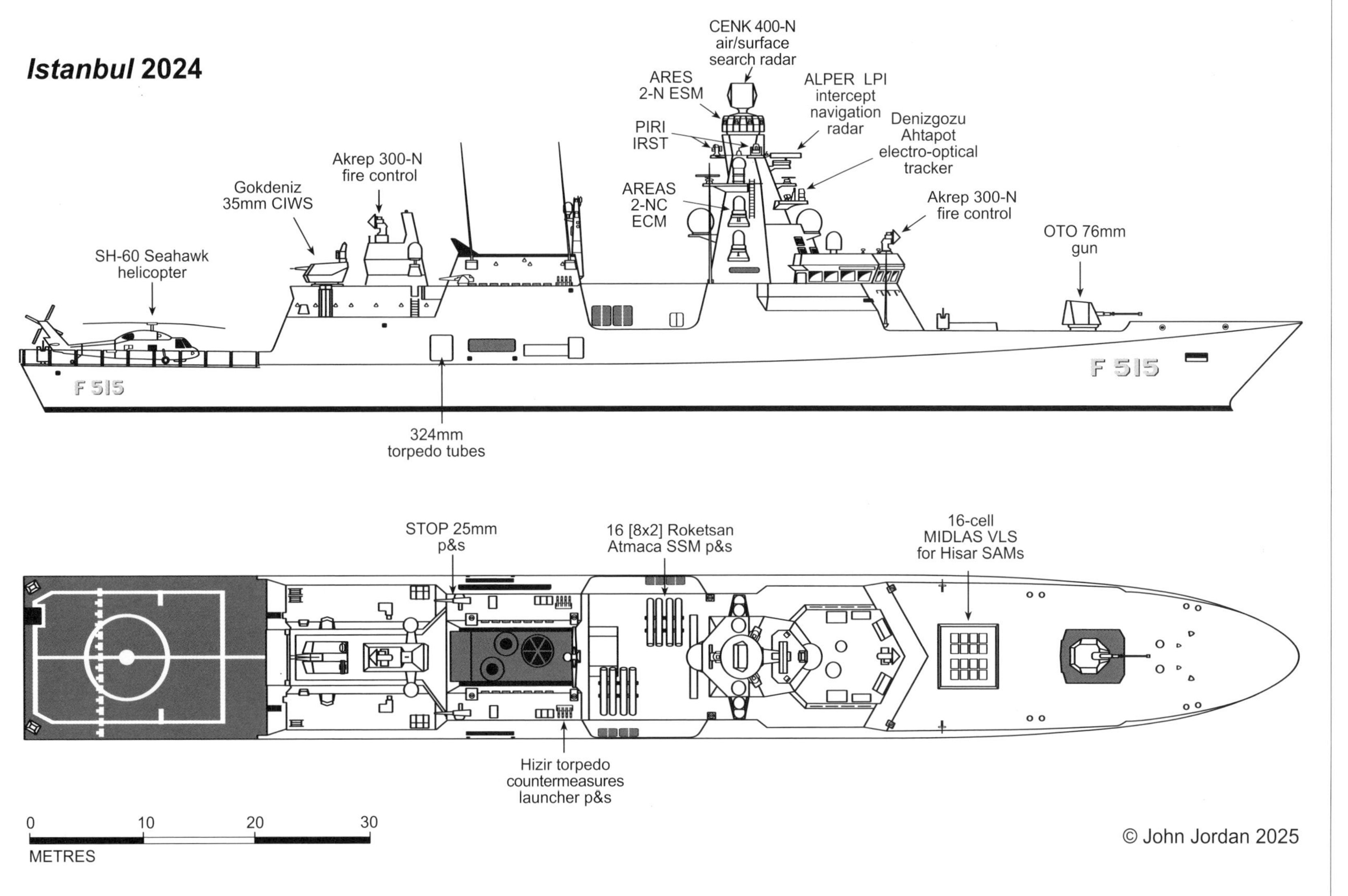

functions and supports a range of fire-control applications, including both pre-action and in-action calibration. Additional features include track splitting, weapon launch alerts, operator-selectable wartime waveforms and frequencies, RF/laser prohibit zones, and an interface compatible with electronic support measures and laser warning systems. The system also includes infrastructure for X band continuous wave illumination to support semi-active missile guidance.

Additional onboard sensors include the Aselsan ALPER LPI intercept navigation radar. Operating in the X band, this is a low power, low-probability-of-intercept radar that can detect surface targets in all weather conditions up to a distance of around 65km. Amongst other significant equipment are the company's PİRİ infrared search and track (IRST) system and its Denizgözü Ahtapot electro-optical reconnaissance, surveillance and targeting system. Specifically designed for naval applications, the latter includes a high-performance infra-red camera,

This direct stern view of *İstanbul* provides a particularly good view of her Aselsan Gökdeniz CIWS with its twin 35mm KDC-02 cannon and integrated radar and electro-optical systems. Immediately forward and above is one of the two Aselsan Akrep 300-N fire-control radars. The two STOP RWS, each armed with a single 25mm KBA cannon, can be seen to port and starboard. Note also the positions for manually-operated light machine guns on either side of the hangar deck. *(Devrim Yaylali)*

Many of *İstanbul*'s electronic systems are pictured in this view of her forward mast. Amongst the most significant is Aselsan's CENK 400-N air and surface radar, which is located at the masthead. Some of the eight main antennas for the company's ARES 2-N series ESM system are positioned immediately below. Two of the three units that form the PİRİ infrared search and track (IRST) system can be seen on the platforms a level below. An ALPER LPI intercept navigation radar on a platform forward of the mast is largely obscured. The domed antennas located to either side of the lower mast structure belong to AREAS-2NC ECM jamming system. *(Devrim Yaylali)*

a full HD TV camera, a shortwave infrared (SWIR) camera, and an eye-safe laser rangefinder. The ships are also fitted with LİAS 200-D laser warning receivers (LWRs). These are improved over the LWRs in the 'Ada' class, having two sets of sensors instead of one.

Like their 'Ada' class counterparts, the 'İstif' class frigates are equipped with an Aselsan ARES 2-N series ESM system. This system, incorporating eight prominent antennas mounted below the CENK 400-N radar, provides 360-degree coverage. It can detect, intercept, classify, and track electromagnetic emissions in the 2-18 GHz frequency range. By analysing the received signals, the system determines their characteristics and origin, assisting operators in emitter classification and identification. This capability is supplemented by Aselsan's AREAS-2NC ECM system, which is carried in radome-like antennas on either side of the forward mast. This is described as a modular electronic attack system designed to deliver jamming and deception capabilities in dynamic maritime threat environments. It employs directional radio frequency radiation and a high-power solid-state amplifier to execute both noise and deceptive jamming

The 'İstif' class is fitted with Aselsan FERSAH 100-N/MF hull-mounted sonar to detect underwater threats. This is described by the manufacturer as a mid-frequency anti-submarine sonar with high source level and array directivity. The system has active and passive ASW, as well as mine-like object avoidance (MAS), modes.

All weapons and sensors are integrated through the Havelsan ADVENT (*Ağ Destekli Veri Entegre Savas Yönetim Sistemi*) combat management system. ADVENT is described as a network-centric command and control platform, fully compliant with NATO standards. A significant evolution from the G-MSYS CMS used in 'Ada' class corvettes, ADVENT incorporates full data link support, enhanced situational awareness, support for joint engagements, and multi-domain operational capabilities. It is designed to leverage the capabilities of all platforms involved in a mission, thereby facilitating real-time interoperability across task forces.

This general view of *İstanbul* at anchor in August 2024 provides a good perspective of her overall arrangement. In addition to the visually apparent upgrades over the 'Ada' class, all the 'İstif' class frigates will benefit from the latest ADVENT iteration of Havelsan's combat management systems, which are also gaining considerable export success. *(Devrim Yaylali)*

The two 'Hisar' class offshore patrol vessels *Akhisar* and *Koçhisar* under construction at Istanbul Naval Shipyard in 2023. The two vessels were launched in an unusual joint ceremony on 23 September 2023. The 'Hisar' class vessels are based on the 'Ada' class hull design but use a different propulsion system and a 'fitted for but not with' equipment approach. *(ASFAT)*

'HİSAR' CLASS OFFSHORE PATROL VESSELS

The 'Hisar' class offshore patrol vessels are the most recent iteration of the Milgem family destined for Turkish Navy service. The project is being led by ASFAT under a contract signed in November 2020 and aims to enhance the Turkish Navy's patrol and security capabilities through the construction of modern and cost-effective constabulary warships. The OPVs are based on a modified Milgem 'Ada' class corvette hull that has been tailored for patrol missions. Up to ten units are planned.

Programme Status: ASFAT performed a first steel cutting ceremony for the lead ship of the class, TCG *Akhisar*, at INS in August 2021. Work commenced on a sister, *Koçhisar*, in November 2022. The two vessels were launched on the same day on 23 September 2023 in a joint ceremony that was claimed to be a first for Turkish shipbuilding. *Akhisar* subsequently commenced sea trials at the end of 2024 prior to expected delivery in 2025. A tight project schedule influenced ASFAT to rethink previous construction processes. As a result, the ships are the first Turkish warships built with pre-outfitted modules, with cableways, piping and systems installed inside modules before assembly on the slipway. This is an advance over previous programmes, where internal systems were largely installed after hull integration.

A defining feature of the 'Hisar' class is its 'fitted for but not with' design. Accordingly, the ships are configured to accommodate systems such as the Atmaca anti-ship missile, Gökdeniz CIWS, ASW rockets, and a specially-developed four-cell module for the Hisar air defence missile if required with only minimal modification. When fully outfitted with this equipment, they could function as light corvettes. The ships are equipped with the ADVENT CMS, which can readily integrate core and optional systems.

Platform Description: The 'Hisar' class vessels displace 2,300 tonnes and have a length of 99.6m and a beam of 14.4m. They retain the overall hull design and general layout of the 'Ada' class but have a reconfigured superstructure and mast layout, as well as enhancements to their internal arrangement. They are principally designed for constabulary intelligence surveillance and reconnaissance (ISR) and security operations. They can also support a range of secondary missions that extend to maritime interdiction and amphibious operations. There is sufficient accommodation for 104 personnel.

Propulsion and Performance: A notable difference from other Milgem variants is the class's use of a combined diesel-electric or diesel (CODELOD) propulsion system. This incorporates two MAN 20V175D diesels (each producing 3.7MW) and a domestically-produced electrical motor (rated at 1MW) on each of two shafts. The motors are powered by the ship's four diesel generators via its electrical distribution system. This allows the vessel to cruise efficiently at lower speeds, also reducing its acoustic signature. The main diesels can be used when higher speeds of up to 24 knots are required. It is also possible to use the electrical motors as generators via a power take-off (PTO) arrangement. The 'Hisar' class are the first Turkish Navy ships that use such an electrical propulsion system. Operational range is some 4,500 nautical miles at economical speed, whilst endurance is 21 days.

Weapons and Sensors: The class's main gun is a MKE-manufactured Denizhan 76/62mm mounting, sometimes also referred to as the National Naval Gun. It has an effective range of 16km with standard ammunition, extendable to 20km with advanced rounds, and an elevation range of -15° to +85°. It can fire up to 80 rounds per minute. The gun is similar to the ubiquitous OTO 76mm mountings that equip many Turkish warships, with *Akhisar* being the first ship that the new mounting has been installed in from build. The 'Hisar' class is also the launch platform for the Unirobotics Targan RCWS.

The class's hangar and flight deck can support one S-70B Seahawk helicopter.

Primary radar coverage is provided by the Aselsan CENK 100-N fixed-face AESA radar. Operating in the X band, it is optimised for short-range surveillance and fire control, with specific capabilities for detecting small, low radar cross-section (RCS) threats such as UAVs. Electronic warfare is managed by TÜBİTAK's Yelkovan ESM system. Specifically developed for the 'Hisar' class, it features a modular, lightweight design and a digital architecture integrating both wideband and narrowband receivers. It enables precise direction finding and parameter extraction in dense RF environments.

TCG *UFUK*

Ufuk is a one of its kind among the ships that are based on the Milgem design. It traces its origins to a contract for the construction of a test and training ship that was signed with STM – as main contractor – in December 2016. Actual construction was allocated to the privately-owned Istanbul Shipyard, a subsidiary of Türkiye's SNR Holding, which commenced work on the project in 2017.

The production of a test and training ship made sense given that the Turkish defence industry is developing a wide array of naval weapons, sensors and other systems which would benefit from a dedicated platform for testing and evaluation. However, during his speech at the ship's launching ceremony on 9 February 2019, Turkish President Recep Tayyip Erdoğan, stated that *Ufuk* would serve as the 'eyes and ears' of the nation at sea, contributing to early warning and surveillance activities across the Mediterranean, Aegean and Black Seas. The speech was the first official indication that *Ufuk* was not merely a test and training ship but the first domestically-built intelligence-gathering ship intended for the Turkish Navy.

Ufuk is based on the 'Ada' class hull and has similar dimensions to these ships. Her displacement is approximately 2,250 tonnes. Further details are provided in Table 3.1.2.

The ship is driven by two MTU 20V 4000 M93L diesels of the same type found in the 'İstif' class. Maximum speed is some 18 knots and endurance 45 days. The design evidences considerable attention to stealth; for example, the four 750kW diesel-generators that produce the vessel's electrical power are installed within an acoustic housing provided by the Turkish company İsbir.

The most sensitive equipment aboard *Ufuk* is her intelligence-gathering equipment. This is largely provided by Aselsan and mostly located on the forward mast. The shape of the mast is formed by the antennae for ESM electronic countermeasures

The intelligence-gathering ship *Ufuk* pictured in December 2021 during the final stages of her trials. She was commissioned on 14 January 2022. Like the 'Hisar' class, she shares the same hull and basic configuration of the 'Ada' class but uses a different propulsion system. Whilst her basic silhouette is similar to that of the corvettes, her various communications arrays give her a different appearance. *(Devrim Yaylali)*

This photograph of *Ufuk* was taken in June 2022 a few months after she had entered service. The ship is unarmed except for light weapons, acting as a platform for an array of sensitive intelligence-gathering equipment manufactured largely by Aselsan. The surveillance radar on the stub mainmast atop the aft superstructure is a Terma Scanter 6002. *(Devrim Yaylali)*

and the ship's signals intelligence and communications intelligence systems. There are also two Denizgözü Ahtapot surveillance systems on this mast. The main surveillance radar is Terma's Scanter 6002, which is located on a stub mast at the aft end of the ship's superstructure. The ship is only armed with small calibre machine guns for close range self-protection. There is also a landing deck that can support a medium-sized helicopter but no hangar.

Ufuk formally entered into service with the Turkish Navy on 14 January 2022.

BABUR CLASS CORVETTES (PAKISTAN)

The considerable export success that is now being achieved by the Milgem family commenced in July 2018, when a contract for four corvettes was signed between Pakistan's Ministry of Defence Production and ASFAT. This milestone built upon a history of naval cooperation between Türkiye and Pakistan, including the construction of the logistical support ship PNS *Moawin* and the modernisation of the country's 'Agosta 90B' submarines. At the time, the agreement represented Türkiye's largest defence export contract with an estimated value of c. US$1.5 billion. The contract became effective on 11 March 2019, encompassing the construction of two ships in Türkiye and two in Pakistan over a six-year period.

Programme Status: Construction of the *Babur* class programme got underway on 29 September 2019, when steel was cut for the lead ship, PNS *Babur*, at INS. Her keel was laid on 4 June 2020 and she was launched on 15 August 2021. Delivered to the

This photograph of *Babur* was taken around the time of her delivery voyage to Pakistan. From this angle, the Pakistan Navy ship is difficult to distinguish from her Turkish Navy counterparts, although the 'mushroom heads' of her forward VLS installation are a notable point of detail. *(Pakistan Navy)*

Pakistan Navy in September 2023, she underwent a significant period of trials and training in Turkish waters before arriving in Pakistan in June 2024. She was formally inducted into Pakistan's fleet on 6 September that year.

The second vessel of the class, named *Badr*, was laid down on 25 October 2020 at Karachi Shipyard & Engineering Works (KSEW), from where she was launched on 20 May 2022. Her delivery is expected during the coming twelve months following completion of final outfitting and sea trials. Within this timeframe, she will be joined by the third ship, *Khaibar*, which was laid down at INS on 30 April 2021 and launched on 25 November 2022. The keel of the final ship, *Tariq*, was laid at KSEW on 5 November 2021 prior to her launch on 2 August 2023. The ship is also in the outfitting phase, with delivery scheduled for 2026.

The Pakistani Milgem project also includes a collaborative design initiative. As part of this offset agreement, ASFAT's design office and the Pakistan Navy's Platform Design Division have begun the joint development of a next-generation frigate to meet the Pakistan Navy's evolving operational requirements under a transfer of technology deal. These ships will be known as the 'Jinnah' class in the Pakistan Navy.

Platform Description: The *Babur* class corvettes share a comparable silhouette with the 'Ada' class. However, they have been 'stretched' by nearly 9m, ostensibly to accommodate a VLS for air defence missiles.[9] Accordingly, the ships have a length of 108.2m, a slightly increased beam of 18.8m and a

This profile view of *Babur* taken whilst she was undertaking post-delivery working-up in April 2024 gives an impression of the 'stretched' nature of her design compared with the original 'Ada' class. Although this has been reported as being due to a decision to install the CAMM-ER based Albatros NG surface-to-air missile system forward of her bridge, her bridge structure and, particularly, amidships section have also been extended to meet Pakistan Navy requirements. Otherwise, her outfit of sensors has much in common with that which equips vessels of the Turkish Navy's Milgem series. *(Devrim Yaylali)*

draft of 4.1m. Their full load displacement is approximately 2,950 tonnes.

Propulsion and Performance: The ships have a similar combined diesel and gas (CODAG) propulsion system to that used in the 'Ada' and 'İstif' classes. The *Babur* class's additional length likely compensates for the ships' higher displacement, producing a broadly equivalent top speed and endurance to that found in the 'Ada' class.

Weapons and Sensors: The *Babur* class utilise a Leonardo OTO 76mm/62 mounting equivalent to that found in most of the Milgem series vessels. Immediately aft are two groups of sextuple vertical launchers for the MDBA Albatros NG surface-to-air

Table 3.1.2: 'ADA' CLASS COMPARISONS

VARIANT	'ADA' TN (*HEYBELIADA*)	'ADA' PN (*BABUR*)	*UFUK*
Displacement:	2,400 tonnes	2,950 tonnes	2,250 tonnes
Dimensions:	99.5m x 14.4m x 3.6m	108.2m x 14.8m x 4.1m	99.5m x 14.4m x 3.6m
Propulsion:	CODAG, 32 MW combined, c. 29 knots	CODAG, 32MW combined, c. 26 knots +	Diesel, 9MW, c. 18 knots
Principal Armament:	1 x 76mm OTO gun, 2 x 12.7mm RWS	1 x 76mm OTO gun, 2 x 25mm RWS	Light weapons only
	1 x RAM SAM	12 x Albatros NG SAM	Helicopter deck only
	8 x Harpoon/Atmaca SSM	6 x Harbah SSM	Intelligence gathering equipment
	2 x twin 324mm torpedo tubes	2 x triple 324mm torpedo tubes	
	Helicopter deck and hangar	Helicopter deck and hangar	
Principal Sensors:	1 x search, 1 x fire control, 1 x sonar	1 x search, 1 x fire control, 1 x sonar	1 x search
Crew:	94 core	Not known	Up to 110
Number of Vessels:	4	1	1

missile system, which is based on the CAMM-ER missile. The system has an effective range of around 40km and incorporates a soft-launch design that minimises the need for deck penetration and reduces structural stress. These weapons are supplemented by two Aselsan 25mm STOP RCWS located to either side of the funnel.[10]

It is believed that the class's primary offensive armament will comprise six Pakistan-manufactured Harbah anti-ship cruise missiles.[11] Each missile is 6.8m long, 0.5m in diameter, and weighs about 1,350kg. Their launch canisters will be installed between the forward superstructure and the funnels. The missiles have an estimated range of 280km and are capable of engaging both land and sea targets.

Anti-submarine warfare armament is based on two lightweight 324mm torpedo launchers. As in the 'Ada' and 'İstif' classes, there is a flight deck and hangar sized to sustain medium helicopter operations. This will most likely be the Harbin Z-9 in the first instance.

The outfit of sensors has much in common with that which equips vessels of the Turkish Navy's Milgem series. For example, the main surveillance radar is the Thales SMART-S Mk 2 (manufactured under licence by Aselsan) used in the 'Ada' class. Operating in the S band, it can detect surface targets up to 80km away and air targets up to 250km away. The class's Yakamos sonar system – operating in both active and passive modes and capable of detecting and tracking submarines, torpedoes and other underwater threats – is also common with the 'Ada' class corvettes, whilst their Aselsan Hızır torpedo countermeasures system equips some of the later members of the 'Ada' class, as well as *İstanbul*. The use of these, and other, systems vividly demonstrate the value of the wider Milgem project to the Turkish naval sector.

There is some use of equipment sourced from Pakistan industry. For example, the electro-optical sensors located to each side of the bridge's roof are navalised versions of the 'stabilised optical tracker system' manufactured by Dyntek Engineering, a state-owned entity based in Rawalpindi, Pakistan. The company claims that the system is capable of automated detection and tracking of aerial and surface targets, and is fitted with high-resolution infrared and colour cameras. It is said to possess anti-jamming capability due to its passive sensors and can operate effectively both day and night. It appears

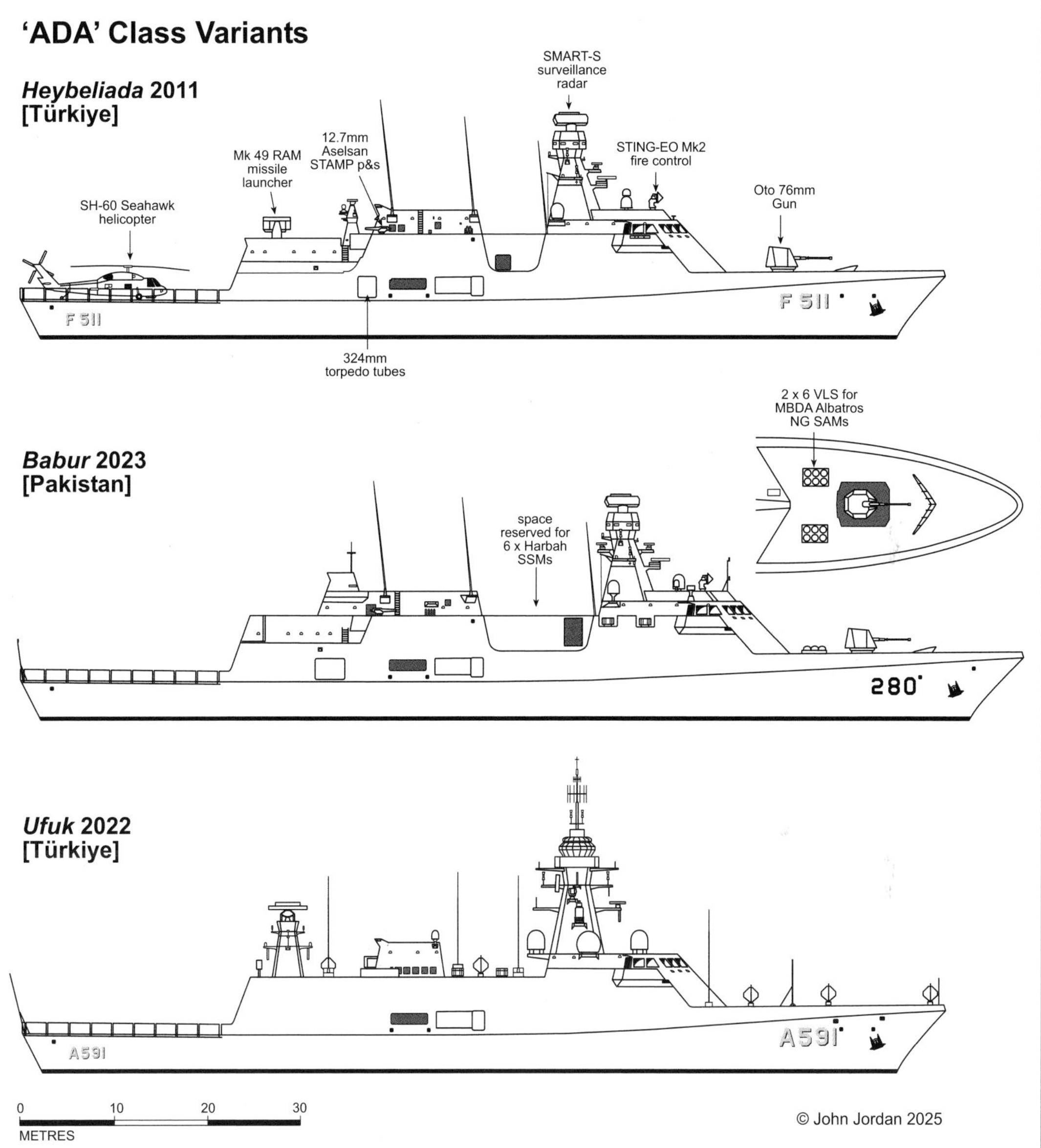

that only the casing of the system will differ between domains, with minimal engineering changes involved.

Combat management is undertaken by the ADVENT CMS that has also been previously described.

MAZEPA CLASS CORVETTES (UKRAINE)

The Milgem programme's expansion to serve Ukraine was formalised in December 2020, when Türkiye and Ukraine signed a bilateral agreement for the co-production of 'Ada' class corvettes and unmanned aerial vehicles. This collaboration was intended to enhance the capabilities of the Ukrainian Navy, which had suffered a period of decline following Russia's seizure of Crimea and years of underinvestment.

Initially, four corvettes were planned. The first two were to be constructed in Türkiye, while the remaining two were to be built in Ukraine. The Okean Shipyard in Mykolaiv was selected to build the second batch of ships, as well as for final outfit-

Hetman Ivan Mazepa is the first of what was originally intended to be four 'Ada' type corvettes ordered for the Ukrainian Navy as part of efforts to rebuild its capacity after Russia's annexation of Crimea in 2014. The subsequent Russo-Ukraine War disrupted the programme but the construction of two vessels in Türkiye's has continued. The lead ship was launched by Ukrainian First Lady Olena Zelenska from RMK Marine in Tuzla, Istanbul on 2 October 2022, when these photographs were taken. *(President of Ukraine)*

ting of the first pair. However, the contract signed in December 2020 was only for one frigate. Later a contract amendment was made to add the second ship. The Russian invasion of Ukraine in February 2022 has put paid to construction of the planned Ukrainian-assembled ships, at least for the time being.

Programme Status: STM is designated as the lead contractor for the Ukrainian corvettes. Construction of the first ship is being carried out by RMK Marine in Tuzla, Istanbul. First steel cutting for this lead ship, later named *Hetman Ivan Mazepa*, took place in early 2021, and her keel was laid in September of the same year. Despite Russia's full-scale invasion of Ukraine in February 2022, construction work continued. *Hetman Ivan Mazepa* was subsequently launched in Istanbul on 2 October 2022 during a ceremony attended by Ukrainian First Lady Olena Zelenska and senior defence officials. On the same day, first steel cutting for the second vessel, *Hetman Ivan Vyhovskyi*, also took place. This second unit is being built at the privately-owned Istanbul Shipyard and was launched on 1 August 2024.

STM delivered the first ship in March 2025, with potential deployment in the Black Sea as soon as regional security conditions allow. As of mid-2025, both vessels remained in Türkiye for continued outfitting and integration work.

Design Description: The Ukrainian corvettes closely resemble the original 'Ada' class design, with equivalent hull dimensions and a shared CODAG propulsion architecture. There is also considerable overlap in terms of their equipment. This description therefore focuses on areas where there are significant differences.

The corvettes are fitted with MBDA VL MICA missiles for primary air defence. This compact, vertically launched naval air defence system can engage short to medium range threats. The MICA missile offers two seeker options – imaging infrared (IR) or active radar (RF) – providing flexibility against aircraft, anti-ship missiles, and guided munitions. The system is integrated with the ship's combat management system, eliminating the need for a dedicated fire-control system. Eight missiles are housed in two groups of four launchers positioned on either side of the hangar, just behind the funnel. In the Turkish and Pakistani Milgem type ships, this area is reserved for replenishment at sea. In another change to the original 'Ada' class configuration, VL MICA is supplemented by an Aselsan Gökdeniz CIWS on the centreline at the aft end of the hangar.

The main offensive weapons that will be carried by the Ukrainian ships have not been made public. When the project was first announced, three candidates were mentioned: Ukraine's own Neptune anti-ship missile, the US-made Harpoon and Turkish Atmaca anti-ship missiles. Fitting Harpoon and Atmaca to the ships and integrating them into the combat management system would be relatively easy as both missiles are used in the Turkish 'Ada' class corvettes. The position with respect to Neptune is a little more uncertain, although the flexibility of the ADVENT CMS used in the ships suggests that integration would not be problematic and this may be the most likely choice. The fact that weapons systems such as Albatros NG and VL MICA have already been integrated with ADVENT suggests the technical maturity of the CMS in this regard.

LITTORAL MISSION SHIPS (MALAYSIA)

Malaysia's selection of the 'Ada' design as the basis for Batch II of its Littoral Mission Ship programme is the Milgem family's latest export success. The signing ceremony for a 'MoU on G2G Procurement for Defence Products between Türkiye and Malaysia' and a 'Handing-over Ceremony for the LoA (Letter of Acceptance) of the Littoral Mission Ship (LMS) Batch 2 Project' were held in Ankara in June 2024. The programme encompasses three corvette-type vessels based on the original 'Ada' class.

Programme Status: As is the case for the Ukrainian corvettes, oversight of the Malaysian programme is being undertaken by STM. Physical construction has been allocated to the privately-owned Istanbul Shipyard, which previously built *Ufuk*. Steel for the lead vessel was cut in December 2024 and was followed by a keel laying ceremony on 9 April 2025. Under a tight construction schedule, all three vessels are scheduled for completion by the end of 2027.

Design Description: The LMS Batch 2 vessels share their hull form and dimensions with other members of the 'Ada' class. Displacement is anticipated to be in the region of 2,500 tonnes. Although there will be other significant similarities with the existing vessels, open source information also indicates that there will also be some important differences.

One notable alteration is the use of combined

Ukrainian President Volodymyr Zelenskyy (centre) pictured aboard the corvette *Hetman Ivan Mazepa* in March 2024 during a visit to inspect progress with the new vessel. The corvette subsequently commenced sea trials in the Sea of Marmara in May 2024 prior to delivery in March 2025. Her arrival in home waters inevitably depends on the evolution of the conflict in Ukraine. *(President of Ukraine)*

The Royal Malaysian Navy became the latest to acquire ships from the Milgem family when contracts were signed for the acquisition of three variations of the 'Ada' class to meet the requirements of its Littoral Mission Ship Batch 2 project. Details of the programme that are in the public domain suggest that the new vessels will be similar in dimensions to the Turkish ships, such as *Büyükada* – the second 'Ada' to be completed – photographed here shortly before her delivery in 2013. However, Malaysia has requested significant alterations, including use of all-diesel propulsion and installation of the South Korean K-SAAM surface-to-air missile system. *(STM)*

diesel and diesel (CODAD) propulsion. The Malaysia ships will be equipped with four diesel engines linked via two reduction gears to twin shaft lines. This configuration will enable a maximum speed of over 26 knots to be achieved, while also permitting an efficient cruising speed of 14 knots. The vessels will have a range exceeding 4,000 nautical miles at cruising speed, ensuring good operational endurance.

Weapons and sensors will be derived from both Turkish and international sources. The ships retain the 76mm gun and Atmaca anti-ship missiles of the Turkish ships but will incorporate several new systems. Most significantly, the main air defence weapon will be South Korean Haegung air defence missile produced by LIG Nex1. This is sometimes also referred to as K-SAAM. This missile measures 3.1 metres in length and reaches a top speed of Mach 2 with a maximum range of 20 kilometres. Developed to replace the American-made RIM-116 Rolling Airframe Missile (RAM) on South Korean naval vessels, the Haegung enhances close range defence capabilities. It utilises dual-mode seekers, combining radio frequency (RF) and infrared imaging (IIR), to operate effectively in all weather conditions. The location of these missiles in the Malaysian corvettes will be similar to that seen in the

Table 3.1.3: MİLGEM SERIES LIST

SHIP	PENNANT	FIRST STEEL CUT	LAUNCHED	COMMISSIONED	BUILDER
TURKISH NAVY					
'Ada' (*Heybeliada*) class					
Heybeliada	F511	26 July 2005	27 September 2008	27 September 2011	INS
Büyükada	F512	27 September 2008	27 September 2011	27 September 2013	INS
Burgazada	F513	27 September 2013	18 June 2016	4 November 2018	INS
Kınalıada	F514	8 October 2015	3 July 2017	29 September 2019	INS
Ufuk					
Ufuk	A591	2 May 2017	9 February 2019	14 January 2022	Istanbul
'İstif' (*İstanbul*) class					
İstanbul	F515	19 January 2017	23 January 2021	19 January 2024	INS
İzmir	F516	10 April 2023	10 January 2025	[TBA]	Anadolu
İzmit	F517	10 April 2023	11 January 2025	]TBA]	Sedef
İçel	F518	10 April 2023	[TBA]	]TBA]	Sefine
Four further ships – reportedly named *Akdeniz* (F519), *Karadeniz* (F520), *Ege* (F521) and *Marmara* (F522) – have been ordered. First steel for *Akdeniz* was cut in 2024 and her keel was laid on 17 January 2025.					
***Hisar* Class**					
Akhisar	P1220	15 August 2021	23 September 2023	[August 2025]	INS
Koçhisar	P1221	25 November 2022	23 September 2023	[March 2026]	INS
Up to eight additional ships are planned.					
EXPORT					
'Ada' PN (*Babur*) class					
Babur	280	29 September 2019	15 August 2021	23 September 2023[1]	INS
Badr	281	9 June 2020	20 May 2022	[June 2026]	KSEW
Khaibar	282	23 January 2021	25 November 2022	[September 2025]	INS
Tariq	283	15 June 2021	2 August 2023	[December 2026]	KSEW
'Ada' UN (*Mazepa*) class					
Hetman Ivan Mazepa	F211	2021[2]	2 October 2022	March 2025	RMK
Hetman Ivan Vyhovsky	F212	2 October 2022	1 August 2024	[February 2027]	Istanbul
Work commenced on the first of three 'Ada' MN class littoral mission ships ordered by Malaysia on 5 December 2024.					

Notes

1. Date delivered to the Pakistan Navy in Türkiye. Subsequently formally inducted in Pakistan on 6 September 2024.
2. Exact date of first steel cut not available but is believed to have been in the first half of 2021. Keel-laying was on 7 September 2021.
3. Dates in brackets relate to planned future timelines.

Ukrainian ships, with two VLS cells placed on either side of the ship's helicopter hangar. The Haegung missiles will be quad-packed in each launch cell, allowing up to a total of 16 missiles to be loaded across the four cells.

Close-in defence the ships will be provided by two Aselsan SMASH 30mm remote controlled RCWS. This utilises the 30mm Mk44S Bushmaster II. The gun has dual feed and can fire 200 rounds per minute. SMASH utilises the heaviest-calibre weapon amongst Aselsan's Line-up of RCWS products and this may have influenced Malaysia's selection.

Primary sensors share similarities with the 'İstif' class. The main surveillance radar will be the Aselsan CENK 400-N whilst fire control will be undertaken by the company's Akrep 300-N. Aselsan will also supply its ARES ESM system.

A noticeable omission in Malaysian warships is the sonar. This is not a Royal Malaysian Navy requirement, possibly because anti-air warfare and anti-surface warfare capabilities have been accorded a higher priority in these vessels. As noted previously, however, there will be a helicopter hangar – and flight deck – to support rotorcraft operation.

The frigate *İstanbul* pictured at sea in May 2024. The successful development and evolution of the Milgem family of warships has considerably strengthened the Turkish Navy whilst putting the Turkish naval sector 'on the map'. *(Devrim Yaylali)*

CONCLUSION

The Milgem programme has evolved from a national initiative to modernise the Turkish Navy into a flexible and internationally recognised warship platform. Through various configurations – including corvettes, frigates, offshore patrol vessels, and specialised variants – the original Milgem concept has demonstrated considerable adaptability across operational roles and geographic regions. The project has also exerted a considerable influence on other significant Turkish naval programmes, such as the future TF-2000 class destroyer.[12]

Whether configured for coastal defence, blue-water operations, or electronic intelligence, each Milgem derivative maintains a shared design philosophy: modularity, the maximum use of indigenous, Turkish technology, and mission-specific customisability. As Türkiye continues to invest in domestic defence capabilities, the Milgem family represents a foundational achievement in naval shipbuilding and looks set to become an enduring instrument of the country's national maritime diplomacy.

Notes:

1. Milgem is an acronym of the Turkish words *Milli Gemi* (National Ship). This chapter provides an update to the chapter 'Milgem Class Corvettes: Turkey's "National Ship" supports National Industry' that appeared in *Seaforth World Naval Review* 2016 a decade ago.

2. ASFAT was formed in January 2018 to manage and develop ordnance factories and shipyards that had been previously directly controlled by the Turkish Ministry of National Defence.

3. At times it was envisaged that orders for the 'Ada' class would also encompass options for four further ships, potentially expanding the class to twelve ships.

4. A much more detailed description of the initial 'Ada' class design is provided in the 2016 chapter referenced in note 1 above.

5. As noted previously, the main diesels in the 'Ada' class are the older generation MTU 16V595 TE90.

6. Subsequent members of the 'İstif' class will be equipped with the MKE-manufactured Denizhan 76/62mm mounting.

7. The MİDLAS VLS on TCG *Istanbul* is the 'tactical' variant, while the remaining ships in the class will receive the 'strike' variant. The variant is 1.3m longer, enabling it to house a wider range of missiles.

8. This claim can be found in Aselsan's brochure for the Akrep system, currently available at: wwwcdn.aselsan.com/api/file/AKREP_300N_ENG.pdf

9. A detailed comparison of the two designs suggests that this explanation does not reveal the whole story. Whilst *Babur* has been extended by around 1.7 metres in the area of the VLS, the length of the bridge structure has been increased by 1.4m and, notably, the area between the end of the bridge structure and the funnel by 5.6m. This demonstrates that much of the additional length is in the vicinity of the surface-to-surface missile installation.

10. Although many sources state that the ships are to be equipped with Aselsan's Gökdeniz, pictures of *Babur* taken in her delivery voyage did not show her equipped with this system.

11. This armament was not installed when *Dabur* left Türkiye and will presumably be installed in Pakistan after delivery.

12. The TF-2000 destroyer will be a large, c. 8,000-tonne anti-air warfare destroyer. The lead vessel was laid down at INS on 2 January 2025.

3.2 SIGNIFICANT SHIPS

MOGAMI (FFM-1) CLASS FRIGATES

Japan's Compact Multi-Mission Combatants

Author:
Tomohiko Tada

Until recently, surface combatant construction for the Japan Maritime Self Defence Force (JMSDF) has been focused on the procurement of destroyers of various shapes and sizes.[1] However, a desire to expand the overall size of the combatant force in the face of a more volatile regional security environment has resulted in the decision to acquire a new type of smaller multi-mission frigate, or FFM. Construction of the first pair of the resulting *Mogami* (FFM-1) class was authorised under Japan's FY2018 defence budget, with deliveries of these ships taking place in the first half of 2022.

Initial JMSDF plans envisaged the construction of as many as 22 members of the *Mogami* class. However, it was subsequently determined to halt production at twelve units in favour of building the remaining ten FFMs to an enhanced design. The number of these 'New Type FFMs' has subsequently been increased by a further two units so that this class will also comprise twelve vessels. Taken together, these two classes of 24 frigates will comprise over a third of the JMSDF's future combatant force, representing one of its most significant acquisitions to date.

Left: The lead Japanese *Mogami* class frigate pictured in June 2022, soon after being delivered to the JMSDF. Displacing around 5,500 tonnes in full load condition, the twelve *Mogami* class frigates mark a significant departure from Japan's previous focus on building larger destroyers. They also exhibit a much greater focus on stealth than previous JMDSF ships. *(JMSDF)m*

PROGRAMME BACKGROUND

The origins of the *Mogami* class can be traced as far back as 2005, when a 'Study on the Next Generation Destroyer (DD)' was commissioned from the Japan Defence Industry Association (JADI) by Japan's Maritime Staff Office. This work was heavily influenced by the US Navy's contemporary Littoral Combat Ship concept, most notably its high speed. However, it proved challenging to produce a satisfactory ship within the planned budget, even when the ship's specification was reduced. An important constraint was the use only of equipment in existence at the time of the study as the basis for these cost estimates. Subsequently, a major research and development effort was undertaken to pave the way for the next-generation combatant.

The programme took a significant step forward in December 2013 with the publication of *Japan's National Defense Program Guidelines* for FY2014 and beyond and the associated *Medium Term Defense Program (FY2014-FY2018).*[2] These outlined plans to increase the JMSDF's number of surface combatants through the introduction of, "…new destroyers, with additional multifunctional capability and with a compact-type hull…" The subsequent FY2015 Japanese defence budget allocated a total of 3.6 billion Japanese yen (c. US$25m) for the development of the new, compact ships and, particularly, their 'downsized' radar systems. This work paved the way for the inclusion of the first two ships within the FY2018 acquisition programme. The total cost for both ships was budgeted at 92.2 billion Japanese yen (c. US$650m) plus an additional 13.3 billion Japanese yen (c. US$100m) of non-recurring costs.

The selection of the new ships' shipbuilders was determined through a competitive bidding process managed by Japan's Acquisition, Technology and Logistic Agency (ATLA). Proposals from Japan Marine United, Mitsubishi Heavy Industries (MHI), and Mitsui Engineering & Shipbuilding Co (ME&S) were all deemed to be compliant, with MHI being selected as main contractor and MES being chosen as subcontractor under a decision announced in August 2017 on the basis of the overall evaluation of their bids. Under this arrange-

Agano (FFM-6) pictured at the time of her launch from Mitsubishi Heavy Industries' Nagasaki shipyard on 31 December 2022. Mitsubishi Heavy Industries was selected as main contractor for the *Mogami* class frigate programme in August 2017 after a competitive bidding process. *(JMSDF)*

ment, MHI took leadership of the project whilst ME&S was assigned construction of one of the two initial ships.[3] MHI had reportedly been working on self-funded frigate-type concepts for some time and its success in the procurement process can therefore be seen as a vindication of this approach.

The initial FY2018 orders have been followed by further authorisations at a regular 'drumbeat' of two ships each year through to FY2023, after which orders have shifted to the New Type FFM design.[4] To date, eight members of the class have entered JMSDF service, with the other four being under construction or on order. The vast majority of vessels have been built at MHI's Nagasaki shipyard but FFM-2 from the original order and FFM-8 from the FY2021 approvals have been allocated to the former ME&S Tamano facility. Further details of the class are provided in Table 3.2.1.

The *Mogami* class's designation has undergone several changes over the years, with destroyer (DD) and destroyer escort (DE) nomenclature both being applied at times. The current FFM designation was determined upon in 2018, being a combination of the FF symbol for frigates and the letter 'M' for multi-mission but sometimes also associated with mine warfare. Multi-functionality is at the heart of the new design, whilst mine warfare – both minelaying and mine clearance – is one of its core missions.

OVERALL DESIGN DESCRIPTION

The *Mogami* class frigates utilise a conventional, mono-hull design.[5] Standard displacement is 3,900 tonnes, increasing to 5,500 tonnes at full load. The hull is 133m long and has a beam of 16.3m, a depth of 9m and a draft of 4.8m. In comparison with previous Japanese warship designs, the class is notable for its extensive focus on visual stealth reduction, including the use of an angled hull structure by dint of a 'knuckle' that curves downwards from the forecastle and extends for the hull's full distance to end under the helicopter deck aft.

Mitsui Engineering & Shipbuilding Co. were awarded subcontractor status in the competitive selection process for the *Mogami* class but later sold their naval shipbuilding business to Mitsubishi Heavy Industries. Two ships of the class have been built at their Tamano shipyard, which now operates under the name of Mitsubishi Heavy Industries Maritime Systems Co Ltd, Tamano. This photograph shows the launch of *Yubetsu* (FFM-8) from the facility on 14 November 2023. *(JMSDF)*

Table 3.2.1: MOGAMI CLASS FRIGATES: CLASS LIST

NAME	PENNANT	PROGRAMME	COMMENCED	LAUNCHED	DELIVERED	SHIPYARD
Mogami	FFM-1	FY2018	29 October 2019	3 March 2021[1]	28 April 2022[1]	Mitsubishi Heavy Industries Ltd, Nagasaki
Kumano	FFM-2	FY2018	30 October 2019	19 November 2020[1]	22 March 2022[1]	Mitsubishi Heavy Industries Maritime Systems Co Ltd, Tamano
Noshiro	FFM-3	FY2019	15 July 2020	22 June 2021	15 December 2022	Mitsubishi Heavy Industries Ltd, Nagasaki
Mikuma	FFM-4	FY2019	15 July 2020	10 December 2021	7 March 2023	Mitsubishi Heavy Industries Ltd, Nagasaki
Yahagi	FFM-5	FY2020	24 June 2021	23 June 2022	21 May 2024	Mitsubishi Heavy Industries Ltd, Nagasaki
Agano	FFM-6	FY2020	24 June 2021	21 December 2022	20 June 2024	Mitsubishi Heavy Industries Ltd, Nagasaki
Niyodo	FFM-7	FY2021	30 June 2022	26 September 2023	21 May 2025	Mitsubishi Heavy Industries Ltd, Nagasaki
Yubetsu	FFM-8	FY2021	30 August 2022	14 November 2023	19 June 2025	Mitsubishi Heavy Industries Maritime Systems Co Ltd, Tamano
Natori	FFM-9	FY2022	6 July 2023	24 June 2024	TBA	Mitsubishi Heavy Industries Ltd, Nagasaki
Nagara	FFM-10	FY2022	6 July 2023	19 December 2024	TBA	Mitsubishi Heavy Industries Ltd, Nagasaki
TBA	FFM-11	FY2023	TBA	TBA	TBA	TBA
TBA	FFM-12	FY2023	TBA	TBA	TBA	TBA

Notes

1. A problem with the *Mogami*'s MT-30 gas turbine meant that *Kumano* (FFM-2) was the first of the class to be launched and delivered.

Although *Mogami* (FFM-1) is the lead ship of her class, a manufacturing problem with her main gas turbine delayed her launch and completion by several months. Accordingly, her delivery at the end of April 2022 was actually a few weeks after that of her sister-ship *Kumano* (FFM-2). This photograph was taken shortly after she finally entered service. *(JMSDF)*

This profile view of *Mogami* (FFM-1) taken in June 2022 provides a good indication of the design's main features. The class uses a conventional mono-hull design, with a high premium being placed on visual stealth and compact dimensions. In contrast to previous JMSDF surface combatants, the superstructure extends fully to the ship's sides and there is a marked lack of obvious protrusions. A dominant feature is the forward mast, which is similar to the integrated type increasingly found in European designs and which houses much of the ship's outfit of sensors. *(JMSDF)*

This focus on stealth is also reflected in a monolithic superstructure that extends to the ships' sides from the forecastle to the helicopter deck, eliminating the exposed passageways forward and aft that were a feature of many previous JMSDF surface warships. The forecastle, particularly, is free from protrusions, with bollards, cables and other ship-handling equipment hidden within a fully enclosed deck below. Similarly, workboats and boat-handling equipment are located within the superstructure rather than in the open and shielding is used to mask equipment housed on the main superstructure decks. Bollards and other equipment on the helicopter deck are hidden by hinged screens that are lowered when helicopter operations are underway.

General layout adopts a largely conventional approach, with the main gun forward in 'A' position and space for an initially 'fitted for but not with' vertical launch system (VLS) reserved between this weapon and the bridge. The bridge and main command spaces are located forward, with the ships' sole, pyramid-like mast just aft of the bridge housing much of its electronic equipment. The uptakes for propulsion system are amidships, and a hangar for a single helicopter located in the aft part of the superstructure. There is a well for surface-to-surface missiles between the funnel and hangar. Hatches in the stern provide access to a ramp and handling area under the helicopter deck for uncrewed systems and provide a means of deploying the embarked OQQ-25 surface ship sonar system.

The compact nature of the *Mogami* class design is reflected in a crewing requirement that has been significantly reduced compared with previous destroyers. Core complement amounts to around only 90 personnel; a number that could be reduced to as few as 60 in wartime conditions. This is central to the JMSDF's ambition to increase ship numbers against a backdrop of constraints on overall personnel headcount. Innovations in habitability include use of a shared dining hall for officers and ratings. In line with global trends, there is provision for separate accommodation for female crew members.

PROPULSION

The *Mogami* class used a combined diesel and gas turbine (CODAG) propulsion system comprising two diesel engines for lower speed cruising and one gas turbine for higher speeds. The diesel engines are German designed MAN 12V28/33D STCs, each

This photograph of *Mogami* (FFM-1) was taken in November 2022. The emphasis on stealth reduction measures is evidenced by the monolithic superstructure, which shields the exposed equipment and passageways found in previous Japanese surface vessels. *(Arjun Sarup)*

This photograph of *Noshiro* (FFM-3) gives a good view of the hinged screens that can be raised to obscure bollards and other protrusions around the edges of the helicopter deck when flying operations are not taking place. Note also the opened hatches that provide access to mooring lines. The smaller, port-side hatch in the stern is used to deploy the ship's sonar whilst the larger, central hatch gives access to a stern ramp from which, inter alia, uncrewed systems can be deployed. *(Australian Department of Defence)*

Mogami (FFM-1) pictured at speed off the Japanese coast. She is equipped with a CODAG propulsion system that incorporates two MAN diesels for lower-speed cruising and a Rolls-Royce MT-30 gas turbine for high-speed operation. This is the first time such a configuration has been used in a JMSDF vessel. Maximum speed is reported as being in excess of 30 knots. *(JMSDF)*

with a power output of 6MW, and the gas turbine a Rolls-Royce MT30 with an output of up to 40MW. They are geared to two shaft lines fitted with controllable pitch propellers. Maximum speed is in excess of 30 knots.

The ships are also equipped with an electrically-powered bow thruster in the forward hull that is particularly useful for maintaining station during mine countermeasures operations or utilising small ports. Three MTU-designed diesels supply the onboard electrical distribution network.

COMMAND AND CONTROL

The emphasis given to reducing crewing requirements has been a central influence on the *Mogami* class's command and control arrangements. For example, the integrated bridge system (IBS) fitted in the conventional bridge has reduced the number of bridge crew to just three or four from the much larger numbers seen in ships of yesteryear. However, the drive to reduce crewing is most evident in the class's innovative combat information centre (CIC). This utilises a total ship control system concept to centralise not only conventional combat command and control but also functions such as navigation, machinery and damage control in a single area, thereby dispensing with separate spaces for these activities.

The class's CIC adopts the circular format illustrated in the drawing. Console positions for the OYX-1-29 display system are grouped largely in functional positions around the edge of the room, as well as in the centrally-located command position. The consoles are linked to sensors, weapons and platform management systems by means of a standardised network system utilising open architecture. There are also electronic display tables immediately aft of the command position and a 360° circular screen wall that can display a wide range of imagery for enhanced situational awareness. The CIC incorporates a helmsman's position that allows navigation to be conducted away from the bridge.

The core combat management system (CMS) is the OYQ-1, the latest iteration of a long series of JMSDF tactical data processing systems that date back to the 1970s. Intended to provide unified and effective command and control, its basic functions are:

- **Situational awareness:** It obtains surface, subsurface and air information across the operational area through the ship's sensors (e.g. radar, sonar and electrical-optical devices) and communications technology.
- **Interpretation:** It converts the information obtained by these systems into a usable operational image by interpretation, analysis and evaluation.
- **Planning and decision making:** It helps the command team to plan and take rapid decisions in a complex and fast-moving battle environment.
- **Weapon control:** It provides command and control of a ship's various weapon systems to deal with approaching threats.

The CMS is connected to a range of communications systems that include support for the latest NATO standard Link 22 tactical data link, as well as the sensors and weapons described in the following section. Communications are primarily channelled through the NORA-50 UNICORN (unified complex radio antenna) at the top of the mainmast, which consolidates a wide range of communications functions in a stealthy, shared housing.

SENSORS AND WEAPONS

The *Mogami* class frigates are equipped with the comprehensive range of sensors and weapons outlined in Table 3.2.2. Further details of these individual systems are provided below.

OPY-2 Multi-function Radar: The ships' core sensor is arguably its OPY-2 multi-function radar. An active phased array, this has four fixed arrays installed towards the top of the forward mast's pyramid structure and is used for air and surface surveillance and tracking, as well as for weapons-control. The radar is the latest iteration of Japan's FCS-3 series of active electronically scanned arrays, which are manufactured by Mitsubishi Electric. Further information on the development of the FCS-3 radar for use in JMSDF warships is provided in the text box.

The OPY-2 was developed by combining the functions of OPY-1 C band (NATO G/H band) array installed in the preceding *Asahi* (DD-119) class destroyers with the OPS-48 X band (NATO I/J band) periscope detection radar. The OPY-2 also operates in the X band, improving resolution at the expense of some loss of range. Its main benefit is that

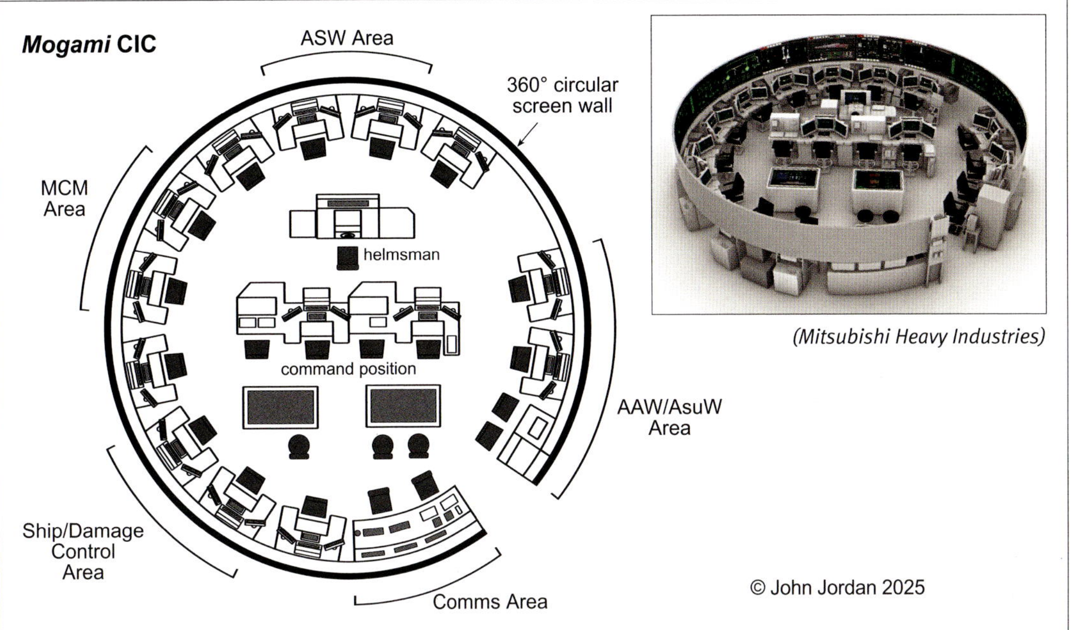

(Mitsubishi Heavy Industries)

This view of the bridge and mast structure aboard *Mogami* (FFM-1) provides a clear view of one of the four, fixed panels used by her primary OPY-2 multi-function radar. There are antennas for the NOLQ-3E electronic warfare system immediately above and below the radar array. Other systems identifiable are three of the six fixed cameras for the OAX-3 electro-optical sensor system in the collar at the top of the mast, which supplement the trainable sensor seen on the forward roof of the bridge. One of the ship's two RCWS is trained to starboard. *(JMSDF)*

JAPANESE ACTIVE PHASED-ARRAY RADAR DEVELOPMENT

The success of the SPY-1 radar, which was adopted by the US Navy for use with the Aegis system, led to widespread recognition of the usefulness of multi-function, phased-array radar. Accordingly, around the time that the first US Navy *Ticonderoga* (CG-47) class cruiser equipped with SPY-1 was commissioned in the early 1980s, the Japan Defense Agency's Technical Research and Development Institute began basic research in conjunction with Mitsubishi Electric into a multi-function radar that could be installed in various ships. The resulting system, which would later be called the New Shipboard Fire Control System (FCS-3), was developed on the basis of using an active phased-array system in the 4,000-8,000 MHz, C band (NATO G/H) frequency. Such an active phased array had yet to be realised anywhere in the world at this time.[1]

Basic research into multi-function radars between 1983 and 1985 was followed by the development of a FCS-3 research prototype between 1986 and 1988. This prototype was configured with multiple active transmitting and receiving modules – using gallium arsenide (GaAs) semiconductors for their high-frequency power amplifiers – on the antenna's face. The antenna was designed to rotate at 60 revolutions per minute so that both fixed and rotating functionality could be confirmed. Whilst factory testing of the prototype was successful, further trials were carried out at the Japan Air Self Defense Force (JASDF) Omaezaki Sub Base overlooking the Pacific Ocean from February 1989 onwards to provide more data in 'real world' conditions. A variety of search, detection and tracking tests against numerous T-33 jets and HSS-2 helicopters confirmed the system's successful performance in both fixed and rotating modes, even in adverse climatic conditions.

The data obtained from the FCS-3 research prototype was fed into work on a developmental prototype that also considered practical factors such as ease of installation and maintainability. Careful consideration was given to the merits of systems comprising one or two rotating arrays, as well as four fixed faces. Miniaturisation of the array's transmitting and receiving modules was another area of focus. Testing of the resulting developmental prototype – which used four fixed faces – commenced in FY1990.

After initial land tests, this developmental prototype was installed aboard the JMSDF's newly-commissioned experimental ship *Asuka* (ASE-6102) prior to the commencement of a series of maritime trials in June 1995. These included detection and tracking tests using JMSDF P-3C patrol and JASDF F-15 jet aircraft, as well as towed targets. The trials also included Japan's first tests using Target Radar Augmented Projectiles (TRAPs); supersonic radar targets with the same shape as a 127mm artillery round that were fired from the destroyers *Tachikaze* (DD-168) and *Hatakaze* (DD-171). Approximately 300 TRAPs were fired at various altitudes between November 1997 and January 1998; all were successfully tracked.

Successful conclusion of testing of the FCS-3 developmental prototype was followed by construction of production models that were further refined to incorporate the results of previous trials. The first ships to be equipped with the system were the helicopter-carrying destroyers *Hyuga* (DDH-181) and *Ise* (DDH-182). Four FCS-3 fixed arrays were mounted on each of these ships' island superstructures, two at the forward end facing forward and to port and two at the aft end facing aft and to starboard. They were supplemented by four smaller X band (NATO I/J band) arrays produced in partnership with Thales Netherlands to provide intermittent continuous wave illumination (ICWI) for the ships' semi-active ESSM surface-to-air missiles, which require high definition radar guidance in the

The experimental ship *Asuka* (ASE-6102) was used to conduct an extensive series of successful trials of the developmental prototype of the Japanese FCS-3 active phased-array radar. *(JMSDF)*

a single radar can be used to handle a broad spectrum of functions, thereby contributing to the overall emphasis on size and cost reduction.

The ships are also equipped with surface navigation radar.

OAX-3 Electro-Optical Sensor: The Mitsubishi Electric-manufactured OAX-3 electro-optical sensor system supplements the *Mogami* class's radar. It is the most recent member of the JMSDF's OAX family. It is intended to monitor the entire circumference of a ship using a combination of fixed and trainable sensors. Six fixed cameras are installed underneath the NORA-50 composite communications antennae at the top of the mainmast to provide 360° coverage. This imagery can provide part of the situational awareness picture provided on the CIC wall, also facilitating navigation from this position. These are supplemented by a trainable sensor encompassing a day and infra-red imaging device and a laser distance measuring system atop the bridge. In addition to supporting surveillance and tracking, OAX-3 can also be used for gunnery fire control purposes.

NOLQ-3E Electronic Warfare System: Another important system is the latest NOLQ-3E iteration of Japan's NOLQ-3 system. Its main antennas are fixed into the sides of the mast pyramid above and below the OPY-2 radar arrays, with additional ESM equipment integrated within the NORA-50 antenna. The system is supplemented by two, six-barrelled Mk 137 launchers for the Mk 36 SRBOC system located aft of the mast on the ship's superstructure.

Anti-Submarine Warfare Systems: The class's anti-submarine warfare (ASW) detection capabilities are provided by the OQQ-25 surface ship sonar system manufactured by NEC Corporation. The system is a variable depth sonar that adds active sonar functionality to a traditional towed-array sonar to improve overall detection and classification capabilities. The sonar is designed to work in conjunction with that aboard other ships to allow the possibility of bi-static or multi-static operation. Whilst there is no hull-mounted ASW sonar, the ships are provided with a hull-mounted OQQ-11sonar array for mine avoidance.

ASW armament comprise two triple HO3-303 launchers for 324mm Type 12 ASW torpedoes, It is likely that the Type 07VLA vertically-launched anti-submarine rocket – an improvement over the US

The first ships equipped with an operational variant of the FCS-3 radar were the two *Hyuga* (DDH-181) class helicopter carrying destroyers. In these ships, FCS-3 was combined with an ICWI fire-control radar produced in conjunction with Thales Nederland; each ship having four fixed arrays of each radar type so as to provide 360° coverage. This photograph is of *Ise* (DDH-182). *(Tomohiko Tada)*

final stages of an engagement. Tests performed by *Hyuga* in 2009 confirmed the radar combination's ability to detect, track and engage multiple targets.

The next variant of the FCS-3 series, the FCS3-A, was installed in the four *Akizuki* (DD-115) class destroyers. The system is also used to control these ships' 127mm gun and incorporates improved range and target discrimination. These improvements were facilitated by changing the semiconductors used in the transmitting element of the transmitting and receiving modules from GaAs to gallium nitride (GaN) technology. Subsequent iterations of the FCS-3 family encompass the OPS 50 used in the *Izumo* (DDH-183) helicopter-carrying destroyers and the OPY-1 of the two *Asahi* (DD-119) class destroyers. As the *Izumo* class are not equipped with weapons that need centralised fire control, the OPS-50 is used for surveillance and air traffic control, with its fire-control function removed. The OPY-1 is largely similar to the FCS-3A used in *Akizuki* and her sisters but has a shorter range due to the *Asahi* class's different, ASW focus.

The next, OPY-2 iteration of the FCS-3 series is described in the main text.

Note

1. Active phased arrays arose from developments in electronics that reduced the size of components, allowing individually energised transmitting and receiving modules to be combined with the phase shifters that control the direction and shape of the radar beam. This contrasts with passive phased arrays such as SPY-1, where the individual phase shifters on the surface of an antenna are connected by waveguides to a centralised power source. Active phased arrays are more flexible in radiating beams across various frequencies than their passive equivalents and less vulnerable to catastrophic failure.

Navy's ASROC – will be used once the Mk 41 VLS is fitted. The ships also typically embark a Mitsubishi SH-60K sea control helicopter.

Mine Countermeasures: As previously mentioned, the performance of mine countermeasures is an important component of the *Mogami* class's multi-role functionality, allowing a reduction in the total number of the JMSDF's bespoke mine countermeasures vessels. With the exception of the OQQ-11 sonar system previously referenced, this capacity will be primarily provided by uncrewed systems – uncrewed underwater vehicles (UUVs) and uncrewed surface vessels (USVs) – for which *Mogami* and her sisters will act as 'motherships'.

The UUV used in the *Mogami* class is the OZZ-5 autonomous underwater mine detector. It has a length of 4m, a diameter of 0.5m and weighs around 900kg. Propulsion is by means of an electric motor powered by lithium batteries, providing endurance of up to nine hours at a cruising speed of four knots and a maximum seven knot top speed. The use of 'X' form control surfaces forward and aft ensure excellent manoeuvrability, with guidance

Table 3.2.2.

MOGAMI (FFM-1) PRINCIPAL PARTICULARS

Building Information:	
Commenced:	29 October 2019 Launched: 3 March 2021 Commissioned: 28 April 2022[1]
Builders:	Mitsubishi Heavy Industries Ltd at their Nagasaki shipyard
Dimensions:	
Displacement:	5,500 tonnes full load displacement (3,900 tonnes standard displacement)
Overall Hull Dimensions:	133.0m x 16.3m x 4.8m. Depth is 9m.
Equipment:	
Armament:	2 x quad launchers for Type 17 (SSM-2) surface-to-surface missiles. 1 x 11-cell SeaRAM launcher for RIM-116 surface-to-air missiles. Fitted for but not with 2 x 8-cell Mk 41 vertical launchers for Type 07VLA vertically-launched ASW rockets.[2] 1 x 127mm Mk 45 Mod4 62 calibre gun, 2 x 12.7mm remotely controlled machine guns. 2 x triple HOS-303 324mm anti-submarine torpedo tubes for Type 12 lightweight torpedoes. Mine-laying capability.
Aircraft:	Flight deck and hangar for 1 x SH-60K sea control helicopter.
Countermeasures:	Include NOLQ-3E electronic warfare suite, 2 x Mk 137 launchers for SRBOC Mk 36 OZZ-5 uncrewed underwater mine detector, uncrewed surface mine removal vehicle.
Principal Sensors:	OPY-2 multifunction active electronically scanned array, navigation radar. OAX-3 electro-optical and infra-red sensor system. OQQ-25 surface ship sonar system (VDS & TASS), OQQ-11 hull-mounted anti-mine sonar.
Combat System:	OYQ-1 advanced combat direction system, OYX-1-29 information processing subsystem. NORA-50 UNICORN communications.
Propulsion Systems:	
Machinery:	CODAG: 2 x MAN 12V28/33D STC diesel engine each rated at 6MW, 1? Rolls-Royce MT30 gas turbine rated at 40MW. 2 shafts fitted with controllable pitch propellers. 1 bow thruster.
Speed:	Designed speed is over 30 knots in full CODAG configuration.
Other Details:	
Complement:	Core crew is 90.
Class:	Eight ships – *Mogami* (FFM-1), *Kumano* (FFM-2), *Noshiro* (FFM-3), *Mikuma* (FFM-4), *Yahagi* (FFM-5), *Agano* (FFM-6), *Niyodo* (FFM-7) and *Yubetsu* (FFM-8) – have been completed. Two named ships – *Natori* (FFM-9) and *Nagara* (FFM-10) – are under construction. Two further ships have been ordered but not yet named.

Notes

1. A problem with the *Mogami's* MT-30 gas turbine meant that *Kumano* (FFM-2) was the first of the class delivered, commissioning on 22 March 2022.
2. Capable of launching other missiles; see text for details.

provided by an inertial navigation system (INS) and GPS. OZZ-5 is equipped with a Thales SAMDIS high-frequency synthetic aperture sonar and a low-frequency synthetic aperture sonar produced by NEC to ensure accurate detection and identification, including of buried mines.

Meanwhile, in the first half of 2023, a series of trials commenced with a water-jet powered USV that was embarked and deployed utilising *Mogami's* stern hatch. The USV is reportedly c. 10m long with a beam of c. 3m and is capable of a maximum speed of 23 knots. The USV would work in conjunction with the OZZ-5 UUV, destroying mines located underwater by means of remotely-controlled, expendable mine disposal munitions.

The *Mogami* class also has a basic mine-laying capacity, utilising a system of rails to deploy weapons stowed in the ships' torpedo magazine.

Missiles: The first six ships of the *Mogami* class are currently 'fitted for but not with' a Mk 41 VLS, which is capable of housing a range of missiles. The system has been fitted from build in the seventh frigate – *Niyodo* (FFM-7) – onwards and will be

Mogami (FFM-1): 2022

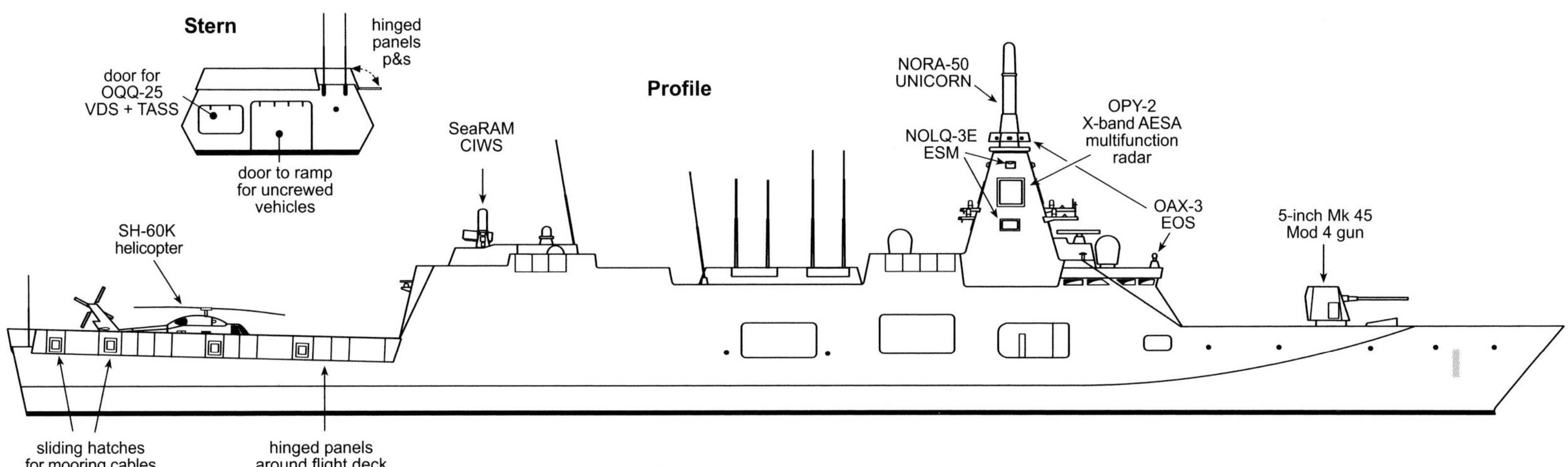

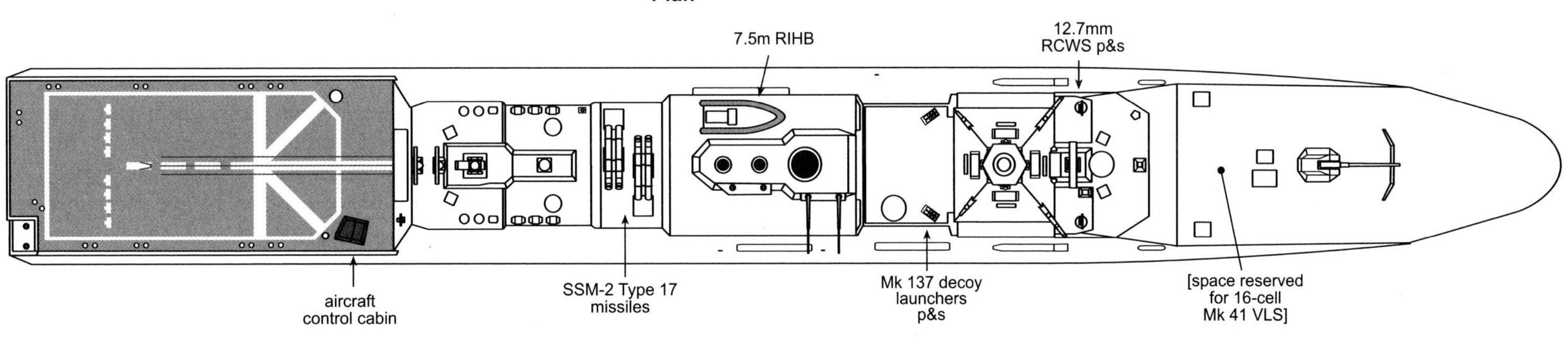

These two photographs of *Kumano* (FFM-2), taken early in 2024, illustrate many of the *Mogami* class's principal weapons. A 127mm (5in) Mk 45 Mod 4 mounting is located in 'A' position, with space reserved for a 'fitted for but not with' VLS between it and the bridge. There are two 12.7mm RCWS located to port and starboard on top of the bridge roof and a SeaRAM CIWS above the hangar. *(JMSDF)*

retrofitted in the earlier members of the class in due course. The system comprises two, 1?Rolls-Royce modules for a total of 16 VLS cells located on the centreline ahead of the bridge. It will initially be used to deploy the Type 07 VLA ASW rocket referenced above but could also be fitted with the US Navy's ESSM in quad pack configuration or with the Type 23 A-SAM, a new Japanese surface to air missile that has been under development since 2017 and is currently in the course of entering service. The 4.9m long, 750kg missile has a reported range in excess of 60km and was subject to successful launch testing from the experimental ship *Asuka* (ASE-6102) in December 2022. Fire control in both cases would be by means of the OPY-2 multi-function radar.

In advance of installation of a VLS-based surface-to-air missile, the primary air defence weapon is the SeaRAM iteration of the RIM-116 Rolling Airframe Missile. This essentially combines the radar and optronics of the Phalanx close-in weapons system with an eleven cell missile launcher to provide an autonomous self-defence capability at short to medium ranges. A single mounting is positioned atop the hangar roof.[6]

The frigates are also equipped with the Japanese-developed Type 17 surface-to-surface missile, which is also sometimes referred to as SSM-2. The 5m long, 750kg missile is able to strike targets at distances out to 400km using inertial guidance until its active radar seeker takes over in an engagement's final stages. It can receive mid-course guidance and is equipped with GPS targeting for potential use against land targets. Two quadruple launchers are installed aft of the funnel.

Gunnery: The *Mogami* class's main gun is a US Navy pattern 62-calibre, 127mm Mk 45 Mod 4 manufactured under licence from BAE Systems. It has a rate of fire of between 16 and 20 rounds per minute and a range of up to 37km (20 nautical miles) with conventional munitions. Fire control can be provided by the OPY-2 multi-function radar or OAX-3 electro-optical sensor.

The ships are also equipped with two remotely-controlled weapon stations (RCWS), which are located to port and starboard on the aft part of the bridge roof. They are equipped with 12.7mm machine guns and used for dealing with targets at close range.

Aviation: Aviation facilities comprise a helicopter

The *Mogami*'s class main gunnery armament comprises a single US Navy pattern 127mm Mk 45 Mod 4 mounting, seen here aboard *Noshiro* (FFM-3). *(JMSDF)*

The *Mogami* class frigates are equipped with a flight deck and hangar to sustain a single SH-60K sea control helicopter. This photograph is of *Kumano* (FFM-2). *(JMSDF)*

deck and hangar in the aft part of the ship. Facilities include a helicopter handling system and a control cabin that protrudes from the starboard side of the deck just aft of the hangar. The ships' helicopter is a Mitsubishi SH-60K; an improved variant of the previous SH-60J model that was, itself, derived from the US Black Hawk/Seahawk series. The type has been in service since 2005 and can be used for both anti-submarine and anti-surface warfare missions. Equipment includes surface search radar and dipping sonar, as well as air-to-surface missiles and ASW torpedoes and depth charges.

THE NEW FFM

The decision to replace construction of the *Mogami* class with a New Type FFM was publicly announced in January 2023 when ALTA solicited proposals from industry for the new vessels, which were to enter the construction programme from FY2024 onwards. The subsequent selection process was similar to that adopted for the original FFM, although consolidation in the Japanese naval sector meant that only Japan Marine United and MHI submitted bids. The result of the competition announced in August 2023 saw MHI once again selected as main contractor and Japan Marine United assigned the sub-contractor role. Two ships – one to be built by each contractor – were subsequently included in the FY2024 defence budget for delivery in 2028 at a total cost of 174 billion Japanese yen (c. US$1.2bn). Current plans involve all twelve members of the class being ordered in the five years through to FY2028, implying an increase over previous two ships per year 'drumbeat'. The Japanese FY2025 budget subsequently included three New Type FFMs for a total of 314.8 billion Japanese yen (c. US$2.2bn).

The New Type FFM, also known as the 'Upgraded *Mogami*' class is a larger design than its predecessor. Standard displacement will increase from 3,900 tonnes to c. 4,880 tonnes, with full load displacement in the region of 6,200 tonnes. Overall length will be about 142m and beam 17.4m. The new vessels share a generally similar layout and design to the earlier class, including their notable focus on maintaining visual stealth. Their CODAG propulsion system consisting of two diesel engines and one gas turbine driving twin shaft lines to produce a maximum speed of over 30 knots is another area of similarity with the original *Mogami* class design. Some reports suggest that generator capacity will be increased in line with greater electrical requirements.

The increased size of the new design will allow a doubling of Mk 41 VLS capacity from the 16 cells intended for the *Mogami* class to a total of 32. In contrast to their predecessors, all the new frigates will receive their VLS systems from build. The increased cell count means that it will be easier to accommodate the Type 23 A-SAM surface-to-air missile alongside the Type 07VLA ASW rocket, as well as increasing the scope for other missiles to be deployed. Other weapons systems are likely to be broadly similar to the earlier ships.

Another area of difference will be the incorporation of the OPY-2A multifunction radar, which is an improved variant of the existing OPY-2 active phased array. The new system retains the four fixed antenna of its predecessor but these will be shifted by 45 degrees in the New Type FFM, which will incorporate a larger, octagonal mast. The area in the vicinity of the command spaces will also be enlarged, increasing the size of the CIC.

EXPORT OPPORTUNITIES

The New Type FFM has already emerged as a leading candidate for the Royal Australian Navy's (RAN's) requirement for up to eleven 'Tier 2' surface combatants as part of its plans for an *Enhanced Lethality Surface Combatant Fleet* published in February 2024.[7] These new frigates will have general purpose capabilities but have an undersea warfare emphasis. Acquisition of the vessels is currently being taken forward as part of Australia's Project Sea 3000. They will serve alongside the existing *Hobart* class air defence destroyers, the new *Hunter* class frigates and a projected class of large, optionally crewed surface vessels.

The *Mogami* class was specifically cited as one of four 'exemplars' of ships that should form the basis of a selection process for the new RAN frigates, the

The *Mogami* class frigate design was selected by the Australian government as one of four 'exemplars' that could be adopted for a new general purpose frigate for the Royal Australian Navy. *Noshiro* (FFM-3) was subsequently dispatched to Australian waters in early 2025 to promote the Japanese proposal to meet the requirement, which is seemingly based on the 'Upgraded *Mogami*' class design. *(Australian Department of Defence)*

others being the German MEKO A-200, South Korean *Daegu* class FFX Batch II and III, and Spanish ALFA 3000 designs. Subsequently, in November 2024, it emerged that the German and Japanese ships had been shortlisted for further consideration, with the Japanese proposal increasingly being based on the Upgraded *Mogami* design. It is intended that the selected ship will be built with only minimal changes from the Japanese design, with the first three built by the existing builders and the remaining eight at the Henderson yard in Western Australia. A final decision is expected to be made before the end of 2025.

There have been reports that Indonesia is also interested in acquiring FFM type vessels under a partnership arrangement with Japan.

CONCLUSION

The development of the *Mogami* class FFMs marks something of a new direction of travel for the JMSDF. The increasingly pressing need to expand the navy's size to meet increased security risks has resulted in an innovative approach to produce compact vessels that Japan can afford to build and crew in greater numbers. The prowess of Japanese industry in implementing technological solutions that are enabling this objective to be achieved whilst still enhancing combat capability has been a key component in the programme's success.

The shortlisting of the design to meet the RAN's requirement for a general purpose frigate is another significant development, representing the first time since the Second World War that Japanese industry has been a major contender to export a surface combatant to an overseas navy. Every indication suggests that Japan is doing all that it can to secure the contract. Notably, in February 2025, third member of the class, *Noshiro* (FFM-3) departed Japan for a mission to Australian waters. There it called at the *Stirling* naval base in Western Australia and conducted training with the RAN before returning home by way of Subic Bay in the Philippines – participating in further exercises with allied navies – on 16 April 2025. The deployment was part of a wider public relations campaign, including hosting Australian journalists to view the launch of *Nagara* (FFM-10) at MHI's Nagasaki shipyard the previous December.[8] If successful, these efforts will also extend the FFM design's influence beyond the JMSDF, giving *Mogami* and the New Type FFM broader international significance.

Noshiro (FFM-3) pictured in company with the helicopter-carrying destroyer *Izumo* (DDH-183) in July 2024. The entry of the new *Mogami* class frigates into service represents a new direction of travel for the JMSDF and could have wider significance if current export campaigns are successful. *(JMSDF)*

Notes:

1. These ships have included the two pairs of *Hyuga* (DDH-181) and *Izumo* (DDH-183) 'helicopter-carrying destroyers', the eight Aegis-equipped destroyers of the *Kongou* (DDG-173), *Atago* (DDG-177) and *Maya* (DDG-179) classes, and various general purpose (DD) destroyers. Two of these classes, the *Hyuga* class helicopter-carrying destroyers and the *Akizuki* (DD-115) general purpose destroyers have been described by the author in, respectively, the 2014 and 2019 editions of *Seaforth World Naval Review.*

2. Both Tokyo: Government of Japan, 2013. They can currently be found online at: www.mod.go.jp/en/d_act/d_policy/national.html

3. Mitsui Engineering & Shipbuilding sold its naval shipbuilding business to MHI in October 2021 as part of its plans to withdraw from the ship construction sector. The business – based on the Tamano works – is now known as Mitsubishi Heavy Industries Maritime Systems.

4. The class is often also referred to as the 30FFM class. The 30 relates to the thirtieth year of the Heisei era, corresponding with the reign of the former Japanese Emperor Akihito.

5. Utilisation of a trimaran hull was considered during the 'Study on the Next Generation Destroyer (DD)' but ultimately rejected.

6. Chapter 4.3 in this edition provides a more detailed description of the RAM system's development and capabilities.

7. *Enhanced Lethality Surface Combatant Fleet: Independent Analysis of Navy's Surface Combatant Fleet* (Canberra: Australian Government, 2023). It and other related materials can currently be found at: defence.gov.au/about/reviews-inquiries/independent-analysis-navy-surface-combatant-fleet.

8. A report on the visit was provided in Kym Bergmann's 'Mogami frigate – fast and stealthy, like a ninja' posted to the *Asia Pacific Defence Reporter* site – asiapacificdefencereporter.com – on 29 December 2024.

R11

3.2 SIGNIFICANT SHIPS

VIKRANT

India's Project 71 Indigenous Aircraft Carrier

Author:
Mrityunjoy Mazumdar

On Wednesday, 4 August 2021 India's first home-built aircraft carrier, *Vikrant,* slipped her moorings in the Indian port city of Kochi. Escorted by tugs, she sailed past the historic district of Fort Kochi and out into the open sea to commence initial sea trials. The ship's voyage marked a historic day for the Indian Navy (IN), representing the fruition of a more than three decades-long national endeavour to complete an indigenous aircraft carrier (IAC). Subsequently commissioned on 2 September 2022, *Vikrant* marks India's arrival amongst the select group of nations that can design, build and operate these most powerful of surface warships.

Described as the largest and most complex surface warship to be designed and constructed in India to date, *Vikrant* is emblematic of the Indian Navy's long standing drive for self-reliance in naval construction. Her name and pennant – R11 – are a tribute to India's first carrier, a British-built *Majestic* class vessel launched as HMS *Hercules* in 1945 but finally completed for Indian service in March 1961. The first *Vikrant* played an important role in the modern IN's formative years, being particularly celebrated for her crucial role in the December 1971 war with Pakistan that led to the creation of Bangladesh from what had previously been East Pakistan.

Maintaining a carrier capability has long been a crucial element of India's 'blue water' maritime ambitions. Fixed-wing carrier aviation has been a consistent feature of IN's operations since the first *Vikrant*'s arrival; for a long time India was the only emergent Asian navy to operate such ships. The induction of a second carrier, *Viraat* (the former Royal Navy *Hermes*), in 1987 allowed the development of two carrier operations; a concept that has long been central to IN doctrine but which has only been achieved from time-to-time. The capability was 'gapped' between the first *Vikrant*'s decommissioning in 1997 and the arrival of *Vikramaditya* – the reconfigured former Soviet Project 1143.4 *Kiev* class vessel *Admiral Gorshkov* – in 2013. After another gap following *Viraat*'s decommissioning in 2017, this capacity has now been restored with the new *Vikrant*'s arrival.

Left: The Project 71 Indigenous Aircraft Carrier *Vikrant* is the largest and most complex surface warship to be designed and constructed in India to date. Equipped for STOBAR operations, she carries an air group centred on the Russian MiG-29K multi-role fighter. Fifteen of these aircraft can be seen on her flight deck in this recent image. *(Indian Navy)*

This photograph of India's second aircraft carrier *Viraat*, formerly the Royal Navy's *Hermes* of Falklands War fame, was taken from a US Navy warship during the 'Malabar 2007' exercises. *Viraat*'s induction into Indian Navy service in 1987 allowed India to develop two-carrier operating concepts. *(US Navy)*

PROJECT 71 IAC ORIGINS

Design studies for an indigenous Indian aircraft carrier can be traced back many decades and have evolved through multiple iterations.[1] In 1979-80, the IN's Directorate of Naval Design (DND) undertook exploratory work on producing a helicopter carrier utilising the hull form of the passenger ship MV *Harshavardan*; a process that failed to gain traction through lack of official interest. Later, in 1985, staff requirements were drawn up as part of a more formal project for what was intended to encompass a class of at least two locally-built aircraft carriers. Referred to as sea control ships, these were to displace in the region of 35,000 tonnes.[2] France's DCN (Naval Group) was subsequently contracted to provide concept designs in 1988; their report, produced in 1990, included both conventional, catapult assisted take-off but arrested recovery (CATOBAR) and ski-jump based short take-off and vertical landing (STOVL) options displacing some 37,500 tonnes. As eventually transpired in the case of *Vikrant*, the resultant ships were to have been built at Cochin Shipyard Ltd (CSL), with the first to be delivered in 2001. Funding constraints meant that neither option was pursued. Instead, the government directed the IN to develop a less ambitious proposal.

In the face of this setback, the Directorate of Naval Design pursued alternative carrier design studies throughout the early 1990s. In line with government mandates, these were focused on a smaller and, hence, cheaper concept known as the Air Defence Ship (ADS).[3] Various, progressively larger designs displacing from 16,000 to 24,000 tonnes were produced against a backdrop of evolving IN thinking about the configuration of the air groups their future carriers would likely operate. Although the initial focus was on the Sea Harrier STOVL aircraft then used aboard the first *Vikrant* and *Viraat*, the possibility of adopting short take-off but arrested recovery (STOBAR) operation steadily gained traction. A navalised variant of the indigenous Light Combat Aircraft (LCA) was proposed for this role. However, the subsequent decision to acquire the Project 1143.4 *Gorshkov* and convert her to operate MiG-29K multi-role fighters under Project 11430 saw a requirement for a further evolution of the ADS design to support the larger Russian jet so as to ensure a common air group. This resulted in a significantly larger ship.[4]

Government approval for what was then known as the Project 71 ADS was finally received in mid-1999, with government-owned CSL being allocated the shipbuilding project. However, the approved design did not take full account of the emerging requirement to operate the MiG-29K, resulting in a need to obtain further authorisation at the end of 2002 for the larger ship that was now envisaged.[5] This was followed by the requisite financial approvals in January 2003. After conclusion of functional and detailed design, a formal first steel-cutting ceremony was held at CSL on 11 April 2005. The programme was re-designated as the Project 71 Indigenous Aircraft Carrier on the same day.

As finally envisaged, the MiG-29K-equipped IAC displaced approximately 37,000 tonnes at full load. It would have a near 830ft (252m) flight deck, including an angled landing runway equipped with three arrestor wires capable of handling aircraft weighing up to 22 tonnes. Aircraft would be launched by means of a 14-degree ski-jump via a (maximum) 600ft deck run from positions equipped with blast deflectors and hydraulic chocks. Propulsion would be by means of four gas turbines in combined gas and gas (COGAG) configuration, producing a maximum speed of 28 knots. The IAC would carry an air group of around 30 aircraft and helicopters and be crewed by approximately 1,500 personnel. Many of these details continued to evolve during the lengthy construction process that followed, particularly as understanding of the operating requirements of the MiG-29K came to be better understood.

The Indian Navy decision to acquire MiG-29K multi-role fighters to operate in STOBAR mode from the reconfigured former Soviet-era Project 1143.4 class vessel *Admiral Gorshkov* – renamed *Vikramaditya* in Indian service – had a significant impact on IAC concept studies, eventually leading to the design adopted for the ship that became *Vikrant*. Here, *Vikramaditya* is pictured in the North Arabian Sea in November 2020 during that year's iteration of the 'Malabar' series of exercises. *(US Navy)*

IAC DESIGN AND CONSTRUCTION

In general terms, the basic and functional design of the IAC was carried out by the IN's DND – now known as the Warship Design Bureau – with CSL being responsible for detailed design, the generation of production drawings, systems-integration and construction. CSL was issued with a letter of intent (LOI) to design and construct the ship immediately after financial approval was granted in January 2003, with an order for design and pre-production activities – including procurement of long-lead items – being signed the following year. The LOI optimistically envisaged completion of preliminary design by the end of 2003, commencement of ship construction by early 2004, finalisation of detailed design and integration by 2007, and delivery of the ship in 2010.[6]

Design: The design process presented serious challenges to both the DND and CSL, not least in recruiting sufficient numbers of qualified personnel to undertake the relevant work. An important consideration was the fact that CSL had previously focused on building commercial (merchant) vessels, with little to no experience of warship design and construction. Whilst it had dry docks of the size necessary to build the carrier, additional investments in infrastructure and changed ways of working were required by the shipyard to realise the project. This included the

An overhead view of *Vikrant* under construction at Cochin Shipyard Ltd (CSL). Whilst CSL had docks large enough to support *Vikrant*'s assembly, the yard had previously focused on merchant-ship construction. As a result, investment in new facilities and the adoption of new ways of working were needed. Construction was based on the assembly of pre-outfitted blocks, with over 1,100 of these assemblies eventually being used in the ship's construction. *(Indian Navy)*

establishment of a dedicated design group for the project separate from its commercial activities.

CSL's commercial background did, however, provide important experience. For example, its expertise in using pre-outfitted blocks in the construction process was adopted in the build plan for the new vessel. Production planning also benefited from the use of Tribon software for 3D modelling, facilitating the creation of production drawings and assisting with subsequent inspections.

Despite the largely indigenous nature of the IAC design, certain aspects of the process were supported by consultancy services provided by overseas companies. Notably, Italy's Fincantieri assisted with development of the ship's build strategy and provided assistance with propulsion system integration. Another important contract placed through Russia's Rosoboronexport in 2006 related to the design of the ship's Aviation Facilities Complex (AFC) by the Nevskoye Design Bureau. The DND developed-hull form was tested at the Maritime Research Institute Netherlands (MARIN) research centre.[7]

A notable feature of the design process was the decision to commence construction before detailed design had been concluded. This concurrent design and production approach – not uncommon at the time – was intended to avoid construction delays, particularly in the light of a still-evolving understanding of MiG-29K operating requirements. However, the lack of a 'frozen' design caused increasing problems as construction progressed, particularly due to protracted delays in finalising the specification of key items of equipment. The resulting costly, time-consuming changes that had to be made to shipboard equipment and structures

This bow view of *Vikrant* at CSL shows the ship slowly taking shape. The advantages inherent in the planned use of pre-outfitted blocks was somewhat negated by delays in finalising detailed design and receiving key items of equipment. These delays had a material impact on the overall delivery schedule, requiring significant changes to contract phasing. *(Indian Navy)*

These two photographs were taken at the time of *Vikrant*'s formal launch on 12 August 2013. She had previously entered the water in December 2011 to allow the construction dock to be freed for other work whilst delayed equipment was delivered. The photographs indicate that there was still considerable outfitting work to be completed at this stage. An interesting detail in the images is the pontoon structures that were attached to the ship's hull to provide additional buoyancy during the launch process. *(Indian Navy)*

negated any advantage gained from the concurrent approach. A 2016 report noted that the IN had made more than 2,720 changes to the ship's general arrangement (GA) by that time.[8] The design of the island's top deck and many key operational spaces was not finalised until as late as 2019/20.

Construction: CSL's design and pre-production agreement was followed by signature of a first phase production contract in May 2007, some years after the largely ceremonial first steel cutting event had been held. As a result of a decision taken in 2006, it was determined to contract for the carrier's construction in two distinct phases; one for the hull structure and preliminary outfitting to the ship's technical launch and the other to take work through to completion. At this stage, it seems that launch was expected in 2010 and completion in 2014.

Subsequently, in 2010, the delays in finalising equipment details referenced above – particularly with respect to the AFC and weapon systems – led to CSL proposing that the latter construction phase be further split into two elements. The new Phase II, eventually signed in December 2014, encompassed key items such as completion of the propulsion train and power distribution system but excluded aviation facilities, weapons and sensors. These were to be completed in the new Phase III, only finally contracted in October 2019, which was also to cover ship trials and post-delivery support.

Keel laying for the IAC took place on 28 February 2009, nearly four years after the first steel-cutting ceremony. Progress had been delayed by the need to source indigenous supplies of warship-grade steel, although it should be noted that block production had commenced in November 2006 and, accordingly, many of the carrier's constituent blocks had been fabricated by this time. Whilst early media reports referenced to the use of some 874 blocks in the ship's construction, later official accounts suggest a larger total of some 1,100 of these assemblies. Infrastructure improvements at CSL to facilitate assembly included the erection of a 300-ton gantry crane over the dry dock, purchase of a plasma cutting machine for cutting plates and a plate bending roller for shaping plates, as well as the provision of enhanced facilities for transporting and storing completed blocks. Integration of the blocks to form *Vikrant*'s complete hull ('grand assembly) commenced on 4 October 2009.

Vikrant entered the water for the first time in a

The second phase of *Vikrant*'s construction saw her return to dry dock for further outfitting, including the installation of underwater equipment. She was in a much more complete state when she re-entered the water on 10 June 2015, when this photograph was taken. The openings in her island superstructure would eventually be used to facilitate installation of the MF-STAR multi-function radar arrays. *(Indian Navy)*

low key 'technical launch' on 29 December 2011, being temporarily floated out of the building dock to free it for other work pending the delayed receipt of important elements of her propulsion and generating systems.[9] After re-docking in February 2013 to receive the missing equipment, formal launch followed on 12 August 2013 in a ceremony presided over by Elizabeth Antony, wife of the then Indian defence minister. This effectively marked the end of Phase I of the construction process. An IN press release at the time stated that induction into the IN was now envisaged in 2016-17, although a further delay in delivery to December 2018 would soon be agreed.

Phase II construction saw *Vikrant* return to dry dock for the installation of shaft lines and other underwater equipment. The ship's island and sponsons had also been fitted by the time the carrier re-entered the water on 10 June 2015. However, progress continued to be delayed by late orders and receipt of important equipment, leading to tensions between the IN and CSL as to when delivery could be achieved.[10] Contemporary press reports suggest that harbour trials finally commenced towards the end of 2019. However, progress was subsequently further delayed with the outbreak of the Covid-19 pandemic in 2020, with travel restrictions on equipment suppliers' representatives impacting the setting-to-work and testing process. The IN reported that basin trials were finally concluded by CSL in November that year, paving the way for the commencement of sea trials on 4 August 2021.

Vikrant pictured departing Kochi on 4 August 2021 at the beginning of her maiden voyage. She eventually completed four phases of trials between August 2021 and July 2022. *(Indian Navy)*

Vikrant welcomed her first aircraft on the day her sea trials began. This photograph captures the arrival of Sea King Mk 42C, serial IN 559, at the time of this historic event. The photograph also provides a good overall view of the carrier's island, including the Selex RAN-40L surveillance radar atop the lower part of the mast structure, the TACAN navigation system at the mast head and the arrays associated with the Resistor-E air traffic control complex at the end of the aft superstructure. However, much equipment has still to be fitted. Ultimately, around 100 sensors and antennae from around 20 manufacturers were located atop the island structure. *(Indian Navy)*

Sea Trials & Commissioning: *Vikrant*'s sea trials encompassed four phases completed over the course of nearly one year between August 2021 and July 2022.

- **Phase I:** Held over five days between 4 August and 8 August 2021 during India's monsoon season, this phase saw initial testing of the performance of the ship's propulsion and other critical systems. The carrier reportedly achieved full power in Sea State 4 in the course of these tests. Over 20 helicopter landings were also performed, commencing with the arrival of a Sea King Mk 42C (serial IN 559) piloted by the IN's Flag Officer Naval Aviation, Rear Admiral Philipose G Pynumootil, on the day sea trials began.
- **Phase 2:** The second phase of sea trials commenced on 24 October 2021 and lasted over a period of ten days, ending on 2 November 2021. This period saw extended testing of the carrier's machinery and other ship systems.
- **Phase 3:** The ship's third sortie began on 9 January 2022 and was completed on 16 January that year. It included tests of communications systems and sensors, as well as more complex manoeuvring trials.
- **Phase 4:** The final phase of trials took place between 2 July and 10 July 2022 and were focused on integrated trials of the majority of equipment and systems onboard. Some testing of the AFC was also completed during this time.

Vikrant was subsequently delivered to the IN on 28 July 2022 prior to an official commissioning ceremony in the presence of Indian Prime Minister Narendra Modi on 2 September 2022. At this time, the carrier had yet to receive its MF-STAR multi-function radar and associated Barak 8 surface-to-surface missiles; these were subsequently fitted during the second half of 2023. Many months of further trials and tests were to be required before the ship obtained operational status, including the first landings of fixed-wing aircraft on the carrier's deck on 6 February 2023 during air certification and flight integration trials.

The completed *Vikrant* had experienced considerable change when compared with the design that existed when steel was first cut in 2005. Displacement had grown from the initial 37,500 tonnes to nearly 45,000 tonnes in full load condition, whilst length had increased by around ten metres to 262m overall. There had also been significant changes to sensors and weaponry, including the use of the Israeli MF-STAR radar and Barak 8 missile combination in place of the Russian equipment that featured in early project drawings.

Project Challenges & Costs: The ongoing revisions to *Vikrant*'s design and equipment were important contributors to the project challenges and cost overruns that the IAC programme ultimately experienced. Underlying these problems was insufficient institutional experience of a project of this scale, leading to a significant underestimation of the challenges involved in such a 'first time' endeavour. Despite attempts to establish a robust oversight structure, overall project management controls seem to have been lacking, with orders for important items of equipment sometimes delayed for many years beyond the dates envisaged in the initial programme strategy. For example, the design contract for the crucial AFC was only placed in April 2006, some 16 months after the design was due to be completed. In the end, the AFC's design was only finalised in January 2009; some five years later than planned. This had knock-on effects on many other elements of the ship's design, including power generation capacity and the heating ventilation and air conditioning system (HVAC). Moreover, the resultant delay to AFC procurement was a key factor in the delayed implementation of Phase III construction.[11]

IN explanations of the programme's delays tend to highlight tardy delivery by overseas contractors, as well as a failure of some local suppliers to engage with a somewhat bespoke project, sometimes having to be 'cajoled' to come onboard. Much of this criticism seems to be somewhat disingenuous given the project management deficiencies noted above. However, it is also clear that there were significant supply chain difficulties. An early problem related to the supply of warship-quality steel after commercial discussions relating to planned purchases from Russia reached a commercial impasse. This resulted in a decision to create an indigenous production capability, with India's Defence Metallurgical Research Laboratory (DMRL) developing an appro-

This photograph shows *Vikrant* returning to Kochi at the end of her relatively short first trials voyage. Although flight deck markings are in place, it seems that the arrestor gear has yet to be fitted. Delayed receipt of equipment for the ship's aviation facilities complex (AFC) was one of a number of significant production challenges that needed to be overcome in the course of *Vikrant*'s construction. *(Indian Navy)*

Vikrant pictured at sea shortly before her official delivery on 28 July 2022. At this time, she still lacked important items of equipment and had yet to undertake trials of fixed wing aircraft. *(Indian Navy)*

priate high-tensile steel that was then put into production by the state-owned Steel Authority of India Limited (SAIL). Eventually, three qualities of the resultant DMR 249 formulation were manufactured; DMR 249A plates for the hull and interior structures, DMR 249B for the flight deck, and DMR 249 AZ65 for the machinery space decks. All-in-all, SAIL are believed to have produced up to 30,000 tonnes of steel for the carrier project. However, establishing this new capacity took considerable time, further contributing to programme delays.[12]

The production challenges of the IAC project, coupled with the steady growth in the carrier's size, inevitably impacted the overall programme cost. When first approved in 1999, the ADS was anticipated to cost INR 17.3 billion (c. US$200 million at mid-2025 exchange rates). However, the evolution to the larger, MiG-29K-capable carrier saw projected costs almost double to INR 32.6 billion (c. US$375 million) when the revised, c. 37,000-tonne design was approved at the start of 2003. A further INR 6.5 billion (c. US$75 million) was to be expended upgrading CSL. By 2014, a more realistic assessment of project costs saw a further substantial leap to INR 193.4 billion (c. US$2.25 billion), a figure that was approved by India's Cabinet Committee on Security in July that year. Whilst this figure has never been officially revised subsequently, it seems inevitable that costs will have risen further over the following decade.

Indigenisation: An important element of the IAC programme – often trumpeted by the Indian government – is its contribution to the nation's quest for *Atmanirbhar Bharat*; a self-reliant India. The overall indigenous content of *Vikrant* has been estimated at 76 percent. Moreover, CSL has stated that construction of the IAC has contributed significantly to the overall Indian economy, generating demand in both 'upstream' industries, such as steel and electro-mechanical equipment, as well as in

These two photographs of *Vikrant* taken during her initial sea trials provide a good overview of the new aircraft carrier, which is believed to displace around 45,000 tonnes at full load. Despite being justifiably trumpeted as a product of a self-reliant India (*Atmanirbhar Bharat*), the vessel also exhibits a number of overseas design influences. These include her Russian-designed aviation facilities complex and her propulsion arrangement, the latter being influenced by the Italian aircraft carrier *Cavour*. *(Indian Navy)*

'downstream' sectors, such as infrastructure and services. Approximately 550 Indian vendors supported the construction of the IAC, around 100 of which were medium and small enterprises.[13]

Extensive lists of IAC suppliers encompassing major industrial groups such as Bharat Electronics Limited (BEL), Bharat Heavy Electricals Limited (BHEL), Garden Reach Shipbuilders & Engineers (GRSE), Kerala State Electronics Development Corporation Limited (Keltron), Kirloskar, and Larsen & Toubro have been publicised by the IN. However, the underlying reality is a little more complex, with much equipment either built under licence or comprising 'pass through' imported products that have only been partly manufactured or, simply, assembled locally. Despite this, elements of local industry have undoubtedly secured substantial benefits from the programme. The development of a capability to manufacture appropriate high tensile steels highlighted above is a case in point, allowing indigenisation of a key aspect of future warship production.

Most importantly, the institutional knowledge gained since the inception of the IAC project has been immense. In addition to the experience obtained by India's industrial base in providing materials and equipment to the latest naval standards, the programme's key stakeholders have achieved the knowhow and confidence to execute the most complex warship design and construction projects at scale. All this is contributing to a steady improvement in the performance of the indigenous warship construction sector.

SHIP DESCRIPTION: OVERVIEW

As of mid-2025, *Vikrant* is the largest combatant to have been built in India and – with the possible exception of the *Arihant* class strategic submarines – also the most complex. Further details are provided in Table 3.3.1.

Vikrant has an overall length of 262.5m, an overall beam of about 62.5m and a draught in excess

of 8.8m at a full load displacement of nearly 45,000 tonnes. Waterline dimensions are approximately 236m (233m between perpendiculars) by 32.5m. Depth is some 25.5m from the keel to the flight deck, increasing to nearly 62m to the top of the main mast.

General Arrangement: Only limited information on the carrier's internal layout has entered the public domain.[14] It is known that there are a total of 14 main deck levels, five of which are contained within the island superstructure. The latter comprise Deck 01 to Deck 05, with Deck 05 corresponding to the superstructure's roof. The main navigating bridge and flying control position are located at Deck 04 level, with a flag bridge incorporated a level below. There are additional decks in the carrier's mainmast, one of which is believed to house an emergency control position. The outlets for the uptakes to the ship's gas turbines and diesel generators are located to the starboard side of the island structure, with a replenishment-at-sea (RAS) position in between.

Vikrant's flight deck is at Deck 1 level, with further levels running downwards through to Deck 9. The keel forms an additional level and the waterline is located between Decks 6 and 7. Large sponsons stretch for much of the carrier's length underneath the flight deck to both port and starboard, extending downwards as far as Deck 4. These principally serve to increase the breadth of the flight deck but also provide platforms for weapons and a range of other equipment, whilst housing facilities for the ship's boats. Similarly, there is an enclosed forecastle below the ski-jump containing anchor handling equipment.

A large proportion of the upper hull is taken up with the ship's hangar, which extends for three deck levels in depth below the flight deck at Deck 4 level for almost half the carrier's length in the centre part of the ship (see further under Aviation Facilities Complex below). Much of the accommodation is located at lower deck levels closer to the waterline,

Table 3.3.1.

VIKRANT (R11) PRINCIPAL PARTICULARS

Building Information:	
Laid Down:	28 February 2009[1] Launched: 12 August 2013[2] Commissioned: 2 September 2022
Builders:	Cochin Shipyard Ltd (CSL), Kochi, India
Dimensions:	
Displacement:	c. 45,000 tons full load displacement.
Overall Dimensions:	262.5m x 62.5m x 8.8m. Waterline dimensions are 236m x 32.5m.
Equipment:	
Aircraft:	Typical air group of 30 fast jets and helicopters. Flight deck equipped with 14° ski jump, 3 arrestor wires and 6 helicopter spots.
Missiles:	Two groups of 2 x 8-cell vertical launchers for Barak 8 surface-to-air missiles.
Guns:	3 x 30mm AK-630M CIWS. 5 x RCWS.
Countermeasures:	Includes Shakti integrated R-ESM and ECM. ELK-7036 communications intelligence. 4 x Kavach Mod II decoy launchers. Surface ship torpedo defence system.
Principal Sensors:	1 x ELM-2248 MF-STAR multi-function radar. 1 x RAN-40L surveillance radar. Resistor-E radar complex. TACAN.
Combat System:	CMS-71 combat management system. CEC (JTF mode of Barak 8). Advanced Composite Communication System. Link 2 Mod 3 datalink.
Propulsion System:	
Machinery:	COGAG. 4 x GE LM-2500 gas turbines producing c. 88MW (118,000hp) through two shafts.
Speed:	Designed maximum speed is c. 28 knots. Endurance is c. 7,500 nautical miles at cruising speed.
Other Details:	
Complement:	Typical crew is around 1,700, including between 170 and 200 officers. Accommodation is provided for up to c. 2,000 personnel.

Notes:

1. A formal first steel-cutting ceremony was held on 11 April 2005. Block assembly commenced in November 2006.
2. A temporary 'technical' floating out had previously occurred on 29 December 2011. This was essentially a low key launching event but the IN insisted on delaying a formal launch ceremony until the carrier was more complete.

with a broad passageway that runs for almost 240m providing forward-to-aft transit along the length of the ship on Deck 5. The lower deck spaces are largely occupied by the propulsion train and solid and liquid stores.

Little has been revealed about *Vikrant*'s lateral sub-division, although some reports suggest that the carrier is divided into nine or ten independent fire zones, each with its own independent HVAC system. These presumably have some correlation with the ship's damage control zones. No details have been provided on passive protection, although the limited information that is available suggests that some armour has been incorporated into the design.

All-in-all, the ship has some 2,300 separate compartments linked by 12km of passageways and lobbies, as well as more than 700 ladders. Given the number of compartments, a ship's officer briefed local media that it can take three months for personnel to become familiar with the ship's layout.

Propulsion and Power Generation: *Vikrant* utilises a twin-shaft combined gas and gas (COGAG) propulsion system. Two General Electric LM2500 gas turbines, each rated at c. 22MW, are located in each of the forward and aft engine rooms, providing c. 88MW of propulsive power overall. The two engine rooms are physically separated for damage control purposes, whilst the gas turbine exhaust uptakes running from each engine room are fitted with infrared suppression systems to reduce the ship's heat signature. The gas turbines were assembled in India by Hindustan Aeronautics Limited (HAL).

The two gas turbines in each engine room are connected to one of the twin shaft lines by a Renk BS 2*252 gearbox. Each of the two gearboxes weighs around 90 tonnes and includes some components manufactured by India's Elecon Engineering. The gearbox in the forward engine room is connected to the port shaft line, which – at some 100m in length – is the longest in any Indian warship. Similarly, the aft engine room powers the shorter, starboard shaft.

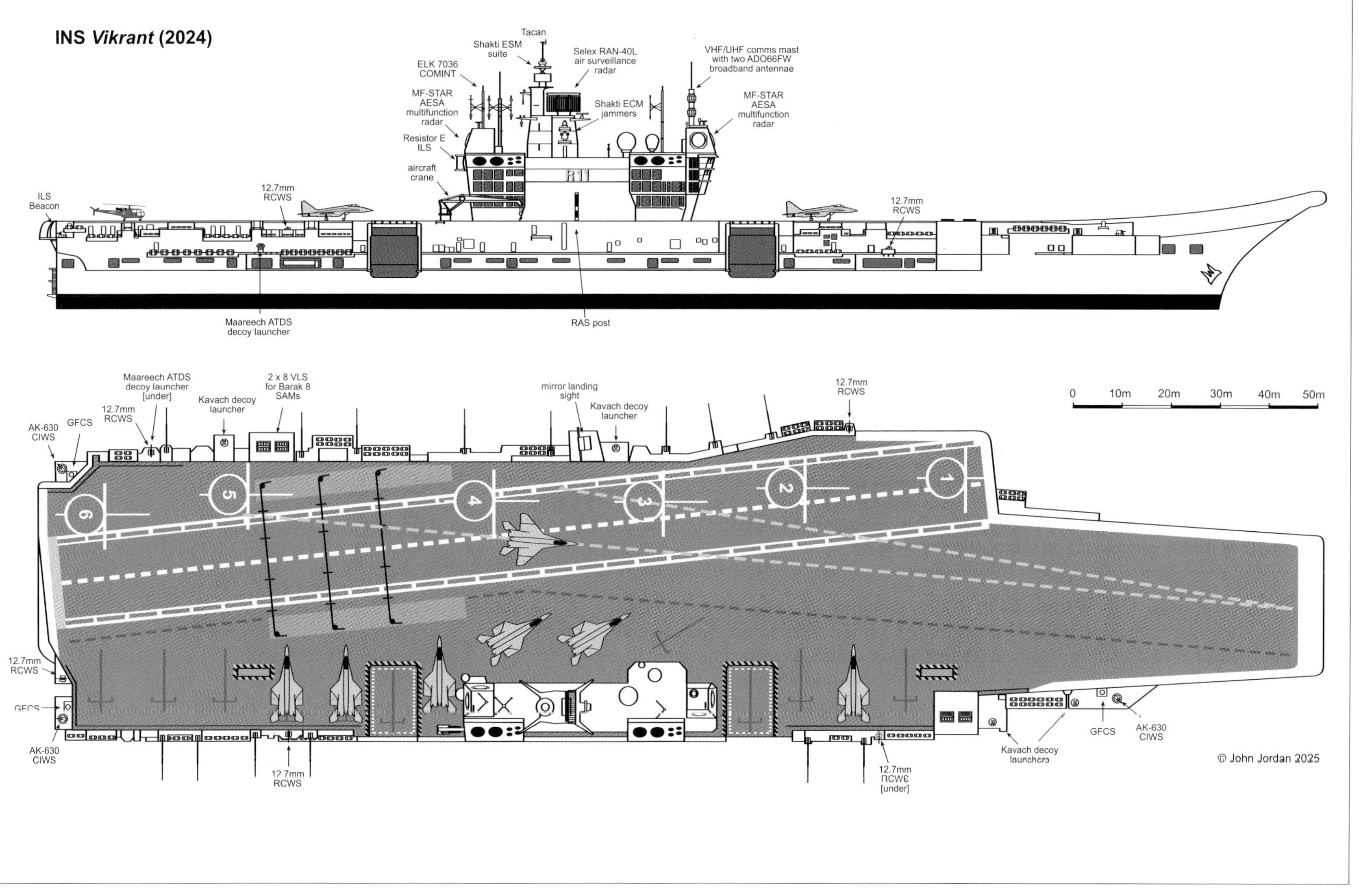

This stern view of *Vikrant* was taken whilst the carrier was underway during early sea trials. The image gives a good impression of the way that sponsons have been used to maximise her flight deck area. *Vikrant* can achieve a maximum speed of 28 knots from a COGAG-type propulsion system that is controlled by an integrated platform system manufactured by India's BHEL working in partnership with Avio of Italy. *(Indian Navy)*

The shaft lines are fitted with Wärtsilä CPP 5C20 five-bladed, controllable pitch propellers. Maximum speed is in the region of 28 knots. Manoeuvrability is provided by twin rudders.

Power generation capacity is provided by a total of eight Wärtsilä diesel generators; believed to be the company's 12V26 model. Each generates around 3MW of power, providing 24MW capacity overall. Four generators are housed in each of the forward and aft generator/alternator rooms that are again physically separated for reasons of survivability. The generators provide power to a main switchboard complex manufactured by Larsen & Toubro Electrical that, in turn, feeds several energy distribution centres located throughout the ship. The electrical power system is controlled by an automatic power management system (APMS) module that forms part of *Vikrant*'s broader integrated platform management system.

Integrated Platform Management System (IPMS): *Vikrant*'s IPMS was supplied by BHEL working in partnership with Avio of Italy. It provides a high level of automation in connection with the management and control of various critical ship systems through a number of functional modules. The IPMS's main functions include propulsion and manoeuvring, the aforementioned automatic power management, auxiliary system control, battle damage control, flying systems control, onboard training, and equipment health monitoring. It also encompasses a network of CCTV cameras and integrates with other systems, such as the carrier's integrated bridge system (IBS). In similar fashion to other modern IPMS, the system has an open architecture and utilises a distributed digital data network.

The focal point for IPMS control is the Ship Control Centre (SCC); the hub for the monitoring and control of propulsion, power generation and other shipboard systems. It is equipped with numerous operator consoles and large-screen displays. It is supplemented by secondary control positions and several dozen remote terminal units (RTUs) located throughout the ship. These serve as 'process level' data collection units, receiving information from thousands of equipment and hazard detection sensors linked by the data network. Importantly, the IPMS allows operation of a comprehensive range of systems from any operator station.

Damage Control: An important component of the IPMS is the battle damage control system (BDCS). This receives data from a network of fire and flood detection sensors and acts as a decision-making aid during damage control operations for the damage control headquarters and zonal damage control teams. The BDCS also includes a stability management element that, for example, can guide counter-flooding measures.

A comprehensive list of damage control hardware is headed by a SEM-SAFE high-pressure water mist fire-fighting system in the two engine rooms. This utilises a dry pipework system and does not require crew evacuation prior to release. It is supplemented by the supplier's bilge foam protection system. The ship's Johnson Controls-suppled HVAC system potentially forms another important element of the damage control response, being equipped with a smoke extraction system that operates independently in each fire zone. Its extensive ducting system incorporates remotely operated shut-off valves that help to maintain the watertight integrity of the ship's various sections in case of flooding.[15]

Accommodation and Habitability: *Vikrant*'s complement is variously reported as being between 1,600 and 1,700, potentially surging to almost 2,000 if required.[16] There are separate cabins for female officers and accommodation areas for female enlisted sailors. The crew accommodation was outfitted by UK-based Varivane – also a contractor for the *Queen Elizabeth* class carriers – under sub-contract to principal supplier Maritime Montering (Marinor) India. Varivane produced and supplied a complete set of accommodation furniture in accordance with the specifications of Def Stan 02-128. Constructed from steel, this included two and three-tier bunks, various lockers and cabinets. Marinor was also responsible for supplying the 'wet spaces' – 92 sanitation areas equipped with showers and vacuum toilets – that are distributed throughout the ship. Its website states that there are sufficient facilities for 1,950 crew, in line with the surge capacity previously referenced.

Vikrant seen operating with the Project 15A destroyer *Kolkata* around the time of the carrier's delivery. Although not installed in *Vikrant* at the time, both ships are now fitted with the Israeli Barak 8 surface-to-air missile system and associated MF-STAR multi-function radar, which – inter alia – provides missile guidance capabilities. An increasing number of Indian Navy warships are being fitted with this equipment, which supports a cooperative engagement capability under which missiles launched from one ship can be directed by another. *(Indian Navy)*

The ship has three main galleys; one for officers and two for ratings. They utilise electricity for all cooking purposes and incorporate a high level of automation. Crewed by between 30 and 50 sailors working in watches, they can serve over 5,000 meals each day. Meals are eaten in eight dining halls or messes, with officers having separate spaces.

Vikrant is equipped with a comprehensive medical complex typically crewed by five doctors and 15 paramedics. It encompasses two modular operating theatres, two intensive care units, a dental facility, medical laboratories and – in a first aboard an IN warship – a CT scanner. There are sufficient beds for 16 patients. Other crew facilities include a laundry, gym, libraries and recreational spaces.

SHIP DESCRIPTION: COMBAT AND AVIATION SYSTEMS

Whilst *Vikrant*'s primary combat capability is obviously provided by its embarked air wing, this capacity is supported by a complex network of integrated systems and sensors to achieve its full capacity.

Combat Management System (CMS): *Vikrant*'s CMS-71 was developed as a collaborative effort between India's Tata Power Strategic Engineering Division (TPSED), the IN's Weapon Equipment and Systems Engineering Establishment (WESEE) and Russia's MARS JSC. The Russian company reportedly supplied the Lesorub-E CMS installed in *Vikramaditya* and there is likely a degree of similarity between the two systems. The CMS is linked to the carrier's various weapons and sensors via the BEL-supplied SDN-71 Ethernet-based ship data network. Information provided from the sensors is displayed on the usual multi-function consoles and large displays associated with these systems that are located in the operations room and other command spaces such as the various bridges.

Weapons Systems and Sensors: Other than her air group, *Vikrant*'s primary weapons system is the Israeli Barak 8 surface-to-air missile. Somewhat confusingly, this is described in IN literature as both a medium-range (MRSAM) and long-range surface-to-air missile (LRSAM). The missile works in conjunction with the Elta EL/M-2248 MF-STAR multi-function radar, whose four fixed arrays are located in the island structure. Each array has a

This photograph of *Vikrant* gives a good view of the forward and starboard arrays of her MF/STAR multi-function radar in their specially designed housing atop the forward part of her island structure. The system was installed during a post-delivery refit in the second half of 2023. Other equipment in evidence includes the ship's forward starboard AK-630M CIWS positioned slightly back from her bow and the starboard, 16-cell silo for the Barak 8 missile system further aft. A Sea King helicopter hovers over the flight deck, *(Angad Singh)*

bespoke version of BEL Mk XII IFF antenna mounted above it. There are two groups of two, eight-cell Barak vertical launch system (VLS) modules, with one group each located to the port and starboard of the carrier's flight deck for a total 32-cell capacity. The system is equipped with datalinks providing a cooperative engagement capability (CEC) with other similarly-equipped IN units; the Project 15A and Project 15B destroyers and Project 17A frigates. Neither missiles nor radar were installed when *Vikrant* was first delivered, being retrofitted during a subsequent refit in the second half of 2023.[17]

Close-in defence is in the hands of three, license-built AK-630M close-in weapons systems (CIWS), each directed by a BEL-manufactured optronic fire control system. They are supplemented by five positions for 0.5in (12.7mm) remotely-controlled weapons stations, supplied by Israel's Elbit but assembled locally. Hard kill defences include four Kavach Mod 2 decoy launchers and two additional launchers for torpedo defence; either the long-established Mareech or the new Ultra-Mahindra Defence Systems Integrated Anti-Submarine Warfare Defence Suite (IADS). There is likely to be an associated towed sonar system. Earlier plans to fit four OTO 76mm guns were seemingly dropped at some point during construction.

Beyond the EL/M-2248 MF-STAR, a Selex RAN-40L L band (NATO C/D band) long-range surveillance radar is amongst the more important sensors. This can detect and track aerial targets out to a range of around 400km. There are a number of additional navigational radars, whilst official releases state that diver detection sonar is also fitted.

The ship's principal electronic warfare (EW) system is BEL's integrated Shakti. This incorporates a radar-electronic support measures (R-ESM) antenna mounted below the tactical air navigation (TACAN) antenna towards the top of the mainmast and two pairs of electronic countermeasures (ECM) jammers towards the bottom of the mast structure. Amongst a range of other sensors – some previously unseen – is a mast towards the aft of the island for Elta's ELK-7036 communications intelligence system.

Communications: *Vikrant*'s external communications are undertaken by a BEL-manufactured Advanced Composite Communication System (ACCS); an IP-based integrated communication system that provides ship-to-ship, ship-to-shore and ship-to-air communication via radio and satellite links. The radio sub-system works over the entire spectrum whilst the satellite component operates in the Ku, C, S and UHF bands in conjunction with terminals that link with the IN's bespoke Rukmani Integrated Communication Network System (ICNS) and commercial satellite services. As might be expected, a full-range of internal communications systems are also provided.

The primary tactical data link is the Link 2 Mod 3 system, which is also supplied by BEL. The company describes it as being used to share tactical pictures in near-real time between ships, aircraft and shore-based Maritime Operations Centres. The system permits exchange of voice, video and imagery data along with tactical and messaging information amongst units at a published data rate of 2Mbps. It is fully integrated with the ACCS and the CMS-71 combat management system.

The decision to use the Russian MiG-29K (including the MiG-29KUB twin-seat variant) multi-role fighter as the centrepiece of *Vikrant*'s air group was the fundamental determinant of the configuration of her aviation facilities complex. This photograph shows an aircraft from Indian Naval Air Squadron (INAS) 303 'The Black Panthers', one of two squadrons which operate the type, aboard the carrier. *(Indian Navy)*

Aviation Facilities Complex (AFC): The Nevskoye Design Bureau-designed AFC, laid out over 600 compartments, comprises the equipment required for onboard aircraft operations. It encompasses 32 major systems, over half of which are of Russian origin.

The flight deck has an area of c. 12,500 square metres. Its STOBAR layout features a prominent 14-degree ski jump similar to that on the IN's other serving carrier, *Vikramaditya*. There are two take-off axes; a short take off runway of 145 metres for lightly-laden fighter aircraft and a long take off runway of 203m for aircraft with heavier payloads.[18] This enables the near-simultaneous launch of two fighters, one after the other. Fighters are held back by two hydraulic restraining systems (chocks) manufactured by RAC MiG as they power up for their take off runs. In a revision to the original IAC design, there are no jet blast deflectors. The landing runway is 191m long and angled at approximately six degrees from the ship's centreline. The configuration does not permit simultaneous take-offs and landings. The runway uses a Svetlana-2 three wire hydraulic arresting gear system supplied by Proletarsky Zavod in Russia. It is built to handle planes weighing in excess of 20 tonnes and to decelerate them during landing without exceeding a force of 4.5 times the force of gravity. This low deceleration limit ensures a smoother landing experience. There are six landing spots for helicopters marked 1 through 6, as well as parking spots for aircraft during flying operations. The Saturn flight deck lighting system – also called the light signalling system – is supplied by Russia's AeroSvet.

The hangar, located three decks below the flight deck, is the ship's largest compartment. It measures 119m by 22m and is over 6m in height. The hangar deck's floor area is approximately 2,600 square metres in area and it can accommodate up to 20 aircraft and helicopters. It is subdivided into two zones by a metallic fire curtain supplied by Darchem. Aircraft are moved to and from the flight deck via two 30-tonne side lifts supplied by Mac Taggart Scott. These measure 10m in width by 14m in length. The lift openings can be closed by hydraulically-operated, armoured doors when not in use. Two 8.95m turntables, supplied by Cargotec AB, align with the aircraft lifts and serve to rotate aircraft and position them for parking. Mototok LB7500 remotely operated tugs are used to move the aircraft whilst in the hangar. The hangar is well-equipped for aircraft refuelling, maintenance and servicing. Notably, it is equipped with a twelve metre long, four tonne, double beamed Pellegrini CPB 4-12 overhead maintenance gantry crane mounted transversely that travels on rails.

The Russian Resistor-E radar complex is used for air traffic, precision approach and landing control. Designed by Russia's NIIT-RK Institute, the system encompasses an azimuth-rangefinder radio beacon, a secondary radar, a glide path landing system, a dual-channel landing radar system and a flight control sub-complex. The last-mentioned provides navigation and digital flight data to shipborne aircraft operating at extended ranges from the carrier. The precision approach guidance system helps fighters on approach to be directed down on a glideslope to a distance of 30m short of the flight deck, after which the pilot uses visual cues from the JSC Elektropribor supplied Luna-3E Optical Landing System (OLS) for the terminal phase of landing. The Resistor-E precision approach radar system is also installed in *Vikramaditya* and a variant in the Russian carrier *Admiral Kuznetsov*.

A pancake-shaped TACAN antenna supplied by Moog – now Thales – sits atop the main mast. It is assumed that the TACAN antenna works in conjunction with other elements of the Resistor-E system.

The Luna-3E OLS's light system is housed in a cabin with protruding arms located on the port side of the flight deck aft of landing spot 3. It comprises ten datum lights on a horizontal bar, five vertically oriented lights (two yellow, one green, two red) to indicate the correct glideslope angle, and two wave-off lights. In daytime, these lights are visible to about 2.5km to 3km and up to 5km at night. The IN wants lights that can be seen farther out and at better resolution. India's Central Scientific Instruments Organization (CSIO) has tested an improved system that is being put into production.

The MTK-201E TV tracking system, from Russia's FSUE TV Research Institute, monitors aircraft taking off, landing, and moving on the flight deck. It also supports visual monitoring of the radar blind spots on the sea surface directly in front of and behind the ship. The TV tracking system, which can operate in twilight (or full moon conditions), auto tracks incoming aircraft established on the approach glideslope from 4.5 to 5km away and provides range and deviations in approach path about three kilometres before touchdown. The system includes five colour cameras housed in protective cases.

The Ilmen inertial navigation system (INS) data transfer system and GUVK gyroscopic initialisation system supplied by Russia's Electropribor provides pre-flight 'transfer alignment' of the carrier's positional data to an aircraft's INS to 'initialise' the aircraft's position and orientation relative to the moving carrier. Performed shortly before launch, this data is crucial for the aircraft's safe and effective navigation from launch through to recovery, allowing it to navigate accurately, perform tactical

Vikrant's Aviation Facilities Complex (AFC) was designed by Russia's Nevskoye Design Bureau. This photograph shows a night landing being conducted by a MiG-29K fighter whilst guided by the JSC Elektropribor supplied Luna-3E Optical Landing System, which can be seen to the left of the aircraft's tail. The Saturn flight deck lighting system – also called the light signalling system – is supplied by Russia's AeroSvet. *(Indian Navy)*

manoeuvres and find its way back to the mothership.

Control of flight deck operations and of aircraft in the carrier's immediate vicinity is provided from the flying control position ('flyco') at Deck 04 level. This interfaces with an Air Direction Room that manages the overall air situation picture, providing air traffic control and command of carrier-borne and other Indian airborne assets in the carrier's operational area. BEL/Motorola supplied the flight deck communications system.

Air Group: As has already been explained, *Vikrant* has been primarily designed around an air wing centred on the MiG-29K STOVL multi-role fighter. This seemingly explains some unusual design decisions, notably the 'tight' dimensions of the carrier's lifts. Other aircraft envisaged for operation onboard the carrier during the design phase included the naval variant of the diminutive LCA – which was ultimately to be the first fixed-wing aircraft to land on the ship – and a range of helicopters. As a result of a decision taken in 2016, the IN does not intend to acquire the LCA for operational use.

A typical air wing is believed to encompass about 30 fixed-wing aircraft but more could be embarked, dependent on mix and the operational scenario. The IN currently operates around 40 single-seat MiG-29K and two-seat MiG-29KUB jets in two squadrons. Imagery shows as many as 15 of these aircraft aboard *Vikrant*'s deck at any one time. Other commonly embarked types include Westland Sea King Mk 42B ASW and Kamov Ka-31 airborne early warning helicopters, as well as the venerable Chetak light utility type. Visiting aircraft have included the new Sikorsky MH-60R and naval variants of the HAL Dhruv.

The IN has had a less than stellar experience with MiG-29K operations, suffering serious reliability and serviceability issues. To date, five of the 45 aircraft it acquired in two batches have been lost to accidents. A lengthy process to select a replacement saw the US Navy Super Hornet pitted against the French Rafale M. The latter type's selection in mid-2023 was followed by signature of a contract for 26 aircraft in April 2025. Deliveries are set to commence in 2028-9. Questions have been raised in the local media about the Rafale's ability to fit on *Vikrant*'s narrow lifts, although this was apparently achieved during trials.[19]

These photographs of *Vikrant* (foreground) sailing with the older *Vikramaditya* in the course of 'two carrier' operations in June 2023 highlights some of the similarities and differences exhibited by the two STOBAR equipped carriers. Whilst the overall configuration of the two ships' Russian-designed aviation facilities are similar, *Vikrant*'s purpose-built design – including her twin side lifts – means that she is able to perform fast jet operations more efficiently. *(Indian Navy)*

In March 2025, *Vikrant* exercised with the French *Charles de Gaulle* carrier strike group in the 'Varuna 2025' exercise, when this photograph was taken. The integration of the French Rafale M into *Vikrant*'s air wing from the late 2020s onwards will increase her overall potential as an instrument of Indian 'blue water' naval power. *(Kevin Auger/ Marine Nationale)*

Further down the line, *Vikrant*'s airwing is expected also to include the planned Twin Engine Deck-Based Fighter (TEDBF), which is currently under development at HAL. Current plans anticipate a first flight in 2028 and entry into service from 2035; targets which appear optimistic on past experience. A new Utility Helicopter Maritime (UHM) derived from the Dhruv is expected to fly within the next twelve months.

INTO SERVICE

Vikrant's commissioning in the presence of Prime Minister Modi in September 2022 was only the first step along the road to the carrier obtaining full operational status. As noted previously, full integration and testing of the AFC as part of air certification and flight integration trials formed an important part of this process, commencing with 'touch and go' landings. Subsequently, on 6 February 2023, the LCA Navy variant NP-2, piloted by Commodore Shivnath 'Dax' Dahiya, landed aboard *Vikrant*, and then took off. A MiG-29K piloted by Commodore Biplab Hota also 'trapped' aboard the *Vikrant* the same day. Subsequently, day and night landing trials of various aircraft and helicopters continued. The first night 'trap' by a Mig-29K took place 24 May 2023. The following month, *Vikrant* operated with *Vikramaditya* to showcase the IN's return to dual carrier operations.

Vikrant subsequently returned to CSL for a post-delivery refit and installation of additional equipment that included the MF-STAR /Barak missile combination. The carrier returned to sea at the end of 2024 to commence final operational clearance work-up. In February 2024, *Vikrant* again operated in company with *Vikramaditya* as part of the 'MILAN 2024' international exercise. In September that year, it was reported that the carrier had joined India's Western Fleet, again conducting dual carrier operations. In December 2024, the IN confirmed that full operational capability had been achieved.

The first half of 2025 proved to be busy for the new carrier. In March, she exercised with the French *Charles de Gaulle* carrier strike group in the 'Varuna 2025' exercise, thereby underscoring the deepening relationship between the two navies. In May, the short four-day conflict between India and Pakistan (7 May to 10 May 2025) saw *Vikrant* deployed operationally in the western Indian Ocean as part of the overarching Operation 'Sindoor'. Although the IN carrier group saw no combat, the deployment served to highlight the navy's increasing ability to operate in a complex threat environment under the protective 'bubble' of a layered air defence capability whilst holding enemy targets at risk of long-range precision attack.

Vikrant's deployment as part of Operation' Sindoor' during the brief conflict with Pakistan in May 2025 demonstrated the Indian Navy's increasing ability to operate in a complex threat environment. More broadly, her construction has provided India's naval sector with the institutaional knowledge to execute further projects of this type. *(Indian Navy)*

NEXT STEPS

Vikrant's entry into operational service marks a return to IN two carrier operation and an important step towards the ultimate goal of a three carrier-strong fleet. In line with this ambition, the IN has long been studying a project for a second indigenous aircraft carrier (IAC-2), allocated the provisional name of *Vishal*. Information entering the public domain suggests that the navy's preference was for a larger, conventional CATOBAR-configured ship benefiting from recent US Navy launch and recovery equipment. However, institutional opposition to the expense of this programme within the Indian Ministry of Defence and from other branches of the armed forces has seen the plan for a large IAC-2 fail to gain traction.

The IN has seemingly changed tack in the face of this opposition, proposing a smaller carrier as a replacement for *Vikramaditya*, thereby shifting the short-term narrative to maintaining the existing force structure. Press speculation suggests that the revised plan for IAC-2 might result in procurement of an evolved variant of the *Vikrant* design. This would capitalise on the experience Indian industry has gained from the Project 71 design and construction process.

Vikrant has certainly demonstrated the ability of the Indian naval sector to build a ship of this complexity, overcoming a myriad of challenges in the 17 years that elapsed from first steel cutting in 2005 to commissioning in 2022. The institutional knowledge obtained from this journey means that the country's warship building ecosystem is now better placed to undertake a similar programme of this nature. In the meantime, as recent events have demonstrated, *Vikrant*'s arrival has enhanced the navy's goal of being the pre-eminent 'net security provider' across the Indian Ocean Region whilst significantly advancing its blue water ambitions.

Notes:

1. Principal sources for this section include (Vice Admiral) Anup Singh's history *Blue Waters Ahoy! – The Indian Navy 2001-2010* (Noida: Harper Collins Publishers India, 2018), pp.34-50 and (Admiral) Arun Prakash, 'India's Quest for an Indigenous Aircraft Carrier' in *RUSI Defence Systems Summer 2006* (London: RUSI, 2006), pp. 50-52. Admiral Prakash was India's Chief of the Naval Staff at the time, Information in these and other sources is not always entirely consistent.

2. The information on a planned two carrier programme is contained in contemporary editions of *Jane's Fighting Ships*. It seems that up to two additional ships might have been ultimately envisaged, with the IN long seeking to maintain at least three carriers so as to have two operational and one in refit or reserve. Sources on the required ships' displacement vary – Prakash states around 25,000 tons, *Jane's* 28,000 tons and Singh 35,000 tons. Singh's figure is supported by a subsequent report into the IAC programme by India's Comptroller and Auditor General.

3. In a strategy reminiscent of the invention of the term 'through deck cruiser' for the British Royal Navy's *Invincible* class light aircraft carriers, the euphemistic 'Air Defence Ship' was seemingly adopted to lessen opposition to the IN's carrier programme from other branches of the Indian Armed Forces.

4. Although the contract to acquire what became *Vikramaditya* was not signed until early 2004, an understanding of MiG-29K operating requirements had been obtained from years of prior negotiations.

5. It has been speculated that the IN purposely sought concrete authorisation for a smaller and cheaper carrier knowing that it would then be easier to obtain a revised approval for the larger and more expensive MiG-29K-capable variant once that ship's design had been fully developed.

6. These details are provided in *Blue Waters Ahoy!*, p.39.

7. There are similarities between *Vikrant's* propulsion train and that used in the Italian aircraft carrier *Cavour*. Moreover, the AFC designed by the Nevskoye Design Bureau has significant commonality with that used in the modernised *Vikramaditya*.

8. See the Comptroller and Auditor General of India (CAGI), 'Performance report on construction of Indigenous Aircraft Carrier' in *Report No 17 of 2016 (Navy and Coast Guard)* (New Delhi; The Comptroller and Auditor General of India, 2016), p.27. This is currently available by searching the web. The report is an excellent source of information on progress with the project up to this time.

9. More specifically, delivery of the ship's eight diesel generators from Wärtsilä India fell behind schedule due to changes in the tender process, exacerbated by damage to two of the sets in an accident during transit. In addition, defects in components for the carrier's two gearboxes arising from production and quality control problems at the Indian contractor needed rectification, resulting in considerable delay.

10. By late 2014, CSL expected delivery to be delayed to as late as 2023 whilst the IN continued to press for a December 2018 date. Whilst delivery to the IN finally took place in 2022, it is worth noting that some important equipment was installed during a further period in shipyard hands after this date.

11. There is insufficient space to detail all the factors contributing to delayed delivery. The CAGI's *Report No 17 of 2016 (Navy and Coast Guard)* – pp.15-68 – provides many more examples.

12. The quantity of steel reportedly supplied by SAIL varies considerably from source to source. The company was unable to produce bulb flats (plate stiffeners) of sufficient quality for the project and these were eventually sourced from Russia.

13. This information was provided in a CSL press release, 'CSL delivers Indigenous Aircraft Carrier, Project 71 (Vikrant) to the Indian Navy' released on 28 July 2022.

14. Much of the information in this section has been collated and/or inferred from a combination of official briefings, tender documents and less formal press reports; as such some is open to revision.

15. The HVAC system is arguably one of the most complex aboard *Vikrant*. It comprises seven elements, viz. (i) a machinery ventilation system, (ii) a mechanical ventilation system; (iii) an aircraft cooling system, (iv) a smoke extraction system, (v) a chilled water system, (vi) a comfort cooling system, and (vii) a control system, which is integrated with the IPMS.

16. Documentation produced by CSL has suggested a crew of 1,614 (171 officers and 1443 sailors) but other sources quote higher numbers.

17. More details of the MF-STAR/Barak 8 combination are provided in the author's 'Kolkata Class Destroyers' in *Seaforth World Naval Review 2024* (Barnsley: Seaforth Publishing, 2023), pp.120-135.

18. An examination of photographs and drawings suggests that the longer take-off run might be a few metres longer than this, possibly reflecting an increase in the MiG-29Ks maximum take-off weight.

19. The MiG-29K and Rafale M designs are both described by David Hobbs in 'World Naval Aviation', *Seaforth World Naval Review 2011* (Barnsley: Seaforth Publishing, 2010), pp.163-79.

4.1 TECHNOLOGICAL REVIEW

Author:
David Hobbs

WORLD NAVAL AVIATION

A Review of Recent Developments

2025 saw the deployment – during separate periods – of carrier strike groups from Italy, France and the United Kingdom to the Indo-Pacific, underlining the fundamental importance of the region and the need to for allies to work together to protect trade and the rule of law. The largest of these was the Royal Navy's (RN's) Carrier Strike Group 25 (CSG25) based on HMS *Prince of Wales*. Significantly, it is anticipated that full operational capability (FOC) for F-35B carrier operations will be declared during the course of the deployment. This review also describes the rapid increase in the number of specialised drone carriers entering service and takes as its specialist topic the challenges encountered by navies that have procured the F-35B strike fighter for operation at sea.

The British Royal Navy aircraft carrier *Prince of Wales* pictured in April 2025 at the start of the CSG25 'Highmast' deployment to the Indo-Pacific. She will operate varying numbers of between 18 and 24 F-35B Lightning II strike fighters from two squadrons during the course of the mission. 'Highmast' is just one of three European CSG deployments to the Far East during 2024-5. *(Crown Copyright 2025)*

UNITED KINGDOM: ROYAL NAVY

In July 2024, a F-35B Lightning II of 809 Naval Air Squadron (NAS) carried out the unit's first sortie to be generated, dispatched, flown and then recovered by its own personnel. The achievement was described by its commanding officer, Commander Nick Smith RN, as 'not a small task for what is still a small, growing team'.[1] Subsequently, in October 2024, the squadron embarked in *Prince of Wales* with its sister F-35B unit – the Royal Air Force (RAF) badged 617 Squadron – to commence training in preparation for the Pacific deployment, which has been designated Operation 'Highmast'. In line with well-established arrangements that see personnel for F-35B drawn roughly equally from the RAF and Fleet Air Arm (FAA), the latter squadron is commanded by Lieutenant Colonel Mike Cary Royal Marines. He noted that his appointment demonstrates the degree of integration achieved within the Lightning force.

Training began at an elementary level since around 60 percent of 809 NAS' personnel including pilots, aircraft maintainers and support staff had never been to sea before. Pilots obtained their day and night carrier qualifications (CQs) and technicians learnt to integrate with carrier operations, which differ significantly from the routines carried out at RAF Marham, their UK base. Whilst the limited sea experience of the fixed-wing squadrons is striking it is, however, encouraging to learn that there are more aircraft technicians per aircraft embarked than was the case in *Queen Elizabeth*'s group deployment in 2021; a lesson seemingly learned from that experience.[2]

After completion of the training period, the CSG participated in Exercise 'Strike Warrior' off Scotland. This culminated in an operational readiness inspection (ORI), after which the whole CSG was declared as ready to deploy. *Prince of Wales* is to embark between 18 and 24 aircraft from the two F-35B Lightning squadrons during 'Highmast'; the exact number embarked being varied at different phases of the deployment to achieve exercise requirements whilst meeting the need to demonstrate the ship's ability to operate the higher number. She will also embark seven Merlin HM 2s of 820 NAS – four in the anti-submarine warfare (ASW) role and three in the airborne surveillance and control (ASaC) role – together with three Merlin HC 4s of 845 NAS in the commando, combat SAR and COD roles. Other ships in the strike group are to embark two ASW Merlin HM 2s of 814 NAS in the ASW role and two Wildcat HMA 2s of 815 NAS in the ASW and surface strike roles.[3] Deep maintenance – when necessary – and technical support for the embarked aircraft is to be provided by detachments from 1700 and 1710 NAS

Positively, the Merlin ASaC helicopters of 820 NAS with their Crowsnest avionics reached FOC shortly before Operation 'Highmast' commenced; a milestone described as hugely significant by Commander James Stone RN, the Crowsnest programme director. He described the ASaC role as one of the three pillars of carrier strike; the carrier itself, the fighters that deliver strike capability and ASaC which provides overarching co-ordination and maritime force protection.[4]

A novel feature of the 'Highmast' deployment is the embarkation of nine remotely-piloted, uncrewed air systems (UASs); Malloy T-150 octo-copters operated by 700X NAS. These are to be distributed

F-35B Lightning II strike fighters from 809 Naval Air Squadron and Royal Air Force 617 Squadron were embarked for training in *Prince of Wales* in October 2024, participating in the 'Strike Warrior' exercise off Scotland. This was the first time 809 NAS – reformed in December 2023 – has embarked in a *Queen Elizabeth* class aircraft carrier. *(Crown Copyright 2024)*

A Malloy T-150 octo-copter from the Royal Navy's 700X Naval Air Squadron drone unit seen in advance of being deployed aboard the carrier *Prince of Wales* for the CSG25 'Highmast' deployment. Nine of these systems will be used to transfer stores weighing up to 68kg between ships during the course of the operation. *(Crown Copyright 2025)*

A Wildcat HMA 2 helicopter on the deck of the Type 23 frigate *Iron Duke* during a night flying exercise. Wildcat capabilities continue to be improved, with the first guided firing of a Sea Venom missile from the type taking place in October 2024. The helicopter will also use the new Stingray Mod 2 ASW torpedo, an order for which was announced in 2025. *(Crown Copyright 2025)*

between three ships, including the carrier, and tasked with replacing crewed helicopters to provide a delivery service between ships. Malloy Aeronautics is a UK-based firm – now owned by BAE Systems – that has worked extensively with the British Ministry of Defence (MOD). Its T-150 has eight rotor blades, each about 2ft in length, powered by eight individual battery-operated electric motors. The batteries can be changed quickly to enable rapid turn-round times and it has an endurance of up to 36 minutes. It needs a team of two to operate it; a remote pilot and a second team member who monitors the command unit. It can be flown under direct control or autonomously to designated way points with an underslung cargo of up to 150lbs (68kg). Cruising speed is 58 knots. When not in use it can be folded into a protective case that can be carried by a single sailor.

The detachment commander, Lieutenant Matt Parfitt RN, stated that statistics from previous group deployments show that 95 percent of stores transferred between ships weigh less than 110lbs. The T-150 is, therefore, a much more efficient means of delivery and its use on this scale will help to expand knowledge of how to integrate uncrewed air systems into the operational airspace around the CSG. 700X NAS is also 'pushing the boundaries' of RN practice in the way that sailors are being trained as remote pilots qualified to fly drones and supervise others doing so. A typical 700X NAS remote pilot is Able Seaman Michael Page who began his RN career as a naval airman aircraft handler and is now qualified to 'fly' and supervise others on Puma and T-150 UASs. He briefed the media that he takes great pride in this responsibility and the fact that others take note of his skill, not his rank.[5]

After sailing on 22 April 2025, the CSG operated under NATO command for Exercise 'Neptune Strike' 2025-1 in the Mediterranean before training with an Italian carrier force headed by the carrier *Cavour*. After transiting the Suez Canal, the group is to conduct exercises with navies from the United States, India, Malaysia, and Singapore in the Indian Ocean before taking part in Exercise 'Talisman Sabre' in Australia. Training will be carried out with the Japan Maritime Self Defence Force (JMSDF) and other allies before returning to the United Kingdom via Suez at the end of the year.

Away from news related to CSG25, the first guided firing of a Sea Venom missile from a Wildcat HMA 2 took place in October 2024 against a target designed and built by QinetiQ engineers who positioned it in the Aberporth range area off the Welsh coast. The firing was organised by 744 NAS, the RN test and evaluation squadron, and every aspect of it went well. The smaller Martlet missile system is intended for use against small, fast targets and Sea Venom now complements it for use against targets up to corvette size. It has a 66lb (30kg) warhead and a range of just over ten nautical miles. A two-way data link displays the images 'seen' by the missile's infrared seeker on the Wildcat observer's tactical display and allows several control options. It can be fired in an autonomous 'fire-and-forget' mode against a target detected by the helicopter but the man-in-the-loop, monitor-and-control facilities allow the observer to re-target the missile in flight, correct the final point of aim if necessary or order a safe abort. Sea Venom can also be used against targets on land, even in a complex littoral environment.

In February 2025 the RN made its first operational use of a remotely-piloted helicopter from the deck of an RN warship, the Type 23 frigate *Lancaster*, which is deployed in the Middle East. The air vehicle was an Austrian-built Schiebel S-100 Camcopter, named Peregrine in RN service and allocated airframe number ZP 526. It is 10ft (3m) long, has a maximum take-off weight of 243lbs (110kg), and has an endurance of over five hours at ranges beyond the parent ship's visual horizon. A team from 700X NAS operate the type, typically for sweeps of the Indian Ocean and Gulf of Oman, downloading live radar pictures and clear imagery to displays in the frigate's operations room. Ideal for long, monotonous patrols by day and night, Peregrine's use leaves the crewed Wildcat HMA 2 free for interdiction or strike missions.

Despite Peregrine's success, the RN has no plans to procure any more of the type because it is working with Leonardo on a project to develop a larger uncrewed helicopter named Proteus. This is a more advanced air vehicle with a projected maximum take-off weight of 6,600lbs (2.7 tonnes), which forms a key element of the RN's Maritime Aviation Transformation (MATx) strategy. It features advances in autonomy, modular payload capability and rotorcraft manufacturing and design techniques. First flight is scheduled for mid-2025 and, once its flight properties and systems have been proven, it is to be evaluated first in the ASW role. The RN sees Proteus as being adaptable between a wide range of potential missions since the modular payload bay allows different loads ranging from mission-specific equipment such as sonobuoys, extra fuel or weapons – including the Stingray Mod 2 torpedo – to be carried.

The RN announced in 2025 that Stingray torpedoes, the primary ASW weapon used by Merlin and Wildcat helicopters, are to be upgraded to Mod 2 standard by BAE Systems. The Mod 0 entered service in 1983 and the Mod 1 in 2001. The latter is widely regarded as a superior weapon to the US Mark 54 against fast, deep-diving nuclear-powered submarines but its use against small targets in shallow, congested waters was limited by the time taken to initiate its search pattern after entering the water. It is this shortcoming that is believed to have been addressed in the Mod 2, which is also likely to have improved lethality against small, stealthy uncrewed underwater vehicles that have become a significant threat. Stingray Mod 2 is designed to be compatible with P-8A Poseidon maritime patrol aircraft (MPA) software and is to be made available for export to all P-8A operators.

UNITED STATES

The US budget plans for Navy and Marine Corps aircraft acquisition in FY2026 that were published in late June 2025 are set out in Table 4.1.1. As is often the case in a new presidential administration's first year, the figures only showed planned procurement for the year ahead rather than for the longer, five year period of the Future Years Defense Program (FYDP). Whilst overall year-on-year spending – which includes modifications, spares and support equipment – has increased, the actual number of aircraft requested is much lower than for FY2025, and also compared with the previous Biden administration's plan for the year. It seems that this, at least in part, reflects a decision to focus available funding on addressing problems with the roll-out of the F-35 Lightning II's Block 4 standard software, described more fully later in this chapter.

Table 4.1.1: US NAVY PLANNED AIRCRAFT PROCUREMENT FY2026

TYPE	MISSION	FY2024 FUNDED[1]	FY2025 FUNDED[2]	FY2026 2025 PLAN[3]	FY2026 CURRENT PLAN[4]	CHANGE FY2026 (NEW V OLD)
Fixed Wing (Carrier Based)						
F-35B Lightning II JSF	Strike Fighter (STOVL)	16	13	13	11	-2
F-35C Lightning II JSF	Strike Fighter (CV)	19	17	14	12	-2
E-2D Advanced Hawkeye	Surveillance/Control	2	0	0	4	+4
Fixed Wing (Land Based)						
P-8A Poseidon	Maritime Patrol	10	0	0	0	0
KC-130J Hercules	Tanker	3	2	0	0	0
UC-12W Huron	Logistics	3	0	0	1	+1
T-45 Replacement [5]	Training	0	0	10	0	-10
T-54A [6]	Training	26	27	0	0	0
Rotary Wing						
CH-53K King Stallion	Heavy-Lift	15	20	18	12	-6
C/MV-22/B Osprey	Transport	5	0	0	0	0
Uncrewed Aerial Vehicles						
MQ-25 Stingray	Refuelling	0	0	3	3	0
MQ-4C Triton	Maritime Patrol	2	0	0	0	0
MQ-9A Reaper	Surveillance/Strike	5	0	0	0	0
Total		106 (US$19.8bn)	79 (US$15.9bn)	58 (N/A)	43 (US$17.1bn)	-15 (N/A)

Notes
1. Authorised FY2024 programme
2. Authorised FY2025 programme
3. FY2026 programme in the Biden administration's FY2025 five-year, Future Years Defence Program (FYDP)
4. FY2026 programme requested by second Trump administration
5. Refers to replacement of the T-45 Goshawk training aircraft.
6. The T-54A is the replacement for the T-44 Pegasus twin-engine turboprop trainer. Both are part of the King Air series of aircraft.
7. US$ figures represent the 'Total Aircraft Procurement' line in the Trump administration's FY2026 budget.

US NAVY: The Huntington Ingalls Industries (HII) shipyard at Newport News, Virginia currently has three *Ford* (CVN-78) nuclear-powered aircraft carriers under construction, with the *Nimitz* (CVN-68) class carrier *John Stennis* (CVN-74) also undergoing refuelling and complex overhaul (RCOH) at the facility. The yard continues to struggle to deliver ships to time in a reflection of the wider woes being experienced by the US naval industrial base.

According to testimony by Rear Admiral Casey Moton USN, Programme Executive Officer for Aircraft Carriers, to the Senate Armed Services Seapower and Projection Forces Sub-committee in April 2024, *John F Kennedy* (CVN 79) – second ship of the *Ford* class – was nearly 95 percent construction complete at that time. However, there was significant pressure on the contracted delivery date of July 2025 due to challenges with the carrier's weapons elevators and advanced arresting gear (AAG); issues that had also previously impacted *Ford*. It now seems that completion is likely in late 2026. The next ship, *Enterprise* (CVN-80) – some 44 percent complete in April 2025 – is also suffering delays, with delivery now anticipated to slip from 2029 to 2030. She will be followed by *Doris Miller* (CVN-81) – around 20 percent complete and less impacted by scheduling issues – in 2032. Current costs of the three ships are US$12.9 billion for CVN 79, US$13.5 billion for CVN 80 and US$14.0 billion for CVN-81. In January 2025, outgoing US President Joe Biden announced that the next two carriers would be named *William J. Clinton* (CVN-82) and *George W. Bush* (CVN-83), although neither vessel is yet under contract. The latter name potentially creates confusion with the existing *George H. W. Bush* (CVN-77), which will likely still be in service when CVN-83 is delivered.

At the other end of the spectrum, *Nimitz* is due to complete her last deployment in April 2026. She is scheduled to decommission at Norfolk, Virginia in May 2026 after which the hull will be moved to Newport News where HII will begin the lengthy process of deactivating her.

Meanwhile, the high tempo of carrier operations has continued, with aircraft from *Harry S. Truman* (CVN-75) being notably active as part of Operation 'Prosperity Guardian'; the ongoing mission to protect Red Sea shipping from Houthi attacks. In the course of these operations in December 2024, a F/A-18F Super Hornet of VFA-11, the 'Red Rippers' – part of Truman's Carrier Air Wing 1 (CVW-1) was shot down in error by a missile fired by the cruiser *Gettysburg* (CG-64), the CSG's own air defence co-ordinator. This 'friendly-fire' incident occurred at about 0300 local time on Sunday 22 December; the aircraft's two aircrew ejected successfully and were recovered quickly. Initial assessments revealed that one had suffered only minor injuries. A full investigation was begun immediately.

Subsequently, on 12 February 2025, *Truman* was involved in a collision with the merchant vessel MV *Besiktas-M* near the entrance to the Suez Canal. The carrier suffered a pierced hull above the waterline on the starboard quarter and damage to a sponson located aft of number three lift. The exterior bulkheads of two storage compartments and a maintenance space were also damaged. Repairs were carried out quickly by a US Navy emergent repair facility at Souda Bay, Crete, and she was under way again by the end of February. On 20 February the navy announced that the ship's commanding officer had been removed due to a loss of confidence in his ability to command following the collision. Further mishaps led to two other Super Hornets being lost accidentally during the deployment; one slid off a

The fast combat support ship *Arctic* (T-AOE 8) sails alongside the *Nimitz* (CVN-68) class aircraft carrier *Harry S. Truman* (CVN-75) during a replenishment-at-sea conducted whilst the vessels were participating in NATO exercise 'Neptune Strike 2024-2' in October 2024. The aircraft carrier lost a total of three Super Hornets in various accidents in the course of an eventful deployment that involved significant combat action against Houthi rebel forces in the Red Sea. *(US Navy)*

side-lift with its tractor as the ship carried out a hard turn to evade an incoming Houthi attack in April and the other went over the side on landing in May after failing to catch an arrester wire. Both aircrew ejected successfully. A collision and the accidental loss of three fighters will be of great concern to the US Navy and this deployment is likely to be closely analysed to discover the underlying reasons.

A statement announcing the successful contractor for the development phase of the US Navy's next generation air dominance (NGAD) F/A-XX fighter had been widely expected in early 2025. This sixth generation aircraft is intended to form the focal point of a new generation of fighters and lower-cost drones within a manned-unmanned teaming (MUM-T) concept. It is described as a crewed replacement for F/A-18E/F Block II airframes as they reach the end of their effective lives in the mid-2030s, with a vision statement for F/A-XX written in 2021 indicating that it will have both greater range and speed than the Super Hornet to complement the F-35C in carrier air wings. To date, little has been said about the uncrewed aerial vehicles (UAVs) that are to form the MUM-T relationship with F/A-XX. In June 2025, it emerged that FY2026 funding would be limited to completing the initial F/A-XX design effort, deferring a decision on the next stage of the programme to some date in the future. Instead, the US has decided to prioritise the US Air Force's (USAF's) own NGAD programme. The contractor for this sixth-generation fighter has already been determined, with President Trump announcing on 21 March 2025 that Boeing had been awarded the deal for what is now identified as the F-47.

Somewhat closer to hand than the F/A-XX is the uncrewed Boeing MQ-25A Stingray. Vice Admiral Daniel Cheever USN, Commander Naval Air Forces, confidently told the WEST 2025 Conference in January 2025 that a production example would fly in 2025 and operate from a carrier in 2026 when the USN will 'start integrating

A prototype MQ-25 Stingray uncrewed refuelling aircraft seem at Scott Air Force Base, Illinois in May 2023. Production examples of the type are scheduled to be embarked for carrier operations in 2026 after considerable delay. *(US Air Force)*

that thing'.[6] He acknowledged that the aircraft has greater potential than the tanker role the US Navy has initially planned for it but said that he was just 'going to turn the weapons tactics instructors loose and they will figure out how to operate this thing seamlessly in a manned unmanned teaming thing'. The carrier trials projected for 2026 come thirteen years after the Northrop Grumman X-47B made the first carrier landing by an uncrewed aircraft. Since then the US Navy appears to have moved with almost glacial slowness as it makes preparations to operate uncrewed aircraft from carriers.

Quality control issues have delayed the delivery of the first production MQ-25As but these are being resolved. Stingray is specified to operate at up to 500 nautical miles from the carrier with 15,000lbs of transferable fuel to extend the radius of action of the carrier's strike fighters, but its airframe was not originally optimised for the tanker role. Aircraft carriers are being fitted with ground stations to operate them but the MQ-25A is a big aircraft with a length equivalent to a Super Hornet and a wingspan close to that of a Super Hawkeye; there are clearly some senior officers who have reservations about integrating it into crewed carrier operations. Admiral Cheever ended his presentation by stressing that MQ-25A 'unlocks the future of manned-unmanned teaming' and other speakers agreed that this teaming could include collaborative combat aircraft that can provide 'adjunct magazines' for fighters. However, Rear Admiral Keith Hash, Commander of the Naval Air Warfare Centre's weapons division seemingly adopted a more conservative tone when he spoke of making sure that that 'you can take an unmanned platform and put it on a carrier'. His centre's work is to include evaluation of Stingray operations within the air wing; new systems that should go on the aircraft in the future' and what new roles they could play as they become part of the air wing.

Whereas the US Navy is moving quite slowly to integrate UAVs into carrier air wings, it has demonstrated that weapons for which it sees a clear and immediate need can be introduced quickly. Since the withdrawal of the F-14 Tomcat and its Phoenix missile system in 2006, the US Navy has lacked a fighter capable of fighting the outer air battle against potentially hostile bombers armed with stand-off missiles such as the Chinese Xian H-6, a derivative of the Russian Tu-16 'Badger'. These can carry up to six missiles which outrange the AIM-120D, the beyond-visual-range (BVR) missile carried by F/A-18E/F Super Hornets. Analysts highlighted this shortcoming and the US Navy has responded with the AIM-174B. This was first seen carried by Super Hornets from CVW-2 embarked in *Carl Vinson* (CVN-70) when they took part in RIMPAC 24. Known as the 'Gunslinger', AIM-174B is an air-launched derivative of the USN's Raytheon SM-6 missile which arms cruisers and destroyers and has a range in excess of 200 nautical miles. Launched from a high-speed aircraft at altitude, AIM-174's range could be even greater, potentially destroying bombers before they launch their missiles against a carrier group. The missile can be used against targets beyond the range of the F/A-18's own APG-79 radar since the naval integrated fire control-counter air (NIFCCA) system can use radar data from surface ships and airborne E-2D Hawkeye ASaC aircraft to provide information for the 'shooter' to engage targets at extreme range.

A F/A-18E Super Hornet (rear) attached to Strike Fighter Squadron 192 (VFA-192), the 'World Famous Golden Dragons' and a F/A-18F Super Hornet, attached to Strike Fighter Squadron 2 (VFA-2), the 'Bounty Hunters', prepare to launch from the flight deck of the *Nimitz* (CVN-68) class aircraft carrier *Carl Vinson* (CVN-70) in May 2025. The Super Hornet's combat capabilities are being enhanced by introduction of the new AIM-174B 'Gunslinger' air-to-air missile, which is based on the Raytheon Standard SM-6 missile and has a reported range in excess of 200 nautical miles. *(US Navy)*

US MARINE CORPS: Two years on from the loss of a USAF CV-22 Osprey that crashed in Japan in 2023 killing eight airmen, the US Marine Corps (USMC) and US Navy Osprey fleets still operate under restrictions despite the Naval Air Systems Command lifting of the type's complete grounding in March 2024. They must operate within 30 minutes flying time from a diversion airfield at all times, posing obvious challenges for embarked aircraft. Commenting on the situation in early 2025, Captain Drew Beard USN, Deputy Commodore of the USN Fleet Logistics Multi-Mission Wing told USNI that the restrictions just have to be incorporated into plans.[7] The initial grounding meant that aging C2A Greyhounds had to replace the CMV-22B carrier onboard delivery (COD) aircraft that were to have embarked in the *Theodore Roosevelt* (CVN-71) and *Abraham Lincoln* (CVN-72) during scheduled deployments. The C-2As are due out of service in 2026 but there has, as yet, been no statement about plans to extend their lives. Both the navy and USMC have few options other than to get their Ospreys working, as both intend to operate them until the late 2040s. Whereas the navy only plans to procure 48 Ospreys, the Marines' program of record is for 360. The 2025 Marine Aviation Plan describes new sensors to make the proprotor gearbox more reliable as an essential next step.[8] During the grounding the USMC used CH-53E helicopters for assault support but, later in 2024, managed to deploy MV-22Bs to the Baltic with the *Wasp* (LHD-1) amphibious ready group (ARG) within the stated restrictions.

Congress has refused to fund the Marine air-ground task force uncrewed expeditionary, medium-altitude, high-endurance uncrewed air system previously known as MUX but the USMC has retained its enthusiasm for the concept. It now seeks to achieve the aim using a family of systems including MQ-9A Reaper drones, amphibious ships and ground-based assets. In mid-2024 Marine Unmanned Aerial Squadron 3 (VMU-3), the 'Phantoms', achieved a significant step forward at Marine Corps Air Station (MCAS) Kaneohe Bay, Hawaii, when it carried out the first 'all Marine' launch of an MQ-9A remotely using satellite communications rather than line-of-sight control. Previously the Marines had to rely on the US Air Force or US Army for this expertise.[9] The USMC initially leased MQ-9s for evaluation from 2018 and has subsequently purchased more. By 2024 it had ten in service with ten more due for delivery in 2025. VMU-3 achieved operational status in 2023 and its aircraft are used primarily for intelligence, surveillance and reconnaissance (ISR). MQ-9As can fly for 20 hours or more at altitudes up to 25,000ft. Later in 2024 it was announced that up to six USMC Reapers are to be based at Kadena Air Base in Okinawa and used for ISR missions over the Ryukyu archipelago south-west of Japan.

The USMC made further progress introducing the F-35C when Marine Fighter Attack Squadron 311 (VMFA-311), the Tomcats, reached initial operational capability (IOC) at MCAS Miramar in August 2024. It is expected to reach FOC after it has received a further aircraft but, at present, it is not assigned to a carrier air wing. The USMC announced in its 2025 Air Plan that it now intends to procure 140 F-35Cs, an increase from an original target of 67. To compensate, the number of F-35Bs to be procured is to be reduced from 353 to 280, of which 183 have already been delivered, reflecting USMC unhappiness with the F-35B's limited remote area landing capability and enthusiasm for the F-35C's all-round better capabilities. The F-35Cs are to be divided initially between four squadrons; two on each coast. VMFA-314, the 'Black Knights', and VMFA-311, the 'Tomcats', are already in existence as part of the west-coast-based 1 Marine Expeditionary Force, (MEF) and two deactivated F/A-18 Hornet squadrons, VMFA 251, the 'Thunderbolts', and VMFA-115, the 'Silver Eagles', are to be reactivated as F-35C units in the east-coast-based 2nd Marine Air Wing, II MEF.[10] The next batch of F-35Cs delivered to VMFA-311

US Marine Corps' MV-22B Osprey tiltrotor operations have been constrained by restrictions that remain in place following a deadly US Air Force crash involving the type in 2023. Here, two MV-22B Ospreys assigned to Marine Medium Tiltrotor Squadron 364 (VMM-364), the 'Purple Foxes', are pictured in an exercise in the Philippines in May 2025. *(US Marine Corps)*

A US Marine Corps MQ-9A Reaper UAV assigned to Marine Unmanned Aerial Vehicle Squadron 3 (VMU-3), the 'Phantoms', seen during the Corps' first satellite communications launch and recovery mission at Marine Corps Air Station Kaneohe Bay, Hawaii on 20 June 2024. The USMC claimed that the process, '...minimises logistical constraints, enables operations from short airfields over vast distances, and supports the flexibility required for modern expeditionary operations'. *(US Marine Corps)*

and the new units will be delivered to Technical Refresh 3 (TR 3) standard. This will upgrade displays and processing power although the lack of a solution to the problem of hardware cooling will limit aircraft performance. The planned Block 4 software improvements that TR 3 was intended to support are still some way off, however, and this will limit the Corps' ability to use TR 3 aircraft operationally. A USMC spokesman briefed the press that eventually the majority of the USMC's earlier F-35Cs are to be upgraded to TR 3 standard but since this involves expensive changes to the engine to support the thermal management system this is unlikely to happen for some time.

CHINA: PEOPLE'S LIBERATION ARMY NAVY (PLAN)

The PLAN's new 80,000-ton Type 003 aircraft carrier, *Fujian*, has continued to carry out an extensive programme of sea trials over the past year and is expected to enter service in 2026. She is fitted with three Chinese-designed electromagnetic catapults and arrester gear, capable of operating a wider range of fixed-wing aircraft than China's earlier, ski-jump equipped aircraft carriers. These are expected to include KJ-600 airborne early warning and control aircraft as well as squadrons of J-15 and the new J-35 fighters. The PLAN has adopted a concept of operations within which aircraft carriers fulfil a central role as task force command platforms. PLAN officers are trained to understand the importance of aircraft carriers in the projection of national power and Chinese military scholars are taught about the decisive use of aircraft carriers from World War Two, through the Cuban Missile Crisis to the South Atlantic War to liberate the Falkland Islands in 1982. For the PLAN and the wider Chinese public, aircraft carriers are seen as a powerful symbol of China's return to what they see should be its rightful place in the world order. The two existing carriers *Liaoning* and *Shandong* have continued to engage in extensive training and other exercises over the last year whilst the next generation of vessels is awaited.

Analysts at the US Middlebury Institute of International Studies have reported that China has built a prototype naval nuclear reactor.[11] In addition, recent satellite images have shown that the PLAN has commenced building an even bigger aircraft carrier than *Fujian* at the Dalian shipyard at a pace that no other country in the world can rival. This ship is believed to be the first Type 004, a potentially 120,000-tonne, nuclear-powered aircraft carrier capable of operating more than 100 aircraft including both J-15 and J-35 fighters, KJ-600 airborne early warning and control aircraft, helicopters and GJ-II jet-powered drones. It is reported to have four electromagnetic catapults, advanced arrester gear and impressively large hangars, workshops and magazine spaces.

New PLAN aircraft are at an advanced stage of development prior to operation from the Type 003 and 004 aircraft carriers. These include the Project 1810, known at first as the F-60 and then as the FC-31. Now known as the J-35 with the same name, Gyrfalcon, as the J-35A intended for service with the PLA Air Force, the naval variant is described as a new type of stealth fighter independently developed in China. It reportedly has a raised cockpit to give a better view for deck landing and a deeper fuselage – to allow more internal fuel – than the land-based variant. It also differs in having twin nose wheels with an oleo strengthened to allow nose-tow catapult launch and a retractable arrester hook. The first production versions are to be powered by two WS-19 Haungshan turbofan engines which allow the

China's Type 002 aircraft carrier *Shandong* (pictured) and her Type 001 counterpart *Liaoning* have remained busy whilst sea trials of the next generation Type 003 vessel *Fujian* have been steadily progressing through a lengthy series of phases. China sees aircraft carriers as powerful symbols of the nation's return to its rightful place in the world order and is developing the means to deploy a balanced carrier fleet. Moreover, development of a wide range of other 'flat tops' – including both large deck amphibious assault ships and specialist UAV carriers – is also underway. *(People's Liberation Army Navy)*

aircraft to cruise at supersonic speed without using reheat; something the Lockheed-Martin F-35 Lightning is said to be incapable of achieving because of its short but wide fuselage shape.[12]

In addition to the effort being put into aircraft carriers and their aircraft, China also appears to be undertaking considerable work on dedicated UAV drone carriers. In mid-2024, reports emerged of such a vessel under construction at the Jiangsu Dayang Marine Shipyard on the Yangtze River. It appears to have a widely-spaced catamaran hull, an axial runway to port and an island structure to starboard. Satellite imagery suggests it has a flight deck that is not very high above the waterline but that the deck is wide enough to operate UAVs with a wingspan of up to 65ft (20m). The exact role of this ship is not yet clear but the building yard has extensive experience of constructing simulated enemy ships for the PLAN – including high-tech target barges and smaller drone motherships – so the vessel could be intended as a sophisticated target simulation. Alternatively it could be an experimental platform for testing new drones under realistic sea conditions. Subsequently, in November 2024, a larger, experimental vessel of some 200m in length and 40m in beam carrying flight deck markings for vertical take-off and landing (VTOL) drones commenced trials from the Guangzhou International Shipyard near Shanghai. Seemingly controlled by the China State Shipbuilding Corporation (CSSC) rather than the PLAN, it has been speculated that the ship is a technology demonstrator intended to pave the way for operational variants.[13]

Yet another new 'flat-top' design hit the water in December 2024 when the lead Type 076 amphibious assault ship *Sichuan* was launched from Hudong–Zhonghua Shipbuilding in Shanghai. Significantly larger than the previous Type 075 design, the c. 50,000-tonne vessel is also bigger that the US Navy's *America* (LHA-6) class amphibious assault ships or the Japanese *Izumo* (DDH-183) class helicopter-carrying destroyers. Utilising two islands in similar configuration to the United Kingdom's *Queen Elizabeth* class carriers and Italy's *Trieste*, the design is also noteworthy for the incorporation of a single electromagnetic catapult on the forward part of the ship's axial flight deck. Unlike the earlier Type 075 design, the flight deck is not interrupted by centreline lifts. Instead, two deck-edge lifts allow an unobstructed runway for fixed-wing operations. These may be drones launched for long-endurance ISR or strike missions, or the configuration may be intended to allow fighter operations when required. If so, some form of arrester system would be needed. However, even if the new ship is limited to drone operations these could include the growing number of Chinese uncrewed aircraft including the GJ-11 stealth combat drone, WZ-7 reconnaissance drone and the CASC Rainbow Strike uncrewed combat air vehicle (UCAV). Analysts have noted Chinese UAVs carrying out test launches from a catapult installed at a naval air station near the Northern Chinese city of Huludao. The Type 076 can reportedly carry 1,000 marines capable of assault landings by helicopter or seaborne assault in air-cushion landing craft carried in a floodable dock aft. By any yardstick the Type 076 is a formidable fighting ship capable of air and amphibious operations, as well as providing joint command across the world's oceans.

FRANCE: MARINE NATIONALE

The French Armed Forces Minister, Sébastien Lecornu, informed a Parliamentary hearing on 14 October 2024 that an order for the next-generation, nuclear-powered aircraft carrier at present known as the *porte-avions de nouvelle generation*, (PANG), intended to replace the current *Charles de Gaulle*, is to be included in the 2025 defence budget. He added that this will be a programme with a major impact. Likely to cost in the region of €10 billion (US$ 11.5 billion) by the time it is completed in the 2030s, the PANG is to operate both fighters designed as part of France's future air combat system (FACS) and UCAVs.

In the latter half of 2024, *Charles de Gaulle* completed a four month refit to to prepare her for the 'Clemenceau 25' deployment to the Indo-Pacific region. In October she carried out a three-week training period in the Mediterranean to regain operational certification for her ship's company and aircrew. During this period the French Navy's Centre for Practical Experimentation and Reception of Naval Aeronautics (CEPA) carried out test flights aimed at bringing the Rafale M fighter up to the future F4.1 standard. This capability is to be fielded by both the French Navy and French Air Force and includes software upgrades, new systems and new weapons. There

Sailors prepare to refuel a Rafale Marine F4 fighter jet assigned to the aircraft carrier *Charles De Gaulle* on the flight deck of the *Nimitz* (CVN-68) class aircraft carrier *Carl Vinson* (CVN-70) in the Philippine Sea in February 2025 during a cross-deck exercise. The event took place during the French carrier's 'Clemenceau 25' deployment to the Indo-Pacific, a deployment which also saw her operate alongside India's *Vikrant* for the first time. *(US Navy)*

A detailed view of the island structure of the Indian Navy aircraft carrier *Vikramaditya* – formerly the Russian Navy *Admiral Gorshkov* – taken whilst she was exercising with the US Navy in 2020. She is to undergo a docking and short refit at Cochin Shipyard Ltd, hopefully resolving some of the reliability problems that have reportedly marked her Indian Navy service. *(US Navy)*

An underbelly view of an Indian Navy MiG-29K multi-role fighter launching decoy flares whilst participating in the Operational Demonstration event scheduled to mark India's Navy Day on 4 December 2024. The Indian Navy's finalisation of a contract to acquire 26 Rafale M fighters from France in April 2025 means that MiG-29K's importance in Indian Naval aviation is likely to diminish. *(Arjun Sarup)*

are currently 41 Rafale M's in Aeronavale service, all of which should have been brought up to F4 standard by the end of 2025. A further upgrade to F5 standard is planned for 2030 onwards to enable the Rafale to use the ASN4G future hypersonic nuclear missile and to operate in collaboration with UCAVs. In addition, the Aeronavale's present three E-2C Hawkeye airborne early warning and control aircraft are to be replaced by three E-2D Advanced Hawkeye aircraft from 2028.[14]

The *Charles de Gaulle* CSG's deployment departed for the Indo-Pacific in November 2024. It was intended to develop allied interoperability from the Mediterranean to the Pacific Ocean as well as contributing to France's capacity for autonomous situation assessment and crisis management. During the deployment the CSG carried out NATO-oriented operations in the Mediterranean and visited ports in the Western Indian Ocean. Next it led the French Navy-organised 'La Perouse' exercise in co-operation with navies of other nations that border the Indonesian archipelago. Beginning in January 2025 this exercise was divided between three locations – the Malacca, Sunda and Lombok Straits – demonstrating maritime safety in the these critical areas through co-operation with international partners. In the Pacific the CSG participated in Exercise 'Pacific Stellar' with US and Japanese aircraft carriers to increase the level of interoperability with them.

In January 2025, the CSG disembarked three Rafale M fighters to Darwin in Australia to carry out several days of air combat training with Royal Australian Air Force (RAAF) F-35As. The following month, the French carrier aircraft carried out cross deck operations with the *Carl Vinson* CSG in the Western Pacific. These included F/A-18E/F Super Hornets and a CMV-22B landing on and being launched from *Charles de Gaulle* and Rafale Ms landing on and being launched from *Carl Vinson.* The 'Varuna 2025' exercise with the Indian Navy took place in March 2025 and included a variety of bilateral drills including air-to-air combat training between Indian Navy Mig-29K fighters and French Rafale Ms, together with anti-submarine, replenishment-at-sea and surface warfare exercises. The exercise marked the new Indian aircraft carrier *Vikrant*'s first opportunity to work with the French CSG. The CSG returned to France on 25 April 2025, three days before the Indian Navy confirmed the purchase of 26 Rafale M jets in a sign of ongoing defence collaboration.

INDIA: INDIAN NAVY

Vikrant was declared fully operational towards the end of 2024 and now forms an integral part of the Indian Navy's Western Fleet.[15] India's other aircraft carrier, *Vikramaditya*, carried out a dual carrier strike group exercise with the Italian Navy's *Cavour* CSG during Exercise 'Malabar 24' in October 2024. The training period focused on a range of operational capabilities including air, surface and anti-submarine warfare with an emphasis on improving situational awareness. In November 2024, a c. US$140m contract was signed with Cochin Shipyard for a refit and dry docking of the Russian-built ship, which has reportedly suffered from persistent reliability problems since her delivery. Local news reports suggest that she may well be replaced by the planned second indigenous aircraft carrier (IAC2) in due course, postponing the Indian Navy's ambition to become a three-carrier force.

As previously mentioned, the long-running negotiations for the purchase of 26 Rafale M fighters from France for the IN were concluded successfully in April 2025. The Indian Air Force already operates Rafale B and C models which share more than 80 percent commonality with the Rafael M, including the same software and weapons capabilities. This commonality is expected to reduce maintenance, repair and training costs significantly.

ITALY: MARINA MILITARE

The Italian Navy's CSG deployment to the Indo-Pacific region in 2024 centred on the aircraft carrier *Cavour* and included an air group of six Italian Navy and two Italian Air Force F-35B strike fighters, as well as seven AV-8B Harrier II Plus jump jets, a single EH-101 and three NH-90 helicopters.[16] Aircraft from *Cavour* carried out exercises with the RAAF as part of the Pitch Black exercise around Darwin in July 2024 and later with the US Navy carrier *Abraham Lincoln* (CVN-72) in the Philippine Sea. During the former, *Cavour*'s aircraft flew sorties on 22 days. This amounted to 180 hours' flying time across 110 missions, which included ground attack, in-flight refuelling, air interception, suppression of enemy air defences, escort and air control sorties. On completion of these exercises, the Italian Navy announced that its carrier-based F-35B force had achieved IOC four months ahead of schedule. The Italian Navy Chief of Staff, Admiral Enrico Credendino, embarked on *Cavour* in Yokosuka to mark the occasion. He described IOC as a significant step toward Italy's ability to project forces from the sea for extended periods of time together with complete interoperability and interchangeability in joint operations with allies and partners. This had been one of the main objectives of the deployment in the Indo Pacific he added. After departing Japan, *Cavour* conducted further exercises and operational visits to Singapore, India, Pakistan, Oman and Saudi Arabia before returning to her home port at Taranto in Italy. Whilst on passage a second set of drills with *Abraham Lincoln* were carried out in October, this time in the Indian Ocean.

The Italian Navy aircraft carrier *Cavour* undertook an extended deployment to the Indo-Pacific region in 2024 with a mixed air group focused on F35B Lighting II strike fighters and AV-8B Harrier II Plus jump jets embarked. This photograph was taken in August 2024 when she was operating with the US Navy's *Abraham Lincoln* (CVN-72) in what a US Navy press release described as, 'the first-ever bilateral Multi-Large Deck Event (MLDE) in the Indo-Pacific'. *(US Navy)*

The Italian Navy's *Gruppo Aerei Imbarcati*, known as 'Grupaer', plans to receive 15 F 35Bs. A similar number are to be operated by the Italian Air Force alongside its 60 land-based F-35As, although both forces aim to increase their F-35B complements to at least 20. Rear Admiral Giancarlo Ciappina, who commands the *Cavour* CSG, briefed the US Naval Institute in October 2024 that eventual FOC is to be based on several benchmarks that include the number of F-35Bs in service, reaching targeted sortie generation rates, training sufficient pilots, reaching full capabilities in weapons' delivery and management of complex logistic information systems. Whilst these would not require *Cavour* to deploy to the United States for a further series of flying trials following its 2021 deployment, the amphibious assault ship *Trieste* will need to be operationally certified in American waters given that she, too, is designed to operate F-35Bs. *Trieste* was commissioned on 7 December 2024 and will act as an alternative 'flattop' to *Cavour*, replacing the veteran *Giuseppe Garibaldi* after that ship's retirement on 1 October that year. Meanwhile, the Italian Navy plans to continue operating Harriers until around 2028-30, by when it is expected that the F-35Bs will have achieved FOC.

JAPAN: JAPAN MARITIME SELF-DEFENCE FORCE

After completion of the initial stage of its two-phase modification – encompassing a new bow and heat-resistant flight deck coating – to enable F-35B operations, Japan's largest warship, *Kaga* (DDH-184), carried out extensive F-35B trials off San Diego in 2024. The aircraft were provided by Air Test and Evaluation Squadron 23 (VX-23), the 'Salty Dogs', from the integrated test force based at NAS Patuxent River, Maryland, which has test pilots from all the nations that operate F-35Bs. Accordingly, one of the pilots that operated from *Kaga* was Lieutenant Commander Nick Baker RN. Her sister-ship *Izumo* had previously undergone a more limited first-stage modification but in 2025 she entered dockyard hands for a more comprehensive work package which included fitting her with the new bow design together with interior changes to facilitate F-35B operations and the storage of air weapons. Work is expected to be complete in 2026 by which time the *Kaga* trials will have been analysed so that any design modifications found necessary can be incorporated before she returns to the fleet. *Kaga* will then be taken in hand to be brought up to the same standard. Japan has followed the experiences of other F-35B operators closely. JMSDF officers attended *Prince of Wales*' F-35B trials – which extended their operating envelope – off the Eastern USA in 2023 and delegations toured *Queen Elizabeth* and *Cavour* during their visits to Japan. The different ways in which the nations that have procured F-35Bs operate them are described later in this chapter.

Although the JMSDF's Fleet Air Arm already operates both fixed and rotary-wing aircraft, the Japanese MOD has decided that the Japan Air Self Defence Force (JASDF) is to operate F-35Bs as part of a programme to procure 105 F-35As and 42 F-35Bs. Eight F-35Bs are expected to be operational by the end of 2025, growing to 30 with the formation of a second operational squadron by 2029. They are eventually to be based at a new airfield on the small, uninhabited island of Mageshima but this is not expected to be complete until 2029. In the interim they are to be based at Nyutbaru air base on the main island of Kyushu. However, noise pollution – and its impact on the nearby civilian population – is expected to limit the amount of vertical landing training that can be carried out until the new base is ready.

The JMSDF 'helicopter-carrying destroyer' *Kaga* (DDH-184) pictured entering San Diego, California on the conclusion of F-35B Lightning II certification trials in November 2024. Although her flight deck has been extensively modified for this purpose, further internal changes will be necessary in a planned second phase refit before the jet can be operationally deployed from the ship. Nevertheless, *Kaga's* visit likely represents the first time a Japanese fixed-wing carrier has operated in US waters. *(US Navy)*

SMALLER NAVAL AIR POWERS

BRAZIL: Brazil is expected to demonstrate the versatility of big-deck amphibious ships before the end of 2025 by conducting trials of an indigenously-produced Albatroz uncrewed aircraft onboard the amphibious helicopter carrier *Atlântico*, the former Royal Navy *Ocean*. Albatroz is designed by Stella Technology and has a maximum take-off weight of 330lbs (150kg) with a wingspan of 23ft (7m). It is powered by a 22hp, avgas-fuelled, piston engine which gives an endurance of 24 hours and the ability to carry 66lb (30 kilogramme) modular payloads. These can comprise either electro-optical, synthetic aperture radar or electronic warfare suites and the aircraft is controlled remotely with what is described as a seamless handover capability between stations.

INDONESIA: The Indonesian defence company Republkorp announced a joint venture agreement for the production of 60 Bayraktar TB3 and 9 Bayraktar Akinci UCAVs from Türkiye's Baykar in April 2025. This has strengthened a rumour that the Indonesian Navy is interested in purchasing the Italian aircraft carrier *Giuseppe Garibaldi*, which has been laid up since its withdrawal from service. If her hull and machinery are found to be in good condition, she would seem to be an ideal ship for Indonesia to introduce uncrewed aircraft operations at sea.

The Portuguese Navy is one of a number of fleets preparing to enter the drone carrier club, with its multi-functional naval platform – *D. João II* – currently under construction at Damen's Galati shipyard in Romania. Damen has unveiled a new 'family' of ship designs based on this vessel; its Multi-Purpose Support Ship (MPSS) range. This currently incorporates 7,000 and 9,000-tonne versions, both seen in this graphic. The family is described in a press release as combining 'the vision of the Portuguese Navy, with Damen's proven process of shipbuilding, using standardised solutions wherever possible'. *(Damen)*

IRAN: In January 2025 the Iranian Revolutionary Guard Corps Navy (IRGCN) commissioned what it described as the 'the world's first purpose-built drone carrier' designed specifically to launch and recover wheeled, fixed-wing uncrewed air vehicles. Named *Shahid Bagheri*, the ship is actually a converted container ship rebuilt with an angled deck which runs from port to starboard and is sited forward of the original, central bridge superstructure. She has a ski-jump at the forward edge of the runway at the bow. Small lifts connect the flight deck with a storage area or hangars below. She is apparently designed to operate Ababil-3 and Mohajer-6 surveillance drones as well Qaher-313s, which are described as combat UAVs. The large flight deck also makes it possible for the ship to operate a range of helicopters including the Mi-17, Bell 412 and Shahad 278. *Bagheri*'s air group therefore has the potential to conduct anti-surface vessel, anti-submarine and ship-to-shore strike operations. She is fitted with short range Kowsar 222 anti-aircraft missiles and anti-ship missiles, and can carry up to 30 small 'Tareq' class fast attack craft.

Her impressive appearance has led analysts to speculate on the way in which she might be employed. The spy-ship *Behshad* has been used for some time to provide data in the Gulf of Aden and the approaches to the Bab el Mandeb. A drone carrier could expand that ISR capability significantly and *Bagheri* has sufficient fuel to do so much further afield if required. For some years, the IRGC has used drones and fast attack boats to harass shipping, simulating an attack only to veer away at the last moment. This leaves defenders wondering when this might turn into the real thing and provides the IRGCN with valuable data on reaction times, weapons and tactics. *Bagheri* allows such grey zone manoeuvres to originate from a much larger sea space, thereby posing a greater threat.[17]

PORTUGAL: The Portuguese Navy is another preparing to enter the drone carrier club, with its multi-functional naval platform – *D. João II* – currently under construction at Damen's Galati shipyard in Romania after a keel-laying ceremony in October 2024. Her design features include a large starboard-side island and an axial flight deck capable of operating both drones and helicopters. Containers, boats or uncrewed surface vessels are to be embarked as well via a stern ramp and the ship is to be capable of accommodating up to almost 200 personnel. Her stated role is to support ISR, humanitarian/disaster relief, oceanographic and environmental monitoring missions.

TÜRKIYE: Türkiye continues to progress development of Bayraktar TB3 UCAVS for operation from its amphibious aircraft assault ship *Anadolu*, a ship based on the Spanish *Juan Carlos I* design built under licence. Since the US Government expelled Türkiye from the F-35B programme in 2019 after it bought Russian S-400 air defence systems, Türkiye has focused its attention on the ship's development as a drone and helicopter carrier. The TB3 is developed from an earlier land-based drone, the TB2, with improvements to allow it to operate at sea. These include folding wings, a strengthened undercarriage for deck landing and an enhanced, variable payload. It has a short take-off and landing capability enhanced by *Anadolu*'s ski-jump at the bow but does not need arrester wires for landing. In addition to a range of ISR options, the TB3 can be fitted with external pylons capable of carrying up to 600lbs of weapons for use in the anti-surface vessel strike role. A TB3 prototype carried out the first take-off and deck landing on the *Anadolu* in November 2024. Another UCAV is also being developed for operation from *Anadolu*; the Bayraktar Kızılelma. This is a larger jet-powered aircraft described as having an air-to-air combat capability, presumably with either radar or infrared-guided air-to-air missiles.

The full extent of Türkiye's naval aviation ambitions were revealed at the beginning of 2025 with the holding of a first steel cutting ceremony for the new MUGEM national aircraft carrier on 2 January. The ship will be 285m long and 75m in beam, with its planned displacement of some 60,000 tonnes being more than twice that of *Anadolu*. The ship will be constructed to a short take-off but arrested recovery (STOBAR) configuration, utilising a ski jump. Design illustrations show a single island on the starboard side and three possible take-off positions. The shortest one, located in line with the bridge on the centreline is for the TB-3 UCAV. The second runs diagonally across the ship from her port side abaft the island to the centreline and is for the Hürjet piloted aircraft. An extension to a third take off position on the port quarter is for the Kızılelma. To land the aircraft there are three arresting wires and an angled deck.[18]

THE F-35B LIGHTNING II – THE EXPERIENCE TO DATE

To date, four services have procured the F-35B for operation from a variety of big-deck flat tops; each of them choosing to administer the aircraft in different ways. The USMC is by far the largest user and was the driving force behind the requirement for the STOVL capability that the F-35B airframe provides. By the end of 2025, the USMC will have taken delivery of 183 F-35Bs, operating them in ten to twelve-strong squadrons that form part of the USMC's command structure. Some embark in amphibious assault ships such as *America* in detachments of about six aircraft alongside helicopters but up to 22 have been operated with the number of helicopters reduced. Others are based ashore.

The United Kingdom has elected to operate its F-35Bs as a joint force with equal numbers of personnel provided by the RN and RAF. This attempts to provide both land-based and carrier-borne strike fighter forces with the same operational squadrons. They cannot be in two places at once, however, and this approach arguably means that the force excels at neither role.[19] As noted previously, the Italian Navy has procured 15 F-35Bs, with a further 15 procured for the Italian Air Force that are capable of embarking to back up the small number of dedicated naval aircraft. The JMSDF has not operated fighters in the fast-jet era and, thus, the Japanese government has elected to concentrate all its F-35s, including the F-35Bs, within the JASDF. However, the 'B's are to be earmarked primarily for operation from the two *Izumo* class 'helicopter-carrying destroyers'.

Theoretically, the key benefits of the 'B' variant compared with the conventional carrier-based 'C' variant from a naval perspective are its ability to operate without catapults or arrester wires, as well as the potential to disembark from the host ship to operate alongside amphibious expeditionary forces using improvised landing strips as the AV-8B Harrier II did. However, both impose considerable restrictions on the aircraft's operating envelope compared with other variants. The F-35B's extremely hot exhaust requires specially-treated surfaces, such as those installed at airfields where training takes place. Ships that operate F-35Bs require areas of steel flight deck where the aircraft land coated with a heat-resistant material to prevent the deck from melting. Photographs of the F-35Bs of any nation operating from remote-area landing strips have been noticeably absent from press releases and the logistic support of these aircraft and their delicate stealth coatings in such a location would, presumably, be difficult for

Japan is one of the four countries that have, to date, procured F-35B Lightning II strike fighters for short take-off and vertical landing (STOVL) operations from big deck flattops. This November 2024 photograph was taken when a joint team consisting of F-35 Patuxent River Integrated Test Force flight test members, US Navy and Marine Corps personnel, and the crew of the *Izumo* class helicopter carrying destroyer *Kaga* (DDH-184) were executing developmental sea trials in the eastern Pacific Ocean to certify the class for F-35B operation. *(US Navy)*

anything but a detachment of short duration. This is possibly the reason why the USMC has decided to reduce the number of F-35Bs it procures and increase the number of F-35Cs.

The origins of the F-35B date back to an Anglo-American study into a potential short take-off and vertical landing (STOVL) strike fighter originally intended to replace the AV-8B Harrier in USMC service and the Sea Harrier FA 2 in RN service and operate from small carriers or amphibious flat tops. The design that ultimately emerged was deeply compromised by the American political decision to produce a common airframe for the land base-operated USAF F-35A variant, the STOVL F-35B for the USMC, and the larger-winged tailhook-fitted F-35C variant for the USN. The dimensions of this common airframe were limited by tight USMC and RN requirements. The former limited the wingspan to 35ft to match parking areas in amphibious assault ships forward and aft of their islands. Whilst the USAF accepted the same wing for their 'A' variant – even though it led to high landing speeds on its runways – the USN wanted a lower landing speed for arrested carrier landings, stipulating an increased wingspan of 43ft for the resultant F-35C. The length of all three variants was restricted to less than 54ft (it is c. 51.5ft in practice) to allow them to fit onto the mid-deck lifts of the RN's then *Invincible* class carriers. The engine in all three variants had to be fitted close to the aircraft's centre of gravity so that the 'B' variant would be balanced in jet-borne flight whilst hovering and the use of two engines was completely ruled out because the loss of either one in the hover would cause a catastrophic departure from controlled flight. Consequently, the F-35B's dense mass of electrically-actuated systems and sensors had to be tightly packed around the engine in the short fuselage of all three variants; these generated considerable amounts of heat and all of them had to be cooled. In earlier fighters the heat generated by the engine, avionics and electrically-actuated systems is dissipated into the outside air but this is unacceptable in a stealth design as it would allow infrared detection at considerable distance. In the F-35B coolant circuits were built into the avionics to dissipate heat into the fuel tanks in a complex system known as the power and thermal management system (PTMS). As fuel in the tanks is used, the system becomes less efficient.[20]

The requirement to achieve stealth has had a major impact on the design of every F-35 variant.

This photograph shows the three variants of the F-35 strike fighter; from left to right the US Navy F-35C conventional carrier variant, the US Marine Corps F-35B STOVL variant, and the US Air Force F-35A land-based variant. The political decision to utilise the same basic airframe to meet three disparate requirements arguably resulted in compromises that undermined the effectiveness of the F-35 design. *(Lockheed Martin)*

Multi-spectrum situational awareness had to be provided for the pilot with minimal use of active radar transmissions. This was to be achieved by using digital sensor fusion to integrate radar and electro-optical sensors, flight control, navigation, communication and electronic warfare functions in real time. However, when development began in the 1990s this could only be achieved by using a large, centralised supercomputer to control every function. At first designers assumed that upgrades could be incorporated easily on the flight line but this has not proved to be possible. The latest phase of F-35 development, known as continuous capability and development delivery (C2D2), grew into such a large programme that it requires a completely new integrated core processor known as hardware technology refresh 3 (TR 3) that has been fitted in all F-35 deliveries from Lot 15, which began in 2023. It was supposed allow software to a new Block 4 standard to be installed to give significant increases in operational capability including a new APG-85 radar, new electronic warfare suite, 'next-generation' defensive aids suite and a wider range of weapons. From a British perspective it was to integrate the MBDA Meteor BVR missile as the primary air-to-air weapon. This has been in service with French Navy Rafales from 2015 onwards and with RAF Typhoons since 2018. The UK also hoped to integrate the MBDA SPEAR 3 air-to-ground missile.

Early tests with TR 3 showed that the new computer generated far more heat than its predecessor, limiting the aircraft's stealth until a more powerful PTMS can be devised. The only solution which offers full TR 3 operational capability across every US and international F-35 customer is an engine and PTMS upgrade which is some years from achievement in new production and would require an expensive adaptation in all earlier aircraft. The project is known as the Engine and Power Thermal Management System Modernization (EPM) program and is likely to require replacement of the engine's high-pressure compressor, turbine and combustor under an Engine Core Upgrade (ECU). These are the hottest and most expensive parts of the F-35's F-135 engine, which already has a unit cost of around US$12 million and takes over a year to manufacture. Even with the more limited TR 3/Interim Block 4 software configuration in current production aircraft, the engine has to provide more bleed air for cooling than that required in its original specification and this has operational consequences. The time spent in the warmer part of the flight envelope low and fast has to be minimised and sortie length has to be reduced by the need to retain sufficient fuel in the tanks to act as a viable heat sink. It seems that the full suite of Block 4 upgrades – and any further blocks – cannot be progressed until EPM is implemented over the rest of the decade.

Two F-35B Lightning jets land onboard *Prince of Wales* during Exercise 'Med Strike' with the Italian Navy's *Cavour* and other warships; part of the wider CSG25 deployment. The operational use of F-35Bs by international partners such as the United Kingdom and Italy is likely to be adversely impacted by problems relating to the roll-out of the F-35's TR 3 hardware technology refresh and associated delays to the Block 4 software upgrade. *(Crown Copyright 2025)*

Lockheed Martin F-35 strike fighters under production at its Fort Worth factory in Texas. The Trump presidency's focus on tariffs risks disrupting the complex international supply chain for the aircraft, increasing production costs. *(Lockheed Martin)*

Upgrading early TR 2/Block 3 aircraft to TR 3/enhanced Block 4 standard is believed to be possible but will be time consuming and expensive. Meanwhile the use of these early-standard aircraft against sophisticated opposition such as the fighters now being deployed by the PLAN becomes questionable. The F-35B is a decades-old design with dated software.

The F-35 Joint Project Office (JPO) ordered Lockheed-Martin to stop delivering new aircraft in July 2023 when the thermal management issues came to light and it was decided that the new operating system was not stable enough to fly the aircraft safely or use sensors and weapons. It took a year to solve some of the problems, by which time there were more than 100 aircraft in storage. Even after deliveries resumed with the new TR 3/interim Block 4 software in July 2024, these F-35s were specifically excluded from combat missions. They are safe to fly but can, apparently, only be used for training. By the end of 2025 the United Kingdom expects to have had all of the 48 F-35Bs ordered so far delivered. Of these 34 were to TR 2/Block 3 standard, one of which ditched from *Queen Elizabeth* in 2021. The balancing 14 are built to the TR 3/interim Block 4 standard described by the British MoD as having a robust training capability. Some analysts believe that these aircraft are unlikely to become fully operational before 2030 and, maybe, not even then with the United Kingdom's weapons of choice. Other operators face similar problems and the expensive need to upgrade or replace their TR 2 aircraft if they are to have a viable operational capability into the 2030s. Whilst countries with TR 2 hardware have operational capability at the moment, the supply chain that delivered and supported TR 2 components effectively ended with Lot 14 deliveries, so this hardware presumably has a finite life.

In addition to problems with software, the hardware needed to drive it and the EPM required to maintain stealth, sovereignty has been an issue for F-35B export customers. As early as 2006 the United Kingdom threatened to withdraw from the programme if it was not given access to the aircraft's software source-code or the ability to generate its own mission data files. By 2009, however, it conceded that all programming support would remain under US control. There has been much talk about the existence of a 'kill switch' with which the US Administration could prevent export customers from operating their F-35s if it disagreed with their policies. Whilst this has been denied by both the Pentagon and Lockheed Martin, it is clear that the withdrawal of programming support for the aircraft's software would likely render it unable to operate effectively over time.[21]

President Trump's outspoken criticism of nations that had considered the United States to be their ally has been covered elsewhere in this edition. In terms of the F-35 specifically, the impact of his tariff policies might add to the aircraft's unit cost. For example, every F-35 rear fuselage is manufactured in the United Kingdom by BAE Systems at Salmesbury at a cost of US$10 million each. Accordingly, a ten percent tariff would add US$1 million in taxes to each fuselage imported into the United States for aircraft assembly. Whilst this danger has been averted for the time being by a tariff deal between the United States and the United Kingdom, many other F-35 components are also made outside the United States by countries that have yet to reach such an agreement. It may be that the tariffs are intended to centralise all production in the United States in line with the Make America Great Again (MAGA) agenda, but that would take time and funding to achieve.[22]

Software problems, the need to cool hot hardware to retain stealth capability and the consequent inability to integrate weapons of choice and doubt about whether operations that are not approved by the USA would lead to software being blocked are among many factors of concern to export customers for the F-35B. There are others, and only time will tell how things will play out. One cannot but wonder, however, how the compromised and troubled F-35Bs compare with the later and potentially more user-friendly designs coming into operational service in China, which might well offer more than just a training capability throughout the remainder of the 2020s.

Notes

1. See, 'F-35 milestone as 809 Naval Air Squadron completes first independent sortie' mission' posted to the Royal Navy website – royalnavy.mod.uk – on 15 July 2024.

2. The problems that lack of maintenance personnel created for *Queen Elizabeth's* CSG21 deployment were outlined in the author's comments on the loss of F-35B strike fighter ZM 152 contained in his previous review of world naval aviation for *Seaforth World Naval Review 2025* (Barnsley: Seaforth Publishing, 2024), pp.149-50.

3. These numbers were provided to the author by Royal Navy public relations. Published sources differ slightly in the number of helicopters embarked for the 'Highmast' deployment.

4. See, 'Royal Navy helicopters with Crowsnest early warning capability make their entrance for global mission' posted to the UK Defence Equipment and Support's website – des.mod.uk – on 25 April 2025.

5. See, 'Royal Navy turns to drones to support carrier task group mission' posted to the Royal Navy website on 7 April 2025.

6. The remarks on Stingray were reported by Sam LaGrone in 'MQ-25A Stingray 2026 Debut Will Unlock Unmanned Aviation for Carrier Strike Group, Say Officials' posted to the *USNI News* site – news.usni.org – on 29 January 2025.

7. See Mallory Shelbourne, 'Navy, Marines Learning to Make Do as V-22 Restrictions Endure' posted to *the USNI News* site on 11 February 2025.

8. *2025 Marine Aviation Plan* (Washington DC: Department of the Navy – USMC, 2025). This is currently readily available by searching the web.

9. For further detail, see Todd South, 'Drone crew conducts first all-Marine satellite comms launch, recovery' posted to the *Military Times* – militarytimes.com site – on 27 June 2024.

10. The *2025 Marine Aviation Plan* ultimately envisages the formation of four further USMC F-35C squadrons – VMFA-232, VMFA-323, VMFA-112 (Reserve), and VMFA-134 (Reserve) – to make a total of six frontline and two reserve USMC F-35C squadrons. There will also be twelve frontline F-35B squadrons. Each of these squadrons will eventually be equipped with 12 aircraft. Additional aircraft will be assigned to training – Fleet Replacement Squadrons (FRSs) – and for developmental and operational testing.

11. The report was carried by several news outlets. For example, see Maya Carlin's, 'Evidence is building China wants a nuclear powered aircraft carrier' posted to *The National Interest* site – nationalinterest.org – on 14 November 2024.

12. Recent developments with respect to the J-35 programme were highlighted by John Lake in an article, 'A first official photo of China's new F-35 clone' carried by the *Aerospace Global News* site – aerospaceglobalnews.com – on 6 November 2024.

13. More information on recent Chinese UAV carrier developments can be found in two articles on the *Naval News* website; navalnews.com. See HI Sutton, 'China Builds World's First Dedicated Drone Carrier' posted on 15 May 2024 and Alex Luck, 'Chinese Experimental Aviation Platform And Combat USV Emerge In Detailed New Imagery' dated 7 November 2024.

14. See, Dzirhan Mahadzir, 'French Navy Carrier Charles De Gaulle Prepping for Deployment, Italian Carrier Cavour Returns Home' posted to the *USNI News* site on 7 November 2024.

15. A fuller review of *Vikrant* is contained in chapter 3.3.

16. See again Dzirhan Mahadzir, 'Carrier Cavour's Pacific Deployment Extends Italy's Reach in the Pacific, Say Admiral' posted to the *USNI News* site on 11 October 2024.

17. See Tom Sharpe, 'Iran's new dedicated drone carrier' posted to the *Australian Naval Institute* site – navalinstitute.com.au – on 20 February 2025 based on an article first published in *The Daily Telegraph* and reproduced with the author's permission.

18. See Devrim Yaylali, 'Turkish naval programmes: status report' published in *European Security & Defence* 05/25 (Bonn: Mittler Report, 2025), pp.112-15 and also currently available at: euro-sd.com/profile/print-issues

19. RAF administrative control of what is supposed to be a joint force is taken to such lengths that 809 NAS is the only RN squadron not to have 'Royal Navy' painted on its aircraft, unlike the USMC which has 'Marines' on its F-35Bs and Italian Navy aircraft which have 'Marina' markings.

20. A critical assessment of the F-35's development and its problems can be found in Bill Sweetman's *Trillion Dollar Trainwreck* (Arlington VA: Valkyrie Strategic Solutions, 2024).

21. For more detailed analysis see David Cenciotti's and Stefano D'Urso's article, 'The F-35 "Kill Switch": Separating Myth from Reality' carried by *The Aviationist* site – theaviationist.com – on 10 March 2025.

22. See Tim Ripley, 'Trump Tariffs – Which F-35 suppliers will take the hit?' posted to the *Defence Eye* news site – defenceeye.co.uk – on 10 April 2025. The article was written before a tariff agreement between the United Kingdom and the United States was reached.

4.2 TECHNOLOGICAL REVIEW

RIM-116 ROLLING AIRFRAME MISSILE

Ship Self-defence for the Close-in Fight

Author:
Richard Scott

Half a century after the United States and the Federal Republic of Germany began to explore the joint development of a new lightweight, quick-reaction ship self-defence missile system, the RIM-116 Rolling Airframe Missile (RAM) programme endures as an outstanding example of transatlantic armaments co-operation. Developed to meet Cold War requirements for close-range, anti-ship missile defence (ASMD), the Mk 31 Guided Missile Weapon System has, over time, undergone a staged evolution in order to counter an expanded target set, while at the same time maintaining its primary role against the latest generation of anti-ship cruise missile (ASCM) threats. Almost 1,000 RAM missiles have been fired to date in developmental flight tests and operational firings.

RAM is also an industrial success story. The United States' Raytheon and Germany's RAM-System GmbH (RAMSYS) – a joint venture of Diehl Stiftung (25 percent), Diehl BGT Defence (25 percent) and MBDA Deutschland (50 percent) – share production and qualification activities to feed a single production line meeting the needs of the two navies, and the additional demands of export customers. As of mid-2025, variants of RAM were also in service, on order, or selected by the naval forces of Canada, Egypt, Greece, Japan, Qatar, the Republic of Korea, Mexico, the Netherlands, Saudi Arabia, Türkiye, and the United Arab Emirates (UAE). RAM variants are today deployed on more than 165 ships worldwide – ranging from 500-tonne fast attack craft to 95,000-tonne aircraft carriers – with more than 6,500 missiles produced to date.

RAM was conceived in the Cold War to provide inner layer 'hard kill' against anti-ship missiles that had penetrated outer screens of air defence. This graphic is a contemporary image of the system concept. *(Raytheon)*

INCEPTION

The origins of the RAM programme go back to the early 1970s. Recognising the growing anti-ship missile threat, the US Navy issued a mission need statement in November 1973 for an 'inner layer' system able to defeat ASCMs that had evaded outer layers of air defence. To meet requirements for all-weather 'fire and forget' operation, thinking came to favour the development of a self-contained weapon guidance system that could exploit the active RF signals emitted by the active radar seekers used by the majority of ASCMs for target search and homing. Such a weapon system would not require any additional ship support – such as a tracking radar or illuminator – beyond an initial target cue. To prove the concept, Johns Hopkins University Applied Physics Laboratory (JHU APL) was tasked by the US Navy to refine an interceptor concept embodying dual-mode guidance – a passive radio frequency (RF) interferometer used to point a terminal infra-red (IR) seeker – in a rolling airframe.[1]

Why a rolling airframe? First, because the passive RF tracking system (using twin interferometer antennas) could only measure phase interference in a single plane, 'rolling' the interferometer would permit the antennas to look at all planes of incoming energy. Second, a rolling airframe meant only one pair of steering canards would be required, so simplifying control hardware requirements.

JHU APL, acting as prime contractor, worked with the Pomona Division of General Dynamics to demonstrate the dual-mode concept utilising 2.75in diameter Redeye IR-homing missiles produced by General Dynamics. Firing trials using these experimental missiles demonstrated the viability of the dual-mode seeker head and the feasibility of a rolling airframe. Subsequently, a decision was taken in 1974 to adopt a larger (5in) missile airframe to enable broader frequency coverage and enhanced lethality. The choice initially fell on the Chaparral missile. However, the US Navy later opted to use the airframe of the AIM-9 Sidewinder air-to-air missile. The US Navy formalised its operational requirement in May 1975, and a programme office was established in the Naval Sea Systems Command (NAVSEA).

In the meantime, the Federal German Navy had also identified a requirement for a ship self-defence system to counter the growing ASCM threat. Recognising a common interest, the US Navy signed a memorandum of understanding (MoU) with Germany in July 1976 to jointly fund an Advanced Surface-to-Air Missile System test flight validation programme as the precursor to a full-scale engineering development (FSED) effort. The cost sharing arrangement for this initial development activity saw the US and Germany each contribute 49 percent of funding. Denmark, which also had an interest in a lightweight ship self-defence missile system, assumed the remaining two percent. These three partner nations signed a MoU for the FSED phase in May 1979.[2] The following month General Dynamics was awarded a contract to move ahead with full development.

At that stage, the programme envisaged two different launch configurations. One was to be a modified Mk 132 NATO Seasparrow launcher in which two of the eight RIM-7 Seasparrow missiles were replaced by two guide inserts, each containing five RAM rounds. The other, as part of what was then dubbed the EX-31 Mod 0 Guided Missile Weapon System, was a traversable 24-round Guided Missile Launching System (GMLS) based on the mounting and servo electronics of the Mk 15 Phalanx close-in weapon system (CIWS) already under development by General Dynamics. In the event, the GMLS concept associated with EX-31 Mod 0 evolved to become the 21-round Mk 49 GMLS. Development of the modified Mk 132 launcher was not pursued.[3]

General Dynamics was nominated as prime contractor for RAM. German industry – represented by RAMSYS (then a consortium of AEG Telefunken, Bodenseewerke Gerätetechnik and Diehl) – functioned as subcontractor and cooperative partner.

Reflecting the cooperative nature of the development, the RAM Program Office (RAMPO) became a joint US/German programme office. RAMPO – today staffed by personnel from the Program Executive Office Integrated Warfare Systems (PEO IWS) 11.0 in NAVSEA and the Federal Office of Bundeswehr Equipment, Information Technology

An image of a prototype General Dynamics Rolling Airframe Missile (RAM) launcher on San Nicolas Island, Pacific Missile Test Center in January 1982. The Pomona Division of General Dynamics was heavily involved in developing the RAM concept and subsequently became prime contractor for the programme, operating in cooperation with the German RAMSYS consortium. The trials launcher has a distinct similarlity with the 21-round Mk 49 GMLS that was subsequently used in the RAM production phase. *(US National Archives NAID 6368630)*

and In-Service Support (BAAINBw) – was established and is periodically re-authorised via memorandums of understanding and agreement signed by the US and German governments (these cover co-operation across development, production, and in-service support). Design authority also resides with RAMPO. The original industrial arrangements have endured, albeit corporate identities have changed over time. Raytheon and RAMSYS have their own agreements covering workshare which are reviewed and updated periodically in the best interest of the overall programme.

A production MoU for the EX-31 (now Mk 31) Guided Missile Weapon System was signed in August 1987, with series production activities commencing in 1989. It had originally been intended to establish parallel production lines – one in Germany, one in the United States – with open competition for combined German/US orders. However, the end of the Cold War, and a commensurate decrease in planned RAM production offtake, saw the industry partners in June 1992 conclude a cooperative production agreement for a single integrated production line located in Tucson, Arizona, with each contractor building specific sub-assemblies.

RE-USE AND RE-PURPOSE

The original RIM-116A (Block 0) missile was, quite deliberately, engineered so as to reduce cost and minimise technical risk. This approach meant re-using many subsystems common to either Sidewinder or the FIM-92 Stinger man-portable air defence system (the successor to Redeye). For example, the Mk 112 Mod 1 rocket motor, Mk 20 Mod 2 active optical target detector (AOTD), and WDU-17B annular blast/fragmentation warhead were all re-used from AIM-9, while many of its IR seeker components (seeker head assembly, gyro-optics, reticule and IR detector) were common to Stinger. In both cases, only minor modifications were made to reflect the operating environment and mission requirements specific to RAM. The signal processing electronics were also identical to Stinger, except for the removal of some components to avoid compromising the Stinger IR counter-countermeasures techniques.

While RAM owes much to Sidewinder and Stinger, there were some notable changes from the outset. For example, Sidewinder's aerodynamics were altered with the introduction of two movable canard fins and four folding tail fins (the latter being used to keep the missile spinning in flight, roll having been imparted at launch through helical lands in the launch tube). Furthermore, the missile guidance section fitted forward reflected the adoption of a dual-mode RF/IR guidance solution pairing a passive RF receiver with the rosette scan IR seeker from Stinger. Target RF energy, angle and amplitude was captured using single-plane interferometry (using the twin forward-facing antennas mounted on the front of the missile). The roll motion of the missile meant that angle information

A RAM launcher fires a RIM-116 missile from the *Nimitz* (CVN-68) class aircraft carrier *Abraham Lincoln* (CVN-72) during a live-fire exercise in April 2024. The original RIM-116A (Block 0) missile was deliberately engineered to reduce cost and minimise technical risk by re-using many sub-systems common to either the Sidewinder air-to-air missile or the Stinger man-portable air defence system. *(US Navy)*

A test firing of a RAM Block 0 missile from the now-retired amphibious assault ship *Nassau* (LHA-4) in 1993. In this view the missile has ignited for launch but is still contained within the RAM launcher. Tests from *Nassau* and her sister shup *Peleliu* (LHA-5) in 1993 paved the way for RAM to enter operational service. *(US National Archives NAID 6491763)*

could be obtained in the entire forward sector. Two more RF antennas were fitted at the rear of the missile. These served to reject signals coming from the rear hemisphere, so preventing them interfering with target acquisition.

Use of a wide field of view RF seeker was designed to make RAM insensitive to launching errors and designation uncertainties. It also endowed the RIM-116 missile with a useful 'shoot around the corner' capability (+/-15 degrees) for targets shadowed by the ship's superstructure.

In Block 0, the passive RF seeker achieved target lock-on after launch, performed mid-course guidance, and pointed the IR seeker towards the target. After lock-on, the IR seeker used proportional navigation to home into the inbound threat. In the event that IR lock-on was not achieved, the guidance system retained a reversionary RF all-the-way mode.

Technical Evaluation (TECHEVAL) flight testing performed in 1989 saw RAM Block 0 missiles score eleven hits out of eleven firings against single and multiple targets. Key features demonstrated, among others, included the performance of 'RF all the way' guidance, IR mode operation in difficult background scenarios, and RF seeker immunity to multipath effects. Additional tests were conducted during 1993 from the US Navy amphibious ships *Peleliu* (LHA-5) and *Nassau* (LHA-4) within the scope of their combat ship system qualification tests; an initial operating capability (IOC) was declared on 9 June 1993 following four successful RAM firings from *Peleliu*.

The German Navy F122 class frigate *Niedersachsen* subsequently completed test firings in Roosevelt Roads, Puerto Rico, in March 1994. Five Block 0 missiles were fired, achieving five direct hits.

MK 31 GUIDED MISSILE WEAPON SYSTEM ARCHITECTURE

While the name Rolling Airframe Missile has gained currency, the full Mk 31 Guided Missile Weapon System is much more than just its effector. Alongside the missile itself, a RAM ship system also comprises launching equipment and associated below-decks electronics. A target cue – for launcher train/elevation and missile initialisation – is provided by ship's sensors via the combat management system.

Each RIM-116 missile is stored and transported in a sealed canister, designated as the Mk 44 Guided Missile Round Pack (GMRP). The Mk 44 GMRP has a nominal 10-year storage life, with no testing or maintenance required.

The other main component of the Mk 31 Guided Missile Weapon System is the Mk 49 GMLS. This combined the above-decks Mk 144 Guided Missile Launcher (GML) unit, hosting 21 RIM-116 missiles, with three below-decks enclosures: the Mk 406 Weapon Control Panel; the Mk 202 Launcher Control Interface Unit; and the Mk 201 Launcher Control Servo Unit.

The original Mk 49 Mod 0 GMLS was succeeded in service by the Mod 1 standard equipment, which addressed obsolescence and launcher affordability.[1] The Mod 3 variant introduced support for the Block 1A helicopter, aircraft and surface (HAS) capability and, through later software updates, added Block 2 and then Block 2A compatibility. It also addressed obsolescence.

The Mk 49 Mod 5 has introduced Block 2B compatibility, and an increased rate of fire, while additionally addressing obsolescence. Most recently, the Mod 7 is a stowed kill improvement project that builds upon the missile-to-missile data link to increase battlespace awareness of the missiles in flight, therefore improving performance against complex raids and other targets of interest.

Sailors load a Mk 44 Guided Missile Round Pack (GMRP) into a Mk 144 Guided Missile Launcher (GML) on board the amphibious transport dock *San Diego* (LPD-22) in August 2024.The Mk 144 GML is the above-decks component of the Mk 49 (Guided Missile Launching System) GMLS, itself a major element of the full RAM-based Mk 31 Guided Missile Weapon System. *(US Navy)*

Note

1. The Mk 49 Mod 2 is a lightweight launcher which marries the standard Mk 49 mounting with the 11-round missile guide pannier originally developed for the Mk 15 Mod 31 SeaRAM launcher. This variant is currently unique to the two *Arialah* class offshore patrol vessels serving with the UAE Critical Infrastructure and Coastal Protection Agency. It appears the Mod 4 and Mod 6 designations were never allocated.

THE BLOCK 1 UPGRADE

One constraint of the original RAM Block 0 system was the need for the target to radiate in order for the missile to achieve passive RF acquisition for initial guidance: the IR seeker used in the Block 0 missile was a narrow-field device, capable of terminal target acquisition only. This meant that the missile was ineffective against ASCM threats employing passive terminal guidance methods.

To address this shortfall, development was initiated of an improved Block 1 missile (RIM-116B) incorporating a so-called IR Mode Upgrade (IRMU). The IRMU modification – introducing a completely new image-scanning mid-waveband seeker with an 80-element linear detector array and intelligent digital signal processing – conferred an 'IR-all-the-way' guidance capability to enable the engagement of non-RF-radiating targets out to the missile's maximum range.

The seeker upgrade additionally endowed improved performance against crossing targets, improved resistance to countermeasures, and better performance in severe IR background conditions. The modification was designed such that existing Block 0 missiles could be cost effectively upgraded to Block 1 configuration through a guidance section exchange.

The Block 1 missile retained all capabilities of the Block 0 missile while adding two guidance modes: IR only; and IR Dual Mode Enable (IRDM). The IR mode guides all the way on the thermal signature of the ASCM target, while IRDM guides on the IR signature of the threat while retaining the capability to utilise RF guidance if the RF signature of the ASCM becomes adequate to guide on.

Another change introduced with Block 1 was a redesign of the AOTD to provide superior low altitude performance against 'sea-skimming' targets. Coincident with this, enhanced signal processing was developed to improve capability in 'aerosol' environments (such as dense fog).

RAM Block 1 Developmental Testing was initiated in May 1999 at the US Navy's Atlantic Fleet Weapons Training Facility using the *Whidbey Island* class dock landing ship *Gunston Hall* (LSD-44). Missile exercises were conducted to evaluate the ability to fire Block 0 missiles from a Block 1 launcher, the new Block 1 IR-only capability, the Mk 20 Mod 2 low-altitude AOTD design; and the Block 1 missile's retention of the Block 0 capability. All four missiles fired (two Block 0 and two Block 1) scored direct hits.

The Block 1 development programme was successfully completed in August 1999, with an Operational Evaluation completed using the Self-Defense Test Ship EDDG-31 – the former destroyer *Decatur* (DDD-963/DDG-31) – to demonstrate the system's introduction maturity. Firing against real-world threats and threat-representative targets, RIM-116B missiles engaged and defeated singular Vandal supersonic diving and sea-skimming manoeuvring targets, a supersonic stream raid, and singular subsonic non-manoeuvring targets (including a target inbound through a sun-glint corridor). A total of 17 RAM Block 1 missiles and 11 targets were expended for all events, with Harpoon, Exocet and Vandal supersonic (Mach 2.5) target missiles intercepted and destroyed under realistic conditions. According to NAVSEA, RAM Block 1 achieved first-

The German Navy's K130 class corvette *Ludwigshafen am Rhein* pictured firing a RAM Block 1A missile during Exercise Spartan Arrow in the Mediterranean in September 2024. Germany has been a joint partner in the RAM programme throughout its life. Its need for a capability to engage slow aircraft and helicopters was a key factor in the development of the HAS (helicopter, aircraft and surface) upgrade that resulted in the development of RAM Block 1 to the revised Block 1A iteration. *(Bundeswehr/Tom Twardy)*

The amphibious transport dock *Green Bay* (LPD-20) fires a RAM Block 1A missile during a combat system ship qualification trial off the coast of Hawaii in September 2009. RAM Block 1A was an upgrade of the RAM Block 1 missile to deliver a helicopter, aircraft and surface (HAS) capability. *(US Navy)*

shot kills on every target in its presented scenarios, including sea-skimming, diving and highly manoeuvring profiles in both single and stream attacks. A Milestone III approval for Block 1 full-rate missile production followed in January 2000.

While Block 1 development was still progressing, both the US Navy and the German Navy identified requirements to expand the RAM target set so as to address emerging asymmetric threats in littoral environments. In the former case, the US Navy needed a weapon that could defeat small boats, such as those operated by the Iranian Revolutionary Guards; in the latter, the German Navy sought a capability against slow aircraft and helicopters.

The two navies harmonised their respective requirements in 1997, recognising that the image scanning capability introduced with the IRMU upgrade could, with software changes, deliver a helicopter, aircraft and surface (HAS) capability for the engagement of slow-flying air targets and surface vessels. Development of the HAS upgrade – taking the Block 1 missile up to a Block 1A standard – began in 1999, with testing completed in 2002.

Deliveries of the Block 1A missile to the US fleet began in 2004. First tests against a surface target, conducted in May 2004, saw two direct hits in flight tests at the Pacific Missile Test Range in California. Alongside new production missiles, Raytheon and RAMSYS were also contracted to recertify and upgrade a significant proportion of US and German RAM Block 0 inventories to Block 1A standard.

The RAM Block 2 missile (RIM-116C) significantly expands the weapon's effective engagement envelope through the introduction of a larger dual-thrust rocket motor and an independent four-canard control actuator system. Block 2 also embodies an updated passive RF seeker in its guidance section. *(Raytheon)*

ENTER BLOCK 2

The next major upgrade for the Mk 31 Guided Missile Weapon System, known as RAM Block 2 (RIM-116C), involved the development of kinematic and guidance upgrades designed to counter a new generation of high manoeuvring ASCM threats. In parallel, this improvement effort provided an opportunity to address certain obsolescence issues. Informed by threat assessments, Raytheon had previously established a Pre-Planned Product Improvement (P3I) programme aimed at introducing performance upgrades matched to the evolving threat. Engineering analyses and risk reduction studies performed under the P3I umbrella provided the basis for Block 2 design and development.

The US and German governments signed a MoU in May 2007 for the co-operative development of RAM Block 2, sharing costs on a 50/50 basis. Block 2 remains the kinematic baseline for all subsequent production variants. Raytheon was awarded a US$105.5 million System Design and Development (SDD) contract by NAVSEA/PEO IWS the same month. This SDD contract included the manufacture of 20 engineering missiles, and 35 missiles to support Development Testing/Operational Testing (DT/OT).

RIM-116 ROLLING AIRFRAME MISSILE: SPECIMEN BLOCK CHARACTERISTICS[1]

VARIANT	RIM-116 BLOCK 1A	RIM-116 BLOCK 2
Weight	164lbs (74.4kg)	194.4lbs (88.2kg)
Length	9.3ft (2.83m)	9.45ft (2.88m)
Diameter	5in (0.127m)	6.25in (0.159m)
Wingspan	17.5in (0.445m)	12.65in (0.322m)
Warhead (explosive weight)	7.9lbs (3.6kg)	7.9lbs (3.6kg)
Date Deployed	1999	2015
Range[2]	0.8km minimum/9km maximum	0.4km minimum/15km maximum

Note

1. Missiles are fired by the 21-round Mk 49 GLMS. This has an above-deck weight of 11,466lbs (5,201kg) when loaded with Block 1 missiles and 12,081lbs (5428kg) with Block 2 missiles. Below-Deck Weight is 2,068lbs (938kg). The mounting can train 360 degrees and can elevate from -25 degrees to +80 degrees.
2. Not officially released. Based on open source information

Building on the RAM Block 1A missile, Block 2 significantly expands the effective engagement envelope through the introduction of a larger dual-thrust rocket motor and an independent four-canard control actuator system. Together, these measures serve to increase effective missile range by about 50 percent, and deliver a threefold improvement in manoeuvrability. Block 2 also embodies an evolved passive RF (ERF) seeker in its guidance section. The ERF provides increased sensitivity and discrimination.

A digital autopilot is introduced to support the additional engagement envelope afforded by the kinematic and sensor update. Other engineering changes resolve obsolescence in IR seeker hardware; a new processor to re-host existing algorithms in more modern hardware; an all-sapphire seeker dome; and an aluminium mirror piece part, replacing the previous titanium component.

The launch canister associated with the Mk 44 GMRP is externally unchanged. However, its inner

The amphibious transport dock *Anchorage* (LPD-23) fires a RAM Block 2 missile during a live-fire exercise in the Pacific Ocean in February 2022. Developed between 2007 and 2015, the RAM Block 2 (RIM-116C) missile shot down 27 out of 28 targets in developmental and operational testing. *(US Navy)*

sides are re-engineered so as to increase diameter to accommodate the larger Block 2 missile.

The incorporation of a larger diameter (6.25in) rocket motor – the increased size allowing the missile to carry more propellant for extended range – was an upgrade that Raytheon had initially explored back in the early 1990s. Indeed, the company had gone so far as to perform two risk reduction firings using a Hercules metal-cased dual-thrust rocket motor. The first, a launch test vehicle, was fired at the White Sands Missile Range in July 1993; the second, in November 1994, was an instrumented test vehicle that executed some pre-programmed manoeuvres in flight. Under the Block 2 SDD programme, Alliant Techsystems – today badged as Northrop Grumman Innovation Systems – was contracted to develop a new, insensitive munition, 6.25in solid-propellant boost/sustain rocket motor. A graphite-fibre composite case design was adopted that would reduce overall weight, and withstand high g-force manoeuvres.

ERF development for Block 2 was undertaken by MBDA Deutschland (as part of RAMSYS). Increasing the sensitivity of the receiver, in combination with digital signal processing, enables improved identification and tracking of low probability of intercept RF seekers.

The revised aerodynamics of the Block 2 missile obliged Raytheon to perform wind tunnel testing of the new missile configuration (using a fully operational 75 percent spinning missile model). Testing occurred in NASA's Ames' supersonic and transonic wind tunnels in California; aerodynamic data was captured during 164 wind tunnel test hours spanning four-and-a-half weeks. A Raytheon-produced, one-of-kind data acquisition system and model interfaced with the Ames' computer systems to provide important tunnel facility safety interlocks. The data acquired was then transferred to a NASA server for post-processing: NASA Ames built and programmed a custom computer system for post-processing of the data, along with other interfaces between the model and facility systems.

A series of Controlled Test Vehicle (CTV) flight tests – designated DT-B-1 – were completed between April and October 2009. These firings were focused on the Block 2 rocket motor, airframe, and the control section and autopilot software.

The follow-up DT-B-2 series was planned to comprise a series of three Guided Test Vehicle (GTV) over-water firings performed from a

The *Nimitz* (CVN-68) class aircraft carrier *Abraham Lincoln* (CVN-72) launches a RAM Block 2 missile during combat system ship qualification trials. The US Navy is pursuing the integration of the latest RAM Block 2B (RIM-116E) iteration into the Mk 15 Mod 40 CIWS RAM Defense Capability (CRDC) that is specific to the *Nimitz* class. *(US Navy)*

launcher test stand on San Nicolas Island (located within the Point Mugu Sea Range off the California coast). In actual fact, the failure of GTV-1 obliged four tests. GTV-1A (a re-test of GTV-1) and GTV-2 were conducted in December 2011, both against BQM-34 targets. Subsequently, GTV-3 – conducted from San Nicholas Island in September 2012 – saw two RAM Block 2 missiles launched in salvo against separate BQM-74 air target vehicles (each augmented with RF transmitters simulating an ASCM seeker). Both engagements resulted in direct hits.

The DT-B-2 campaign rounded off the development flight test programme, fully demonstrating the system's upgraded kinematic performance, guidance system and airframe capabilities. It also verified the first-time use of RAM Block 2 production hardware. SDD phase activities were formally concluded in early November 2012 with the finalisation of missile-level qualification testing and delivery of final test reports.

DT/OT of RAM Block 2 was undertaken by the US Navy on the Point Mugu range between May 2013 and March 2015. Testing was primarily conducted using the Self-Defense Test Ship EDD-964 – the former destroyer *Paul F. Foster* (DD-964). However, one test was performed from the *San Antonio* (LPD-17) class landing platform dock *Arlington* (LPD-24) to validate supportability, training and fleet configuration for the Block 2 system. DT/OT firings of RIM-116C missiles were performed to demonstrate performance against representative targets in a variety of stressing high fidelity threat scenarios. These included a number of tests from the SDTS in which dual salvos of Block 2 missiles defeated 'stream raid' scenarios representative of supersonic, high-manoeuvring and low level threats. According to PEO IWS, RAM scored 27 out of 28 in DT/OT firings.

IOC for RAM Block 2 on board *Arlington* was declared on 15 May 2015.

EVOLUTIONARY DEVELOPMENT

Work to further enhance the Block 2 missile has been driven by a need to improve performance in complex multi-threat engagements. Going back to 2015, a multiple RAM live firing as part of testing of the Ship Self-Defence System (SSDS) Mk 2 combat system revealed scope for improvement in complex 'raid' situations. While the exact nature of these remains classified, they drove the US Navy to pursue two efforts designed to further improve overall 'Probability of Raid Annihilation' (PRA) performance.

The first of these, known as the RAM Block 2A Fire Control Loop Improvement Project (FCLIP), introduced new multi-threat missile software design improvements and a software modification to improve fire detect-to-engage coordination in SSDS Mk 2. FCLIP was successfully tested from EDD-964 in 2016, with the Block 2A missile variant designated as RIM-116D.

RAM Block 2B – also known as the Raid Engineering Change Proposal – is a further evolutionary development specifically designed to improve PRA performance in multi-threat ASMD scenarios. It introduces a missile-to-missile link (MML) capability, plus a further improved IR seeker, while maintaining the proven capabilities of previous RAM variants (Block 0/1/1A/2/2A) with regard to accurate terminal guidance, high lethality, and 'fire and forget' operation post-launch. In essence, the MML embodiment gives RAM Block 2B (RIM-116E) missiles the ability to talk to one another. This is seen as an important enhancement for two reasons. First, it ensures that missiles cooperate in target allocation/prioritisation, and do not inadvertently go after the same targets in complex, multi-threat scenarios; second, it should mean that fewer missiles are expended.

RAM Block 2B deliveries to the US Navy and the German Navy began in 2024, with fielding following in 2025. Production of RAM Block 2 and Block 2A rounds is expected to complete in the first half of 2026, leaving only the Block 2B configuration in active and ongoing production thereafter. However, Block 1A, Block 2, and Block 2A rounds will continue in their upgrade, maintenance, and routine recertification cycles.

The modified Block 2B guidance and control section – which accommodates the electronics and antennas associated with MML – offers substantial

INTRODUCING SEARAM

The RIM-116 missile is also fielded as part of the SeaRAM autonomous inner-layer defence system. Conceived by Raytheon in the late 1990s as a cost-effective upgrade for the existing Mk 15 Phalanx CIWS, SeaRAM was developed with three key drivers in mind: first, extended engagement range and reduced reaction time to address ASCM threat developments; second, earliest possible detection to achieve 'outer boundary' engagements at the limit of the range envelope; and third, the need to minimise through-life costs.

SeaRAM sought to satisfy these aims by combining the Phalanx Block 1B high resolution multi-sensor suite, and integral threat evaluation and weapon designation capability, with the superior accuracy, extended range and high manoeuvrability afforded by the RIM-116 missile. To achieve this, the six-barrel M61A1 20mm gun (including its supporting electronics and mechanics) associated with the CIWS is replaced by an eleven-round guide assembly (all electronics associated with the missile being incorporated in a small fairing below the missile guide).[1]

The existing Phalanx Block 1B mounting and control panel are retained, as are the Ku (NATO J) band search-and-track radar and long-waveband thermal imager. To enable autonomous or semi-autonomous operation an electronic surveillance measurement system (ESMS) is added to the mount to measure and characterise threat emitter information, and then deliver that threat information to the RAM missile prior to launch.

Fast reaction time ('detect to engage') is achieved by coupling the high-data-rate Phalanx sensor suite directly into the RAM launcher: most notably, superior low-elevation radar performance provides for the firm track ranges required for maximum-range engagements.

This hybrid approach – melding elements from two existing self-defence weapon systems – creates a weapon system that is able to automatically detect, evaluate, track, engage, and perform kill assessment against ASCMs and high speed air threats around the ship (SeaRAM can also be integrated into ship combat control systems to provide additional sensor and fire-control support to other installed ship weapon systems). According to Raytheon, SeaRAM expands the engagement envelope by a factor of three compared to CIWS,

The *Freedom* (LCS-1) variant Littoral Combat Ship *Nantucket* (LCS-27) transits the Menominee River in northern Wisconsin, during acceptance trials in December 2023. In common with other littoral combat ships, she is equipped with a single Mk 15 Mod 31 SeaRAM mounting, which is located prominently atop her hangar. SeaRAM combines the Phalanx CIWS Block 1B sensor suite, plus its embedded threat evaluation and weapon designation capability, with a RAM 11-round launcher guide assembly on a single mount. *(US Navy)*

spare computing capability to facilitate continuous software improvements throughout the system's lifecycle. A RAM 'Software Factory' has been established with the navy to provide end users with rapid missile software updates incorporating improvements identified through real-world events, trade studies, modelling and simulation, and test firings.

Another initiative being pursued by the US Navy is the integration of RAM Block 2B into the Mk 15 Mod 40 CIWS RAM Defense Capability (CRDC) specific to the US Navy's *Nimitz* (CVN-68) class nuclear-powered aircraft carriers. The Mk 15 Mod 40 configuration, originally fielded in 2020, is currently limited to utilising the RIM-116C missile: introducing the latest RIM-116E missile variant into CRDC will provide an enhanced ship self-defence capability against complex stream raids and emerging threats.

Notes

1. See Emily C. Elko, James W. Howard, Richard C. Kochanski, Thu-Phuong T. Nguyen, and William M. Sanders, 'Rolling Airframe Missile: Development, Test, Evaluation, and Integration' in *John Hopkins APL Technical Digest*, Volume 22, Number 4 (Laurel MD: John Hopkins APL, 2001).

2. Denmark ended its participation in the programme in May 1985, assuming observer status thereafter. It has not yet procured RAM.

3. Industry also funded development of a ten round RAM Alternate Launching System (RALS) specifically designed for smaller surface combatants. An engineering development model was completed but RALS did not go into production.

and provides for a true multi-threat engagement capability.

A pre-production operational suitability model (OSM) completed manufacture in 2000 and was subsequently offered to prospective customers for installation, integration and compatibility testing. The British Royal Navy took advantage of this facility, with the OSM (using production-representative hardware and a generic baseline threat-evaluation and weapon-assignment program) fitted aboard the Type 42 Batch 3 destroyer *York* in 2001 for a Fleet Equipment Trial.

SeaRAM (under the designation Mk 15 Mod 31) was subsequently selected to equip the US Navy's Littoral Combat Ship (LCS). Both *Freedom* (LCS-1) and *Independence* (LCS-2) variants are equipped with a single Mk 15 Mod 31 mounting. In addition, the US Navy has fitted SeaRAM on board *Arleigh Burke* (DDG-51) class Aegis-equipped guided missile destroyers forward-deployed to Rota, Spain. This iteration – Mk 15 Mod 33 — replaces the aft Phalanx Block 1B and stems from an Urgent Operational Needs Statement raised by the US Sixth Fleet in February 2015.

The Japanese Maritime Self Defence Force is, for the time being, the only other navy to have fielded SeaRAM. At present, the system is installed on its *Izumo* (DDH-181) class helicopter carrying destroyers and *Mogami* (FFM-1) class frigates. However, the Royal Saudi Naval Forces is set to become the third SeaRAM operator. In this case, each of its four new, US-built Multi-Mission Surface Combatants will receive a single Mk 15 Mod 31 weapon system.

In February 2025, NAVSEA contracted RAMSYS to develop a common electronic support measurement system (cESMS) for integration into SeaRAM. Designed as an upgrade to the legacy ESMS, the cESMS engineering modification – together with the exploitation of the RAM Block 2B MML as an uplink/downlink – is intended to improve RAM Block 2B mid-course guidance and kill assessment by providing an increased probability of missile intercept, and therefore economise on missile expenditure.

A sailor from the *Arleigh Burke* class guided-missile destroyer *Paul Ignatius* (DDG-117) sprays down the ship's SeaRAM weapon system during a wash down of the ship in September 2022. *Paul Ignatius*, based in Rota, Spain, is one of four US Navy destroyers assigned to Commander, Task Force 65 in support of NATO's Integrated Air Missile Defense architecture. These ships are fitted with the Mk 15 Mod 33 iteration of SeaRAM as a result of an Urgent Operational Needs Statement raised by the US Sixth Fleet in February 2015. *(US Navy)*

Note

1. SeaRAM fits the existing Phalanx footprint, offering over 80 percent commonality in parts and structures, and uses the same power supply.

4.3 TECHNOLOGICAL REVIEW

SHIP-BASED ASW

Anti-submarine Warfare Weapons for Surface Ships

Author:
Norman Friedman

The sea control helicopter has increasingly become the platform of choice for seaborne anti-submarine warfare (ASW) operations, offering a flexibility and range that few other systems can match. However, surface ship ASW continues to make full use of a range of other, ship-based weapons. These weapons can be divided into categories by range, which in effect means by the range and character of the supporting sensors. At the shortest range are anti-torpedo weapons, none of which, it appears, have yet been proven. These weapons are important because submarines can attack from increasing ranges, with effective homing torpedoes.[1]

The British Royal Navy early Cold War-era Type 14 anti-submarine warfare frigate *Pellew* carried two triple-barrelled Limbo ASW mortars as her primary weapons; visible prominently towards her stern in this October 1966 photograph. This type of salvo-firing anti-submarine weapon was widely used at this time but fell out of favour as increases in reliable sonar range allowed submarines to be engaged at longer distances. *(Crown Copyright 1966)*

SHORT-RANGE ASW

Next are quick-response weapons that are intended to embarrass and drive off submarines which appear suddenly at short range. The existence of such weapons is testimony to the incomplete capacity of shipboard sonars (as well as submarine sonars; the submarine may be as surprised as the surface ship). In Western navies the typical embarrassment weapon is a ship-launched lightweight torpedo, generally automatically fired from a ship's combat information centre or operations room. These weapons are unlikely to destroy a suddenly-detected submarine, but the submarine will have to flee to avoid destruction.

At one time many Western warships were armed with salvo-firing anti-submarine weapons, most prominently the British Royal Navy's Squid and Limbo. They were principal ASW weapons when reliable shipboard sonar ranges were about 1,000–2,000 yards, but fell back into the embarrassment category as sonar ranges increased beyond that. By the 1980s they had largely been replaced by lightweight homing torpedoes. In theory, a lightweight torpedo may be able to detect targets as much as 2,000 yards away; whether it can catch them depends on how fast they are and when they detect the torpedo.

The only new weapon in this category seems to be BAE Systems' (BAE's) Kingfisher, a device which can carry alternative payloads and can be fired by a standard 5in Mk 45 gun. BAE began working on Kingfisher as a private venture in 2018. The shell cannot accommodate a very heavy payload, but BAE suggests it as a means of attacking submerged unmanned vehicles and also incoming torpedoes. At least in theory, a gun can react very quickly, and

LESSONS FROM THE FALKLANDS WAR

The 1982 Falklands War between Argentina and the United Kingdom illustrated an important, but rarely mentioned, aspect of close-in anti-submarine warfare (ASW) weapons: target classification. That is the problem of deciding that something indicated by sonar is or is not a valid target. Sonar is quite different from radar in that it is far more susceptible to false targets. Real targets are often missed, largely due to the complexity of the environment. When it steamed south to engage the Argentines, the Royal Navy found itself in a very unfamiliar environment, in largely shallow water crowded with obstructions on the bottom. Moreover, it was facing small diesel submarines rather than the nuclear submarines it faced in northern European waters. Diesel and other non-nuclear submarines can bottom in shallow water. Nuclear submarines avoid bottoming for fear of sucking mud into their condensers and thus immobilising them. How do you distinguish a small diesel submarine sitting on the bottom from a shipwreck there? The diesel submarine is not running its machinery, so it is not producing characteristic noise. The Royal Navy, which was considered the best ASW force in NATO, had not practised against small diesel submarines of the type the Argentines had.

The crews of the British task force were understandably nervous, particularly because there were so few escorts to shield the two carriers and other high-value units. It later turned out that there was a tendency to fire lightweight torpedoes at apparent targets as soon as they were tentatively detected, and therefore long before they could be classified as real targets; better to do that than to become a torpedo target. However, the task force had only a limited number of lightweight torpedoes, and little prospect of receiving more from bases 8,000 miles away.

Simple weapons like the British Limbo mortar were valued. No one expected that a Limbo salvo would destroy a bottomed submarine, but at the least it would probably cause the submarine to run, hence to become detectable and vulnerable to a lightweight torpedo. Limbo rounds were far less expensive than torpedoes (though in fact there were not all that many salvoes available). The alternative to Limbo rounds was the helicopter-delivered Mk 11 depth charge. Observing the war, the US Navy considered adopting something like Limbo, but instead bought a depth charge fuze for its standard aircraft bomb.

For a time, there was a NATO requirement for a 'classification weapon', a lightweight bomb which could be dropped on or near a suspected bottomed submarine. This requirement seems to have lapsed at the end of the Cold War, although it was actually the sort of weapon needed in the post-Cold War world, when the West faced Third World non-nuclear submarines operating in littoral waters. The US Navy – and presumably others – became interested in means of visualising the bottom of a shallow area in order to detect bottomed submarines. In its case, that involved the use of explosive sound sources and passive sonobuoys, with appropriate signal processing.

What would it take to convince a submarine commander sitting on the bottom to expose himself by running? An Argentine account of the operations of the submarine *San Luis* mentions that her commander once kept her on the bottom for about 20 hours to avoid exposing her, while the British dropped numerous weapons nearby. It is not clear how or why the small depth bombs offered by Kingfisher or, for that matter, by the Russian RBU, would be more persuasive as classifiers. All that can be said, it would seem, is that because the bombs would be numerous, there would be a much better chance that some would land close enough to a bottomed submarine to be a real threat.

The British Royal Navy Type 42 destroyer *Sheffield* pictured after being hit by an Exocet air-to-surface missile in May 1982 during the early stages of the Falklands War between Argentina and the United Kingdom. The Type 21 frigate *Arrow* can be seen alongside the destroyer's port side providing assistance with the ship's own fire-fighting efforts. A Sea King anti-submarine warfare helicopter is also visible. False classification of underwater threats reportedly hindered fire-fighting efforts, repeatedly forcing another frigate, *Yarmouth*, to break off the task to utilise her anti-submarine warfare weapons. This reflected a wider problem of accurate target classification in the face of stealthy Argentine diesel-electric submarines and unfamiliar waters, resulting in heavy expenditure of finite ASW munitions against seemingly false targets. *(Crown Copyright 1982)*

The BAE Systems Kingfisher device allows alternative payloads, including anti-torpedo and anti-uncrewed underwater vessel munitions, to be fired from a standard gun. This graphic illustrates a Kingfisher shell engaging an incoming torpedo. *(BAE Systems)*

shells can reach an approaching submarine far more quickly than a lightweight torpedo with a speed of perhaps 45 or 50 knots. Firing quickly – at about 15–20 rounds per minute – the gun might be able to lay down a pattern of shells which would likely ensure one or two hits, something like the wartime Hedgehog. Although the warhead in a carrier shell is small, a hit by a shaped-charge projectile might be enough to penetrate the pressure hull of a small submarine. However, Kingfisher may be most interesting as an anti-torpedo weapon, a requirement that is discussed later in this chapter.

ASW AT EXTENDED RANGES

The next category consists of ship-launched ASW weapons with ranges comparable to the direct-path ranges of low-frequency active sonars. For example, in the 1950s the US Navy developed the 5 kHz SQS-23 series, which was credited with a reliable range of 10,000 yards. The associated weapon was ASROC, an unguided (ballistic) rocket with roughly that range, carrying either a homing torpedo or a nuclear depth bomb. In theory the associated sonar could locate a submarine precisely enough that a homing torpedo dropped on its position – at the time of launch – would have a good change of homing on and hitting the submarine. There was no provision for adjusting the aim point while the rocket was in flight. ASROC was widely installed on board US Navy and some foreign ships throughout the 1980s.

Another approach to exploiting shipboard direct-path sonars was a helicopter controlled by the attacking ship, the British MATCH system. An alternative was a weapon controlled by the ship: the Anglo-Australian Ikara and the French Malafon. Radio control offered the possibility that control could be passed to a second ship which might be better placed to track a target submarine. France and Italy collaborated on a follow-on to Malafon, MILAS, based on the Otomat anti-ship cruise missile, with a considerably longer range. It has been adopted only by Italy.

Lower-frequency sonars can see considerably further, but beyond about 20,000 yards their beams

A MILAS anti-submarine missile seen during checkout after assembly. ASW weapons such as the Anglo-Australian Ikara and the French Malafon, of which MILAS is a Franco-Italian developed follow-on, were similar to the US Navy ASROC in seeking to match the direct-path ranges of low-frequency active sonars. However, they offered potentially greater accuracy by dint of being radio-controlled. *(MBDA)*

bend down, coming back up at convergence zone ranges.[2] Unfortunately convergence zones are typically about five nautical miles wide, so it is pointless simply to fire a missile at a submarine in one. It seems to follow that the maximum useful range for a shipboard ASW missile is about 20,000 yards, although in some special circumstances – in which signals are trapped in layers – it may be greater. The US Navy planned an Extended-Range ASROC (ERA) to work with its long-range SQS-26 sonar, but development was stopped during the Vietnam War. Much later SQS-26 was developed into the current SQS-53 series, and a new vertically-launched ASROC (VLA: RUM-139) was developed to match its 20,000-yard direct-path range. It entered production about 1996, and has been adopted by both the US Navy and the Japanese Maritime Self-Defense Force. Japan produces an equivalent rocket (Type 07VLA) carrying its indigenous lightweight torpedo. South Korea produces another equivalent missile, named Red Shark. This carries its indigenous White Shark lightweight torpedo.

China and India have both claimed the development of much longer-range weapons, the 50km Chinese Yu-8 and the Indian SMART (Supersonic Missile Assisted Release of Torpedo). The claimed 50km range of Yu-8 suggests that it is intended to hit convergence-zone targets or, perhaps, targets locatable in an extended direct path in particular places. There was once a proposal for an ASW cruise missile based on the US Tomahawk. It would have deployed sonobuoys in the indicated target area, cruising overhead while monitoring them and then dropping its torpedo accordingly. It is not clear whether this weapon was abandoned as impractical or as too expensive.

SMART is credited officially with a range of 350 or 400 nautical miles. It employs inertial navigation with mid-course update via a data link. Some writers have speculated that SMART is intended to prosecute targets detected by an Indian equivalent of the

A July 1991 view of the bow of the *Spruance* (DD-963) class destroyer *O'Bannon* (DD-987), showing the ship's eight-cell Mk 46 ASROC anti-submarine rocket launcher in the foreground. The launcher was used to deploy a homing torpedo or nuclear depth bomb by means of an unguided rocket whose aiming point could not be adjusted after launch. Later iterations of the ASROC system were capable of longer ranges in line with improvements in sonar detection and were fired from a vertical launch system. *(US Navy)*

A test launch of an Indian SMART (Supersonic Missile Assisted Release of Torpedo) in October 2020. The system is designed to deploy lightweight ASW torpedoes at considerable ranges, employing inertial navigation with mid-course updates via a data link. It is intended to be launched from surface warships and truck-based batteries. *(Indian Ministry of Defence)*

One major limitation on shipboard ASW weapons has been the finite and competing space for weapons in relatively cramped destroyers and frigates. The US Navy's answer to this was the development of the Mk 41VLS, which is capable of launching a wide range of weapons that include the vertically-launched variant of ASROC. This photograph shows a missile being launched from the aft set of VLS cells aboard the *Arleigh Burke* class destroyer *Fitzgerald* (DDG-62) during a training exercise in March 2017 *(US Navy)*.

US SOSUS underwater sensing system. However, no undersea sensing system is likely to offer the sort of precision that a missile-borne torpedo needs at the end of its long flight. This suggests that SMART is part of a larger system which would include additional sensors closer to its target.[3]

At one time some surface ASW ships were armed with wire-guided ASW torpedoes, which the ship could theoretically guide using her long-range sonar. The most extreme version of this idea was the plan to install tubes for Mk 48 torpedoes on board *Knox* (FF-1052) class frigates. It was dropped because – due to the financial stress of the Vietnam War – not enough Mk 48s were being made to arm both US Navy submarines and the frigates. The idea was not revived when American naval finances recovered.

All of these shipboard weapons are subject to limitations inherent in a ship's configuration, and also to limits on the extent to which she can be replenished at sea to keep fighting. A frigate has only so much length and volume in which to stow weapons. Anti-submarine warfare is usually only one of several possible roles. In the 1950s and 1960s, when long-range ASW weapons were introduced, they competed, if at all, with anti-aircraft weapons. The first multi-role launcher (ASW and AAW) was on board large US Navy *Belknap* (DLG-26) class cruisers. The situation worsened with the introduction of anti-ship missiles beginning in the 1970s. At about the same time frigate-based helicopters were introduced, with their demand for hangar and flight deck space.

The US solution to the problem was the multi-role Mk 41 vertical launcher. Its multiple cells can accommodate anti-aircraft missiles, strike missiles, and vertically-launched ASROC rockets (as well as their Japanese and Korean equivalents). At present the great drawback of Mk 41 is that it cannot be replenished at sea, although work to solve this problem is ongoing. Thus, a ship leaves port with a set distribution of weapon functions.[4]

Late in the Cold War Western navies, led by the US Navy and the Royal Navy, introduced towed-array sonars, initially passive devices, which could reach out to multiple convergence zones. They were expected to be effective mainly against nuclear submarines, which necessarily produced detectable sounds because they had to run some machinery continuously. By way of contrast, diesel submarines may be noisy at times – e.g., when snorkelling – but very quiet at others; e.g. on batteries or on an AIP power plant. The solution was to add a low-frequency pinger to a towed array. This combination is exemplified by the Type 2087 sonar currently found on board ASW-configured Type 23 'Duke' class frigates. They tow both the pinger and their low-frequency arrays, and they retain their active bow sonars. All of these devices feed into a common set of processors. The low-frequency pinger is said to provide effective performance against all submarines. Presumably its long wavelength makes it difficult for a submarine to locate the pinging ship.

Very long range detection in turn requires that the area in which the submarine has been detected be searched, which in turn currently means a helicopter using either or both of sonobuoys and a dipping sonar. There is no longer a replenishment problem; torpedoes can easily be transferred at sea for stowage near the hangar.

SOVIET AND RUSSIAN WEAPONS

During the Cold War the Soviets developed their own range of ASW weapons, in rough parallel to the Western weapons described here. Their immediate-response weapons were unguided rockets (RBUs) fired from multiple launchers. These weapons are also advertised as anti-torpedo measures. RBU-6000, introduced as long ago as 1960-1, still arms current Russian frigates and corvettes. The Russians describe it as both an anti-submarine and an anti-torpedo measure; maximum range is about 5,000m or around 5,450 yards. It seems unlikely that it can hit a fast submarine at maximum range because the pattern of explosions it produces is too small.[5] Nor is it likely to be very effective against torpedoes, for reasons elaborated below.

For many years the Soviets did not have light-weight torpedoes equivalent to Western ones, although now the Russians have a 324mm (12.75in) Paket torpedo. Many Russian surface combatants have 21in torpedo tubes, which may fire multi-purpose – including wire-guided – torpedoes. These tubes may also launch long-range ASW missiles similar to the US Navy's Cold War era SUBROC, a long-range submarine-launched ASW missile. The US missile had a nuclear depth bomb warhead, but the Russian equivalent also had a torpedo-carrying version.

The Soviets developed a number of ship-launched ASW missiles, such as SS-N-14. This was broadly equivalent to Malafon but much heavier, because its torpedo payload was much more massive. A few surviving Russian Cold War units are still armed with this weapon.

TORPEDO COUNTERMEASURES

Western navies first became interested in anti-torpedo measures during the Second World War. Some merchant ships were fitted with anti-torpedo nets, which on occasion proved effective. Many escorts were given towed noise-makers as a counter to German acoustic homing torpedoes. Current towed torpedo decoys are the much more sophisticated descendants of these devices.

After the war, the U.S. Navy and the Royal Navy invested heavily in hard-kill anti-torpedo measures because, at least until the late 1950s, submarines were credited with the ability to attack formations from beyond their sonar ranges. The Royal Navy, for example, conceived two countermeasures; Camrose and Ruler. Camrose fired a salvo of high-speed

The Russian Navy Project 133.1M 'Parchim II' corvette *Kazanets* pictured at Saint Petersburg in 2016. Two RBU-6000 ASW rocket launchers, which fire unguided rockets, can be seen ahead of her bridge. She is also equipped with two pairs of 400mm (15.75in) torpedo tubes for ASW torpedoes; other Soviet-era warships were fitted with larger, 533mm (21in) diameter tubes. *(Conrad Waters)*

The Indian Navy Project 15 destroyer *Delhi* pictured firing a salvo of unguided rockets from her RBU-6000 ASW rocket launchers. Despite being introduced in the 1960s, the system remains in widespread use in Russian and overseas navies. *(Indian Navy)*

One of two decoy launchers that form part of the British Royal Navy's Surface Ship Torpedo Defence (SSTD) system – also known as Sonar 2170 and Sea Sentor – pictured aboard the now retired amphibious transport dock *Albion* in September 2022. The ship was firing a 96-gun salute to mark the death of the late British queen, HM Queen Elizabeth. Systems like SSTD, which also includes a passive towed array (to detect incoming torpedoes) and a towed decoy, typically use a 'soft kill' approach to lure away homing torpedoes. However, a 'hard kill' approach may be required to combat the wake-following type torpedoes developed by the former Soviet Union, *(Crown Copyright 2022)*

torpedoes and Ruler fired a mortar. Neither came close to entering service, because neither seemed likely to be effective.

At high speed, say 45 knots, a torpedo covers three-quarters of a nautical mile every minute. Reliable sonar range in the early 1950s was about two nautical miles at best. That gave an anti-torpedo system perhaps three minutes to engage and destroy the attacking torpedo. The short time available appeared to demand that the device attacking the incoming torpedo be projected through the air. Unfortunately torpedoes, or at least straight and pattern runners, are hard targets. Among other things, they are designed to be fired in salvoes, meaning that each must function even after a nearby torpedo explodes. Moreover, unguided torpedoes are controlled by gyros, which will try to keep the torpedo on course even after it has been distorted by an explosion. In one test, a standard British torpedo kept going after a depth charge was exploded nearby. Possibly, however, homing torpedoes are vulnerable to nearby explosions which can damage or confuse their guidance sensors.

As sonars improved, it appeared that submarines could be kept a considerable distance from potential targets. It seemed to follow that torpedoes meant to attack high-value units had to be guided. Western torpedo developers concentrated on passive acoustic guidance, which could presumably be tuned to concentrate on the right targets. Hence the interest in towed acoustic devices, which might attract a homing torpedo or confuse it.

Unfortunately there was another way to guide a homing torpedo to attack ships: wake-following. At any kind of speed a ship creates a very detectable wake. A torpedo crossing the wake can detect its onset and its other side, and it can turn so as to re-cross the wake, closing with its target as it repeatedly crosses the wake. Wake-following was conceived by wartime German torpedo developers, but they never put it into service. Post-war, it was tried by several navies, including the US Navy and the Soviet navy. With very limited interest in anti-ship homing weapons, the US Navy abandoned this type of homing. The Soviets did not; by 1965 they had a wake-following torpedo. Later it turned out that wake-following was the only type of anti-ship homing the Soviets employed, hence the only type they sold to their client states.

Perhaps the best evaluation of the wake-following problem came in the 1960s. A US Navy report confirmed that wake-following would work quite well, and that countering it would be difficult or impossible. It would be best if the United States abandoned work on wake-following in a hope - that was to be frustrated – that it was not adopted by anyone else. The sole US wake-follower of the Cold War period seems to have been an adapted Mk 45 torpedo sold to Türkiye in the early 1970s. Delivery was cancelled due to the 1974 Cyprus crisis, and it does not seem that any other customer bought the weapon.

Unfortunately there seems not to have been any obvious way to create a false wake, no analogue to a towed decoy. The French Navy developed a rocket-thrown explosive decoy. Possibly a line of explosions in the water can appear to a wake-following torpedo to be a wake. The false wake can lead away from the target ship, but a limited number of explosions can create a false wake of only limited length. When the torpedo reaches the end of the line of explosions, presumably it begins to search again for a wake to follow.

Some years ago the US Navy stated a requirement for an anti-torpedo measure effective against wake-followers. At least initially, it tried conventional lightweight torpedoes; for a time US Navy carriers were to have been provided with a version of the then-standard Mk 46 torpedo specifically for anti-torpedo use. This weapon was abandoned, presumably because of the time problem: it would not have had enough time to reach an incoming torpedo.

The next step was to develop a much smaller homing torpedo, which presumably could be fired in salvo against incoming weapons. This weapon had half the diameter of the standard lightweight, and it probably weighed about a third as much. Presumably the issues were whether the controlling system could detect an incoming torpedo quickly (and unambiguously) enough and whether the anti-torpedo torpedo could be guided into position to kill the attacking enemy torpedo (or torpedoes). The

This picture of the Chilean Navy's frigate *Almirante Williams* – the former British Type 22 frigate *Sheffield* – operating with the US Navy destroyer *Momsen* (DDG-92) and the Chilean FFG-7 type frigate *Capitán Prat* (ex HMAS *Newcastle*) in October 2023 shows the tell-take wakes that wake-following torpedoes use for targeting. There is no easy way to create a false wake, spurring efforts to develop torpedo-killing countermeasures. *(US Navy)*

anti-torpedo programme died, but the ultra-lightweight weapon remains interesting for more standard homing torpedo roles, particularly for carriage aboard unmanned vehicles.

The Royal Navy currently claims that its anti-torpedo programme includes a classified means of dealing with wake-following torpedoes. Similarly, the French have claimed the ability to deal with these weapons, again on a classified basis. In each case, presumably some means of throwing off the guidance of the wake-following torpedo is envisaged. The danger is that operators of wake-following torpedoes may become aware of what is intended, and modify guidance to circumvent it. That makes a hard-kill countermeasure attractive; albeit it has to solve a very difficult problem.

One such system was displayed at the Euronaval 2022 show by DSIT, a spin-off from the Israeli Rafael company. For some years Rafael has publicised its torpedo defence system for submarines, employing both a decoy and a lethal weapon. This was already unusual; submarine self-defence systems generally employ only decoys. Presumably that is because of fear that a lethal device intended to attack a torpedo may turn on the submarine firing it, as that submarine manoeuvres violently to avoid an incoming weapon.

DSIT offered a version of the Rafael system as a torpedo-killing countermeasure to protect surface ships. The company attacked the time problem by firing its anti-torpedo weapon through the air, from a multi-round box launcher. The incoming torpedo would be tracked by an active sonar, and the anti-torpedo weapon would be activated by a proximity fuze. Because the system can fire rounds rapidly through the air, it can keep shooting as it evaluates its success on each salvo. It is not yet clear how well a proximity fuze-armed countermeasure can perform against a hard torpedo.

Notes

1. The prospects for anti-torpedo weapons will be further discussed at the end of this article.

2. In the Atlantic, these are typically multiples of about 35 nautical miles.

3. It has not been suggested that, like the proposed ASW Tomahawk, SMART deploys and monitors sonobuoys.

4. The other current Western stand-off ASW weapon, MILAS, can be fired from the standard Otomat canister launcher, which takes up substantially more lengthwise space than a vertical launch cell, but can be accommodated on board a smaller ship.

5. Western navies gave up on pattern weapons such as Limbo at much shorter ranges.

4.4 TECHNOLOGICAL REVIEW

ROLLING OUT THE FUTURE

HMS Venturer's Launch Highlights Evolving Shipyard Techniques

Author:
Conrad Waters

On the morning of Tuesday 27 May 2025, *Venturer* – the first of the Royal Navy's new Type 31 'Inspiration' class frigates – was rolled out of the construction hall at Babcock's shipyard in Rosyth, near Edinburgh, in preparation for her 'launch' by floating barge. The event served to highlight the modernisation that is taking place in British warship construction, as well as the ongoing process of change that has been impacting naval shipbuilding over recent years.[1]

The sixth and final Type 45 destroyer, *Duncan*, hits the waters of the River Clyde on 11 October 2010. Changed ways of working mean that dynamic launches are now a thing of the past for British warship construction. *(BAE Systems)*

THE DEMISE OF DYNAMIC LAUNCH

The most noteworthy feature of *Venturer*'s unveiling was the absence of the traditional dynamic launch by means of a slipway that has marked the arrival of previous British warships. This process typically sees ships positioned in launch cradles and held in place by restraining props until released to travel down greased launch ways into the water, where they are restrained by heavy chains. The last Royal Navy major surface combatant that was launched in this way was the sixth and final Type 45 destroyer, *Duncan*. She entered the River Clyde from BAE Systems' Govan yard some 15 years ago, on 11 October 2010.

Although undoubtedly creating an impressive spectacle, dynamic launch has a number of downsides. Most significant, perhaps, are the risks involved in the process. These were recently vividly demonstrated by the high-profile mishap that left the second North Korean *Choe Hyon* class destroyer partially capsized during a launch event at the Chongjin Shipyard on 21 May 2025.[2] Whilst other methods of launch are not without their hazards, it is generally possible to model and plan for these more effectively than for some of the less predictable vagaries impacting the traditional dynamic process.

Dynamic launch has other downsides. Notably, it involves putting greater stresses on a ship's hull than those it would normally experience during operational service. This can result in the need for temporary internal strengthening until the launch takes place. These stresses can also act as a constraint on

A drone shot of Babcock's Rosyth facility taken in the course of HMS *Venturer*'s roll-out from the 'Venturer Building' on 27 May 2025. The Malin Augustea barge *CD01* that was used for her subsequent float-off can be seen in the foreground. *(Babcock International Group)*

launch weight; a particularly negative limitation when considering the drive to achieve efficiencies by increasing the amount of outfitting that is completed before a ship enters the water. Although not incompatible with construction under cover, dynamic launch can complicate the positioning and assembly of the new generation of ship halls that are becoming increasingly common to facilitate fabrication of ships in controlled climatic conditions.

ALTERNATIVE WAYS OF WORKING

The steady reduction in the use of dynamic launch has been balanced by the increasing popularity of alternative means of delivering a warship into the water; many of which are already well established. These include construction in a dry dock that is then flooded up; a method used, for example, for the launch of the Royal Navy's *Queen Elizabeth* class aircraft carriers and long adopted by many of the larger commercial shipbuilding yards. The use of mechanical ship-handling systems, such as those pioneered by Syncrolift, has also proved popular for both new construction and – especially – maintenance applications, particularly for smaller ships. Both methods typically involve heavy, upfront capital expenditure. A more recent trend, first introduced in China in the 1980s, is the use of marine airbags to support a ship's hull as it is slowly rolled into the water. This method is essentially a variation of the dynamic launch approach and requires less investment in fixed infrastructure than other methods.

Both British shipyards currently involved in the construction of major surface combatants – BAE Systems at Govan and Babcock International Group at Rosyth – have now adopted a construction process in which ships are assembled and subject to initial outfitting in a covered construction hall prior to being transported via a hard-standing area to be loaded onto a semi-submersible barge. This is then towed to an area of water sufficiently deep to allow float-off to take place prior to the commencement of final outfitting and system commissioning. The use of a semi-submersible barge for float-off is now a widespread practice for warship launches across the globe. This possibly reflects the fact that the volume of warships passing through a naval shipyard is generally lower than that for a facility building merchant ships, thereby making it more cost-effective to utilise a barge that can be redeployed for other tasks in between launches.

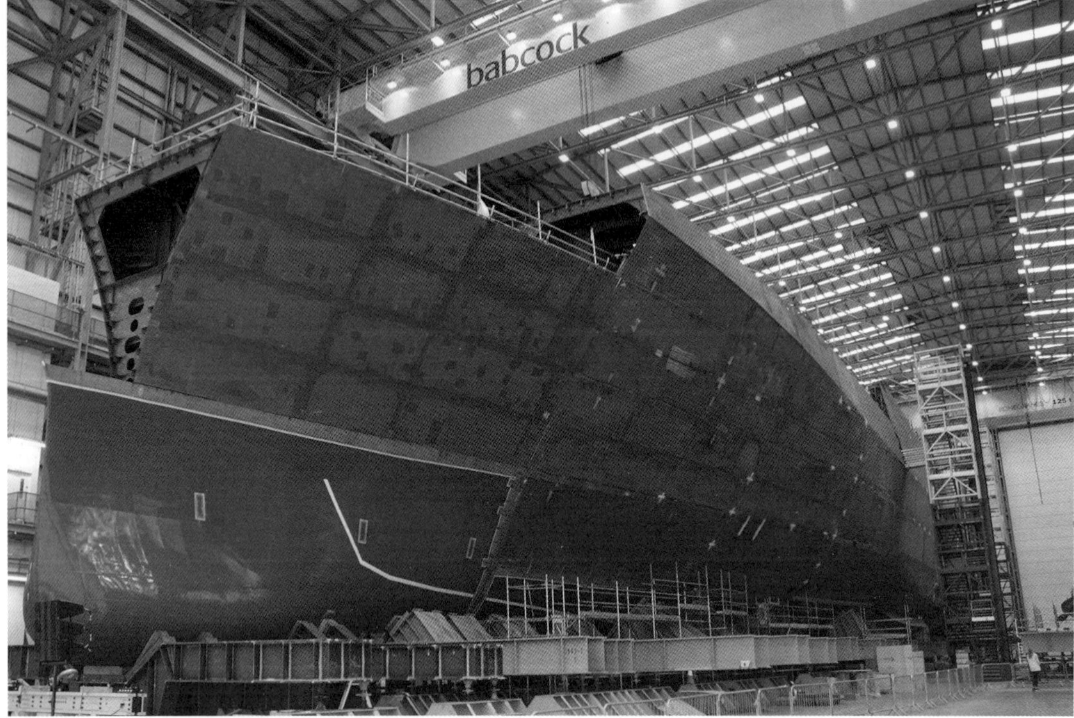

Two pictures of *Venturer* taken in the course of her assembly in the ship hall at Rosyth during the course of 2023. The construction and transportation cradles that were used to carry her weight during assembly and, subsequently, to facilitate the transportation process are readily apparent. *(Crown Copyright 2023/Conrad Waters)*

The new shipbuilding hall at Rosyth was built to support the construction of the Type 31 frigates following the award of the programme to Babcock in November 2019. The hall is intended to provide a state-of-the-art shipbuilding facility that encompasses the latest manufacturing and information management processes. Completed in November 2021, the 147m by 62m facility is large enough to accommodate the simultaneous assembly of two frigate-sized warships. The advantages of an enclosed facility in a location that is often subject to adverse weather are self-evident, helping to drive efficiency and productivity. The improvement in working conditions has also doubtless assisted recruitment of the new generation of shipbuilders that work at the yard.[3]

INTO THE LIMELIGHT

The construction of *Venturer* commenced in September 2021 prior to her formal keel-laying on 26 April 2022. Initial plans envisaged that she would enter the water before the end of 2023. However, delays resulting from changes in the assembly plan that resulted in a greater amount of outfitting taking place whilst she was still in the assembly hall and, doubtless, the disruption of the Covid-19 pandemic meant that it was not until mid-2025 that the new frigate was ready to enter the limelight. Her roll-out on 27 May 2025 was described by Babcock as, '…signifying the transition from the construction phase into final preparations for her entry into water'.[4]

The transportation of the frigate from the Venturer Building to the semi-submersible launch barge that was to be used for her launch and the subsequent float-off process had been long preplanned as part of the overall construction strategy adopted for the class. These operations were carried out under Babcock's overall control and coordination in association with a number of expert subcontractors. In advance of the roll-out, the Type 31 project team's preparations had considered every element of the operations, not only aboard the vessel but also across infrastructure, logistics and support systems. Importantly, the frigate was made structurally complete, weathertight, and watertight to enable the ship to safely transition out of the build hall and into the water.

Roll-out and float-off are inevitably complex operations. As such, comprehensive risk reviews were carried out to ensure appropriate safety measures were in place across personnel, equipment and

Venturer emerges into the daylight from the confines of Babcock's ship hall at Rosyth on 27 May 2025. Her movement out of the assembly hall was undertaken by a 'grid' of self-propelled modular transporters (SPMTs), which were positioned beneath the cradles that supported her hull. *(Conrad Waters)*

This detailed view of *Venturer's* hull shows the Mammoet self-propelled modular transporters (SPMTs) that were used to move the frigate from the ship hall to the semi-submersible barge used for her float-off. *(Conrad Waters)*

procedures. Extensive planning ensured that any potential challenges were mitigated; for example operations were split into manageable durations, with built-in hold points to enable each phase to be carefully and safely managed. Whilst inclement weather posed an unpredictable risk, contingency plans were built into the schedule to mitigate this.

Photographs of *Venturer* in the course of assembly show her resting on the specially designed cradles that were later to facilitate her move out of the build hall. The specification of these cradles was an important element of the overall Type 31 shipbuilding process and they form a visible representation of the extensive pre-planning that is a requisite of programmes of this type. Their design had to take account of the requirements of carrying *Venturer*'s weight during construction, interfacing with the equipment used to transport her to the water, and then supporting her hull during the float-off phase.[5]

Venturer's move from hall to barge was performed by self-propelled modular transporters (SPMTs), which are designed to move large and heavy objects with very high levels of precision. They were placed into position underneath the cradles shortly before the move was due to take place. The SPMTs used were supplied by Mammoet, a Netherlands-based company that played a significant role in developing the concept.[6] Their modular transporter units can be supplied in modules with four, five, six or eight axle lines that can be mechanically connected both head-to-tail and side-by-side to form a mobile platform of the requisite size. They can also be operated in a dispersed but harmonised fashion by means of datalink. The 'grid' of SPMTs is powered by a number of power pack units (PPUs) that are equipped with an engine and a steering control system. Photographs of *Venturer*'s roll-out suggest that four separate groups of SPMTs, each formed of transporters linked together in head-to-head formation and comprising 240 axle lines in total, were required to transport the frigate. Each of these groups of SPMTs was powered by a PPU at the front and rear of the formation, the total of eight power units being confirmed in a Babcock media handout.

The design of the Mammoet SPMTs allows each set of wheels to be steered independently across 360 degrees. This facilitates performance of a wide number of steering options, such as transverse, carousel and crab-like movements. Their tires are air rather than foam filled, resulting in a lower ground bearing pressure. This reduces the need for additional reinforcement of the hardstanding and reduces the risk of damage to the working surface. *Venturer* was manoeuvred through the relatively narrow doors of Babcock's ship hall with seeming ease, completing the move from the hall to the hardstanding in less than an hour under the supervision of a single operator using a remote control unit. Whilst the movement was made to look easy, the complexities of transporting a 139m-long hull with a displacement of some 5,700 tonnes can be readily imagined.

After performance of various checks, *Venturer* was subsequently wheeled onto *CD01*, the semi-submersible barge that was to be used for her float-off. This operation took approximately eight hours in total. The barge had been pre-prepared with supports on which the cradles holding the frigate's hull could rest. The SPMTs are able to adjust their deck height hydraulically by up to 60cm to allow the

The movement of *Venturer*'s c. 5,700-tonne hull from the 'Venturer Building' to the external hardstanding was completed within an hour under the supervision of an operator using a remote control unit. *(Conrad Waters)*

cradles to be lowered onto these supports, after which they are driven off the barge to allow the next stage of the launch process to commence.

MALIN AUGUSTEA BARGE *CD01*

The *CD01* semi-submersible barge used for *Venturer*'s float-off is operated by Malin Augustea, a joint venture between Scottish Malin Group's Malin Abram heavy lift subsidiary and the Italian shipping company Augustea. The barge was originally built in China in 2010 and subsequently lengthened and strengthened at the Hat-San Shipyard in Türkiye before commencing its new working life with the joint venture. The barge is registered at Glasgow and based on the River Clyde, where it is available to support a wide range of projects. Before arriving at Rosyth for *Venturer*'s launch, it had previously been used to support the float-off of the first two Type 26 frigates *Glasgow* and *Cardiff* in the deep waters of Loch Long after completion of their initial assembly at BAE System's Govan shipyard. The Malin Group has a long track record of transporting and/or floating off Royal Navy vessels over many years, including Type 45 destroyer and *Queen Elizabeth* aircraft carrier sections, as well as the Batch 2 'River' class offshore patrol vessels. As described previously, the float-off technique – one of the group's specialisms – is more controlled than dynamic launch and allows ships to enter the water in a more complete state.[7]

With a deadweight of some 21,800 tonnes and an overall length of 137m, *CD01* is described as one of the largest barges of her kind operating in Europe. She can submerge to a maximum eleven metres over her deck, allowing her to float off cargos with up to 9.5m draught. Internally, the ship is divided into 24 watertight ballasting compartments and a separate pump room by seven transverse and three longitudinal bulkheads. There is also a non-watertight swash bulkhead along the centreline to reduce the

Venturer pictured on the hardstanding of Babcock's Rosyth shipyard awaiting final checks prior to being loaded onto the Malin Augustea barge *CD01* for float-off. One of the blocks for her sister ship *Formidable*, third member of the Type 31 class, can be seen awaiting transportation into the ship hall space that had just been vacated *(Conrad Waters)*

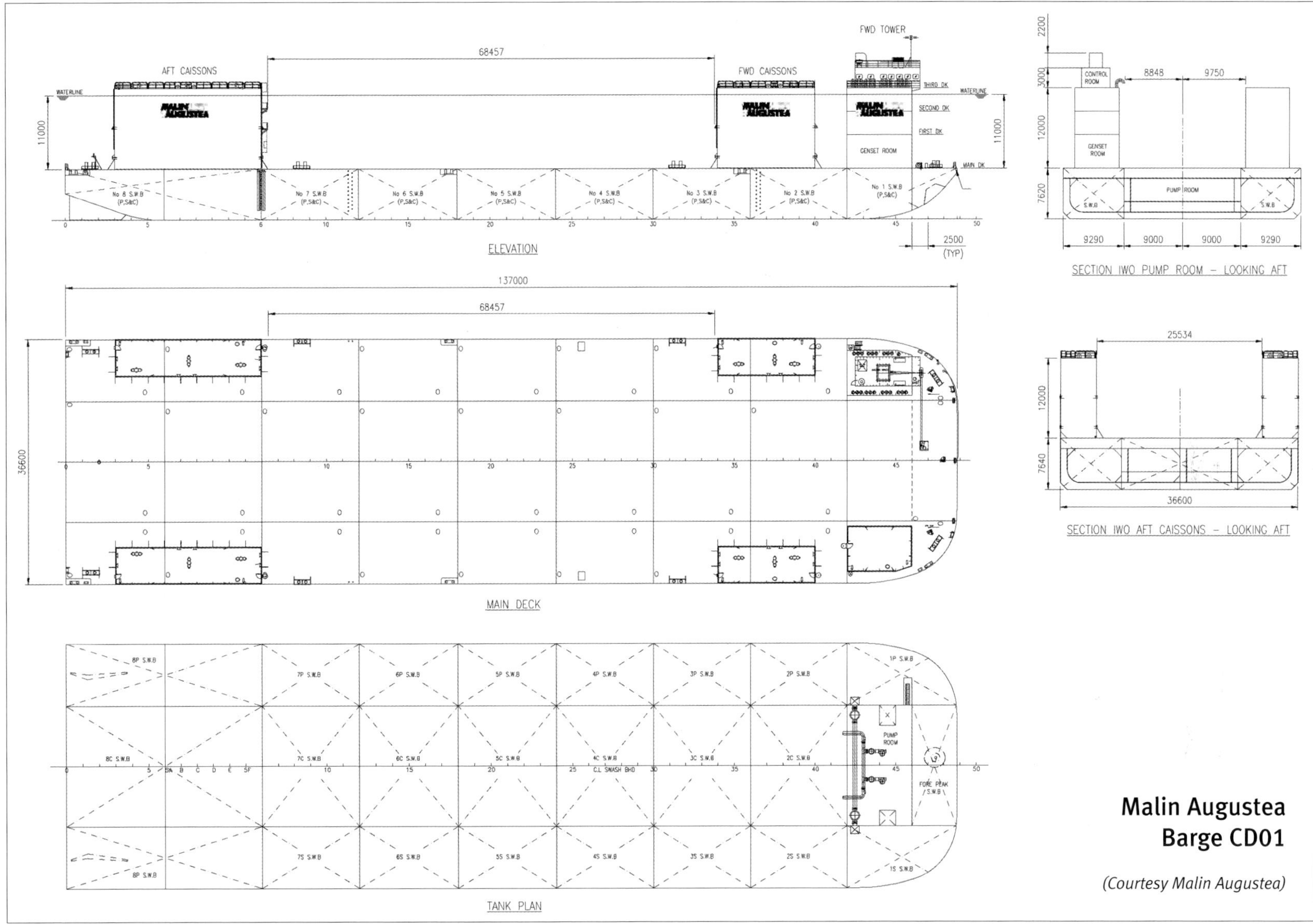

Malin Augustea
Barge CD01

(Courtesy Malin Augustea)

movement of water within the central compartments, thereby helping to maintain stability. Water is pumped into and out of the ballast compartments by two Hamworthy pumps, with the system being controlled by means of a series of hydraulically operated valves linked to the barge's control room. Electrical power is provided by two 480hp (358kW) Caterpillar diesel generators, with propulsion relying on the use of tugs or similar craft.

Just as was the case for *Venturer*'s roll-out, loading the ship onto and off the barge was a complex operation that required careful preparation. An important initial step was securing the transportation

Table 4.4.1: SEMI-SUBMERSIBLE BARGE CB01 – PRINCIPAL PARTICULARS

Construction:	China 2010, modification in Türkiye completed 2022. Registered in Glasgow, United Kingdom
Displacement:	21,806 tonnes at maximum draught
Dimensions:	137.0m x 36.6m x 5.8m (maximum). Depth is 7.6m. Deck area is 4,200m^2
Machinery:	2 x Caterpillar diesel generators each rated at 358kW 2 x Hamworthy pumps with a maximum capacity of 1,000m^2 per hour
Handling capabilities:	Can submerge to 11m and float off cargoes with us to 9.5m draught
Mooring:	1 x anchor windlass with a bow anchor of 3.5 tonnes

The Malin Augustea barge CD01is seen ballasted down off Leith port prior to *Venturer's* float-off on 14 June 2025. *(Babcock International Group/Peter Devlin)*

cradles firmly to the barge prior to her move from the quayside to the area designated for float-off. Once this process was complete, *CD01* was towed from the basin at Rosyth on Monday 9 June 2025, subsequently passing under the Forth bridges to the Port of Leith, near Edinburgh. Here, the barge was moored alongside the Charles Hammond Berth near the port's East Breakwater; an area of water that was sufficiently deep to allow *Venturer*'s float-off to be safely undertaken. Once tidal conditions were suitable, CD01 was slowly ballasted down to allow the frigate to enter the water for the first time. *Venturer* was released from the barge and then towed the short distance back to Rosyth on Saturday 14 June 2025. Afterwards, the final stage of her outfitting process commenced. Speaking after the launch was complete, the Chief Executive of Babcock's Marine Sector, Sir Nick Hine, released a statement noting the importance of the event, '*HMS Venturer*'s first entry into the water is a clear demonstration of UK sovereign capability in action and the depth, resilience and expertise within Babcock's Marine business. This latest milestone exhibits the excellent progress being made across our multi-build programme, which will see us deliver five complex warships for the Royal Navy within a decade. This is engineering at its best, delivered, together with our partners, with pride, purpose and precision.'

THE END OF THE BEGINNING

Venturer's successful launch marked only the end of the beginning for Babcock's Type 31 construction programme. *Venturer* herself will likely remain in dockyard hands for around a further 12 months to allow the installation of her main weapons and sensors, followed by the sometimes difficult task of combat systems integration. This latter process will be led by Thales UK, which is a key member of the Babcock 'Team 31' tasked with delivering the project. Thales has already completed factory acceptance tests of core system elements and de-risked the shipboard installation process through use of a shore-based testing facility. As of mid-2025, it was hoped to commence *Venturer*'s sea trials in the course of 2026; a challenging target for an already ambitious project.

There remain another four Type 31 frigates to deliver by 2030 if the programme is to achieve its planned completion timetable. The second unit, *Active*, has been under construction in the ship hall since January 2023, whilst work on the third ship, *Formidable*, commenced in October 2024. The roll-out of *Venturer* released space within the Venturer Building to allow her constituent blocks – several of which could be seen in the open at the roll-out – to be brought into the hall so that work on her assembly could commence. Despite the many challenges ahead, the Type 31 programme appears to be gaining momentum as it continues to benefit from Babcock's investment in modern shipbuilding infrastructure and application of the latest industry practices.

With float-off complete, *Venturer* is pictured being towed under the Forth bridges and back to Rosyth on 14 June 2025 prior to the commencement of final outfitting. *(Babcock International Group/Peter Devlin)*

Notes

1. The editor thanks Babcock International Group Plc for the opportunity to witness the roll-out event. He is also grateful to Helenor Fisher and Chloe Walters of, respectively, the Malin Abram and Babcock International Group communications teams for their assistance in the preparation of this article.

2. For further information on this event, please see Chapter 2.2. British shipyards have also suffered less significant mishaps in relatively recent times; for example damage suffered to the portside 'A' shaft bracket of the amphibious helicopter carrier *Ocean* when she was launched from Govan on 11 October 1995.

3. The editor's article, 'Overseeing the Royal Navy's Rejuvenation' in *Seaforth World Naval Review 2025* (Barnsley: Seaforth Publishing, 2024), pp.175-82 provides more background on the two new ship halls built by BAE Systems and Babcock, as well as the Type 26 and Type 31 frigate programmes they are intended to support.

4. Babcock press release dated 27 May 2025. The Type 31 contract has not progressed entirely smoothly, with Babcock being required to take provisions totalling £190 million (c. US$260 million) on the fixed-price contract due to higher than expected rates of inflation and a number of execution issues. These problems are not entirely unexpected given the challenges involved in creating a new shipbuilding facility from scratch and have been partly counterbalanced by successes in licensing the 'Arrowhead 140' design on which the Type 31 is based to Indonesia and Poland.

5. The importance of build and transportation cradles was highlighted in an article by Malin Abram's James Bowie, 'In the Yard: Designing Ship Build and Transport Cradles' posted to the Marine Link site – marinelink.com – on 8 December 2020. Malin Abram, one of the two joint venture partners supplying the semi-submersible barge, provided Babcock with project management, operations management and technical engineering support for the overall transportation and launch strategy. The scope of this work encompassed mooring analysis and 'seafastening' design, as well as load-out and float-off engineering. Seafastening related to the design and delivery of the means of securing *Venturer* so as to ensure no movement during transit. Key considerations in seafastening include the cargo type and load distribution, as well as likely sea conditions.

6. Mammoet means 'mammoth' in Dutch. Considerable information about its SPMTs can currently be found on its website at: mammoet.com/equipment/transport/self-propelled-modular-transporter/spmt/

7. Further information on the *CD01* barge and the Malin Augustea joint venture can currently be found on Malin group's website at: malingroup.com/malin-abram-2/malin-augustea/

Contributors

Richard Beedall: Richard is an IT consultant with an interest in the Royal Navy and naval affairs in general. He served in the Royal Naval Reserve as a rating and officer for 14 years, often in the Arabian Gulf working with the US Navy and local naval forces. In 1999 he founded *Navy Matters,* one of the earliest websites on the Royal Navy. He has contributed to *Seaforth World Naval Review* since the initial 2010 edition and has written on naval developments for publications such as *AMI International*, *Naval Forces, Maritime Defence Monitor* and *Warships IFR*. He lives in Ireland with his wife and daughters.

James Bosbotinis: Dr James Bosbotinis is a freelance specialist in defence and international affairs. He has particular expertise in the study of contemporary maritime strategy, assessing naval and air force developments, geopolitical analysis, and generating understanding of the connections between maritime strategy and national policy. Dr Bosbotinis has extensive experience encompassing academic and policy-relevant research and analysis for a range of customers, including United Kingdom government bodies. He has written widely on issues including the development of British maritime strategy, maritime airpower, Russian maritime doctrine, naval and wider military modernisation, and China's evolving strategy. He is the Book Reviews Editor of *The Naval Review* and an Associate Member of the Corbett Centre for Maritime Policy Studies, King's College London.

Norman Friedman: Norman Friedman is one of the world's best-known naval historians and the author of over forty books. He has written widely on issues of military interest, including an award-winning account of the Cold War, and with respect to warship development. Amongst recent works, *Winning a Future War: War Gaming and Victory in the Pacific War* – a description of how war gaming at the US Naval War College helped the US Navy prepare for the Pacific War – produced for the Naval History & Heritage Command stands out as a notable contribution to naval history. His latest book, *The British Aircraft Carrier in Two World Wars,* forms part of a wider series on British warship types, whilst his *Cold War Anti-Submarine Warfare* is soon to be published. In June 2022, he received the Anderson Medal for lifetime achievement from the Society for Nautical Research and, in August that year, the Dudley W. Knox medal for lifetime achievement in naval history from the (US) Naval Historical Foundation. The holder of a PhD in theoretical physics from Columbia, Dr. Friedman is a regular commentator on television and lectures widely on defence issues. He resides with his wife in New York.

David Hobbs: David Hobbs is a naval historian with an international reputation. He has written numerous books, the most recent of which, *Aircraft of the Royal Navy since 1908*, describes over 450 types of fixed-wing, rotary-wing and lighter-than-air aircraft, and was published in 2024. He has also written for a large number of journals and magazines, winning the award for the Aerospace Journalist of the Year, Best Defence Submission at Paris in 2005 and the essay prize awarded by the Navy League of Australia in 2008. Besides lecturing on naval aviation topics worldwide, he has been broadcast in several countries. He served in the Royal Navy for 33 years and retired with the rank of Commander, qualified as both a fixed and rotary-wing pilot with 2,300 flying hours in his log book with over 800 deck landings, 150 of which were at night. For eight years he was the Curator of the Fleet Air Arm Museum at Yeovilton and his next book, *The Fleet Air Arm in the Korean War 1950-53*, is due to be published in 2027. He lives in Northumberland with his wife Jandy, a former WRNS Officer.

Mrityunjoy Mazumdar: Mr Mazumdar, who studied applied physics and mechanical engineering, has been a regular contributor to *Seaforth World Naval Review* since its inception. His interests are the sea services of South and Southeast Asian countries, as well as the lesser known naval and air forces around the world. His words, pictures and research have appeared in many naval and military aircraft publications including *Jane's Navy International,* IQPC's *Defence Industry Bulletin, Shephard Media, Ships of the World, Warship Technology, Air Forces Monthly* as well as the standard naval reference books. Having grown up in India and Nigeria, Mr Mazumdar lives in the 'wine country' north of San Francisco with his wife.

Richard Scott: Richard Scott has been a UK-based analyst and commentator on naval operations and technology for over 25 years, with particular interests in the fields of naval aviation, guided weapons and electronic warfare. He has held a number of editorial positions with Jane's, including the editorship of *Jane's Navy International* magazine, and is now group Consultant Editor – Naval. Mr Scott also regularly contributes to other periodicals, including the *AOC Journal of Electromagnetic Dominance* and *Warship World.*

Tomohiko Tada: Tomohiko Tada was engaged in the development, manufacture and project management of defence equipment for the JMSDF (Japan Maritime Self Defence Force) at a major Japanese electronics company for more than 30 years. Following retirement, he has studied the history, current status and future trends of defence technology. He is currently a defence technology researcher and military writer for the monthly magazines *Japan Military Review*, *Ships of the World*, *MARU* and the weekly magazine *World Weapons*. He is author of *The World's Warship Catalogue* and *Shipboard Weapons of the World* and co-author of the *United States Navy Handbook*, *The World's Near Future Weapons*, *21st Century Weapon Technology: Naval Ships and Aircraft*, the *Review of Today's European Navies*, the *Japan Maritime Self Defence Force Destroyer Perfect Guide* and others. He is a guest commentator on television and lectures on naval defence issues and ballistic missile defence.

Devrim Yaylali: Cem Devrim Yaylalı is a freelance defence journalist based in Istanbul, with a degree in economics from the University of Istanbul. His lifelong passion for naval matters began with photographing warships visiting the Bosphorus, and his first images were published in *Jane's Fighting Ships* in 1991. Since then, his work has appeared in numerous leading Turkish and international defence publications, including *Defence News*, *Jane's*, *Warships IFR*, *European Security & Defence*, *Combat Fleets of the World*, and *Seaforth World Naval Review*. He is also the founder of the blog www.devrimyaylali.com, where he shares insights and reporting on naval affairs. He lives in Istanbul with his family.